POLITICAL SYMBOLISM
IN MODERN EUROPE

POLITICAL SYMBOLISM IN MODERN EUROPE

Essays in Honor of George L. Mosse

Edited by
Seymour Drescher, David Sabean, and Allan Sharlin

Transaction Books
New Brunswick (U.S.A.) and London (U.K.)

Copyright © 1982 by Transaction, Inc.
New Brunswick, New Jersey 08903

All rights reserved under International and Pan-American Copyright
Conventions. No part of this book may be reproduced or transmitted in any
form or by any means, electronic or mechanical, including photocopy,
recording, or any information storage and retrieval system, without prior
permission in writing from the publisher. All inquiries should be addressed
to Transaction Books, Rutgers — The State University, New Brunswick,
New Jersey 08903.

Library of Congress Catalog Number: 80-26544
ISBN: 0-87855-422-X
Printed in the United States of America

Library of Congress Cataloging in Publication Data

Main entry under title:
Political symbolism in modern Europe.

　Includes index.
　CONTENTS: Introduction: Drescher, S., Sabean, D., and Sharlin, A.
George Mosse and political symbolism. — The language of cultural crisis:
Nye, R.A. Degeneration and the medical model of cultural crisis in the
French Belle Époque. Rabinbach, A. The body without fatigue in
nineteenth century utopia. Keck, T. Practical reason in Wilhelmian
Germany. Aschheim, S.E. Caftan and cravat. Gross, D. Myth and symbol
in Georges Sorel.—[etc.]
　1.　Power (Social sciences) — Addresses, essays,
lectures.　2.　Symbolism — Addresses, essays, lectures.
3.　Mosse, George Lachmann — Addresses, essays, lectures.
I.　Mosse, George Lachmann.　II.　Drescher, Seymour.　III.　Sabean,
David Warren.　IV.　Sharlin, Allan, 1950–
JC330.P64　306′.2　80-26544
ISBN 0-87855-422-X

Contents

Acknowledgments

Many people have helped make this book possible. We must first thank the authors of the essays. They endured with remarkable patience and good humor detailed letters outlining the theme of the book, long-winded critiques and requests for revisions, delays due to our location in three different cities and sometimes in three different countries, and incessant deadlines. In addition a number of George Mosse's students, friends, and colleagues generously offered enthusiasm, help, and advice. We would like to thank Renzo De Felice, Howard Fertig, Paul Grendler, Fred Harvey Harrington, Thomas Nipperdey, Robert Soucy, Victor Trescan, and especially Robert Berdahl. Irving Louis Horowitz encouraged and supported us in our belief that this *Festschrift* could be more than a miscellaneous collection of essays.

George Mosse provides the occasion for this volume. To him we all — editors, contributors, and friends — owe countless debts, intellectual and personal. This volume is a small token of our admiration and affection.

Seymour Drescher, David Sabean, Allan Sharlin

Grateful acknowledgment is made to the following for allowing the reprinting of published material:

"Darwinism and the Working Class in Wilhelmian Germany," from *The Descent of Darwin: The Popularization of Darwinism in Germany, 1860–1914*, by Alfred H. Kelly, The University of North Carolina Press, 1981. By permission of the publisher.

We would also like to note the following books which have been dedicated to George Mosse: Seymour Drescher, *Dilemmas of Democracy: Tocqueville and Modernization* (Pittsburgh, 1968); Richard Soloway, *Prelates and People: Ecclesiastical Social Thought in England, 1783-1853* (London, 1969); Robert Soucy, *Fascism in France: The Case of Maurice Barrès* (Berkeley, 1972); Paul Grendler, *Culture and Censorship in Late Renaissance Italy and France* (London, 1981).

INTRODUCTION

George Mosse and Political Symbolism

Seymour Drescher, David Sabean, and Allan Sharlin

Usually people have false rather than true consciousness ....
(Mosse, in *Nazism*, p. 117)

How can a good man survive in an evil world? Machiavelli's question runs throughout George Mosse's teaching and writing.[1] This eternal human problem acquires new urgency through the twentieth-century experience of mass murder and the final solution. As a refugee from Nazi Germany, George Mosse emphatically rejects inner migration. Mosse takes up the issue of survival in the context of religious and ideological commitment. His special concern lies with how such commitments engage reality where the fight for an alternative reality is most intense.

How are the urgent demands of religious and political idealism adjusted to the exigencies of everyday life? Mosse first examined this problem in his study of seventeenth-century Puritan casuistry, and its conclusions bear a strong resemblance to his judgment of left-wing intellectuals in the Weimar Republic.[2] In *The Holy Pretence* Mosse suggests that Christianity requires continual reformulation in its relationship to everyday human affairs, for there is an unresolved contradiction in the need to live in this world while striving for the next. To sustain both virtue and physical survival demands a balancing of the practical logic of action with a capacity for judging action on the basis of absolute values — in Biblical terms, "the endeavor to combine the Serpent and the Dove does not imply hypocrisy."[3]

From a similar perspective, Mosse later criticizes Weimar left-wing intellectuals for their inability to descend from the level of absolutes to the practical theater of everyday political life. "These men were not content to build bridges from the present to the future, but rather sought to bypass such dreary work and leap across the stormy river."[4] The critique of the Weimar intellectuals lies in their failure to develop a twentieth-century casuistry. In their idealism and concern to seek "salvation" through the pu-

1

rity of their values, they were unable to find a spring for action to deal with a world that would not bend to their own vision. Unable to act in a manner called for by the moment:

> German left-wing intellectuals removed themselves ever further from the realities of their times. The result was a Marxist impulse translated into the realm of idealism, a "Marxism of the heart" rather than one based on the rational analysis of existing facts . . . . The German case is especially tragic because there a Republic had to be saved and a growing menace from the right had to be countered . . . . In condemning compromise, existing politics, and the exploitation of realistic possibilities, the left-wing intellectuals put forward a vision of society that seemed incapable of realization.[5]

While maintaining his basic question of the survival of good men, Mosse, in shifting his focus from the early modern to the modern period in European history, has given the old question a new and pressing formulation. How is it that evil has triumphed? How is it that masses of men and women could cooperate in the extermination of a people? And, more specifically, how did the Holocaust come to pass? While his earlier focus allowed Mosse to examine how Puritan divines accommodated to the world, this new interest has drawn from Mosse a series of studies on facism, nationalism, and racism involving secular nationalists, utopians, scientists, racialists, and socialists. In shifting from the early modern era, Mosse has also moved from the study of Christians to Jewish idealists, be they Zionists, liberals, or left-wing intellectuals. The subject is a tragedy of almost incomprehensible proportions, and Mosse attempts to dig deeply into the cultural and institutional roots of the story.

In doing so he forsakes the path of traditional intellectual history. Mosse emphasizes that nineteenth-century democratization and industrialization imposed a new form of politics, characterized by mass movements and mass agitation. This "seemed to transform the political process itself into a drama which further diminished the individual whose conscious actions might change the course of his own destiny."[6] Where liberal and socialist historians have often attempted to place mass antidemocratic ideologies within a spectrum derived from the nineteenth-century classical period of formation, Mosse attempts to understand the new politics on its own terms. Building on his earlier insights into the baroque, Mosse's conception of political symbolism assumes central analytical importance. How are ideas comprehended, shaped, and applied by the masses? Here Mosse perceives that ideas do not take form through formal, rational analyses but through experimentation in the popular arena. Symbols are the means through which political movements develop and ideas are given concrete form. Therefore, his analysis of the impact of the baroque continues to be analytically relevant to a more secularized era. The religious forms that defined how people perceived their world retained an analogous function when transposed into the institutionally autonomous world of modern politics. In Mosse's perspective the masses were drawn into the political arena not only through the political organizations that fostered and developed these symbols, but at least as much through a wide range of cultural creations: festivals, myths, monuments, art, novels, music, and theater.

To understand this approach to political symbolism, it is useful to begin with Mosse's understanding of politics. Politics is more than the formal political process. It is even more than behavior of men in institutions indirectly related to the state, in cultural, economic, and military organizations. In everyday life, all human interaction is thoroughly permeated with political implication.[7] Methodologically, this view makes Mosse skeptical of analyses of political action that content themselves with the in-and-out trays of a foreign ministry or statistical studies of parliamentary and election votes.[8] Morally, just as Christianity views sin as composed of acts of omission as well as of commission, so it is impossible to be unpolitical. Each person is answerable for the political effects of his/her actions, whether participating directly in the formal polity or attempting to ignore or flee such involvement. Mosse dismisses as self-delusion the ideological cocoon which many a *Bildungsbürger* constructed to wait out the future, while avoiding contact with the perpetual dirty, compromising, often humiliating business of politics. His powerful pedagogical talent barely conceals a fundamental moral indignation against the aspiration to the apolitical.[9]

With this definition of politics, what is the role of symbols? They shape political discourse, and political struggle is partly a struggle to control such discourse.[10] The relative success of political contenders in determining the shape and character of the terms of debate has decisive implications for their ability to gain authority or obedience. Those who can find no way of entering into the discourse are squeezed to the periphery and excluded from direct political influence. Mosse is concerned with who most successfully captured a group or a society's central symbols or found a way to be most closely identified with them. The value of Mosse's approaches to European racism, German Volk ideas, and national identity lies in denoting the groups which captured or successfully institutionalized the symbolic linkages through which debate took place. People fit themselves to words as much as they bend them to their own purposes. Mosse identifies unspoken assumptions, unavoidable terms, and above all, the limits that specific rhetoric, myths, and symbols came to place on the thought and action of audience and speaker. In his analysis of the struggle between ideologies Mosse objects to the notion of *propaganda* as misleading. Leaders do not simply manipulate their followers. They are successful in capturing symbolic assent and compliance.[11] People require symbols because they objectify myths and thereby offer participation, identity, and salvation.

The Nazi road to victory was already paved from the fact that anti-Semitism was part of a symbolic discourse that permeated all social and political questions of the time. The Nazis vied for power using an idiom they only ultimately epitomized. The success of National Socialism cannot be separated from the fact that, despite the socialist and revolutionary Strasser wing, the party under Hitler was deeply attached to the symbols of a middle class desperate to ensure its collective survival in a hierarchic society. Such a movement could promise to overcome alienation on the level to which the ideology had shifted the question: the aesthetic and the affective. For a community that perceived itself on the verge of disintegration, folk and racial ideas held out the promise of a radical reversal, converting a potential social disaster into an aesthetic and emotional revolution against cultural and social outsiders. This diversion, in turn, rested on prior achievements. The educational system, the student and middle-class movements of imperial Germany had already institutionalized the culturally exclusive assumptions of the nation's problems. By 1933 Hitler was supported by physical violence and naked state terror, but the long-run symbolic repression of alternatives in reducing the potential for organized protest and resistance should not be underestimated.

For Mosse, the peculiar characteristic of myths and symbols adopted by large numbers of people in nineteenth- and twentieth-century Germany lies in the very tenuity of contact with reality. An ideology only "vaguely relevant to real problems ultimately became normative."[12] The process is partly explained by the fact that racism, Volk ideology, and fascism all upheld bourgeois values of order, cleanliness, honesty, family life, and hard work.[13] With an educational system upholding the same cultural linkage, *Bildung* reinforced the nationalist nexus of racism and respectability. Just as entrepreneurs of nationalism had appropriated the rituals of formal religion, so they appropriated a middle-class morality that was no longer confined to one class. The "new" German man was the ideal bourgeois.[14] Mosse expresses the effects of the connection thus: "Racism substituted myth for reality; and the world it created with its stereotypes, virtues, and vices, was a fairy-tale world, which dangled a utopia before the eyes of those who longed for a way out of the confusion of modernity and the rush of time."[15] Here in his subjects' confusion of reality and myth, Mosse sounds one of his enduring themes:

> The pragmatism of daily politics [speaking of nationalism] lay within a cultic framework and for most people was disguised by it. But "disguise" is perhaps the wrong term in this context, for any disguise which utilized regular liturgic and cultic forms becomes a "magic" believed by both leaders and people, and it is the reality of this magic with which we are concerned.[16]

Mosse does not separate objective reality and the way it is perceived into two discrete analytic moments. Perception of a thing is as real as the thing itself. In such a process, myth, symbol, and value not only give form to perception, but become currency in themselves and the political system brought into action to valorize the dream: for "many people . . . Hitler was necessary in order that the fairy tale could begin."[17]

Culture is a fundamental rather than a derivative human activity and like politics, entails continuous interaction.[18] It is part of the human condition to think symbolically, although symbols can be simple or complex, mundane or grandiose, relatively isolated or parts of more complex systems. Inherent in all symbols is a masking quality, which follows from the fact that they impose form on their subjects. When it becomes a question of socially imposed symbols, the discernible facts of authority and domination allow the historian to speak of "mystification."[19] For his examples, Mosse always returns to the seventeenth century: "The baroque is full of myth, theater, and symbols which carry you away from the reality of this world. But the very success of the Jesuits was that while carrying you away from this world they really integrated you into their political system."[20]

This suggests Mosse's response to those who have taken him to task for neglecting social and economic contexts. Mosse has always argued for the autonomy of culture and myth but not in the sense that they are the result of higher logical processes or an existential expression of human freedom.[21] Rather, they cannot be considered as existing outside of economic and social contexts and indeed have no function outside of them. While Mosse makes no determination of the desires and myths of people according to their group or class position, no full analysis can be made without reference to collective identity.[22] Mosse remarks that history is made by people with false consciousness.[23] It is the definition of *false* and the paradoxes which arise when one seeks to connect interest with ideas and actions, that he takes as the problem to be addressed. To analyze these interactions, Mosse has described *mediation* as the most useful concept available to the historian.[24] Symbols, culture, myths, and ideas have to be examined in terms of the complexity of interests and actions mediated through them. He tries to show that the obsession of German anti-Semitism had little to do with Jews themselves or with emancipation. Rather, through the symbol of the Jew, middle-class alienation, fears of attacks on hierarchy, aesthetic values, and unease with cities were causally linked.[25] The power of symbols cannot be grasped through the logical categories of the conventional historian any more than such categories can account for the effects of religious liturgy.[26] Without proper understanding of mediation, one fails to grasp that in political discourse objective reality is filtered through myths, values, and attitudes.

In the understanding of symbols as giving or imposing form in specific historical situations Mosse is at his most penetrating. Here he counters some recent anthropological thinking.[27] The latter undertakes the exposure of meaning within symbols, by a kind of loose base/superstructure framework which assumes that with enough understanding of social and economic conditions, of psychological makeup, or of fundamental epistemological categories, the symbols can be explained. Mosse argues that symbols are the meaning in themselves, that they order perceived reality, have multiple dimensions, and mediate between subjects and between subject and object. Historical actors perceive their own interests in distorted form. The very processes actors set in motion for their purposes rarely function exactly as intended and do so under conditions that often mask sources of tension from them. The only way to handle the problem is for the historian to incorporate the dialectic into historical practice.[28]

Mosse's assumptions as a working historian have to be brought together from a number of scattered texts. Refusing to limit himself to the works of great thinkers and seeking unusual sources for examining popular culture, he has laid new ground in determining the role of ideas in history. His method is neither easy to define nor to replicate. Myths and symbols have neither the relative precision of market transactions for the economic historian nor the boundedness of the complete works of systematic thinkers. How is it possible to differentiate dominant political symbols from the transient ideas of every crank? Mosse does this in two ways. First, being oriented toward mass audiences, he seeks out authors who sold books in the hundreds of thousands. These writers must have struck chords in popular consciousness. For example, he explores the works of poular novelists Marlitt, Ganghofer, and May.[29] Second, he considers it important to trace from diffuse exotic beginnings the subsequent development of symbols that achieved institutional resolution. The most obscure writers can thus be grist for Mosse's sensitive reading. His works *The Crisis of German Ideology, The Nationalization of the Masses,* and *Toward the Final Solution* trace the development of Volk ideology, nationalism, and racism from reputable elite beginnings to their triumph under National Socialism. Because Mosse relies on successful conclusions to determine his study of antecedents, he does not turn his attention to historical cases where racial symbolism and aesthetic politics did not capture the forum from other traditional or modern political symbolic systems. He emphasizes that German fascism was not typical of European fascism, but he has not developed that approach in which a variety of possible outcomes are taken as the point of departure.

While many intellectual historians are uneasy dealing with second-rate scribblers and the *outré*, Mosse usually mines writers precisely for their unstated assumptions and aesthetic predilections. Often stringing together a number of unobtrusive aspects of various writings, he offers his judgment about who read them and how they were read. Methodologically, Mosse is interested in the form of communication and the problem of reception. Something of the "oral" quality of his works originally delivered as lectures, reverberates in his texts. He is at his best in "hearing" texts and "seeing" people in action. Because he approaches the subject matter through the producers of cultural artifacts — be they authors, painters, architects, orators, or promoters of popular festivals — Mosse often views audiences as undifferentiated masses. Perhaps his most frequent differentiation for German history is between workers and the bourgeoisie or middle class. He is sympathetic to class analysis, but his approach allows him to make only relatively loose social distinctions.

Mosse has drawn two conclusions from his studies. He refuses to see history as the outcome of logical processes, and denies that historical events can be grasped through the rational categories of traditionally practicing historians.[30] Although he recognizes that bureaucratic organization made the "final solution" possible, he is concerned to demonstrate the nonrational substructure to all internally rationalized institutions — of science, bureaucracy, and education.[31] His aim is to highlight the extrinsic political intentions which inform bureaucratic action or scientific curiosity. Such a viewpoint leads Mosse, for example, to trace the complex interaction between the assumption of classical forms of beauty and such things as the school curriculum, student rituals, and the scientific investigations of linguists, historians, demographers, anthropologists, and biologists.[32] He refuses to separate the political from the religious, the scientific from the aesthetic, and the bureaucratic from the mythological and symbolic.[33]

> Fascist and National Socialist political thought cannot be judged in terms of traditional political theory. It has little in common with rational, logically constructed systems such as those of Hegel or Marx. This fact has bothered many commentators who have looked at fascist political thought and condemned its vagueness and ambiguities. But the fascists themselves described their political thought as an "attitude" rather than a system; it was, in fact, a theology which provided the framework for national worship. As such, its rites and liturgies were central, an integral part of a political theory which was not dependent on the appeal of the written word. Nazi and other fascist leaders stressed the spoken work, but even here, speeches fulfilled a liturgical function rather than presenting a didactic exposition of the ideology. The spoken work itself was integrated into the cultic rites, and what was actually said was, in the end, of less importance than the setting and the rites which surrounded such speeches.[34]

Scholarship is left with the task of attempting to determine the conditions, whether cultural or social, which tend to foster or retard the mythical and the realistic in political discourse. All of Mosse's historical analysis rests on the assumption that it is easy, at least in practice, to draw a fairly clear line between myth and reality in the reconstruction of the thought and behavior of the past. To that extent, Mosse the historian of mystification paradoxically draws on categories of the Western Enlightenment. This humanistic or common-sense distinction between myth and reality is the working assumption that enables him to distinguish between the myths he is investigating and the story he is telling. For all his emphasis on the power of myth and the human need to symbolize, Mosse stands unambiguously in the demystifying and unmasking tradition.[35]

Inherent in such historical reasoning is a thoroughgoing political critique. Mosse has always considered the acts of writing and teaching to be inherently political activities. Historians are always demythologizing or mythologizing, masking or unmasking, demystifying or mystifying, but never neutral, even if commitment to rational procedures hides this characteristic of the activity from themselves.[36] Along with this kind of critical work, Mosse has reflected on several of the important political traditions, two of which can be mentioned here as examples.

Fundamental to historic forms of conservatism has been a distinction between culture and civilization, between, on the one hand, true feeling and inward spirituality and on the other, what is considered artificial and materialistic. Transposed to the plane of a society or nation, the stress on culture, on the inward spirituality of a people, has tended to emphasize its uniqueness and worked against reconciliation with other peoples.[37] The notions of true feeling and genuine character call for opposing symbols. In the historic German case, this meant the Jew — to whom was imputed materialism, rationalism, and a fossilized religion.[38] Mosse argues that:

> German anti-semitism is a part of German intellectual history. It does not stand outside it. Above all, it became involved with the peculiar turn which German thought took after the first decade of the nineteenth century. German thought became at once provincial, in its search for roots, and idealistic in its rejection of mere outward progress, in its belief in the irrationality of culture. Here the Jew was the outsider, and if he could at times gatecrash by assimilation in the nineteenth century, that did not fundamentally alter the emerging image of the Jew. Culture was closed to him, for he lacked the necessary spiritual foundations. This differentiation between culture and civilization, still part of the intellectual equipment of many Germans, is one of the clues to the Jewish tragedy of our times.[39]

In maintaining the distinction between culture and civilization, conservatives played a central role in reinforcing and transmitting the symbolic structure of hostility and nonreconciliation.[40]

> Those who advocated a return to Culture, who embraced a "German revolution" . . . were men and women who wanted to maintain their property and their superior status over the working classes. The notion of a genuine social

revolution was anathema to these people, yet they were profoundly dissatisfied with their world. The tension between their desire to preserve their status and their equally fervent desire to radically alter society was resolved by the appeal to a spiritual revolution which would revitalize the nation without revolutionizing its structure.

While reticent about expressing his own values in his texts, Mosse's own sympathies apparently lie with the liberalism of the Enlightenment and humanistic socialism. Mosse tries to rescue the humanistic core of all movements while recognizing their historical flaws. Fundamental to traditional liberalism is the belief in the efficacy of various modernizing institutions such as education and parliamentary democracy which should serve as the necessary agents for the enlightenment of the population. In his analysis of educational institutions in Germany, Mosse argued that irrational, antidemocratic values penetrated to the very core of educational institutions.[41] As for parliamentary democracy, Mosse expresses fears for its survival in major crises because of its inability to "integrate aesthetic, political, economic, and social desires."[42] By lumping all its enemies together under such rubrics as "totalitarianism," liberalism has waged war against other humanistic alternatives.[43] While very insistent on distinctions between Stalinism and fascism, his critique of the political failure of liberalism during the Weimar Republic applies equally well to social democracy and communism. Perhaps he offers the same insights to both humanistic liberalism and humanistic socialism. Mass movements have dominated the modern era, a fact with which we must all live. His task, as he sees it, has been to analyze these movements at their most extreme,

in order to produce a confrontation between men and masses. It is the task of the historian to destroy old myths in order to encourage new confrontations with reality. History, after all is a process which contains within it possibilities for both good and evil. That the history with which we are concerned saw the victory of evil over the good does not mean that mankind is unable to shed the sea of pain which radical nationalism has caused. To plumb the depth of evil might strengthen the forces of good, to fill man's consciousness with the need to transform consciousness into a humanistic nationalism. If such hope did not exist there would be no sense in the unpleasant task of chronicling the illusions of domination which follow, even if this book also contains men and women devoted to human creativity and liberty, those who refused to follow false gods.[44]

* * *

The essays in this volume deal with many of the themes which have been considered by Mosse and in some respects also break new ground. Most of them deal with the mediation of social and political power through symbolic representation. One aspect of this mediation is found in the central characteristic of symbols. The components of discourse itself are part of the projection of groups or classes. We must distinguish between the object of discourse, which may appear to be subject to logical analysis and dispassionate debate, and the vehicle of that discourse. While the intent of participants in a particular exchange may be directed toward a specific issue or set of issues, the effect of the debate itself might also be to maintain their own positions as leaders on public issues in general. The effect might also be to support a conception of group identity and that group's proper place in the hierarchy of power.

This is one of the implications of Soloway's essay on the eugenics movement in England. In addition to its ostensible purpose of dealing with a dynamics of demography, the vocabulary of the movement reinforced a specific picture of the working class and justified a specific strategy of domination by its superiors. The movement's chosen values of rationality and science were those of professionals — professors, doctors, scientists, and administrators. Its mode of discourse, like similar movements of the time, was an attack on ascriptive power and inherited wealth in favor of the establishment of social domination through the extension of bureaucratic norms. One fails to grasp the social character of the movement if its significance is evaluated by either the relative success of its stated goals or the empirical validity of the arguments it presented. The importance of the movement in terms of political symbolism is related to the experience professionals underwent in their daily thinking, writing, and debating, solidifying and increasing their claims in the shifting patterns of domination and subordination.

In a more general way, Nye attacks the same problem in his approach to the concept of "degeneration" in late–nineteenth-century France. He shows how the medical model of physical decline became widely embedded in cultural and political discourse. Here the binary opposition normal/abnormal gave one group of professionals the crucial power of definition in the conceptualization of social crises. Nye argues that medical vocabulary saturated the "consensual norms, prejudices, and salient anxieties" of French society. They also mediated the social and political power not only of doctors but bureaucrats, criminologists, public hygienists, social theorists, and polemicists. Rabinbach, dealing with metaphors of energy and fatigue in the late nineteenth century, provides a more diffuse approach to the problem of modes of maneuvering for social domination expressed in categories of will, discipline, control, and character — the primary values and symbols of the period. "Energy" and "exhaustion" were symbols deriving their mythological force from scientific discourse. Such symbols were expressive of widespread anxiety about the problem of maintaining social order and expanded through the supposed threat of degeneration of physical and intellectual power.

A second aspect to the mediation of social power through symbols, namely that of mystification or masking, is also taken up in these essays. The distribution of social power, the many facets of domination, and the arbitrariness of rules are only partly apparent to the actors. They are experienced existentially only through the forms which make domination possible by offering seemingly autonomous rules of behavior. Part of the analytical problem is to grasp how what might appear to be a single symbol means different things in different contexts, while maintaining a social continuity of meaning. Keck deals with a transformation of culture, examining academics in Germany prior to World War I. He discusses the fate of the Marburg Kantians who tried to exercise influence on the ideology of German social democracy, showing how the war experience forced them to make explicit loyalties that their situation had allowed to remain equivocal. These thinkers used the notion of culture as a way of summing up a number of aspects which they never consciously expressed. It was a symbol by which the French could be criticized as mediocre and the English as constantly in utilitarian motion, rewarding only the "productive." They defended a society in which their skills of formal analysis were valued together with other forms of "unproductive" production, a symbolic "package" that ensured a crucial role for the university professor of moral philosophy and the gymnasium teacher. In their campaign to get social democracy to accept their symbol, the categorical imperative, as the fundamental value of the movement, they sought to ascribe a central role to their own expertise as intellectuals.

The problem of symbols as mediating social power involves an analysis of reception. There is a gulf between the producer and the user of the product; reading and hearing involve active processing as much as speaking and writing do; and there is a constant exchange between political discourse and everyday life. This implies the need for a multilayered analysis of mass communication. Kelly's assessment of Darwinism and the German working class in the late nineteenth century takes up the nature of workers' reception of Darwinian ideas in favor of those of Marx. Marxism was received as a kind of Darwinian monism, providing workers with their own religious alternative to the established churches. This may account for the fact that while party leaders were ambivalent, they encouraged workers to read Darwinian tracts. The workers would be divorced from traditional power bases and institutional religion. From the leaders' viewpoint, an alternative, secular religion might also have provided a necessary discipline — a not *too* revolutionary proletariat — whereby the vanguard was to lead rather than follow. Yet one is left with the suspicion that in allowing Darwin to stand beside Marx it was the leaders who were following in the process of mass communication.

Other contributors offer reflections on the problem of reception. Koenigsbergertakes up the problem of the substitution of scientific ideology for that of the church during the three centuries after the Renaissance. Noting that intellectuals were socially conservative, he argues that they made no direct attack on the church. If anything, they were in favor of order. Yet the development of an autonomous area of knowledge, of discourse not dominated by revelation, the creation of two cultures (one of science and rationality and the other a "popular" culture) are parallel to the growth of national bureaucracies, with their dependent educational institutions and new leadership criteria organized around the increasingly technical discussion of public policy.

A number of essays in this volume offer a further perspective on mediation, concentrating on the generation and use of symbols in everyday political debate. Looking at discourse in practice, the problem is to discover how ideological structures, myths, and symbols contain, transmit, and alter values and relationships. Scott, in her perceptive analysis of popular theater in late–nineteenth-century France, shows how traditional responses to well-known symbols were redirected through the conscious inversion of received meanings. Her essay draws attention to the fact that mythmaking is not simply a matter of production from above as a means of perpetuating the status quo. Her essay assumes that cultural symbols are protean and that proletarian cultural norms could develop as an extension as well as a rejection of the Christian mythos. Gross' essay on Sorel provides an interesting case study of an attempt to self-consciously fashion a counterbourgeois myth for the working class. Sorel aimed at a fundamental distinction between words as analysis and words as calls to collective cohesion. Yet he was also unconsciously enmeshed in the biosocial characterizations of his age. A degenerating will-less bourgeoisie was pitted against a noble savage proletariat. The Sorelian case also strikingly shows how political symbols are not crystalline signs in the possession of a given group but multiedged weapons whose handle can often be grasped by one's enemy. Just as Sorel could turn bourgeois anxiety about degeneration against its authors, so his own ideas of the fortification of will by myths provided validation, if not inspiration, for the suppression of working-class threats by ultimately more powerful communal myths.

Hermand's essay likewise revolves around a self-conscious use of the masking power of symbols. Hermand takes up the analysis of painting in Germany at the beginning of the nineteenth century, dealing with the political content of the painting of Caspar David Friedrich. Most of the painters worked in a highly coded, allusive form, burying in symbols a range of political ideas and attitudes. Lachance studies generational discourse in France on the eve of World War I and shows that the various political orientations used generational symbols to objectify and shape changes in political balance and focus political debate. This involved mapping a political terrain and provided myths that informed action by orienting minds along particular lines. Pois offers a description of Nazi religious notions in terms of discourse systematically ordered along lines of struggle. He argues that in this attempt the Nazis stood squarely in one of the alternative Western traditions, and their notions cannot be passed off as pure propaganda. Taken together with the essays of Kelly, Scott, and Koenigsberger, serious issues are discussed about the nature of religious symbolism in modernizing Europe, the development of an alternative religious tradition to Christianity in the form of an optimistic monism, and the political dimension of religious commitment.

Aschheim's essay, which deals with one of the central themes of German political symbolism, charts the development of the language of dehumanization to dominance in public discourse. A symbol originally used to describe a set of outsiders with clearly distinguishable characteristics was transformed into an essence designed to create a permanent barrier between groups without any visible differential characteristics. In a parallel way Aschheim neatly shows how what was a consensual symbol of a progressive political outlook in the eighteenth century, the social pathology of the ghetto, ultimately became a symbol of an integral biological pathology for those who were precisely most disturbed by the whole social development which produced the dismantled ghettos. Aschheim emphasizes how extreme inequality of political and social power renders irrelevant the rules of rational analysis. The Jews in Germany futilely expended enormous energies on charting optimum personal and group strategies within the parameters of the consensual *Ostjude* symbol. In Germany the ghetto Jew became *the* political metaphor of the second quarter of the twentieth century.

Many of the essays above focus on the unconscious or latent implications of symbols by their progenitors. But in the hands of both artists and polemicists, who not only recognized the masking power of symbols but exulted in them, a more overt manipulation occurred. Perhaps it is not accidental that one of the most successful and calculating manipulators of symbolic discourse in our century was an originally unsuccessful artist who eventually found a whole continent not large enough to paint the bloodiest canvas in its history.

NOTES

Our thanks to the following for criticism and advice: Peter Reilly, Kenneth Barking, Alf Lüdtke, and Hans Medick.
1. First posed in George L. Mosse, *The Holy Pretence: A Study in Christianity and Reason of State from William Perkins to John Winthrop* (Oxford: Basil Blackwell, 1957), p. 33. On the frontispiece, Mosse quoted from Machiavelli, *The Prince*, ch. 15: "A man who wishes to make a profession of goodness in everything must necessarily come to grief among so many who are not good."

2. George L. Mosse, "Left-Wing Intellectuals in the Weimar Republic," *Germans and Jews* (New York: Grosset & Dunlap, 1970), pp. 171–225, esp. pp. 176, 180, 213, 217. In an interview, Mosse said that the problem he took up in *The Holy Pretence* was much the same he dealt with later when he studied racism and fascism: *Nazism: A Historical and Comparative Analysis of National Socialism* (New Brunswick, N.J.: Transaction Books, 1978), p. 27, cf. 28–29.

3. *Holy Pretence,* p. 154. On Mosse's later use of the notion of hypocrisy see *Germans and Jews,* p. 7.

4. *Germans and Jews,* p. 32. The issues are handled there at length, pp. 3–33, 171–225. Also cf. *The Culture of Western Europe: The Nineteenth and Twentieth Centuries* (n.p.: Rand McNally, 1961), pp. 419–23.

5. *Germans and Jews,* p. 217.

6. George L. Mosse, *Nationalization of the Masses: Political Symbolism and Mass Movements in Germany from the Napoleonic Wars through the Third Reich* (New York: Howard Fertig, 1975), p. vii. See also his *Men and Masses* (New York: Howard Fertig, forthcoming).

7. See the formulations in Mosse, *Culture,* pp. 5–7, 240–41, 278 ff., 419–23; id., *The Crisis of German Ideology: Intellectual Origins of the Third Reich* (New York: Grosset & Dunlap, 1964), pp. 2, 5–8, 171–89.

8. Mosse taught at the University of Iowa in the 1950s where a number of people later to pioneer in the application of statistical methods to the historical study of power were his colleagues — among others, William O. Aydelotte, Allan G. Bogue, and Samuel P. Hays. For Mosse's views on the limitation of statistical methods for the study of politics, see *Nazism,* pp. 109–10; *Germans and Jews,* p. 23. On Marxist approaches, *Nazism,* pp. 47–50, 117; *Crisis,* p. 9; *Nationalization,* pp. 2–3, 11–12. For the influence of Hannah Arendt, see *Nazism,* pp. 77–78.

9. See George L. Mosse, *Toward the Final Solution: A History of European Racism* (New York: Howard Fertig, 1978), pp. 232–37, esp. 235; id., *Nationalization,* pp. 207–16; id., *Culture,* pp. 419–23; id., *Nazism,* p. 74: "I would also say that the corruption of values for which these people [Nazis] stand is not abnormal in our civilization. It's part of a growing brutalization — a part of the idea of a total war which you already have in World War I: The enemy must be killed, and to kill the enemy is a good act. The church blesses it, in fact." See also id., "National Cemeteries and National Revival: The Cult of the Fallen soldiers in Germany," *Journal of Contemporary History* 14 (1979): 1–20.

10. This problem recurs continually in his works. For an introduction to his views see *Racism,* pp. 187, 191 ff., 232 ff.; *Nationalization,* pp. 207ff., esp. 209.

11. *Nazism,* pp. 32, 112: "Facist mass movements were in fact movements of consensus rather than of manipulation."

12. *Crisis,* p. 9.

13. *Racism,* p. 34; *Nazism,* p. 43.

14. *Nazism,* p. 43.

15. *Racism,* p. xiii.

16. *Nationalization,* p. 15.

17. *Nazism,* p. 116.

18. *Nationalization,* p. 211; *Nazism,* p. 109.

19. *Nationalization,* pp. 1–20.

20. *Nazism,* p. 31.

21. See the discussion in the introduction to *Culture*, pp. 1–9; *Nazism*, pp. 108–17; *Crisis*, pp. 1–10; *Racism*, p. x iii.

22. *Nazism*, p. 117; *Crisis*, p. 9; *Nazism*, p. 109: "The true Marxist approach . . . must be based on a dialectic and cannot be based on a universal approach, i.e., *all* economics, *all* politics, *all* social class. This is a static approach. It ignores the essence of Marxism — namely its Hegelian ingredient, its dynamic, its dialectic."

23. *Nazism*, p. 117.

24. *Nazism*, p. 117.

25. *Crisis*, pp. 7–8, 36, 292, 301–2; *Nazism*, pp. 45–46; *Racism*, pp. xii–xiii.

26. Mosse first approached the methodological problem in *Culture*, p. 4: "The intellectual occupies the foreground, for he systematizes thought, making it understandable to historians." This negative judgment on the capabilities of historians and their need for someone to simplify things for them developed into a critique of "liberal," "traditional," or "Anglo-Saxon" historians as he tried to develop the notion of symbol in his later works. See *Nationalization*, pp. 6–20, esp. 9. Cf. *Nazism*, pp. 108–9.

27. For a sharp criticism of the various anthropological approaches to symbolism, see Dan Sperber, *Rethinking Symbolism* (Cambridge, Mass.: Cambridge University Press, 1975).

28. *Nazism*, p. 117: "We must finally discard unmediated and positivist analyses for the examination of a mediated dialectic." Also, p. 30: "Obviously today we cannot be pure Hegelians. We realize, after all . . . that the dialectic is, in fact, between myth and social forces. I would say between myth and what Marx called objective reality, that is social, political, and economic forces." Cf. also pp. 17, 30, 37, 109; *Nationalization*, pp. 15, 208–9; *Racism*, p. xiii; *Crisis*, p. 9.

29. "Was Sie wirklich lassen: Marlitt, Ganghofer, May," *Popularität und Trivialität* (Bad Bomburg, V.D.H., 1974), pp. 101–20.

30. *Nationalization*, pp. 1–20.

31. *Culture*, pp. 8–9; *Crisis*, pp. 149–70, 190–203; *Racism*, pp. 1–34, 234.

32. *Racism*, pp. 35-50, 77, 82, 85, 234–35; p. 2: "The continuous transition from science to aesthetics is a cardinal feature of modern racism."

33. See citations in notes 31 and 32 and remarks in *Crisis*, p. 202; *Nationalization*, p. 28; *Nazis*, p. 72.

34. *Nationalization*, pp. 9–10.

35. See his remarks in *Nazism*, pp. 29–31, 116–17; also *Culture*, pp. 419–23.

36. *Culture*, pp. 1–6.

37. *Culture*, pp. 1–3, esp. 2, 419–23; *Germans and Jews*, pp. 15–18, 34–60, 116–43; *Crisis*, pp. 6–7.

38. *Germans and Jews*, p. 37. On bringing together both antiimages, Jew and red, ibid., pp. 27, 61–76. Also *Culture*, p. 2.

39. *Germans and Jews*, p. 60.

40. *Crisis*, pp. 242–43.

41. Liberalism is discussed at length by Mosse in *Culture*, pp. 93–124. On educational institutions, see *Crisis*, pp. 5, 149–70.

42. *Nazism*, pp. 51, 123; *Germans and Jews*, p. 117.

43. *Germans and Jews*, p. 77. See also remarks in *Nationalization*, pp. 2–4.

44. *Men and Masses*, Introduction.

PART I

The Language of Cultural Crisis

CHAPTER ONE

Degeneration and the Medical Model of Cultural Crisis in the French *Belle Époque*

Robert A. Nye

If the terms *degenerate* and *degeneracy* have been pronounced dead as valid scientific concepts in the twentieth century, this death cannot be made to include their popular uses in a variety of contexts familiar to both Americans and Europeans. Though not as oft-employed as they once were in the popular culture of the West, these terms retain the power to evoke scenes of drunkenness, disorder, and collapsed morality; they sum up the pathetic condition of a fall from some cherished state of perfection. It is simple to trace the uses of degeneracy in popular culture to the frequently reproduced family histories of the Jukes and the Kallikaks and to a number of nineteenth-century literary sources, of which the best known are Émile Zola's *Rougon-Macquart* novels.[1] The "real" and fictional subjects of these sagas are tainted with mental illness and violent emotions, have a fatal weakness for alcohol, weak constitutions, and constantly run afoul of the law.

It is tempting to explain the popularity of degeneracy in moral terms. The period from the 1850s to World War I was one of remarkable moral intensity and degeneracy was an ideal "Victorian" illness; the intemperate and dissolute behavior of the degenerate could be unfavorably compared to the continent and self-regulated ideal of the respectable Victorian gentleman.[2] As the opposite ego of the morally correct gentleman, the degenerate provided an astonishingly corporeal vision of the fatal consequences of drink, sloth, and vice. In popular culture degeneracy was routinely associated with various forms of antisocial behavior because it bolstered "the common sense, man-on-the-street conclusion that criminals are what they

19

are because they don't know enough to understand the hazardous nature of criminality, or the satisfying rewards of law-abiding life."[3]

In France, while the explanation of degeneracy as a negative symbol of Victorian moral rigor is probably a necessary part of any overall account of its popularity, it is not sufficient. The term first appeared in a technical psychiatric context. The pioneer works of this medical tradition, Charles Lucas' *De l'Hérédité naturelle* (1847) and B.H. Morel's *Traité des dégénérescences* (1857), laid foundations on which French and European mental pathologists built elaborate nosological structures in the *fin de siècle*. These theoretical foundations also heavily influenced nineteenth-century criminology, the public hygiene movement, general social theory, and a wide range of racial and eugenical movements. The role that the concept of degeneracy played in these "scientific" contexts, as opposed to its widely recognized use in "decadent" literature, is very poorly understood. It has never been explained how, for instance, degeneration articulated with French heredity theory, with native Lamarckian evolutionism, or how it helped build a conceptual bridge between the psychology of individuals and collective and social theory.[4] This chapter intends to fill that gap by reconstructing these links and showing how they were used by both medical professionals and the general public.

Once we have specified the nature and the ubiquity of these links, we will make a strong case for the argument that the medical and "hygienic" sources of degeneracy were, if anything, more important elements in public discourse than the "moral" notion of degeneracy popularized in literature and criticism. As we shall see, a strictly medical notion of degeneracy could convincingly demonstrate the relationship that was assumed to exist between degenerate individuals and the various social pathologies from which the nation suffered: depopulation, crime, mental illness, prostitution, suicide, and various organic diseases. Embedded in a medical model of cultural crisis, the concept of degeneration played a much more important symbolic and ideological role and had a deeper social meaning to contemporaries than has previously been understood. If medicine has a political and cultural history, as is now widely acknowledged, so do politics and culture have a medical history.

There are two fundamental reasons why the medical model in which degeneracy enjoyed so important a status had a profound appeal in fin-de-siècle France. First, French medicine, which had undergone far-reaching organizational and conceptual transformations during the revolution, was ideally suited for engaging in public discourse. As Michel Foucault has written of the new nineteenth-century medicine: "In the ordering of human existence it assumes a normative posture, which authorizes it not only to distribute advice as to healthy life, but also to dictate standards for physical and moral relations of the individual and of the society in which he lives."[5] In the outlook of French medicine, the health/sickness binary opposition that governed eighteenth-century therapeutics was supplemented by a normality/abnormality one. Where it could be said of the term *healthy* that it implied merely the absence of some illness, the term *normal* was invested with a value that flowed from its opposite, *abnormal*.[6] Conceptually organized in this manner, medical judgments were capable of expressing the consensual norms, prejudices, and salient anxieties of French society.

The gradual process of professionalization in French medicine during the nineteenth century encouraged doctors to act as mediators between medical knowledge and the general public. Prior to the emergence of a modern medical monopoly in the nineteenth century, "the medical secret" was jealously hidden from public view by the folk healers and charlatans who preceded the university-trained medical corps. The power and prestige of modern medicine is built on the existence of a body of rational and systematic, if not scientific, knowledge that is by its very nature public. The long rehabilitation of the reputation of medicine from its medieval and early modern nadir was thus dependent on the widest possible acceptance of a body of standard medical knowledge. From the late eighteenth century, doctors regarded themselves as emissaries of modern scientific culture to the savage hinterlands. Horrified by the backwardness and brutality of peasant society, they explained the pathologies of rural life by viewing cultural "deprivation" as an effect of unhygienic living conditions. As their professionalization advanced and their local prestige as men of knowledge grew, doctors found themselves increasingly treated as notables whose opinions on all matters were held in esteem.[7] After 1875 many rural doctors benefited from the new republican electoral system and were elected to national political office. They were, after lawyers, the most dominant professional group in the political life of the early Third Republic. This is not to argue that their medical views encouraged them to support any given narrow political position; loyal republicans and monarchists alike defended a species of medical politics that acted to enhance the prestige of both the profession and medical knowledge in general.

The second reason for the appeal of a medical model in nineteenth-centuryFrance is the very appropriateness of such a model for a nation whose vital statistics revealed several alarming trends. Chief among these were disquieting demographic figures. Though the first signs of a leveling off of the high population growth characteristic of eighteenth-century Europe were noticed as early as the Restoration, it was not until the Second Empire that the growth began to slow dramatically compared with other European states. In 1872–1911 the French population grew from 36,103,000 to only 39,605,000, an average of 89,700 per year, less than a third the annual growth rate of the period 1821–46. During the same period (1872–1911) the German population grew by 600,000 a year and increased in size by 58 percent to France's 10 percent. Spain had a 20 percent expansion, Italy a 30 percent, Austria-Hungary 38 percent, Great Britain 43 percent, and European Russia 78 percent. The reason for this small growth lay more with a lagging birthrate than with any other cause, and with the decline of mortality by the end of the century France had to contend with the possibility of natural decrease. During one five-year period (1891–95), deaths exceeded births by 300, and there were several single years after 1890 when growth was negative: 1890, 1892, 1895, 1900, 1907, and 1911.[8] Writing just after the war of 1914–18, Michel Huber said of France: "The pathological weakness of its birthrate distinguishes the French population from all other European peoples."[9]

In the realm of material culture, French performance was only a little better. Industrial production had been in the doldrums from the last years of the Empire, and even the spurt of the 1890s and the remarkably high per capita GNP rate could not conceal the fact that the French were falling woefully behind the Germans in the most important categories of economic productivity.[10] By the end of the century many French scientists were lamenting that France had lost its former position of leadership in pure science and in the critical area of applied science and technology.[11]

And what of "moral" statistics? It is more difficult to judge the relative weight of these figures because of the varying definitions and modes of data collection employed throughout Europe. But there were several trends that, in absolute terms, seemed alarming enough to contemporaries to warrant serious concern. Some of these worrisome trends were strictly medical. In the 1890s, for instance, just as victory over cholera and smallpox was being claimed, tuberculosis and syphilis became grave concerns. Doctors, members of the hygiene professions, and many other leaders of public opinion began to speak and write about the dangers to the social organism posed by these diseases as if they were discovering them for the first time.[12]

The most serious problem, if we can judge by the flood of documents attesting to contemporary concern, was alcoholism. It was a widely documented fact that the French were the European leaders in per capita alcohol consumption: in 1901–10 they consumed 17 liters per capita of pure alcohol per year to 15 in Italy, 12.5 in Belgium, and 11.5 in Switzerland.[13] Simplified licensing procedures for *débits de boissons* in the 1880s had led to a growth of drinking establishments, giving France more of these outlets than any other country in the world. Paris led the way for the world's great cities with 11.25 *débits* for every 1,000 residents.[14] French politicians had always enjoyed a cozy relationship with the distilling lobby, and prosecutions for public drunkenness actually fell between 1876–80 and 1901–05, indicating that the police allowed other matters to outweigh their concern about drink.[15] As in the case of venereal disease and tuberculosis in the 1890s, eventually even public officials were forced to acknowledge the wave of public outcry about the threats of alcoholism.

In this area of social pathologies it is more difficult to know with any precision whether French crime rates were worse than, say, those in Germany or England.[16] It is not even a simple matter deciding whether crime increased or decreased in France during the nineteenth century, owing to changes in policing, prosecution and reporting procedures, and the creation or lapsing of whole categories of crime.[17] The same problems might also be said to apply to assertions about relative rates of insanity.[18] There was sufficient latitude in these judgments to allow those who wished to argue the point for absolute or relative increases in these pathologies to make a convincing statistical case. The two areas most reliably labeled and reported, suicide and homicide, gave at least limited support to the growth theory.

As Durkheim pointed out in 1897, European suicide rates were everywhere on the increase, quintupling in some cases rates recorded in the eighteenth century. France had practically the highest suicide increase in Europe, rising in 1826–88 by 385 percent, or from about 2,000 per year to about 8,000 in the decade of the 1880s. This growth increased even further in the first fifteen years of the twentieth century to annual figures between 9,300 and 10,300.[19] Even after allowing for the range of "normal" expressions of social pathology which he permitted in his social theory, Durkheim regarded this increase as dangerously high. In a celebrated passage from *Suicide* he wrote:

> We must not be dazzled by the brilliant development of sciences, the arts and industry of which we are the witnesses; this development is altogether certainly taking place in the midst of a morbid effervescence, the grievous repercussions of which each one of us feels. It is then very possible and even probable that the rising tide of suicide originates in a pathological state just now accompanying the march of civilization without being its necessary condition.[20]

Data on voluntary homicide are much less clear-cut. Howard Zehr gives a figure of 9 percent in the decline in persons tried for homicide in 1830–1900, a number that is even higher in per capita terms.[21] There was an abrupt rise in homicide figures just after the turn of the century that particularly alarmed contemporaries. From figures averaging around 450 per year in the 1893–1903 period, homicides climbed to an average of 611 in the decade before the war.[22] Contemporaries could also read the general figures on crime as supporting the growth theory of social pathology. When all crimes against property from the 1820s onward are averaged, including those tried in correctional courts, there was an increase in offenses reported to the police of 230 percent and at least a 60 percent gain in property crimes going to trial.[23] Personal assaults also rose in the last quarter of the century. In the decade 1875–84, an average of 25,611 cases were tried yearly on this charge. This figure increased to 34,655 yearly by the decade of 1895–1904.[24] Other studies have noted an increase in the number of recidivists apprehended for crimes in urban areas and a general rise in juvenile delinquency near the century's end.[25]

Another litmus test for those terrified of pathology was the growth of a modern pornography industry and of sexually explicit entertainment. French publishers and printers had supplied the lion's share of European pornography for generations, with the consequence that the mother tongue of Bossuet and Racine was the language par excellence of European erotica. Fascination with the perverse that was a major theme in the "decadent" and symbolist literature of the 1880s and 1890s often spilled over into lucrative pornographic hackwork: Appollinaire, poet and pornographer, produced a sizable quantity of erotica for profit (and by inclination). If there was some precedence for ignoring French leadership in the pornographic book trade, there was less tolerance for the belle époque brand of nude display and erotic dialogue that appeared in the cabarets and little theatres of the capital and in the grand shows of the Moulin Rouge, Olympia, and Folies Bergères.[26] These new forms provoked the appearance of lawsuits, press campaigns, and international congresses designed to counteract their influence and put the vice squad on a footing of constant mobilization.

France had its problems, and citizens of any historical society might have been expected to feel alarm at this formidable range of "illnesses" attacking the nation's vitality. But many other European nations were plagued with high rates of alcoholism, disease, mental illness, suicide, and "modern" forms of immorality without undergoing an anxiety crisis about national health such as that in France. What distinguished French reaction to these typically "modern" problems of urbanizing and industrializing societies was the existence in France of two images of the fatherland of near ideological stature in the nineteenth century. These models, against which all progress or decadence was measured by contemporaries, were the image of France as it used to be and its relative status vis à vis neighboring Germany. In the course of geopolitical developments in the period after 1850 the two images became so inextricably linked that no judgment about the stature of France could be made without some reference to that of Germany.

It is a commonplace of French history that the "idea" of France has provided the necessary ideological apparatus for warring political factions throughout the modern period. The monarchist idea consisted of a king, a union of throne and altar, and the dispersion of political power into the hands of landed notables. The Bonapartist idea recalled an authoritarian political regime, a subordinate but "official" church, and a certain military-imperial veneer. And there was of course the idea of the French Republic: Jacobin state centralism, anticlericalism, and popular sovereignty. If Theodore Zeldin's recent argument about the richer vein of analysis being the study of forces uniting the French is correct, what is common to all three "ideas" of France? It is France as The Great Nation, the premier military power on the continent and the most rich, populous, and economically advanced state in West and Central Europe. Within the skein of historical memories in each of these "ideas" lay an enormous pride in the expansion of French arms, culture, and institutions.

Following the humiliating defeat in 1870 at the hands of Prussia, French images of France as it used to be and of newly united Germany underwent some revision. The new nation, already possessed of a much larger population than France in 1870, had also a more substantial birth rate and an astonishing capacity for economic growth that would allow it to surpass France in most significant areas by the 1890s. In Claude Digeon's account, it was the literary generation of 1890 which felt the first clear signs of "a profound anxiety, a consciousness of weakness, a concern about decadence, an obsession with diminution."[27] By the 1890s the image of the lost provinces had begun to take a characteristically corporeal, biological form. Thus, explains Digeon, for Maurice Barrès, "it is certain that the detachment of these two provinces contributed precisely to the orientation of the Lorrainer's reflections toward the idea that the fatherland was first a soil, a frontier, and men, and that it was conditioned by both human and material realities."[28] Organic metaphors and typologies such as this increased in popularity throughout the remaining years of the century; by 1914 they exercised a kind of linguistic imperialism over all efforts to compare the situation of the two nations. One could dispute degrees of illness or health within this clinical frame of reference, but there was no easy way to avoid the medical model of analysis that it invariably entailed.

The "master pathology" in the spectrum of pathologies afflicting France was the sluggishly growing population. It was in this domain that the relative disadvantages of the French were most readily apparent and geopolitical effects most redoubtable. Lucien Prévost-Paradol, writing at the time of Bismarck's consolidation of the North German Confederation, worried about France preserving:

> . . . a material place and a physical force worthy of our rightful pride, deserving still some consideration from the other peoples of the earth, and retaining the respect the glorious name our old France deserves . . . it is to the most numerous nation that the highest military and political rank belongs along with all the material and moral advantages that flow from it. Any projects or hopes to keep France in its relative rank in the world must be considered to be absolutely chimerical if they do not take as their point of departure this maxim: the number of French must rise rapidly enough to maintain a certain

equilibrium between our power and that of the other great nations of the world.[29]

At about the same time, the French medical and scientific community was engaged in spirited discussions on the relative quality of their population; it was in this context that the notion of degeneration as a social question was first raised. It was conceded that the French were less fertile than their neighbors and as a population significantly older, but few were willing to conclude that this signified any inevitable degeneration.[30] Nonetheless, it was generally argued that, in the face of a relative diminution in absolute numbers, the "productive and instrinsic worth" of the population assumed an increased importance: "The fatherland is not in danger at present; it offers a population powerful in numbers and in the productive and personal worth of its individuals, but it is in danger for the future, and, in the place of sleeping tranquilly, we must remain alert and act with energy and in a spirit of patriotic foresight."[31]

As the figures on French natality worsened in the 1890s, there gradually appeared a huge contemporary literature on the problem. In his classic review of this literature Joseph Spengler broke down the causal explanations most commonly employed into two great categories: involuntary and voluntary.[32] In the first category he considered the explanations that seemed biological. These included causes which weaken the "genetic instinct" of the race to reproduce itself, manifested by a depression of "natural fecundity" or the practices of birth deferment, active contraception, abortion, and infanticide. Spengler found that the favored causes in this category were racial, whereby formerly fecund and "pure" races intermixed under the social conditions of modern democracy and thereby lost, in their new genetic identity, the capacity to procreate.[33] Of secondary importance were causes based on equilibrium models, wherein some form of genetic energy essential for reproduction was gradually lost in the movement of the social organism from a homogeneous condition to a heterogeneous form characterized by specialization and division of labor.[34]

In the "voluntary" category, Spengler listed the causes he felt French writers believed to be susceptible of conscious or rational control. Among these was the argument of social capillarity whereby individuals exchanged the social limitations of high birthrates for the lucrative advantages of upward mobility. Another voluntary argument was popular with the Le-Playans and with those who preferred the generalized notion of "civilization" as the most powerful explanation. In Paul Leroy-Beaulieu's words: "The children of our families, one or two in number, surrounded with indulgent tenderness, with delibitating care, are inclined to a passive and sedentary life and do not but exceptionally manifest the spirit of enterprise and adventure, of endurance and perseverance which characterized their ancient ancestors and that the sons of prolific German families possess today."[35]

Apart from a certain circularity of argument, the most notable thing about all these positions is that they tend to burst the bonds of Spengler's voluntary/involuntary dichotomy, expressing instead belief in a generalized sociological determinism that controls all these mechanisms, hereditary and social alike. In the causal explanations offered for low birth rates, as well as those proposed to account for the other social pathologies we have discussed, there was a characteristic compression of biological and socioenvironmental arguments that ignored the classic distinction between them that one intuitively assumes to have prevailed. Though biological causes were often advanced as the proximate source of social behavior, they were usually characterized as the products of some more distant environmental circumstance acting to shape the organism. When doctors and social scientists confronted a pathology in the genotype, they explained it as having arisen from some earlier pathological environment. When two or more pathologies were found to be invariably associated with one another, they were assumed to be linked in a way which tended to telescope hereditary and social causes that was typical of French thought in this period. This is how Émile Durkheim analyzed the relationship between suicide and abnormally low birth rates in 1888: "Tainted nervous systems do not multiply themselves in a group only by means of unfortunate cross-breedings and hereditary predispositions, but also from the bad sociological conditions in which they find themselves placed. Organic causes are often social causes tranformed and fixed in the organism. There are thus social causes common to suicide and natality which are able to explain their relation."[36]

Durkheim did not find it necessary to identify the precise mechanism whereby these environmental influences "fixed" themselves in human organisms because he took for granted the transformist perspective peculiar to French biological and social science in the nineteenth century. This evolutionary theory of species and organic change sprang from Lamarckian roots and was so well established in French biology by mid-century that the later Darwinian variant had no opportunity to displace it. In preference to the Darwinian mechanism of "evolution by natural selection," French neo-Lamarckism was organized on conceptual foundations borrowed from early nineteenth-century embryology, where some of the most convincing proofs for the idea of species evolution had been originally formulated.[37]

Central to this neo-Lamarckian explanation was the conception of the embryo's "organic economy" in which diverse internal elements of the organism exhibit a solidarity of associative bonds which serve the organism in the task of adaptation. In this view the organism possesses some interior force which helps it to determine the "conditions in which it accepts combat."[38] The organism's accommodation to any environment is negotiated between these solidaristic components and the milieu in a way that makes this internal "organic economy" with its efficient division of labor an a priori condition of successful adaptation. Sometimes in the form of equilibrium models reinforced by notions derived from thermodynamics, this concept of organic economy penetrated many areas of French science. It formed the basis of Claude Bernard's idea of the "internal milieu" of autonomous vital forces, and had considerable impact on the human sciences. It was, to quote Durkheim once more, a touchstone of organic health and viability: "For a society to feel itself in good health, it is neither sufficient or always necessary that it use a lot of coal or consume a lot of meat, but it is necessary that the development of all its functions be regular, harmonious, proportioned."[39]

But what if the environment alters in such a way as to produce responses from the organism that are successful in the short-run task of adaptation but potentially dysfunctional to the organism in the long run — an adaptation that the organism experiences as a pathology? It was this problem — a very "modern" one with an intellectual history of its own — that produced degeneration theory. Within the medical model of social pathology, degeneration accounted for the persistence of growth of social illnesses in progressive, industrial societies: increases in mental illness, suicide, alcoholism, crime, and other problems. The appearance of degenerative illnesses in society was the price paid by that society for successful adaptation to a new urban and industrial environment.[40]

In the last half of the nineteenth century, a neo-Lamarckian theory of heredity was elaborated that could successfully explain the inheritance of these human "adaptive" pathologies in a coherent way. The first generation concealed the adaptation as an "aptitude" or "tendency," but later generations experienced it as a debilitating morbid physical condition.[41] In Magnan's classic definition of the syndrome, degeneracy was

> a pathological state of the organism which, in relation to its most immediate progenitors, is constitutionally weakened in its psycho-physical resistance and does not realize but in part the biological conditions of the hereditary struggle for life. That weakening, which is revealed in permanent stigmata, is essentially progressive, with only intervening regeneration; when this is lacking, it leads more or less rapidly to the extinction of the species.[42]

In this standard clinical account of degeneracy there is a characteristic kind of compression of the hereditary and environmental influences that control the syndrome. Unhealthy environments were understood to initiate the syndrome, but once set in motion and in the absence of some determining milieu, the syndrome developed its own hereditary momentum, expressing its progress in worsening behavior and physical signs. Perhaps on account of this unique blend of causes, contemporaries usually regarded a "typical" degenerate sign as both cause *and* symptom of the syndrome, an understandable conclusion in the circumstances. This compression had the effect of endowing the person of the "degenerate" with a double power: he was a painful reminder of the dysfunctional qualities of urban-industrial civilization and the ambiguity of progress, and was a living assurance of its continued moral decline.

Magnan's description of the degenerate syndrome also reveals the belief that a "weakened" condition which lowers "resistance" is the underlying mechanism of the process. The vast literature on degeneration clearly shows that the chief effect of this weakness was its deleterious effect on the human will. Will pathology was a well-recognized effect of certain forms of mental illness in nineteenth-century French psychology.[43] Damage to his will exposed the individual to a wide range of dangers, both biological and social. His inhibitions were catastrophically lowered to instinctive "impulsions" or extreme passions, which swept through him like a whirlwind, compelling him to acts of violence he was powerless to resist. His diminished willpower also made him vulnerable to the sensual appeal of drink and debauchery and the tempting allure of easy or ill-gotten money.

At this point — the weakened ability of the organism to muster resistance to "evil" — degeneration theory intersected the social pathologies most feared by French men and women. Psychiatrists, criminologists, and other members of the "hygiene" professions led the way in forging links between these maladies and hereditary degeneration. The most common linkages were those made between madness, crime, and alcoholism.[44] These "cause-symptoms" were viewed both as sources of degenerate cycles and as certain signs that such cycles were underway; they became so hopelessly confounded with one another and with degeneration itself, in both the technical and popular literature, that they were in practice virtually interchangeable. As the antialcoholic physician Paul-Marie LeGrain argued: "If alcoholism is increasing at the same time as criminality, has not one the right to establish a causal relationship between these two facts as one has already done between alcohol and madness?"[45] In his review of this literature Georges Heuyer has written:

> [The degenerate] is born with a congenital problem in brain operations which takes the form of an emotive instability with obsessive preoccupations, and which is able, in certain circumstances, to lead to crime. A bad education has on them a more pronounced influence than on the normal individual. More than others, degenerates were predisposed to offense or crime, and these predispositions manifested themselves from infancy. Mental degenerescence is a kind of selection, but a selection against the grain.[46]

It was not unusual for students of this syndrome to place degenerates on a *behavioral* continuum, where the degree of seriousness of mental incapacitation corresponded to the degree of seriousness of the crime. According to Thulié, the behavior of the "criminal-madman" varied on a scale of insensible gradations from "the most bestial idiocy to instability of the most subtle type."[47] There were "degenerate assassins" and also "degenerate prostitutes," whose "destiny is to be delivered over to deplorable excesses, to undergo the most abominable miseries, and to fall into the most shameful and abasing degradations whose torments are marked by the perpetual pursuit of new pleasures and the incessant satisfaction of their erotic frenzy."[48] For all these "idiots of the will" [the term of Marandon de Montyel][49] the best assurance of their degenerate status was their manifestation of criminal behavior, alcoholism, mental instability, offensive or "immoral" behavior, or any combination of these.

Concern about these various manifestations of degeneracy was ultimately linked to the "master pathology" of population in two ways. First, there was worry about the presumed effect the spread of these phenomena was having on birth rates. The frequent mixture of biological, social, and equilibrium explanations allowed depopulationists to compress these distinct causes into a general argument which held that the French "instinct" to reproduce (whether conceived as a biological or social force) had been progressively diminished. This position was compatible with the model of degeneracy as a progressive weakening of the vitality of the organism. An editorial writer for *Le Temps*, taking some hope from the relatively stronger natality figures of 1896–1901, concluded that the "degeneration" and "loss of vigor of our race" that had been so discussed was by no means a certainty.[50] Second, there was concern about the influence these pathologies were having on the quality of the population. By the end of the century, the nagging problem of the 1860s had become a national anxiety of grave dimensions.

The effects of this qualitative decline on the army were considered of primary importance. Though they did not always produce their sources of information, popular authors argued that the medical rejection rate for the French army was higher than in Germany, or that the average height of French inductees had declined since 1800.[51] Alcohol, it was also asserted, had become a serious problem in barracks culture.[52] Other depopulationists cited the growth in the number of alcoholics and the mentally ill and the spread of a whole range of diseases which were the more dangerous because of their tendency to become hereditary — thus "hérédo-syphilitiques," "hérédo-tuberculeux," or "hérédo-arthritisme."[53]

By the last decade of the century the metaphors most often used to describe the national condition were drawn from organic models and had a biological, palpable quality. The generality of degeneration theory and of the hereditary mechanisms that governed it consolidated the differences between environmental and genetic causes and made the passage from individual to social pathology and vice versa simple. The medical model of diagnosis and cure seemed the most appropriate to contemporaries. In Émile Durkheim's words: "The duty of the statesman is no longer to push society toward an ideal that seems attractive to him, but his role is that of the physician: he prevents the outbreak of illnesses by good hygiene, and he seeks to cure them when they have appeared."[54]

From the 1890s until the war there was a flood of professional and lay organizations founded to help stem the spread of infection in the social organism. Members of the "hygiene" groups may have been encouraged in their zeal by the bitter atmosphere of political and social strife that dominated this period. These years provided the setting for the Dreyfus affair — the most divisive political struggle in a divisive era — and for the most heavily concentrated and violent strike activity in the history of the republic. The free-thinking, antimilitaristic, and revolutionary socialist dimensions of the working-class movement at the turn of the century added to the anxiety of these hygiene reformers and helped prepare public opinion for a political reading of their medical ideology. It must have seemed to most Frenchmen in those days that the gyroscope that normally stabilized the equilibrium of their society was wildly out of control.

Most of the hygiene groups were ad hoc in nature, addressing themselves to a single problem. There were antidepopulationist groups, antialcoholics, and others that dealt with pornography or diseases of the popular urban classes. In practice, there was overlapping in these movements, since each of these pathologies was understood to be related to the others through the degeneration syndrome. The repopulationists found antipornographic arguments useful in the struggle against the sex manuals of their neo-Malthusian enemies,[55] and antialcohol groups took comfort from the prominent temperance platforms of the other hygiene groups.

The best supported and largest of these groups operated like the great political leagues of those years. The National Alliance for the Growth of the French Population, founded in 1896 by Jacques Bertillon, funded a *Bulletin*, organized a national circuit of public speakers and local action chapters, and acted as a clearing-house for a wide variety of pamphlet literature and lobbying activities. The main antialcohol groups, The National League against Alcoholism and the French Antialcoholic Union, not only carried on all these activities but also managed to persuade the government to allow their conferences to be held in schools and military barracks and their propaganda to be printed in textbooks and training manuals.[56] The French Society for Sanitary and Moral Prophylaxis (1901) lobbied vigorously in favor of continued regulation of prostitution and agitated for the defense of a "family morality." In the words of the founder of the League against Syphilis, Alfred Fournier, "if it should happen that humanity returns to innocence and the golden age, the days of syphilis will be numbered."[57]

Members of these groups hosted national and international congresses in French cities to popularize their causes. An umbrella hygiene conference, the International Congress of Hygiene and Demography, was already holding its tenth annual meeting in 1900.[58] In 1902–03 the École des Hautes Études Sociales devoted all its courses to the "social applications" of "solidarity," many of which were of primary concern to hygienists, and the Academy of Sciences offered a prize for the best work on depopulation in 1909 for which it received twenty-two book-length manuscripts.[59] The public was kept well informed of these developments; newspaper editors presented the most recent data on vital national statistics to their readers in the same spirit of agonizing concern as the media today discuss the "leading economic indicators" for signs of trends in our precious standard of living.

It is impossible in this brief essay to document exhaustively all the conceptual contexts in which pessimistic data appear in popular accounts of French pathologies. But even a cursory reading makes it clear that the same general notions that governed the technical genres were preserved in the process of vulgarization: the medical model of "organic" social analysis, the central idea of degeneracy, the unvarying mixture of environmental and biohereditary causes, and the debilitating effects of these morbid phenomena on the will.

This medical model of cultural decline was embedded in contemporary political discourse, where it played a symbolic role of the highest political significance. In the troubled and conflict-ridden years 1895-1914, this medical model both identified the sources of social illnesses and suggested a cure; its implicit aim of a regeneration of the national organism met with an overwhelming response. For the republican centrists, who had chosen by 1900 a political stance emphasizing class cooperation and solidarity, and a nationlist Right imbued with a hatred of Germany and a terror of class warfare, a doctrine of organic regeneration had an immediate political utility. It provided a powerful set of metaphors for the political groups that fueled the nationalist revival of 1905–14 and set France on a collision course with Germany.[60]

The penetration of these metaphors into various sectors of French civil life — politics, labor, education, and culture — is well known. There is another area that has received much less attention but provides a much more striking continuity with the conceptual terminology of the degenerate medical model and which may have provided a more potent political symbolism for national revival than any other source. This area was the physical culture movement. Nowhere is the confusion of moral and material realms more strikingly represented; nowhere else could the benefits of social action hold the promise of such dramatic benefits to the health of the national organism in so short a time.

In the 1890s, visible evidence of the new popularity of sport could be seen everywhere.[61] As the bicycle increased in popularity and walking came to be more than a means of locomotion, men's and women's clothing changed accordingly. Special periodicals appeared which covered the fine points of the new sporting events, and the great mass dailies covered the array of new activities in great detail. In this age of promotion the first "media events" were born. The Tour de France, the Paris-Nice road race, the annual Seine swimming race, and a host of other events were sponsored, promoted, and then written up as news by the Paris dailies in their apparently insatiable desire for ever larger subscriptions. Not to be outdone, the socialist organ *L'Humanité* entered the sports field with a vengeance, eventually devoting relatively more of its space to sports news than any pre–World War I newspaper. A Frenchman, the artistocrat Pierre de Coubertin, out of a putative concern for the higher principles of internationalism, was the moving force in the modern rebirth of the Olympic games, the first of which was held in Athens in 1896.[62]

It is easy to lose one's way in this explosion of sporting activity if one leafs through a few of the "gentlemanly" sporting magazines or follows only the cycle, horse, or car set through their genteel rituals. Sport, and more particularly physical hygiene, embodied a more profound ideological design and served deeper cultural ends than the fleeting diversion of class or mass. In some quarters nothing less was hoped for in this revival of physical activity than the regeneration of the French race itself. The complete structure of the movement in France remains to be written, but its general outlines may be revealed in a brief review. Many Frenchmen, obsessed with the simultaneous physical and moral decay of their nation, were willing to see in physical hygiene and the moral discipline it demanded a possible source of a sweeping national revival.

The general patriotic design of the movement is apparent from its origins. The National League of Physical Education was organized in the 1870s by Paschal Grousset, a Jacobin nationalist who regarded sport as a curative to the disastrous military defeat of 1870. It was not long before the movement gained a hearing with right-wing nationalists who eventually moved into the leadership positions of the movement.[63] This development coincided with the first appearance of militant hygienists, who progressively became the chief ideologues of the physical culture revival. Philippe Tissié founded the Girondist League of Physical Education. In 1888, a string of Schools of Physical Culture were set up by Desbonnet and his colleague Georges Rouhet, and doctors throughout the country lobbied the government for systematic physical hygiene in schools. The pathologists' appearance changed the emphasis of the movement from simple patriotism to, in Eugen Weber's quaint anachronism, "patriotic and sanitary concerns."[64] In this guise the movement may be seen more correctly as another attempt, with the efforts of the repopulationists, the antialcohol movement, the antipornographic forces, and the eternal battle against crime, to breathe new life into a fatigued and sensual civilization.

Pierre de Coubertin is often cited as a leader and spiritual father of the sports movement in France, and at first glance his conception of the value of sport does not appear to support this emphasis on patriotism and hygiene. The notion of team sport he urged, his ceaseless efforts in the cause of internationalism, and his unaristocratic defense of modern democracy suggest the opposite. But as Eugen Weber has made clear, Coubertin was, in spite of these beliefs, well within the current of the national regenerationists. His aim was to help train a new democratic elite that would lead the nation on the great world stage; sports would build in this youth the qualities of mind and body necessary to this great task. These qualities were the same as those sought by the hygienists. He dedicated the new journal he edited with Gaston Bordat "to those who hope to see science more widely known, criticism more enlightened, a more open horizon, characters more firm, man, in a word, more the master of himself and more free in his movements."[65] The "moral qualities" he and Bordat thought would be built by football were "initiative, perseverance, judgment, courage, self-abnegation, and self-discipline."[66] These characteristics were precisely those habits of self-control and willfulness sought by hygienists and which Coubertin himself hoped would promote a moral revival, counteract depopulation, pornography, egoistic materialism, and physical dissipation.[67]

Victor Margueritte was also concerned with the low natality, alcoholism, and general "vital weakening" of French society.[68] He called for a great national effort in physical education and helped found an organization, Republican League of National Action, to promote physical culture. As was generally true throughout the physical culture movement, Margueritte believed in the direct relationship between mind and body. One must "encourage the culture of the body as this will be the best way to facilitate that of the mind: Physical health, moral purity." The object, Margueritte argued elsewhere, was a "cult of energy" that would save the race and extend its force.[69]

Margueritte's primary concern seemed to be with the biomoral implications of low birth rates and physical disabilities. His concern was well supported after the turn of the century, particularly for the military consequences of these problems. The object of physical education, argued Senator Charles Humbert, "is to augment the value of men since we are no longer able, alas, to augment their number."[70] But this sort of physical education was understood to have a deeper aim and wider significance in France than is implied in the maxim *mens sana in corpore sano*. It was a holistic therapy for the organically related mental and physical ills of the nation. The ultimate goal was the rehabilitation of the degenerate weakness of the will that produced an "insufficiency of force."[71]

The number of hygiene manuals stressing the positve effects of rejuvenated willpower increased in the pivotal years after Tangiers. Exercise, psychotherapy, eugenically sensible marriage, and good diet, insofar as these could be made to reproduce the conditions of a total environment, might overcome the morbid effects of a degenerate inheritance, strengthen the will, and even clean the genetic slate for the next generations.[72] Though we have spoken until now only of the *negative* effects, the neo-Lamarckian emphasis on environmental adaptation by the organism could also account for progressive effects when the environment was beneficent. The hope that they would help the vital forces and will of the nation sustained the public supporters of the hygiene and physical culture movements.

These advertised benefits held a great attraction for the many Frenchmen convinced of their nation's decline, and the promise of a simple and rapid return to vigor and moral health through exercise was an enormously popular alternative. No doubt some middle-aged Parisians were coaxed into the bicycle paths of the Bois de Boulogne by the subliminal appeal of patriotism which lay at the heart of the physical culture movement, but one suspects most adults believed such things were better left to the young. French youth was indeed much taken by the merits of physical culture, and the burgeoning youth movement of the prewar years was permeated by the rhetoric and reality of physical strength, virility, force, and the other presumed benefits of exercise.[73]

In the end the importance of the physical culture movement should not be measured by the number of gymnastic societies it may have generated, nor the boost it may have given the new bicycle manufacturing industry; these phenomena had causes more contingent than any collective desire for national health. The meaning of the movement lies buried in the latent connective tissues of words and things. Physical culture was repeatedly celebrated as a national glory by most observers, with a logic and terminology that dovetailed it smoothly with the national pathologies it was meant to heal. The movement's real significance lies in the rationalizations invoked in its behalf and the precise anxieties articulated therein.

It is difficult to escape the conclusion that by the end of the first decade of the twentieth century there existed, at several levels of thought, the conviction that the nation was grievously ill, suffering from a syndrome that wrenched it from its "normal" path of development. This illness attacked the minds and bodies of Frenchmen and could be made to plausibly explain the relative failings of the fatherland since the defeat of 1870. This great syndrome of degenerative decline was first articulated by doctors, psychiatrists, and other health professionals whose training in science and bourgeois professional outlook encouraged the creation of a hygienic model with cultural and organic dimensions. In a nation deeply worried about its relative vitality, doctors found their medical knowledge selling at a high premium and their social prestige greater than any time in the previous century. They were encouraged to suggest cures for this illness in the same biological discourse in which the symptomatology of the national pathology had been originally constructed.

The existence of a medical model of cultural decline had penetrated the political milieu by 1900. The Chamber established a permanent committee on depopulation, proposed new legislation on the hygiene of urban housing and on the regulation of prostitution. Various ministries undertook inquiries seeking more information on the connections between alcoholism, mental illness, and suicide, and initiated many other activities that touched on national health.[74] For the political class, which was discovering a new resonance in the formulas of national revival and patriotism, the medical model was of great utility. It allowed them to identify crucial problems whose seriousness had already been acknowledged in some cases for generations. It provided republicans of all stripes a ready-made demonstration of the need for class solidarity and social equilibrium. It suggested a cure that was at once moral and physical, and which avoided facing the social and economic aspects of French national decline. As Lion Murard and PatrickZylberman have recently pointed out, this mixture of anxieties and curative processes signals the growth of a peculiarly modern form of political consciousness that has as its ultimate object "materials for the instruction of a new man, a eugenics rising to its climax in a propaedeutics of the masses."[75]

If the politico-medical outlook of "biopower" in France prior to 1914 failed to reach the level of theory and practice it attained in twentieth-century totalitarian systems, we can be sure that a history of degeneracy theory is a necessary prelude to understanding those developments. The manner in which the theory was constructed and the language in which it is expressed enabled it to so integrate the palpable and familiar skein of national pathologies that it escaped the terminological dead end of the clinic and thrived in the arena of public discourse.

NOTES

1. For some of the literary expressions of the term and a discussion of their contemporary appeal see George L. Mosse's introduction, "Max Nordau and His *Degeneration,*" to *Degeneration* (New York: Howard Fertig, 1968), pp. xv–xxiv. Also see Richard D. Walter, "What Became of the Degenerate? A

Brief History of a Concept." *Journal of the History of Medicine* 11 (October 1952), pp. 422–29.

2. Peter Cominos has explained the power of this model of respectability in "Late Victorian Sexual Respectability and the Social System," *International Review of Social History* 8 (1963), pp. 18–48, 216–50.

3. George B. Vold, *Theoretical Criminology* (New York: Oxford University Press, 1958), p. 78.

4. See for instance Koenraad W. Swart, *The Sense of Decadence in Nineteenth Century France* (The Hague: Nijhoff, 1964); A.E. Carter, *The Idea of Decadence in French Literature, 1830–1900* (Toronto: University of Toronto, 1958).

5. Michel Foucault, *The Birth of the Clinic: An Archeology of Medical Preception,* trans. A.M. Sheridan Smith (New York: Pantheon, 1973), p. 34.

6. George Canguilhem brilliantly discusses the historical origins of the notion of "pathological" states as a quantitative variation of "normal" states in nineteenth-century French science and medicine. See his concluding remarks on the problems with this older usage, pp. 155–57 in *Le Normal et le pathologique,* 3rd ed. (Paris: PUF, 1975).

7. Harvey Mitchell, "Rationality and Control in French Eighteenth Century Medical Views of the Peasantry," *Comparative Studies in Society and History* 21 (no. 1, January 1979), pp. 82–112. For an account of the crucial stage of this professionalization see George Weisz, "The Politics of Medical Professionalization in France, 1845–1848," *Journal of Social History* 12 (no. 1, Fall 1978), pp. 3–30. For general accounts of French medicine in the nineteenth century see Jacques Léonard, *La France médicale au XIXe siècle* (Paris: Gallimard, 1978); id., *La Vie quotidienne du médecin de province au XIXe siècle* (Paris: Hachette, 1977).

8. André Armengaud, *La Population française au XIXe siècle* (Paris: PUF, 1971), pp. 47–108.

9. Michel Huber, *La Population de la France pendant la guerre* (Paris: PUF, n.d.), p. 81.

10. Madeleine Reberioux, *La République radicale, 1898–1914* (Paris: Éditions du Seuil, 1975), pp. 196–200; Georges DuPeux, *French Society, 1789–1970,* trans. Peter Wait (London: Meuthuen, 1976), p. 176.

11. See the discussion in Harry Paul, *The Sorcerer's Apprentice* (Gainesville, Fla.: University of Florida Press, 1972).

12. See Alain Corbin, "Le Péril vénérien au debut du siècle: prophylaxie sanitaire et prophylaxie morale"; and Gérard Jacquemet, "Médecine et 'maladies populaires' dans le Paris de la fin du XIXe siècle," *Recherches: l'Haleine des Faubourgs* (no. 29, December 1977), pp. 245–83, 349–64.

13. Michael R. Marrus, "Social Drinking in the Belle Époque," *Journal of Social History* 7 (no. 2, Winter 1974), pp. 120–28.

14. *Ibid.,* pp. 129–31. On the heightened concern about the consequences of this expansion see Jacqueline Lalouette, "Le Discours bourgeois sur les débits de boisson aux alentours de 1900," *Recherches: l'Haleine des Faubourgs* (no. 29 December 1977), pp. 315–47.

15. Maurice Yvernes, "L'Alcoolisme et la criminalité," *Journal de la Société de Statistique de Paris* 49 (November 1908), pp. 400–19. Also Lowenthal, "La Criminalité en France," *Revue du Mois* 6 (October 10, 1908), pp. 410–13.

16. The problematic nature of comparative data on crime rates is discussed in Howard Zehr, *Crime and the Development of Modern Society: Patterns of*

Criminality in Nineteenth-Century Germany and France (Totowa N.J.: Rowman & Littlefield, 1976); Ted R. Gurr, *Rogues, Rebels, and Reformers: A Political History of Urban Crime and Conflict* (Beverly Hills, Calif.: Sage, 1976).

17. On the factors which affect the outcome of criminal statistics, see J.J. Tobias, *Urban Crime in Victorian England* (New York: Schocken, 1972), pp. 256–66; V.A.C. Gatrell and T.B. Hadden, "Criminal Statistics and Their Interpretation." In E.A. Wrigley (ed.), *Nineteenth Century Society: Essays in the Use of Quantitative Methods for the Study of Social Data* (Cambridge: Cambridge University Press, 1972), pp. 336–96; Michelle Perrot, "Délinquance et système pénitentiaire en France au XIXe siècle," *Annales ESC* (January 1975), pp. 67–91.

18. For whatever cause, it is certain that the population of the insane asylums increased dramatically faster than general poulation growth in the last part of the nineteenth century, going from 49,589 in 1871 to 100,291 in 1911. Asile d'Aliénés, "Assistance," *Annuaire Statistique, 1913* (Paris, 1914), p. 33.

19. Émile Durkheim, *Suicide: A Study in Sociology,* trans. John H. Spaulding and George Simpson (New York: Free Press, 1951), p. 367. The data for the period 1900–14 may be found in the "Résumé Rétrospectif," *Annuaire Statistique: Compte Général de l'Administration de la Justice Criminelle* 52 (Paris, 1937), p. 48.

20. Durkheim, *Suicide,* p. 368.

21. Howard Zehr, *Crime and the Development of Modern Society,* pp. 114–115.

22. These averages are computed from the "Résumé Rétrospectif," *Compte Général,* pp. 46–47.

23. Zehr, *Crime and the Development of Modern Society,* p. 36.

24. These are my averages from the "Résumé Rétrospectif," *Compte Général,* pp. 47–48.

25. Denis Szabo, *Crimes et Villes* (Paris: Cujas, 1960), p. 38; Yak-Yon Chen, *Études statistiques sur la criminalité en France de 1855 à 1930* (Paris, 1937), pp. 15–16.

26. See Patrick Waldberg on the nude theater, *Eros in la Belle Époque,* trans. Helen R. Lane (New York: Grove Press, 1969), pp. 90–100. On the pornography tradition see Theodore Zeldin, *France, 1848–1945,* vol. 1 (Oxford: Oxford University Press, 1973), pp. 309–12.

27. Claude Digéon, *La Crise allemande de la pensée française* (Paris: PUF, 1959), p. 431.

28. Ibid., p. 431.

29. Lucien Prévost-Paradol, *La France nouvelle* (Paris: Michel Lévy Frères, 1868), pp. 409–10.

30. See the debate reported at the Academy of Medicine, "Sur la prétendue dégénéréscence de la population française," *Revue des Cours Scientifiques* 4 (April 13–20, 1967), pp. 305–11, 320–31.

31. These are the remarks of Félix-Henri Boudet at the Academy of Medicine reported in *Revue des Cours Scientifiques* 4 (June 29, 1867), pp. 494–96.

32. Joseph J. Spengler, *France Faces Depopulation* (Durham, N.C.: Duke University Press, 1938), pp. 135–74.

33. The best instance of this argument is Vacher de la Pouge, *Les Sélections sociales* (Paris, 1896).

34. Spengler, *France Faces Depopulation,* pp. 138–40. See esp. E. Maurel, *De la Dépopulation en France* (Paris, 1896); and Alfred Fouillée, *Psychologie du peuple français* (Paris, 1898).

35. Paul Leroy-Beaulieu, *La Question de la population* (Paris: Alcan, 1911), pp. 350–51.
36. Émile Durkheim, "Suicide et natalité: étude de statistique morale," *Revue Philosophique* 26 (1888), p. 462.
37. Yvette Conry, *L'Introduction du Darwinisme en France au xixe siècle* (Paris: Vrin, 1974), pp. 39–43.
38. Ibid., pp. 43–44.
39. Durkheim, "Suicide et natalité," p. 447.
40. It was even argued that degenerative "illnesses" should be viewed as advantageous in this process of adaptation. See Gina Lombroso, *I Vantaggi della degenerazione* (Turin: Bocca, 1904).
41. So far as human heredity was concerned, much of the theoretical writing in this field was done by experts in French mental pathology primarily concerned with the inheritance of morbid mental states. Their works regularly catalogue the coeval degenerative-physical effects of these syndromes. Among the major works in the late nineteenth century in this area are Henri Le Grand du Saulle, *La Folie héréditaire* (Paris, 1873); Alexandre Axenfeld, *Des Névrosés* (Paris, 1879); Théodule Ribot, *L'Hérédité psychologique* (Paris, 1873); J. Déjérine, *L'Hérédité dans les maladies du système nerveux* (Paris, 1886); Charles Féré, *La Famille névropathique* (Paris, 1894).
42. Valentin Magnan and Paul-Maurice LeGrain, *Les Dégénérés* (Paris: Rueff, 1895), p. 79.
43. The classic text in this field is Théodule Ribot's *Les Maladies de la volonté* (Paris, 1884). Ribot explained the connection of human will with its organic foundations in the following way: "Volition is not an event coming from no one knows where; it drives its roots into the depths of the unconscious and beyond the individual into the species and the race. It comes not from above, but from below: it is a sublimation of the lower instincts" (p. 150).
44. This literature is enormous and we can only cite the most influential: Charles Féré, *Dégénéréscence et criminalité* (Paris: Flammarion, 1888); Émile Laurent, "Les Maladies de la volonté chez les criminels," *Annales MédicoyPsychologiques* (November 1892), pp. 404–28; Marandon de Montyel, "Les Aliénés dits criminels," *Annales Médico-Psychologiques* (May 1891), pp. 434–50; Émile Laurent, *L'Anthropologie criminelle et les nouvelles théories du crime,* 2nd ed. (Paris: Société d'Éditions Scientifiques, 1893); H. Thulié, *La Lutte contre la dégénéréscence et la criminalité,* 2nd ed. (Paris, 1912); Paul Masoin, *Alcoolisme et criminalité* (Paris, 1891); Paul-Marie LeGrain, *Dégénéréscense sociale et alcoolisme* (Paris, 1895); G.L. Duprat, *La Criminalité de l'adolescence* (Paris, 1909); *Les Causes sociales de la folie* (Paris: Alcan, 1900); Paul Jacoby, *Études sur la selection chez l'homme,* 2nd ed. (Paris: Alcan, 1905).
45. Paul-Marie LeGrain, "L'Année du crime et l'alcool," *L'Alcool* 2 (May 1897), p. 61.
46. Georges Heuyer, "La Point de vue de la médecine psychiatrique," *Revue des Sciences Criminelles* (July 1964), p. 738.
47. H. Thulié, "Assistance des dégénérés superieurs," *Revue Philanthropique* 1 (May 1897), p. 45.
48. H. Thulié, "Premières mésures à prendre contre le développement de la criminalité infantile," *Revue Philanthrophique* 3 (July 10, 1898), p. 303. Like Thulié, most observers saw worsening degeneracy affecting women by miring them ever more deeply in "female" crimes like prostitution. Some believed

that degeneracy signaled the emerging equality of the sexes by bringing women, in the last stages of the disease, to the same condition as men. See Pauline Tarnowsky, *Les Femmes homicides* (Paris: Alcan, 1908). On prostitution and its relation to contemporary medical theory see Alain Corbin, *Les Filles de noce: misère sexuelle et prostitution aux 19e et 20e siècles* (Paris: Aubier, 1978), pp. 436–52.

49. Marandon de Montyel, "Les Pervers et leur assistance," *Revue Philanthropique* 20 (January 1907), p. 287. In this account of his clinical observations, Montyel, head of the asylum at Ville-Avrard and one of the most respected psychiatrists of his day, introduced the term *pervers* as a code word for the last phase of degeneracy.

50. *Le Temps* (January 9, 1902).

51. Victor Margueritte, "La Première des cultures," *Le Journal* (October 24, 1908); A. des Cilleuls, "La Population française en 1800 et en 1900," *La Reforme Sociale* 40 (1900), p. 833.

52. Charles Humbert, "Le Cabaret à la caserne," *La Grande Revue* 48 (April 10, 1908), pp. 417–35.

53. On the appearance of these hereditary syndromes in the medical literature see Gerard Jacquemet, "Médecine et 'maladies populaires' dans le Paris de la fin du XIXe siècle," p. 362. On *hérédo-arthritisme* as a cause of depopulation see E. Maurel, *La Dépopulation de la France* (Paris, 1896). See also Victor Turquan, *Contribution à l'étude de la population* (Lyon: A. Rey, 1902); E. Maurel, *Causes de nôtre dépopulation* (Paris: Doin, 1902).

54. Émile Durkheim, *The Rules of the Sociological Method,* trans. Sarah A. Solovay and John H. Mueller, 8th ed. (New York: Free Press , 1964), p. 75.

55. On the connections between repopulationist and antipornography ideologies see Francis Ronsin, "Liberté-Natalité: réaction et répression anti-malthusiennes avant 1920," *Recherches* 29 (December 1977), pp. 376–88.

56. See J. Lalouette, "Débits de boisson et discours bourgeois," pp. 335–43.

57. Quoted from Alfred Fournier's *Ligue contre la syphilis* in Alain Corbin, "Le Péril vénérien au début du siècle: prophylaxie sanitaire et prophylaxie morale," p. 257.

58. The *procès-verbal* of this meeting lists papers presented on alcoholism, depopulation, prostitution, and all the other "pathologies" (Paris: Masson, 1900).

59. *Les Applications sociales de la solidarité* (Paris: Alcan, 1904); Henri Joly summarizes these depopulationist works in *Séances et Travaux de l'Academie des Sciences Morales et Politiques* 172 (1909), pp. 106–30.

60. See in this connection Eugen Weber, *The Nationalist Revival in France, 1905-1914* (Berkeley: University of California Press, 1959).

61. Marcel Spivak lists the figures for organized sporting activity in France in 1910: 200,000 in general athletic clubs; 200,000 in gymnastic societies; 200,000 in rifle societies; 70,000 in paramilitary societies for military instruction and training; 70,000 more in boxing and fencing societies; and 150,000 in cycling groups. Marcel Spivak, "Le Développement de l'éducation physique et du sport français de 1852 à 1914," *Revue d'Histoire Moderne et Contemporaine* 24 (January-March 1977), pp. 45–46.

62. For Coubertin's role see Richard D. Mandell, *The First Modern Olympics* (Berkeley: University of California Press, 1976), pp. 49–94.

63. John Hoberman has spoken lucidly on this development in his paper "Sport and the French Right," read at the Fourth Annual Meeting of the North American Society for Sport History (University of Oregon, Eugene, June 16,

1976). See also Eugen Weber, "Pierre de Coubertin and the Introduction of Organized Sport in France," *Journal of Contemporary History* 5 (no. 2 1970), pp. 10-11.

64. Eugen Weber, "Gymnastics and Sports in Fin de Siècle France: Opium of the Classes," *American Historical Review* 76 (no. 1, February 1971), p. 87. In his recent article Marcel Spivak indicates the long association of French physical education with military training; the patronage of the army throughout much of the century had kept the movement alive. But Tissié and his fellow hygienists objected to the exclusively military content of this style of physical education as it emphasized only passive skills and the use of arms; the hygienists preferred a more diversified kind of physical education that could develop the moral sources of the individual will. See Spivak, "Le Développement de l'-éducation physique," pp. 40–44.

65. Pierre de Coubertin, *Revue pour les Français* 1 (July 1906), p. 1.

66. Pierre de Coubertin and Gaston Bordat, "La Valeur morale du football," *Revue pour les Français* 2 (January 1907), p. 507.

67. See Pierre de Coubertin, *The Evolution of France under the Third Republic,* trans. Isabel F. Hapgood (New York: Crowell, 1897), pp. 375–85.

68. Victor Margueritte, "L'Éducation physique," *Dépêche de Toulouse* (November 9, 1908).

69. *Le Journal* (November 19, 1908).

70. Charles Humbert, "Pour la Race: l'éducation physique obligatoire," *Le Journal* (October 1, 1907). For this point of view, see also F. Canonge, "L'-Éducation physique," *La Grande Revue* (September 25, 1908), pp. 236–59; Édouard Maneuvrier, *L'Éducation de la bourgeoisie sous la République* (Paris, 1888); Paul Adam, *La Morale des sports* (Paris, 1907).

71. [J.L.], "Le Sport et la neurasthénie," *La Presse* (July 7, 1908).

72. See for instance H. Lavrand, *Traitement de la volonté et psychothérapie* (Paris, 1907); Georges Rouhet and Desbonnet, *L'Art de créer le pur-sang humain* (Paris, 1908); Desbonnet, *La Force physique: culture rationnelle* (Paris: Berger-Levrault, 1901). Berger-Levrault, the publisher of this popular manual, advertised it as necessary for the "future of our nation" and the "regenerescence of the race." The neo-Lamarckian conceptions of heredity which undergirded this physical culture revival are best expressed in E. Contet, *La Régénération des familles et race tarées: prophylaxie et hygiène thérapeutique de l'hérédité morbide* (Paris, 1906). Contet, who had written much on alcoholism, believed that emphasizing the role of heredity could lead to a dangerous fatalism (p. 13). For the section on the will, see pp. 145–51. One of the most popular methods for the cure of "degenerates" at this time was the "methode Bérillon," in the inventor's words a "hypnopedagogic" method designed for the "reeducation of the will and the creation in these creatures of some genuine powers of psychic inhibition." E. Berillon, "Les Applications de l'hypnotisme à l'éducation des enfants vicieux ou dégénérés," *Ve Congrès International d'Anthropologie Criminelle* (Amsterdam, 1901), p. 305.

73. Philippe Bénéton, "La Génération de 1912–1914: image, mythe ou realité," *Revue Française de Science Politique* 21 (no. 5, October 1971), pp. 996–1001.

74. A summary of these activities may be found in Georges Cahen, *L'Autre Guerre: essais d'assistance et de prévoyance sociale (1905-1920)* (Paris: Berger-Levrault, 1920).

75. Lion Murard and Patrick Zylberman, "La Cité eugenique," *Recherches* (no.29 December 1977), pp. 424–25.

CHAPTER TWO

The Body without Fatigue:
A Nineteenth-Century Utopia

Anson Rabinbach

Writing in 1888, Nietzsche asked: "Where does our modern world belong—to exhaustion or ascent?" His characterization of the epoch by the
metaphor of fatigue or exhaustion was, by the end of the nineteenth century, itself symptomatic. It expressed a general fear, shared by the European middle classes, and given full vent elsewhere in Nietzsche's writings,
that humanity was losing its "accumulated energy," depleting itself, and
falling into that sleep which was "only a symbol of a much deeper and
longer *compulsion to rest.*"[1] In the "mobile army of metaphors" which
dominated the late nineteenth century, fatigue held a very high rank. Exhaustion was the constant nemesis of the idea of progress, the great fear of
the "Age of Capital." As George Steiner remarked: "For every text of
Benthamite confidence, of proud meliorism, we can find a counterstate-
ment of nervous fatigue."[2]

Fatigue was a metaphor of decline, inertia, loss of will, or lack of energy.
But it was also a very tangible and ever present mental and physical condition. The portrayal of fatigue as an illness or disorder which, according to
the scientific doctrines of the late nineteenth century, could be treated is of
enormous significance. In one of the few studies to recognize the importance of exhaustion in the mental life of nineteenth-century France, Theodor Zeldin points to the transformation of the old eighteenth-century
passions and sentiments into new diseases as a hallmark of the scientific
mania of the age.[3] Not only physical, but also mental fatigue, and a whole
range of modern disorders classified under such headings as "diseases of
the will," "les maladies d'énergie," and "neurasthenia" were the object of
a vast outpouring of scientific, medical, and popular literature in the last
quarter of the century.[4] Before 1860 there was little interest in the subject

and no medical or scientific studies of fatigue are recorded. By the turn of the century, more than one hundred studies of muscle fatigue alone were listed in the Surgeon General's index and many more can be found under related categories such as " "nervous exhaustion," "neurasthenia," "brain exhaustion," and "spinal exhaustion."[5] Judging from the explosion of research and interest that accompanied this "discovery" of fatigue, we could conclude that medical science was confronted by a disease of epidemic proportions. Doctors were cautioned to "be aware of how a very large number of patients declare that they suffer from overwork." Popular lecturers told public audiences that "our asylums are filled with mad people owing to the overwrought state of the nervous system in the present hard-working age."[6] If these widespread perceptions of the mental and physical state of the populace are to be taken seriously, the late nineteenth century might well be called the age of exhaustion.

Fatigue did not suddenly emerge as a full-fledged illness. Although Cabanis omits fatigue from his taxonomy of relations between physiology and morality, he includes "disorders of the will" under the rubric of "sleep and delirium."[7] It was not uncommon in the first half of the nineteenth century for physiologists to describe the effects of overactivity, particularly of the passions or the intellect, on the emergence of other illnesses. Only in 1875 did fatigue first achieve the status of a disease in its own right. George Poore published an article in the London *Lancet* distinguishing between general and local, acute and chronic symptoms of the disorder. General fatigue was defined as "a disability for performing either mental or physical work," while local fatigue was a "loss of power to a greater or less extent."[8] In France, Carrieu, in his pioneering study *De la fatigue et de son influence pathogénique* (1878), noted that fatigue did not appear in any of the great medical dictionaries, and provided the following auspicious definition: "Un trouble dans l'activité des éléments anatomiques, causé par un fonctionnement exagéré au point que la réparation y est momentanément impossible" (a disorder in the activity of anatomical elements, caused by excessive functioning to a point where repair is momentarily impossible).[9] Significant about these early perceptions of fatigue is the initial identification of a difficulty, disorder, and failure of the mental and physical system. This association of fatigue with discomfort, pain, and the depletion of bodily or mental forces is particularly modern. It contrasts sharply with the premodern image of fatigue, and presents us with new image of the organization of the body, explicitly cast in the language of motion, forces, and energy.

Characteristic of the eighteenth-century view of fatigue is Johnson's admonition of 1782: "Do not continue any day's journey to fatigue."[10] Here fatigue is a natural marker, a warning, an indication of limit, a point beyond which unmeasured exertion would be unwise. For the eighteenth century fatigue marked the point of overexertion, but it was not necessarily an unpleasant experience. Johnson remarks that "the necessity of action" is demonstrable from the fact that men "whose rank or wealth exempt them from the necessity of lucrative labor" have "invented sports or diversions" of "equal fatigue" to the "manual trades."[11] Fatigue is more than a limit, a sign of having utilized body and mind fully, a mark of accomplishment. This notion, which persisted into the nineteenth century as an aristocratic sensibility, sees fatigue as a pleasurable sensation, a luxurious respite from labor or travel, the permitted withdrawal of mind and body from the stimulations and excitements of the world. There is a spiritual element in this vision reminiscent of the medieval image in which "the strength of the soul enters through the *fatagacion* of the body."[12] The *Journal des Goncourt* records this perception as an anachronism, a nostalgic sentiment of earlier epochs: "Excessive work produces a not unpleasant dullness, a feeling in the head which prevents one from thinking of anything disagreeable, an incredible indifference to the pin-pricks of life, a detachment from reality, a want of interest in the most important matters."[13]

The modern image of fatigue opposes this idyll of a natural boundary from the strains of civilization. Now it appears as an obstacle, the source of inhibition or resistance, imposed by physiology. As pain, fatigue is still a limit, but only negatively. It is the horizon of forces and energies within the body: "As the holding back of any power from exercise is positively painful, so its passing into energy, is, were it only the removal of that painful repression, negatively pleasurable."[14] Fatigue is also a consequence of inactivity and despair, which one writer attributed to the "sad passions" accompanying the desperation and ennui of the siege of Paris.[15] Above all, fatigue is both a physical and moral disorder. It is a sign of weakness and the absence of will. As one physiologist proclaimed: "We flee it by instinct, it is responsible for our sloth and makes us desire inaction."[16] If the soul was restored and replenished by fatigue in the consciousness of medieval man, the modern conception subverts this idea. Fatigue is the portal of moral decay. It accounts, in Huysmans' words, for that "diabolic perversion of will which affects, especially in matters of sensual aberration the exhausted brains of sick folks." Here the medieval image is inverted: "It would seem, in fact, that nervous invalids expose fissures in the soul's envelope whereby the Spirit of Evil effects entrance."[17]

The physical horizon of the body was identified with the moral horizon of the species, the moral infirmity of the subject was proportional to the debilitating effects of fatigue: "Fatigue seems to consume our noblest qualities—those which distinguish the brain of civilized from that of savage man. When we are fatigued we can no longer govern ourselves, and our passions attain to such violence that we can no longer master them by reason."[18] As the physical and mental horizon of the body's forces, fatigue is undesirable. It is in this last sense that fatigue represents the threshold of pain which the nineteenth century sought to eliminate. Underlying the anxiety and hostility which surrounded fatigue is a utopian ideal of its supersession. The result would be not only a vast release of mankind's latent energies, a productivity without constraint, but a civilization resistant to moral decay and disorder. Behind the proliferation of scientific and scholarly treatises on all aspects of fatigue lurked a projection, the daydream of the late nineteenth century, the fantasy of a body without fatigue.

The single-mindedness which characterizes the medical, philosophical, and literary concern with fatigue in the second half of the nineteenth century cannot simply be understood as a retreat from the anxieties of urbanism and modern civilization. It reflects a much deeper and profound transformation of consciousness, a new perception of physical reality and nature. The concept of exhaustion is ultimately linked to its opposite, energy, which attained universal significance in both theoretical physics and the practical sciences by the end of the century.[19] The notion of energy as the force present in all matter capable of converting itself into a variety of forms became the dominant motif of the late–nineteenth-century conception of nature. Between 1837 and 1844 a variety of theories simultaneously emerged describing the world of phenomena "as manifesting but a single 'force,' one which could appear in electrical, thermal, dynamical, and many other forms, but which never, in all its transformations, be created or destroyed."[20] By the 1850s this principle of the conservation of energy became the centerpiece of a fundamental reformulation of the epistemological foundation of the natural sciences.

Von Helmholtz, who provided the most lasting formulation of the theory of energy conservation, summarized the doctrine in this way: "The supply of energy, of effective working power, which is operating in the world is a Proteus, capable of being manifested under the most various forms, and of changing from one to another, while still unalterable in its quantity, indestructible, incapable of being added to."[21] The supply of energy in the universe is both finite and constant. Energy is never consumed, only transformed, so that the equivalence between one form of energy or force and another could be located and measured. The principle of motion in the universe was defined almost exclusively in terms of the power to "perform work."[22] Nature was no longer thought of in purely mechanical terms, as in the eighteenth century, or as possessing some vital force or substance which as Kant put it, "resided in the whole" but was inaccessible to experience. Materialism was transformed into a theory of energy in which matter and force were inseparable. The concept of energy provided nature with a transcendental principle of motion: energy was "the other objective reality in the physical universe."[23]

The old image of perpetual motion was denounced as a chimera—no work energy exists that is not transformed natural energy assuming different shapes. With the identity of matter and motion in energy the mechanical world view suffered a defeat that also claimed the theologically motivated search for a hidden principle of motion. Although the social implications of energy conservation were not immediately apparent, the ideal of an inexhaustible reservoir of natural energy and work power underscored the optimistic faith in the productive potential of the age. Nature was seen as a vast cistern of Protean energy awaiting conversion into work. This identification of nature with energy harmonized with the dynamic belief in productivism characteristic of a stage of industrialization based on the harnessing of new forms of power such as electricity, electromagnetism, internal combustion, and on power driven transportation, above all, the railroad.[24] Knowledge of nature was also transformed: the forces of nature enter our consciousness only through their use and conversion into work energy. The new epistemology paralleled the principle of energy conservation: if nature manifests itself as force and energy only after it is transformed, reality is only comprehensible through its transformation into energy.

Nowhere is the change to the doctrine of energy more evident than in the perception of the human body. Whereas eighteenth-century rationalism, following Descartes and La Mettrie, saw the body in terms of mechanical functions and static emotional states, by the middle of the nineteenth century the dynamic language of energy, force, power, and will expressed the new image of the body as a field of forces and motion. Natural philosophy, with its idealist image of the *vis viva* or "life force" was discredited, and especially in Germany, the metaphysical conception of a force greater than the sum of the parts abandoned.[25] Instead the forms of energy within the body had to be discovered along with their precise laws of motion. These forces were conceived in terms of new discoveries in the physical universe, particularly in the theory of light, heat, magnetism, and electricity.

By defining energy or motion as the essence of matter the long accepted dualism of matter and force was overthrown. Emil Du Bois-Reymond, whose essay "Über die Lebenskraft" (1848) led the struggle to establish the doctrine of energy in physiology, illustrated the new principle when he said: "Matter is not like a carriage to which force can be harnessed or unharnessed as we please."[26] The idea of a life force independent of static matter was likewise rejected as a phantasm which, echoing Kant, "brought reason to rest on the cushion of dark qualities."[27] Energy could not exist apart from matter—it had to be sought in those "forces with which the substances of the organism are supplied." Here Du Bois-Reymond clearly delineates the old and new conceptions of motion: "A life force should not be assumed when there are only life forces."[28] Since neither matter nor force could actually be perceived except as abstract categories, their identity could only be comprehended as the necessary precondition for their mutual existence. The relationship of knowledge to nature was revised. In a characteristically neo-Kantian manner, energy or force became a transcendental category. Matter and energy are one because they "complete and presuppose each other."[29] The world was dissolved into spheres of "moving matter," whose essence we could not possibly comprehend."[30] As Von Helmholtz noted: "We can perceive matter only through its forces, never in itself."[31] Knowledge was no longer to be directed toward the ineffable origins of energy, but toward the determination of its laws. "The true kernel of the method," Du Bois-Reymond concluded, lay in bringing "natural appearance under the mathematical principles of causality."[32]

Anatomists and physiologists hoped to demonstrate the identity of the organic structure of the body and the physical laws of the universe. The traditional separation of organic and inorganic nature was seen as arbitrary, "the residue of the theological antinomy between God and World, body and soul." Reflecting the optimism of this new philosophy of nature, Du Bois-Reymond declared that physiology "would one day dissolve completely into organic physics and chemistry."[33] In France, Ribot attempted to give the will a physiological foundation, claiming it to be the "highest force which nature has yet developed."[34] There emerged a conception of the body as a field of forces, as discrete economies of physical, mental, and nervous energies working according to the laws of inorganic matter. William Clifford summed up the impact of the law of energy conservation when he told the Sunday lecture society in 1874: "There is no reason to suppose anything but the universal laws of mechanics in order to account for the motion of organic bodies."[35] This transcendental materialism reflected the principle of energy conservation in its emphasis on the immutable quantity of energy in each sphere: the body was a system of economies with quantifiable rules and available amounts of energy. The consequences of this new physical economy were far-reaching. Not only was the search for the forces of the body, particularly in muscle physiology, the forefront of scientific investigation, but in a much larger sense medicine was directed toward the conservation of bodily energy as its implicit goal. The search for the laws of the muscles and nerves and the attempt to discover the forces at work in emotions, became the leitmotif of the new science of the body.

The optimism produced by Helmholtz's discovery that the supply of natural energy was irreducible was dampened by the almost simultaneous discovery of the second law of thermodynamics. In practical terms, it was revealed that the transformation of energy from one form to another involved a "dissipation" or enthropy: only a fraction of the energy that exists is available for conversion. This created the fear that inefficiency and waste would result in gradual loss of energy that could be converted into productivity. Not only physiologists, but political economists attempted to translate these ideas into socially practical and applicable principles. The social interests of medical and economic research were increasingly directed toward determination of the precise economies of labor power. Marx's contention that medicine constituted one of the "repair costs of labor power," had a general as well as a specific truth.[36]

Nevertheless, Helmholtz's law seemed to support the view that the nation which best conserved and utilized its existing reservoir of the world's energy supply, including both labor power and technology, would also win the race for industrial supremacy.[37] Particularly in Germany and France, competition with the achievements of English steam power made the possibility of more efficient uses of the existing productive capacity of the nation especially welcome. By 1851, when Charles Dupin published his monumental six-volume *Forces productives des nations concurrentes,* surveying the "Création" and "mise en jeu" of the productive forces of the world's nations for the 1851 London exposition—the festival of progress— the value of determining the national supply of productive forces was already a staple of economic theory.[38]

The primacy of energy was not reserved for the bourgeois proponents of national economy. Especially in the last two decades of the nineteenth century, Marxism also absorbed the concept of an equivalence between the productive force of labor and the productive forces of industry and technology. In describing labor as a productive force, Marx did so only in the sense that it becomes a quantifiable and abstract form of energy only by its social character, transformed as a commodity, through the historical development of capitalist production. Marx maintained a utopian vision that through this process of transformation of living labor into the commodity labor power and objectified capital, the expansion of technology would intensify and make possible the ultimate emancipation of labor from the drudgery of physical work forever. In a much narrower sense, Marx's view of human progress is dependent on the level of development of productive forces per se, and indifferent to the qualitative distinction between human labor power and the inorganic forces of nature and technology. By placing such weight on the expansion of productive forces as the absolute subject of social development, he argued that the full development of productive forces would become the "condition of production," the organizing principle of society.[39] Whether Marx saw the development of productive forces as a conscious social process or as a "natural" one is not decisive. Much more important is the later development of Marxism into an ideology which venerated productivity and completely collapsed the distinction between social labor and nature by accepting the energy model as the basis of both nature and economy.

The crucial step was taken by Engels, whose insistence on the natural scientific basis of Marx's theories placed Marxism on the pedestal of energy and transcendental materialism. His unpublished *Dialectics of Nature* (1872–82) and his *Anti-Duhring* (1878) are the canonical texts of the marriage between Marx and Helmholtz.[40] For Engels, the doctrine of energy and its transferability is the basis for a philosophy of nature in which labor power is not only a productive force, but a manifestation of "the true great basic process, knowledge of which comprises all knowledge of Nature."[41] Engels's criticism of eighteenth-century mechanical materialism is ultimately, in accord with Helmholtz, a criticism of the dualism of matter and motion, of its lack of a theory of energy or force. "The motion of matter is not merely crude mechanical motion," he writes, "it is heat, light, electric and magnetic stress, chemical combination . . . and finally consciousness."[42] Marxism is reduced to an ontological materialism rooted in the energetics of matter which, like physics, is based on unalterable laws and principles. Labor power, which for Marx always remained a social category, is transfigured into another mode of work, like heat, electricity, or steam.[43] Muscular force becomes "merely transference" of energy; the distinction between the organic and inorganic forces of production can no longer be upheld. Political economy is transformed into a subordinate science of one form of energy: labor power. It takes its place among the other economies of energy: physiology, physics, and chemistry.

The most profound social impact of the theory of energy conservation is evident in the attempt, after 1850, to describe, locate, and measure the economies of force affecting the supply of energy in the labor power of society as a whole. Intensive focus on the reproduction of labor power and its related economies gave rise to a broad discourse, at once scientific, technical, and political. The factory system, which according to Marx "exhausts the nervous system to the uttermost, does away with the many sided play of the muscles, and confiscates every atom of freedom both in bodily and intellectual activity," did not disappear overnight.[44] There was a growing awareness that a country's labor power was too precious to be wasted by subjecting the laboring body to excessive demands and discarding it when used up. As British reformer Benjamin Ward Richardson noted in 1876: "Excessive physical exertion, then, while it is warranted by necessity and, under necessity, may rank as a virtue, is not absolutely requisite . . . for sustaining the vitality either of individuals or races."[45]

Since modern physics had demonstrated that perpetual motion was a fiction, no system of motion was independent of the total quantity of energy in the universe, and no conception of labor power or human motion could dispense with the problem of its reproduction. The classic Marxist definition of labor power as a social relation necessarily including the costs of its reproduction appeared simultaneously with the new recognition of the economies of the body in production. No longer could the human body be seen as an expendable part of the endlessly recurring circle "which is prescribed by the biological process of the living organism" which ends its "toil and trouble" only with death.[46] Political economy could now be brought into harmony with the doctrine of Protean energy. The energy of the person became "the capital of the body."[47] The theory of value could be explained by considering the body as a commodity, the totality of energies or forces commanded by the individual, his economic "capacity," and production as "the transfer of energy from one body to another." Consequently "the process of exchange is the transfer of energy of physical bodies," and in consumption "the energy passes from the commodity to the owner so that satisfaction is its last economic form."[48] Energy is the universal equivalent of the natural world, as money is the universal equivalent of the world of economic exchange. In labor power these abstract and universal categories are united in a single form. The worker's labor is doubly alienated; first as a commodity and second as energy to be transformed into productive work.

The social application of the principle of energy to the labor process necessitated efficient norms for regulating labor power as well as the search for quantifiable determinations of both the sources and expenditures of energy. This led to the development of a whole new set of sciences solely concerned with the reproduction of labor power. In France, for example, the science of *zootechnie* appeared in the late 1850s and investigated "the animal materials which are the source of energy expended by man in the mechanical or intellectual forms of labor."[49] In Germany, the study of the physiological phenomenon of heat was pursued in order to unlock the mysteries of vegetable growth, animal nutrition, and muscular energy.[50]

By 1870, especially in England, the wasteful expenditure of energy, particularly in the form of labor power, became a source of grave national concern. The increasing costs of labor power resulting from the impact of trade union agitation and a general rise in the working-class standard of living contributed to this concern. Even more important was the recognition that the costs of reproducing labor power could be turned into profit, and the working class constituted a potentially lucrative domestic market, particularly during the years of prosperity after 1871.[51] Reformers like Richardson began to publicly condemn "overwork" and "overanxiety" as "diseases of modern life," while others called attention to the predisposing factor of overexertion in the "fatigue diseases."[52]

The problem of overwork not only affected all areas of social life, but by 1875 appeared to have reached crisis proportions. One London physician even warned that a series of popular lectures entitled "Life at High Pressure" were "having a scaring influence on people" by asserting that "society at large is really suffering from an amount of work, physical and mental, which is injurious to the individual and therefore to the human race."[53] Overwork was not simply an affliction of the working classes or a problem of physical labor. It was evident in mental labor and often had profound physiological and psychological consequences. As one physician reported: "An overworked man, whether his work be mechanical or mental, becomes an over-anxious nervous man."[54] The advances of military medicine, which came into its own during the Franco-Prussian war, established a relationship between fatigue and epidemics of disease, particularly typhus.[55] Simultaneously in England, France, and Germany, the practice of subjecting recruits to long marches came under criticism for "fatiguing the troops" and "subjecting them to sunstroke."[56] George Savage, assistant director of London's Bethlem Hospital, noted that there were increasing cases of "overwork as a cause of insanity" and reported that his caseload included "every variety of mental disturbance from acute mania to profound melancholia" among overworked patients.[57] By 1878 public anxiety about overwork was so extreme that a great debate ensued when a proposal introducing competitive physical entrance examinations for the Royal Military Academy provoked the fear that English boys would "utterly break down" from the combination of physical training and the amount of "brain work required."[58]

The proliferation of overwork and fatigue seemed to be a universal discontent of industrial society. But a closer examination of the cases of overwork and exhaustion reported in medical journals in the 1870s reveals two distinctive characteristics. It was most frequent in men, and second, it was most common in trades or occupations demanding an unflagging devotion to the task or a high degree of emotional pressure. Noting that "overwork rarely, if ever, alone sends us patients on the female side," Savage records the following occupations among his overworked patients showing symptoms of insanity: architect, surveyor, inventor, musician, clergyman, artist, schoolmaster, policeman, and bootmaker. In addition there were seven clerks and two students. He concludes that in all of these cases the patients "fancied that they had not done their duty and were commonly suicidal."[59] In short, overwork and exhaustion were not simply perceived as the result of excessive work per se, they were pathologies of the work ethic, of the compulsion rather than the activity.[60] The toll of the inner drive to work was increasingly acknowledged in those professions which neither demanded submission to the rule of the factory nor promised the reward of effort in monetary terms.

Fatigue, it appears, replaced idleness as the moral infirmity of the will to work. By the second half of the nineteenth century the enforced regularity and introjected time-work discipline, which had to be acquired by the newly industrialized work force of the earlier part of the century, was already an "inner compulsion."[61] By the 1870s, fatigue not only superseded idleness as the quintessential disorder of work, but was established as the disease of time-work discipline itself. In Savage's judgment overwork and its ill effects were not only the result of excessive mental or physical labor, they were a consequence of monotonous, persistent, and continuous work, comparable to those "cases in which continuous railway traveling acted as a cause of nervous exhaustion."[62] If idleness was the sin of irregularity and lack of time sense, fatigue was the result of excessive regularity and the internalization of time as destiny. As Poore noted: "Monotonous repetitions of the same act are acknowledged on all hands, to be the most potent causes of fatigue."[63] Even *Punch* satirists acknowledged this when the rider exclaimed: "its the 'ammer, 'ammer, 'ammer on the 'ard, 'igh, roads."[64]

This shift from idleness to exhaustion as the primary disorder of the will to work explains the new status which fatigue acquired in the cultural and scientific imagination of the 1870s. The concept of labor was completely reevaluated, albeit from different viewpoints. In his brilliant polemic *The Right to Be Lazy,* Paul Lafargue scorned the idea of progress as the perversion of the working class by the "dogma of work," and praised the pleasures of laziness and leisure.[65] Karl Bücher in his important study of the origins of work discipline, *Arbeit und Rhythmus* attempted to undo the effects of centuries of ethnographic literature which claimed that "laziness and savagery are synonymous" by attempting to demonstrate that the principle of economy in human activity is evident from the "inner constitution of our bodies" and therefore "arises out of itself."[66] By studying the ethnographic literature on work and music, Bücher argued that the "natural tendency to rhythmic formation" evident in primitive dance necessarily emerged from the natural organization of the anatomy and physiology of the body.[67] As the factory system and machine labor consumed its first generation, the moral appeal against the scourge of laziness and sloth lost power and credibility.

No longer was resistance to work located in the impurity of the soul. In fatigue it was displaced to the body itself, which now contained the source of resistance in organic nature. Celebration of the identity of matter and motion in the new transcendental materialism did away with the old moral categories by absorbing them into the structure of scientific perception. Fatigue now became the threshold of the body's economy of energies; the horizon of a mechanical universe with its laws of energy and motion. The discovery of these laws could, it was firmly believed, result in the precise determination of the efficiency of the body's interior powers—both muscular and nervous—and therefore in the efficient deployment of its resources.

But if the materialist science of energy and exhaustion became the legitimate heir to the old moral theology of idleness, it remained the servant of the old work ethic. Despite the apparent shift from the soul to the energies of the body, the literature on fatigue often retained clues to its purpose in the moral language of metaphor derived from the old Protestant consciousness of sin and idleness. Here it revealed a moral chemistry in which fatigue, like idleness, was perceived as a cumulative heaping up of corruption, a progressive impurity that ultimately attacked the very center of the individual's being: "Over-fatigue thus means poisoning the organism. The poisons are more and heaped-up, poisoning the muscles, poisoning at last the blood itself, starting in the intricate machinery of the body new poisons in addition to themselves. The hunted hare, run to death, dies not because he is choked for want of breath, nor because his heart stands still, its store of energy having given out, but because his poisoned blood, poisons his brain, poisons his whole body."[68]

The concept of fatigue provided the key to the efficient utilization of the body's energies by determining its internal limit. After 1870, the task of the physiology of fatigue was to provide a systematic understanding of the economies of muscular and nervous force; to quantify that limit. As Richardson pointed out in 1876: "There is hardly a more difficult problem of our time than that of determining the natural bonds of physical labor."[69] To combat fatigue was not merely to discover its limits but as George M. Beard believed to map out the lines of least resistance in the economies of force: "Routine labor requires the evolution and transfer of force along well worn pathways, where the resistance is brought down to a minimum; hence a very slight evolution of force is sufficient to produce the result, just as a very slight amount of electricity will pass through a good conductor."[70] The true purpose of the science of fatigue was, within the "impassible limits" of the law of the conservation of energy, to determine how the energies of the human motor can be liberated and how one form of energy can be tapped and expanded at the expense of others.

This attempt to liberate the body's energies motivated the search for the laws of muscular and nervous exhaustion until the end of World War I.[71] Helmholtz's law was placed at the service of research into the economies of force. As early as 1873, the implications of energy conservation for muscle fatigue were drawn by Hugo Kronecker, who established the principle that fatigue has its own dynamic laws of energy and that the intensity of muscle contractions diminishes with regularity until the organism can no longer function.[72] Angelo Mosso's classic work *Fatigue* (1884) established him as the most important disciple of Helmholtz and the Galileo of modern fatigue research.[73] Mosso's experiments resulted in a theory of muscular energy modeled directly on physics. Fatigue was not dependent on the proportion of work done, but on its own physical principles: "The muscle is not an organ which obeys like a slave the commands transmitted by the nerves."[74] Mosso was the first to calculate and measure the effects of fatigue through his invention of the ergograph. The result of his quantification of the principle of muscular force is summed up in the principle that fatigue is progressive, regular, and independent of the nature of work.

Mosso's discovery of the law of muscle fatigue was paralleled by the attempt to discover a similar logic in the sources of emotional fatigue. In 1868, the American physician George M. Beard published his first study of nervous exhaustion which he called neurasthenia. For Beard, neurasthenia was the "Central Africa of medicine—an unexplored territory into which few men enter."[75] The onset of neurasthenia was accompanied by a feeling of profound exhaustion "as though the body had not strength to hold together."[76] Neurasthenia was probably more like the Grand Central Station of emotional disorders than the Central Africa, however. Beard used the term to refer to "all forms and types of nervous exhaustion," and included more than sixty different "subjective" symptoms from tenderness of the scalp and ticklishness to more than a dozen phobias including anthrophobia (fear of men) and phobophobia (fear of fear). What justified this meeting of so many disparate disorders of the emotional system in one terminus was, in addition to their common pathology and common treatment, the fact that "they are all diseases of civilization, and of modern civilization, and mainly of the 19th century and the United States."[77] For this reason Beard called neurasthenia "American Nervousness."[78]

Nothing exemplifies the passion that accompanied the triumph of energy better than the great panorama of cures and therapies enlisted by science to combat the terrible diseases of physical and mental exhaustion. It was consistent with the principles of modern physics that the energies of the body could be managed and the restoration of energy greatly intensified. At first it appeared certain that the horizon of fatigue could be progressively shifted outward. The possibility of eliminating fatigue and exhaustion blinded those who foresaw an age which no longer had to put up with the external and internal limits of exhaustion to the danger of a collision with the limits of energy conservation. By the 1890s more than one school of fatigue research devoted its full attention to elimination of the disorder.

Here too the old moral principles reassert themselves in scientific clothing. Fatigue like idleness surfaces as a disease of regularity that could be corrected by the reimposition of regularity. In Münsterberg's work, which attempted to give "psychophysics" practical efficacy as industrial psychology, fatigue was seen as the result of a loss of the natural internal "subjective rhythmic experience." Modern technology wasted the body's energy by imposing a form of work discipline antithetical to its natural rhythms. Münsterberg believed that it was both necessary and possible to "eliminate all the factors that injured or reduced the capacity to perform" by rediscovering the proper motions of each muscular movement and applying the law of least resistance to its forces.[79] The greatest practitioner of this approach was Frank Gilbreth, disciple of Frederick Winslow Taylor. Gilbreth's contribution to Taylor's reduction of work motion to quantifiable and scientifically programmed steps (a view of labor that is the result, and not the turning point in the application of positivistic science to the labor process) was to use photography to train the body to internalize precise, unerring, constant, and standardized motions to eliminate "humanity's greatest waste."[80]

If the psychotechnical approach tried to impose regularity on the laboring body to bring it into accord with the external demands of rationalization, the chemical approach sought an antidote to render the body immune to impurities that collect in the blood of the fatigued animal. The goal was the production of a vaccine to "prepare the body to resist the specific fatigue toxins."[81] By 1904 Wilhelm Weichardt succeeded in chemically reproducing the toxins emitted by the muscles, and injected this substance (called antikenotoxin) into white mice, with the startling result that the immunized rodents remained able to work much longer than the normal ones.[82] The effect was euphoric. German scientists began immediately experimenting with the vaccine by converting it to gas and filling their laboratories and even classrooms with the chemical, with equally positive results. The enthusiasm surrounding the fatigue vaccine did not abate until 1914, when scientists finally concluded that previous tests had been faulty.[83] In discovering the illusory powers of the vaccine another even more important discovery was made. In contrast to the antikenotoxin subjects, the control group injected with concentrated caffein exhibited marked spurts in energy and productivity. This further intensified the search for other "nerve whips" or stimulants which, like tea, coffee, or cocaine seemed to erase the signs of fatigue. In the long run these too were found inefficient since they only either masked the real symptoms of fatigue until complete exhaustion set in, or were absorbed by the muscle toxins until they proved ineffective.[84]

In the chemical and technological warfare against fatigue one weapon stood out among the rest: electricity. If fatigue was the disorder of energy, electricity held out the promise of ;estitution. Modern shock therapy can be traced back to 1848 when the *Lancet* published a lengthy defense of the use of galvanic electricity as a therapeutic technique. *Lancet* explicitly placed it "in juxtaposition to mesmerism" and other "advertisements of charlatanry," assuring its readers that cases of patients treated by this method "remains an evidence of what may be effected by medical treatment co-operating with the restorative powers of nature."[85] As a popular form of treatment for nervous exhaustion, electricity was really established in the late 1860s and 1870s, largely due to the efforts of G.V. Poore and George Beard, in England and America. Published in 1874, Beard's *Medical and Surgical Uses of Electricity* included cases of patients suffering from "neurasthenic collapse" who were restored by electrical shock.[86] In Germany, the uses of galvanization for nervous exhaustion were devel-

oped by Althaus, whose case reports also reveal the wondrous future promised by the marriage of medicine and electrical engineering. In 1866, for
example, he treated a young woman whose exhaustion and pain incapacitated her from any movement. As a result of the galvanic treatments "she
had become stouter and could walk for miles without fatigue."[87]

It is not so much in the results of electrotherapy as in its theoretical
premises that the implicit connection between exhaustion and the new
theory of energy that dominated the late nineteenth century becomes fully
transparent. If the doctrine of energy conservation hoped to liberate the
forces of the body, the therapy of electricity sought to replenish the supply.
Because electricity is work, because it is also present in the nerves and
muscles, by reentering the body it could "cooperate with the restorative
power of nature." Beard notes that the treatment of neurasthenia with
electricity had "forced its way into science" with a rapidity that perhaps
has no parallel."[88] His graphic description of the therapeutic powers of
electricity in restoring the body's latent energies underscores the fundamental conviction that the application of energy to energy, the infusion of
force with force, would ultimately lead to the production of work energy.
The principles of Helmholtz and the other pioneers of energy conservation
now formed the basis for a union of medical science and electrical technology: "Electricity is now regarded as a mode of motion analogous to and
correlated to the other great forces, as light, heat, and capable of being
transformed into them. When an electric current passes through the body,
it causes a molecular disturbance—a change, an alteration, by which the
nutrition is modified, and consequently pain relieved and strength imparted. It is not the electricity remaining in the body that accomplishes
this, but the *results* of the passage of electricity through the body."[89]

Despite warnings by more circumspect physicians, that "we ought to be
cautious not to over-stimulate or tire out muscles already exhausted from
disease by the too zealous employment of this agent," the zealous employment of electricity on the physically and emotionally fatigued bodies of
nineteenth-century patients is widely documented.[90] The antipathy to fatigue which the medical and technical literature of the epoch reveals is
only comprehensible in light of the esteem in which the same age held energy and strength of will. The development of the doctrine of energy was
the ultimate social triumph of idealism—not as philosophy, but as a mode
of science and technology dominated by the metaphor of energy.

Faustian idealism was embedded in a materialist substratum, like the
energy that was embedded in the electrical current that pulsated through
Beard's patients. The emergence of fatigue and exhaustion as a leitmotif of
the 1870s illuminates the metaphysics of energy that presupposes it. The
ideal of scientific truth, which made its appearance with the Enlightenment, ultimately consumed everything that appeared to fall outside the

realm of pure reason, including metaphysics. By the end of the nineteenth century the old dualism of spirit and matter was overcome by the digestion of spirit by matter itself. The result, the creation of an idealist materialism that contained its own transcendental principle, also created a new metaphysical monad—the unified body of matter and energy—an energumen. This monism accorded the concept of energy a "trans-sensual" character: the apparent forms of energy belonged to the world of the senses, but energy itself stood above these forms, "like the Platonic Idea over things."[91]

Even the old mechanical materialism, as Engels never tired of pointing out, was based on the ultimate, if hidden, principle that there had to be something beyond matter to explain its movement. Now that there was nothing beyond matter but only matter in motion, energy claimed sole status as a universal principle. The law of energy conservation functioned for the late nineteenth century as the doctrine of a vital force did for the romantic period, or God and the soul in earlier epochs. Perhaps this is what gives the search for a cure for exhaustion its passionate quality, and likens the quest to the hostility of sixteenth- and seventeenth-century Protestants toward the sin of idleness. Here we can recall Max Weber's elegant image of the fate of the work ethic in the modern age: "The rosy blush of its laughing heir, the Enlightenment, seems also to be irretrievably fading, and the idea of duty in one's calling prowls about in our lives like the ghost of dead religious beliefs."[92] What could be a more appropriate body for this wandering spirit than the new science of energy and fatigue? With the emergence of energy as the universal principle of work, the old ghost acquired a material carriage, and Enlightenment seemed to regain a healthy pallor.

In the 1860s and 1870s the metaphors of energy and exhaustion took on a mythic quality. The power attributed to the concept of energy in all spheres of life is the reverse side of the anxiety which haunted the image of exhaustion. The quantification of the body's energies, the isolation and determination of the economies of force in the physical and nervous systems, and ultimately the establishment of a system of equivalences between technological and physical energy all expressed a Promethean idolization of productive force. The effort to bring nature under the general laws of energy resulted in the translation of those laws into the very structures and functions of human activity. Not only did science display an unshakeable conficence in its ability to bring the forces of nature under human control, but it now claimed to be able to bring human nature under the complete control of science. This omnipotence was both similar to and distinct from the old "unshakeable confidence in world domination" which Freud ascribed to magic. Though it shared its omnipotence, control was now predicated on an autonomy of thought which also claimed to be identical with the real material forces. This idealism was the substance of the new materialism of the late nineteenth century.[93]

In this light, exhaustion emerges as the indomitable foe of scientific materialism and the doctrine of energy. It seemed to represent what Freud, in another context, called a "piece of unconquerable nature," a part of our physical and psychic constitution which resists rationalization.[94] Fatigue potentially subverts the utopian belief in the myth of universal energy and a universe completely subject to physical laws. Like idleness it is a form of revolt. As the horizon of pain which seems as insurmountable as original sin, fatigue and exhaustion represent the body's resistance to the attempt to push it beyond its natural limits. They are modes of stubborn defiance against the intense regulation imposed by the machine and the internalized time-work discipline of industrial society. Fatigue is the last line of revolt of the organic against the inorganic.

NOTES

I would like to thank Patrick Zylberman and Lion Murard for their numerous valuable suggestions.

1. Friedrich Nietzsche, *The Will to Power,* trans. Walter Kaufmann and R.J. Hollingdale (New York, 1967), pp. 48, 134.
2. George Steiner, "The Great Ennui," In *Bluebeard's Castle: Some Notes towards the Redefinition of Culture* (New Haven, 1971), p. 11.
3. Theodore Zeldin, *France 1848–1945,* vol. 2, *Intelligence, Taste and Anxiety* (Oxford, 1977), esp. ch. 17, pp. 822–75.
4. See Théodule Ribot, *Diseases of the Will,* trans. M. Snell (Chicago, 1896); Albert Deschamps, *Les Maladies de l'énergie, thérapeutique générale* (Paris, 1908); George M. Beard, *A Practical Treatise on Nervous Exhaustion* (New York, 1869).
5. *Index Catalogue of the Library of the Surgeon General's Office, United States Army,* 2 series (Washington, D.C., 1900), pp. 48, 482.
6. Samuel Wilks, "On Overwork," *The Lancet* (London, June 26, 1875), p. 886.
7. P.J.G. Cabanis, *Rapports du physique et du moral de l'homme* (Paris, 1796–97), p. 289.
8. George V. Poore, "On Fatigue," *The Lancet* (London, July 31, 1875), pp. 163, 164.
9. M. Carrieu, *De la fatigue et de son influence pathogénique* (Paris, 1878), p. 3.
10. James Boswell, *The Life of Samuel Johnson,* 6 vols. (Oxford, 1934), "To Mr. Perkins" (July 28, 1782), vol. 4, p. 153.
11. Samuel Johnson, *The Rambler,* January 8, 1751, no. 85 (London, 1806), p. 78.
12. Hans Kurath (ed.), *Middle English Dictionary* (Ann Arbor, 1952), p. 422.
13. Jules Goncourt and Edmond Goncourt, *Journal des Goncourt: Mémoires de la vie littéraire,* vol. 1 (Paris, 1887), pp. 219–20.
14. William Hamilton, *Lectures on Metaphysics and Logic,* vol. 1 (Boston, 1859), p. 589; cited in Maurice Keim, *De la Fatigue et du surmenage au point de vue de l'hygiène et de la médecine légale* (Lyon, 1886), p. 2. Both authors emphasize Aristotle's theory of pleasure as the concomitant of the unimpeded energy of a natural power, faculty, or acquired habit, as opposed to Plato's view of pleasure as the removal of pain.

15. Keim, p. 25.
16. Ibid., p. 24.
17. Joris K. Huysmans, "Preface—Written 20 Years After the Novel," in *Against the Grain (A Rebours)* (New York, 1969), p. xl.
18. Angelo Mosso, *Fatigue,* trans. M. and W.B. Drummond, 1st ed. 1884 (New York, 1904), p. 238.
19. Thomas Kuhn, "Energy Conservation as an Example of Simultaneous Discovery." In *The Essential Tension: Selected Studies in Scientific Tradition and Change* (Chicago, 1977), p. 68; John Theodore Merz, *A History of European Scientific Thought in the Nineteenth Century,* vol. 2 (London, 1897), p. 96 passim.; Georg Helm, *Die Energetik nach ihrer geschichtlichen Entwicklung* (Leipzig, 1898), pp. 10–50.
20. Kuhn, p. 69
21. Leo Koenigsberger, *Hermann von Helmholtz,* trans. Francis A. Welby (Oxford, 1906), p. 432.
22. Merz, p. 101.
23. Ibid., p. 116.
24. E.J. Hobsbawm, *Industry and Empire* (Harmondsworth, 1969), pp. 109–19; 124.
25. Emil Du Bois-Reymond, "Ueber die Lebenskraft (March 1848)," *Reden,* vol. 2 (Leipzig, 1886), pp. 1–23; see also Everett Mendelsohn, "Physical Models and Physiological Concepts: Explanation in 19th Century Biology," *British Journal for the History of Science* 2 (1965), pp. 201–13; Oswei Temkin, "Materialism in French and German Physiology of the Early 19th Century," *Bulletin of the History of Medicine* 20 (1946), pp. 322–27; and most recently Frederick Gregory, *Scientific Materialism in Nineteenth Century Germany* (Boston, 1977), pp. 29–51.
26. Du Bois-Reymond, p. 17.
27. Ibid., p. 12.
28. Ibid., p. 17.
29. Ibid., p. 14.
30. Ibid., p. 16.
31. Frederick Albert Lange, *The History of Materialism,* trans. Chester Thomas, vol. 2 (New York, 1950, 1st ed. 1865), p. 392.
32. Du Bois-Raymond, p. 6.
33. Ibid., p. 16.
34. Ribot, p. 134.
35. William K. Clifford, "Body and Mind," delivered to the Sunday Lecture Society, November 1, 1874. In C. Harvie, G. Martin, and A. Scharf (eds.), *Industrialisation and Culture, 1830–1914* (London, 1970), p. 215.
36. Karl Marx, *A History of Economic Theories from the Physiocrats to Adam Smith,* ed. Karl Kautsky, trans. Terence McCarthy. Vol. 1 of *Theorien ueber Mehrwert* (New York, 1952), p. 208.
37. George Helms, *Die Lehre von der Energie* (Leipzig, 1887), p. 72. For the theory of energy and national wealth see Leon Walras, *Théorie mathématique de la richesse sociale* (Leipzig, 1883).
38. Charles Dupin, *Force productive des nations concurrentes, depuis 1800 jusqu'à 1851.* In *Travaux de la Commission Française sur l'Industrie des Nations,* Exposition Universelle de 1851, vol. 1 (Paris, 1851).
39. Karl Marx, *Grundrisse der Kritik der politischen Ökonomie* (Moscow, 1941), p. 440.

40. It would be more accurate to describe Engel's scientific theory as a stormy marriage between Helmholtz and Hegel. For Engels the law of the conservation of energy remained the fundamental principle of any materialist theory of nature. But he insisted on integrating this law into the Hegelian philosophy of nature which made dialectics the immanent source of all motion. Engels then used Hegel as the presupposition for his criticism of Helmholtz for continuing to see force as a transmutable form of matter: "Such a primary force would be really no more than an empty abstraction, 1970), p. 215.
41. Frederick Engels, *Herr Eugen Dühring's Revolution in Science (Anti Dühring)*, trans. Emile Burns (New York, 1934), p. 18.
42. Engels, *Dialectics of Nature*, p. 21.
43. Ibid., p. 169.
44. Karl Marx, *Capital: A Critique of Political Economy*, vol. 1 (New York, 1967), pp. 442–23.
45. Benjamin Ward Richardson, *Diseases of Modern Life* (London, 1876), p. 170.
46. Hannah Arendt, *The Human Condition* (Chicago, 1958), p. 86.
47. Helms, p. 72.
48. Ibid. See also, W.S. Jevons, *The Theory of Political Economy* (London, 1879).
49. André Sanson, "L'État Actuel de la Zootechnie," *La Philosophie Positive* (July-December, 1878), p. 336.
50. Merz, pp. 105–6.
51. Hobsbawm, pp. 124–25, 163.
52. See Richardson; George Johnson, "Lectures on Some Nervous Disorders that Result from Overwork and Mental Anxiety," *The Lancet* (July 17, 1875), pp. 85–87; Poore, p. 164.
53. Wilks, p. 886.
54. George Johnson, p. 87.
55. Carrieu, p. 28; see also *Mémoires de médecine militaire* (1876).
56. "Fatiguing the Troops," *The Lancet* (July 13, 1878), p. 60.
57. George Savage, "Overwork as a Cause of Insanity," *The Lancet* (July 24, 1875), p. 127.
58. "Physical Training for the Army," *The Lancet* (August 10, 1878), p. 201.
59. Savage, p. 127
60. See S. Weir Mitchell, *Wear and Tear or Hints for the Overworked* (Philadelphia, 1871), p. 11. Weir Mitchell argues that "mental overwork is harder, because as a rule it is sedentary."
61. For a discussion of the development of work discipline see E.P. Thompson, "Time, Work-Discipline, and Industrial Capitalism," *Past and Present* (no. 38, 1967), pp. 56–97; Edward Shorter, "Towards a History of La Vie Intime: The Evidence of Cultural Criticism in Nineteenth Century Bavaria." In *The Emergence of Leisure*, ed. Michael R. Marrus (New York, 1974), pp. 38–68; Max Weber, "Zur Psychophysik der industriellen Arbeit." In *Gesammelte Aufsätze zur Soziologie und Sozialpolitik* (Tubingen, 1924), pp. 61–255.
62. Savage, p. 127.
63. Poore, p. 163.
64. Ibid.
65. Paul Lafargue, *The Right to Be Lazy* (Chicago, 1907), p. 9.
66. Karl Bücher, *Arbeit und Rhythmus*, 3rd ed. (Leipzig, 1902), p. 298.
67. Ibid.

68. Michael Foster, "On Weariness," The Rede Lecture (Cambridge, 1893). See also Max Weber, *The Protestant Ethic and the Spirit of Capitalism,* trans. Talcott Parsons (New York, 1958), p. 264. Weber describes the symptoms of idleness as follows: "Sloth and idleness are such deadly sins because they have a cumulative character. They are even regarded by Baxter as 'destroyers of grace.' That is, they are the antitheses of the *methodical* life."

69. Richard, p. 164.

70. George M. Beard, *American Nervousness: Its Causes and Consequences* (New York, 1881), p. 12.

71. After the war the English Fatigue Board expressed skepticism about any accurate measurement of fatigue and even demanded that the term *fatigue* be "absolutely banished from precise scientific discussion." See B. Muscio, "Is a Fatigue Test Possible," *British Journal of Psychology* 12 (1921), pp. 31–46.

72. Mosso, p. 82.

73. Ibid., esp. ch. 3, "The Origins of the Energy of the Muscles and the Brain." Mosso notes that Robert Mayer's and Helmholtz's work resulted in "the greatest discovery of the last century," p. 51.

74. Ibid., p. 102.

75. Beard, *Nervous Exhaustion,* p. vi.

76. Ibid., p. 66.

77. Ibid., p. 13.

78. Beard, *American Nervousness,* p. 176.

79. Hugo Münsterberg, *Grundzüge der Psychotechnik* (Leipzig, 1914), p. 382.

80. Frank B. Gilbreth and Lillian M. Gilbreth, *Fatigue Study: The Elimination of Humanity's Greatest Unnecessary Waste* (New York, 1961), p. 7. See also Harry Braverman, *Labor and Monopoly Capital: The Degradation of Work in the Twentieth Century* (New York, 1975). Braverman's thesis that Taylorism deprives workers of the subjective element of work activity is not as important as that it represents one point along a historical continuum in the long-standing attempt of science to exercise control over the human body in the laborprocess.

81. Max Offener, *Die geistige Ermüdung* (Berlin, 1928), p. 9

82. Ibid., p. 10.

83. Ibid. World War I, especially in England, made fatigue a national obsession. The introduction of the twelve-hour day in war work politicized fatigue research and led to the creation of the Industrial Fatigue Research Board. In trench warfare, with its long stretches of inactivity, the emotional aspects of fatigue took precedence over the physical strain of battle, and predisposition to hyperactivity or depression was a constant motif in wartime fatigue discussions. Josefa Ioteyko's influential theory of "Neurasthénie de la guerre" published in France shortly after the war, identified a *"constitution anxieuse"* likely to develop "asthenia of the trenches," a war pathology characterized by lack of attention, depression, and indifference. Fatigue in this guise became the Maginot line between the two great contradictory emotions of war, fear and courage." See E. Farmer, *Reports of the Industrial Fatigue Research Board* (London, 1923); Josefa Ioteyko, *La Fatigue* (Paris, 1920), p. 281.

84. Hugo Münsterberg, *Psychotechnik* (Leipzig, 1914), pp. 388–407.

85. J.C. Christophers, "Observations on the Medical Employment of Electro-Galvanism," *The Lancet* (February 1848), p. 152.

86. George M. Beard and A.D. Rockwell, *A Practical Treatise on the Medical and Surgical Uses of Electricity* (New York, 1875), pp. 386, 455; George V. Poore, *A Text-Book of Electricity in Medecine and Surgery* (London, 1876).

87. Julius Althaus *A Treatise on Medical Electricity: Theoretical and Practical* (London, 1873), p. 621.
88. Beard, *Nervous Exhaustion,* p. 158.
89. Ibid.
90. "Review of G.V. Poore, *A Text-Book of Electricity in Medecine and Surgery," The Lancet* (April 8, 1876), p. 164.
91. Helm, p. 18.
92. Weber, p. 182.
93. Max Horkheimer and Theodor W. Adorno, *Dialectic of Enlightenment,* trans. John Cumming (New York, 1969), p. 11.
94. Sigmund Freud, *Civilization and Its Discontents* (New York, 1962), p. 33.

CHAPTER THREE

Practical Reason in Wilhelmian Germany: Marburg Neo-Kantian Thought in Popular Culture

Tim Keck

A recurring subject of George Mosse's work in cultural history—and at the same time a seminal aspect of his own historiographic contribution—has been that of "popular culture." This term has connoted for Mosse less a rationalistic methodology characterizing the ethereal realm of the history of great ideas and philosophical systems, and more a decidedly historical analysis of ideas and symbols that have moved large numbers of people and supported group identity. More particularly germane to the subject of this chapter is Mosse's emphasis on the pointed reaction of intellectuals, both on the Left and Right, to the seemingly ineluctable ascension of "mass man" as a social and political force in Europe at the turn of the twentieth century.[1]

Among those who took seriously the need to engender "right" thinking through all levels of the increasingly democratized society were the neo-Kantian philosophers—Hermann Cohen and his students—at the University of Marburg in Hesse. From the 1870s—when the Kant revival became well known in German academic circles—to World War I—after which the school lost its character as a unified movement—these thinkers created and developed a system of philosophy based upon aspects of Kant's thought they believed to be of lasting value.

According to this group of intellectuals, Immanuel Kant had stood on the highest pinnacle of thought in the great period of German classicism; he had erected an edifice of ideas that nineteenth-century materialists, positivists, and speculative idealists seemed bent on destroying. Marburg neo-Kantians thought they could help stem this tide in two ways. First, by reintroducing a purified Kantian philosophy and setting German *Wissenschaft* upon a secure epistemological foundation again. Second, they sought to raise the categorical imperative to the status of first principle in German idealist humanism.

For these thinkers—and this will be a recurrent theme of the ideas examined here—German idealism, and more specifically its expression in Kantian ethics, symbolized one of the most fundamental and indigenous verities of German culture. At the same time, Kantian moral philosophy contained a system of ethical principles that, when applied to the current political and social milieu, could provide a valid standard by which the shortcomings of German society could most graphically and convincingly be measured. These principles could also serve as a guide for formulating programs of political and social reform in a society they found far from the ideals of harmony, peace, and social justice. The neo-Kantians' involvement in the practical affairs of politics also reflected what they took to be the proper role of concerned intellectuals actively engaged in bringing their principles to bear upon current affairs. Not content to confine the purpose and scope of philosophy within the categories of pure thought, the Marburg philosophers sought to bring Kant out of the study and into the street.

Neo-Kantians were squarely within the ranks of that extensive cadre of German intellectuals, usually university professors, actively engaged in various attempts to involve academia in the mission to preserve the highest moments of German *Kultur* as well as provide concrete solutions to social problems.[2] Cohen and his students were to go further than most of their colleagues, who shared this enthusiasm and conviction, generally borne of a regular and comfortable income and an overflowing heart. All agreed that the discrepancy between the reality of life in the industrial age and the ideals of a humanistic *Kultur* must be, if not totally eliminated, at least greatly ameliorated.

The following pages are devoted to an examination of two aspects of the attempt to rally the nation around the ethical idealism of Immanuel Kant. Following an initial discussion of the theoretical foundation of neo-Kantian social philosophy, I am concerned first with the efforts of these scholars to gain acceptance for Kantian ethical principles within the official political philosophy of German social democracy. Here the focus is on the ideas and activities of the school's leading intellectuals, Hermann Cohen and his students Paul Natorp and Karl Vorländer.[3] Second, I will turn to these thinkers' reaction to Germany's involvement in World War I. Their practical philosophy as *Kriegsphilosophie* was if anything more intense than their attempt to place Kant in the service of social justice. As they shared a dilemma common among German intellectuals in 1914, their idealistic engagement in the Great War—as in their decade-long search for an ideological home within German social democracy—was concerned with spanning the hiatus between theory and action. In both cases as well, *Kriegsphilosophie* and social philosophy were advanced by thinkers committed to the idea that society in upheaval needed direction and could and must be guided by leaders espousing principles based upon a valid methodological foundation corresponding with true reason and morality.

The essential tenets of Hermann Cohen's social and political philosophy are implicit in his all-encompassing statement: "Socialism is in the right insofar as it is grounded in ethical idealism. And ethical idealism provides the foundation for socialism, [which] loses its validity . . . as soon as it becomes the spokesman for materialism."[4] Ethical idealism, Cohen asserted, found its tradition in the moral philosophy of Plato, and it had achieved its modern expression in Kantian ethics: "Kant expressly called himself an 'idealist'political theorist, [but] he is the true and actual founder of German socialism."[5] The validity, not to mention significance, of such a surprising pronouncement was by no means obvious. The statement seemed to raise more questions than it answered. Unfortunately Cohen never defined what he meant by "socialism," and his argument for the Kantian ground for its German variety found little approbation among SPD party members.

Yet Cohen was suggesting important points that would surface in party debate during the revisionist crisis. He insisted first that a doctrine of socialism could not be validly formulated with an exclusive economic reference, although he was critical of capitalism in its deleterious effect, especially upon the working class. He asserted that the idea of socialism was implicit in Kant's formulation of the categorical imperative from the *Groundwork of the Metaphysic of Morals* that stated: "Act in such a way that you always treat humanity, whether in your own person or in the person of any other, never simply as a means, but always at the same time as an end."[6] Only with the assumption of this moral imperative, Cohen believed, could men become members of a society not founded upon the naturalistic, egoistic, death struggle in the realm of nature.

Cohen was also intent upon going beyond this basic proposition. The possibility of progress entailed not only idealization of the end toward which society strives, it required as well the rejection of a naturalist-materialist foundation as a justification for the existence and viability of socialism.[7] Cohen also insisted that contemporary Marxists tended to obscure the profound ethical impetus inherent in Marx's own writings: "When the socialism of a Marx from its lofty historical perspective seeks to stigmatize the compelling power of material conditions, it unwittingly becomes satire. A fiery ethical spirit motivates all his [Marx's] great works, theoretical as well as practical."[8]

Against Hegel, Cohen argued that his pan-logism had set forth the philosophical foundation for materialism, among other places in his famous thesis from the *Philosophy of Right:* "The actual is the rational."[9] To this the neo-Kantian critique replied that in refusing to distinguish logically between *Sein* and *Sollen,* Hegel had joined the being of nature and the ought-to-be of the ethical imperative in an apparent radically idealistic formulation. Yet, Cohen insisted, the implication was quite the opposite, now the being of spirit itself was firmly anchored in the being of nature—in materialism.

Cohen contended that this Hegelian formulation implied that everything that occurs is necessary, rational, and hence morally good within the limits of Hegel's own logic, or at the very least that all acts were impervious to condemnation on moral grounds. "The actual is the rational," he noted, could be used to justify positions ranging from anarchism to reaction. Here surfaced "the diametrical opposition between Hegel and Kant, for Kant would state: The rational is not actual, but it ought to become actual."[10]

Basic to the neo-Kantian position was Cohen's further contention that this fundamental flaw in Hegel's logic precluded a rigorous critique of the present political and social situation, the most basic institution of which was the state. On the one hand, the preservation of the state was essential, for it was the form in which the process of history, the idea of justice, progress, and morality developed. But the state as it ought to be, that is the state of law, the *Rechtsstaat,* was far from that which existed in Wilhelmian Germany. The contemporaneous Prussian state was clearly a *Machtsstaat,* a power state in which lawless principles obtained in economic and political conditions; the barbarous law of the jungle dominated principles of reasoned ethics, and the egoistic laissez faire concept of economics held sway over individual rights.[11]

Another fundamental aspect of neo-Kantian political philosophy was its morally founded antipathy to capitalism. Cohen felt that the capitalist system as it functioned in Wilhelmian Germany, violated the categorical imperative at the most fundamental level. Not only were workers utilized as means rather than regarded as ends in themselves, on a more concrete level their whole being had become a means to the appropriation of profit. More than their handiwork, the fruits of their labor were being denied these men and women, for the relentless demands of the marketplace had reduced them to nothing more than their capacity to produce. As the products of their labor were in turn appropriated in the marketing process, workers were estranged not only from their value (*Wert*) but more fundamentally and odiously, their human dignity (*Würde*).[12]

If Hermann Cohen provided the basic philosophical methodology and principles for the Marburg neo-Kantian doctrine of socialism, his student Karl Vorländer was the most instrumental in attempting to win acceptance for the doctrine within the party. Delivering a lecture in Vienna in April of 1904 (later published and widely read among German socialists), Vorländer attempted under the banner "Kant and Marx," to outline a program encompassing on idealist grounds his proposal for the unification of theory and practice. Vorländer called for a thoroughgoing synthesis of the economic and historical doctrines of Marxism and the ethics of Kant.[13]

Echoing Cohen, Vorländer asserted that a valid theory of socialism was impossible, either as a consistent doctrine or as a movement capable of enlisting enthusiastic support and dedication, "without ethics . . . without the pursuit of self-posited, consciously anti-egoistic goals." Unlike Cohen, he did not maintain that the materialistic and idealist positions were mutually exclusive, but rather that both were based upon a common conception of the nature and task of philosophy. Philosophy as a science attached preeminent importance to the question of method. Vorländer maintained along with Cohen that the "scientific method" had enabled Kant to establish the principles for an *Ethik als Wissenschaft* (ethics as science), and it enabled Marx to carry forth the same analysis in the fields of historiography and economics. Far from representing antithetical forces in philosophy, with corresponding consequences for political theory and practice, Marxism and Marburg neo-Kantian philosophy formed parts of a greater whole. Kant's ethics, far from paralyzing the socialist movement, was a necessary element in its theory, both for the adequacy and consistence of the doctrine and the practical direction of the movement.[14]

With this observation as a justification, Vorländer was prepared to advance the basic premise for his proposed Kant-Marx synthesis. In Kant's philosophy, besides a systematic ethical theory, there was an epistemological justification for the Marxist view of history. Vorländer admitted that his viewpoint emphasized what was generally regarded as being nonexistent, or at least of little importance, in the works of Marx and Engels. Marx, after all, when asked about the "moral question," had responded with an outburst of derisive laughter, while both Marx and Engels regarded "formal ethics" as completely abstract and thus logically capable of justifying any particular act—and historically an ideological expression of the particular dominant class.[15]

Two points regarding the neo-Kantian theory are essential here. First, Vorländer's argument hinged upon the contention that the economic basis of even a liberalized capitalism (as opposed to socialism) was morally inconsistent with the Kantian idea of freedom. To justify capitalism on the basis of individual freedom would be to prostitute the categorical imperative, for defining autonomy as absolute, or merely freedom from restriction, would be to neglect that essential aspect of freedom consisting in placing oneself under the precepts of moral law. On the other hand, to maintain that moral imperatives could have no force in determining the nature of economic relations would be to deny the universal applicability of moral law itself. Second, and as a correlative to the above, the ever-recurring impetus in Marburg neo-Kantian philosophy consisted of striving for a systematic unified methodology that could serve in formulating doctrines concerning all aspects of man in concrete existence. The philosophy of method of Cohen and his students was extremely rigorous in this respect. Excluding any facet of one's relations with others or in interaction with the environment—denying the possibility, that is, of establishing its philosophical foundation—would be to negate the possibility of philosophy in general. This was the essential defining characteristic of what neo-Kantians called their philosophy as method.[16] This overweening emphasis on rigorous method and the "scientific validity" of their system revealed the extent to which neo-Kantians were bound to the very positivist, materialist intellectual milieu they attempted so vigorously to combat.

What the Marburg philosophers proposed to offer the German social democrats was a "scientific socialism" with a valid foundation and an ethical impetus. Theirs was a cold, logical system with a humanistic face, one which they felt should provide a guide for the course and tactics of German socialism. Within its bounds these tenets formed the foundation for neo-Kantian political philosophy: the ethical basis of socialism as expressed in the Kantian categorical imperative; the dehumanizing effect of capitalism according to these ethical principles; the need for a state within which society could progress toward a higher social and moral order. Particularly Vorländer was to labor tirelessly for their acceptance within the German Social Democratic party.

With all these well-meaning intentions, neo-Kantians found in the party something less than a rousing reception. Among German Social Democrat theorists, Kurt Eisner was the only consistent advocate of the Marburg position. Eisner had come under Hermann Cohen's influence while working as a political journalist for the Marburg *Hessische Landeszeitung* in 1893–97. He agreed that Kant's categorical imperative formed the cornerstone of moral philosophy and that ethics in the theory of socialism, like economics, was scientifically determinable. In the socialist journal *Vorwärts,* Eisner proposed more specifically that the idea of morality was eternal and could not be created and manifested in one period and one set of social conditions. Each society must determine the content of its morality according to existing conditions. At present Kant's ethics could only be developed in a socialist system, whereas Kant's own conclusions, conditioned by his analysis of the French Revolution, were liberal. Kant had developed a framework, Eisner suggested, which Marx filled with his economic and political analysis.[17]

Eisner's theoretical affinity with Cohen's philosophy was obvious. The relationship of the revisionist par excellence, Eduard Bernstein, to neo-Kantian socialist ethics, was not so clear cut. Before 1899, although studying Kant for years in his London exile, Bernstein evoked the name of Kant in only the most general of terms. Even in his "Kant against cant" chapter of the 1898 *Evolutionary Socialism,* the Königsberg philosopher was used as a general admonition to clear thinking and the affirmation of the need for the party to engage in relentless self-criticism.[18]

In 1901, Bernstein defined most clearly his conception of Kantian philosophy in one of his best known and most controversial articles. Titled "How Is Scientific Socialism Possible," Bernstein began by advancing the definition of science as "mere systematically ordered knowledge."[19] "Knowledge is perception of the true nature and reality of things."[20] What Bernstein meant by *nature* and *relations* was unclear, although he did interject a negative qualification: "An intellectual form is not scientific when its presuppositions and purposes contain elements that lie beyond perceptions."[21]

This statement alone was enough to arouse the ire of neo-Kantians, for although Bernstein's analysis would merit approbation from the standpoint of the British empiricist tradition he had been absorbing in London, he clearly had abandoned the essence of the Marburg "critical method."[22] The way was now open for Bernstein to assert that science, or its method, could not be a guide to ethics. As socialism was intimately concerned with "what ought to be," the principles of socialism could not be based upon what the Marburg philosophers insisted was a philosophical method with the same validity as that of other sciences.

Vorländer undertook to criticize Bernstein in a 1902 article published in the respected academic journal *Kantstudien.*[23] Bernstein's terms were not adequately defined, Vorländer noted, and it was therefore impossible to determine what he meant by *science.* More fundamentally, the revisionist socialist's error consisted in his exclusion of the valid application of the scientific method to ethics. Bernstein was correct in asserting that the theoretical aspect of socialism embraced more than an economic and historical analysis, that it necessarily included the "ought" question. But Bernstein incorrectly used this fact to maintain that socialism could not be "scientific" in that there was no basis for a systematic socialist ethics.[24]

In his *Kantstudien* essay, Vorländer commended Bernstein's interest in the moral element of socialism, but the socialist philosopher did not understand the implications of his own doctrine. From 1899 on, when the two began corresponding, Vorländer forwarded to Bernstein a steady stream of articles written by neo-Kantians— including himself. He attempted to explain to Bernstein the systematic foundation of ethics, and also to recommend literature, at times even the works of Kant, to "assist you in your future Kantian studies." Adopting the tone of a tutor, Vorländer apparently hoped to prompt Bernstein to publicly alter his position on the relationship of the natural sciences and ethics. Just as obviously, in his polite but firm refusal to change his views, Bernstein indicated that he did not agree on this point.[25]

This philosophical difference was hardly regarded as significant by party theoreticians. The more radical wing of the SPD was adamant in its identification of Bernstein's revisionism and neo-Kantian thought. Philosophical subtleties aside, they believed that Marburg ethics could entail an ideological paralysis of the worker movement. Especially Franz Mehring wrote in the pages of *Die neue Zeit* criticizing the Marburg philosophers (although he was careful to call them "men of good will"), leaving no doubt that he believed that their influence could only be a negative one within German social democracy. Rosa Luxemburg was less tactful. She wrote to Kurt Eisner in 1905: "Oh anxious ethical colleague, may you drown in the moral absolutes of your beloved *Critique of Pure Reason!*"[26]

August Bebel and Karl Kautsky were also familiar with the Marburg position by 1899, and both were just as adamant as their more radical colleagues, if more polite, in their rejection of the Marburg school's "Kant-Marx synthesis." In 1895 Bebel reviewed in *Die neue Zeit* an article written by Paul Natorp on the "social idealism" of Heinrich Pestalozzi, the eighteenth-century Swiss pedagogical reformer. In his review Bebel expressed interest in Natorp's own social pedagogy, as well as appreciation for one "among our professorial class" who appeared receptive to new ideas and the future of socialism.[27]

Natorp was gratified by this response, and he forwarded to Bebel a copy of his next article, a work on Plato's *Republic,* together with an accompanying letter in which he attempted to define and convey to the socialist leader his position on the social question. "Conditions determine," he wrote Bebel, "but men also determine conditions . . . . Alterations in the conditions of production have as their goal the betterment of the human condition, but ideas once again determine production." For Natorp alteration in the mode and relations of production in a given society could be positive or negative, depending squarely upon the volition, the "ethical will" of those in control of the process.[28]

In his reply to Natorp's letter, Bebel noted that he could agree with much of what the neo-Kantian philosopher had written, both in his letter and the Plato article. Yet the socialist leader then proceeded to reject nearly all the essential points in Natorp's argument. Concerning Plato directly, Bebel insisted that the proposals for education would serve to "maintain the ruling classes." Natorp seemed unaware that the foundation of the state must be brought to earth before that relationship could be altered. Plato's idea for changing the will of the rulers without altering the fundamental social relationship between classes was indeed utopian. Consciousness among workers of the class struggle was essential, he noted finally, but the view should be toward sharpening the conflict and not its melioration, as Natorp had proposed.[29]

Karl Kautsky's attitude toward the whole matter of neo-Kantian philosophy appeared at first surprising. As late as 1898 he wrote: "I must frankly admit that neo-Kantianism at least troubles me. Philosophy was never my strong suit, and even if I stand squarely on the side of dialectical materialism, I believe nevertheless that the economic and historical standpoint of Marx and Engels is compatible with neo-Kantianism."[30]

Later Kautsky addressed the issue of ethics and socialism in greater detail in his 1905 book *Ethics and the Materialistic View of History: An Inquiry*.[31] Here he argued that an adequate understanding of social and economic conditions in historical context would explain the particular role morality played in each society and, by example, indicate the basis for present moral judgements. Acts "regarded today as free activity will be recognized tomorrow as necessary," and therefore the real cause of apparently free ethical choices, governed by moral law, could be determined. The realm of experience, Kautsky insisted, and not Kant's "suprasensible otherworldliness" underlay ethical choice. Acts traditionally regarded as arising in the individual free will were in fact subject to determinate conditions in society. There was also a lesson here for the socialist movement in Germany: workers must not be swayed by "expectations of conditions which merely ought to obtain, which we only wish for and will, but rather anticipations of conditions which must obtain, which are necessary."[32]

Kautsky's analysis was designed to leave no opening for the Marburg philosophers. But as Vorländer eagerly noted, the dean of socialist theoretician's argument implicitly necessitated an ethical expansion of Marxism—precisely where neo-Kantians had been insisting it did. In his concept of freedom and determinism, Kautsky had separated the world of experience, cognition, and causality from that of freedom, the positing of goals (teleology), and free activity. He had failed to deal with the factuality and philosophical foundations of teleology itself. Particular aspirations and moral systems have their determinable basis when viewed from the comfortable perspective of history, but the necessity of positing future goals, which even Kautsky admitted formulating, remained according to his own analysis inaccessible to biological and historical conditions. The essential point was this: Marxism without ethics could provide no grounds for morality, but morality was nevertheless an omnipresent condition of man's existence and an important and necessary force in the present and future acts of moving toward the final goal of socialism, however "necessary" the outcome might be. Kautsky, despite his fatalistic inclinations, found himself admitting that normative guides were integral to human experience—yet he could find no basis in Marxism as he understood it for their foundation.[33]

Kautsky's conclusions, logical and analytical fallacies aside, were both incorporated into and reflected by the official party philosophy concerning the theoretical aspects of the revisionist question. At the 1903 Dresden congress of the SPD, over a dozen resolutions on revisionism were forwarded with the well-known result: revisionism was officially rejected in theory, while its advocates were permitted to remain within the party. All efforts were denounced which "supplant the policy of a conquest of power by overcoming our enemies with a policy of accommodation to the existing order." The issue of a socialist ethics was largely ignored. In all the major speeches of Bebel, Kautsky, and Bernstein, the role of Kantian ethics in the crisis, or even more generally the moral philosophy of socialism with its diverse implications, remained unmentioned. Deviations in theory were attacked because they would destroy party unity, or as Kautsky pointed out, indicated the necessity of a whole new tactical approach. Bebel echoed this judgment and insisted that the party "remain hereafter, as before, in secure isolation and in the sharpest opposition."[34]

The fate of neo-Kantianism within German social democracy was determined not only by the primacy of practical and organizational questions in the revisionist debate, but was also linked to the party view of intellectuals in their midst, as well as academicians who wished to be considered sympathetic fellow travelers. Vorländer had been aware from the beginning of his party involvement that this was a problem. He wrote to Bernstein in 1899 that while his position (as a Gymnasium professor) made party membership impossible, it would also entail "mistrust against me on the part of the party itself."[35]

Kautsky and Bebel expressed the same sentiments in 1903. Kautsky stated: "I am of the opinion that academicians who come to us should go through an initiation period [Karrenzeit] . . . . We have nothing on principle against academicians, but a healthy mistrust (using Vorländer's phrase) is in order." Bebel was as usual more vociferous. "Revisionists are academicians who have unlocked the riddle of the universe and, as 'born leaders' of the proletariat must now forge ahead along their path." These intellectuals, he continued, in league with the liberals, were destroying party unity, splintering its energy, hindering its development, and compelling it to become diverted to other battles.[36] This reaction was in part simply a product of the crisis itself. Bebel was trying to emerge with a unified party, and he could note that much "revisionist" opposition had indeed come from intellectuals, both within and outside the SPD. The label of academician was convenient for discrediting opposition, despite the complexities of their positions.

Neo-Kantians, with little regard for the content of their ideas, found themselves irrevocably relegated to the status of "revisionist," although Vorländer believed it possible for political philosophers intent on establishing the importance of ethics to effect a rapprochement with the more radical party theoreticians (Vörlander drew no distinction between the old guard, Kautsky and Bebel, and younger radicals like Mehring). In this judgment, Vorländer stressed the common methodological foundation of Marxism and neo-Kantianism and relied on his critique of Bernstein's revisionist principles. Yet historically neo-Kantian ethics have been inextricably joined with this theory, and with the failure of revisionist theory to gain party acceptance. Vörlander's synthesis fell apart. As Hermann Lübbe wrote in his excellent work on German political philosophy: "The practical philosophy of Hermann Cohen and his school remained in the relative isolation of the academic study. Its effect exhausted itself, outside the 'school' in the heresies of a party schism . . . dismissed as a bourgeois heresy and attributed to represent the class character of the bourgeoisie."[37]

One wonders if another fate could realistically have been envisioned for the neo-Kantians. The Marburg philosophers' intentions were relatively modest; they sought to take seriously what they viewed as the most profound statement of ethical principles and to insist on a sound methodological framework for the formulation of party principles. But they found a group divided into those who had no time for theory and those who felt that this particular theory would effectively disarm the movement. Cohen's was after all a philosophy of reconciliation, of melioration rather than intensification of class struggle. Their ideas would have and did fit nicely into post–World War II European social democratic platforms. There was, however, no home for them within Wilhelmian socialism.

The issue of revisionism and the ethics of German socialism were resolved in a situation which, in its historical perspective, appeared to demand a revolutionary theory and a revisionist practice. While the party's rejection of Marburg neo-Kantian ethics and ethical socialism may seem inevitable, this outcome was most unclear to participants in the debate. Even as it became increasingly clear that the neo-Kantians were democratic socialists whose ideals could not fit into the mold of revolutionary theory and revisionist practice, their attempt to find a mass base of support for the institutionalization of their ideas continued. Cohen prepared and revised his system of philosophy. Natorp proceeded in the early years of the twentieth century to build his reputation as one of Germany's leading reformist pedagogues. Vorländer continued to work through the century's first decade and a half, if with little success, for the adoption of his Kant-Marx synthesis.

In 1914 all this changed for the neo-Kantians as for countless other German intellectuals.[38] With the coming of the war, a host of German university professors identified a new need for the popularization of philosophical concepts. The nation was at war—and an ideological armament to protect the embattled Reich was needed. This "Spirit of 1914," which academics interpreted in terms appropriate to their chosen disciplines, engulfed the Marburg school as well.

Part of the explanation for the apparently atypical and enthusiastic *Kriegsschriften* of the Marburg professors may be found in the psychological reaction to the conflict common among great numbers of German intellectuals, particularly in the liberal arts and sciences. Here were men "condemned to the pen" who must now react to the needs of the nation, hopefully with the same wisdom and courage—and slightly more success—as their forbears at the 1848 Frankfurt Parliament. It was their great mission to redefine German justification for the preconditions and events of 1914.[39]

The war years did not witness a break in neo-Kantian thought. Essential aspects of Cohen's and Natorp's writings during the conflict were deeply rooted in the philosophy of Marburg neo-Kantianism itself. Both men utilized the philosophy in an effort to impose some meaning on the conflagration before them. Both were involved in the formulation of what became known as the "ideas of 1914," the conscious effort to construct philosophically an alternative to what great numbers of German intellectuals saw as the ideology of the French Revolution and the English "doctrine of Manchesterism."[40] Particularly Paul Natorp was deeply involved in this movement. His *Kriegsschriften,* an attempt to bring Kant and philosophy into the service of the German cause, were read widely in Germany during the war years.

Through this all, Karl Vorländer's reaction was much more moderate. Like many socialists, he reacted to the war at first with a measure of approval if not enthusiasm. But from the beginning his endorsement was carefully measured. Turning to Kant's writings on eternal peace, Vorländer pointed out in a 1915 article that even here Kant had recognized the inevitability and the progress that was often the result of conflict. As to the specific German cause, Germans could be secure in the assurance that their cause was ethically justified, so long as they were fighting for the preservation of "our highest values, our culture, our independence, and our freedom." The German combat soldier, Vorländer noted, was not aware of the categorical imperative, but in his dedication to duty, in his conviction of the justice of the struggle, he exhibited what Vorländer wistfully labeled a "genuine and fundamentally moral enthusiasm."[41]

Vorländer quickly became wary of the war and began to express pacifist sentiments in public as well as private writings. To his friend and fellow neo-Kantian Paul Natorp he wrote in 1916, in response to one of Natorp's more chauvinistic publications:[42]

> I must most vehemently object, that you view matters from the rosy side of your—so to speak—pure, spiritual, idealistic Marburg university milieu. In this regard I believe, insofar as you attribute to the French such a thirst for revenge, that you have allowed yourself to fall into a "national or war psychosis." The French people did not want this war any more than did the Ger-

mans, the Russians, the English, etc. But unfortunately, the governments, spurred on by partially capitalistic and partly chauvenistic circles (including those in Germany) opened the conflict so quickly that an effective opposition was no longer possible.

Hermann Cohen's support of the war effort, which lasted until his death in 1918, was revealed most graphically in a 1915 article entitled "Deutschtum und Judentum."[43] The essay constituted an uncritical and thus uncharacteristic apotheosis of German cultural tradition, which in turn represented, according to the dean of idealist philosophers, the summit to which the human spirit had to that point reached—and which was being threatened on all sides. From the German standpoint, in the struggle for defense of *Kultur* and honor lay the seeds of progress and the actualization of Kant's notion of a federation of states. "A just war," Cohen stated emphatically, "is the preparation for eternal peace," and he exhorted his fellow countrymen to "carry the German classics of Beethoven and Schiller in the depths of their soul."[44]

The Marburg savant's efforts were understandable, insofar as the essential aspect of neo-Kantian method was the intrusion of philosophical principles into worldly affairs. In this case, he like many others surrendered to nationalistic passion, and the application of Kantian categories to the war effort was indiscriminate at best. During this period Cohen seemed to have forgotten the important distinction—his own—between *Sein* and *Sollen*. What he was proposing as the essence of German culture had never been a reality; the formulation of the goals itself may have been the highest achievement of that culture, but never one that could typify Cohen's or any other people.

Cohen's views were not altogether chauvinistic. Germany had developed and expanded in the philosophy of idealism the goals and foundation for a spirit of an age of eternal peace. Cohen believed that this defined the unique German achievement, and it was for this and this alone that the war could be said to be a just struggle. Thus not love of country in itself, but love of a philosophy he believed could lead man to a better world lay at the base of Cohen's patriotism. In this restricted sense, his was a moderate voice of dedication to an ideal whose negation he did not live to witness but whose demise he tragically foresaw. As Cohen wrote to Natorp in 1917: "My patriotism becomes increasingly purely historical, and I despair of what will happen; what will become of our people, yes and even of our spiritual life."[45]

Natorp's writings during the war had none of Cohen's moderation, yet he too had confronted the same dilemma. He had wavered at first between supporting the German cause and the abhorrence of war that was the natural consequence of his philosophical position. Like Vorländer in the autumn of 1914, he preached moderation and attempted in correspondence with Dutch and American friends to set forth the German position of what he hoped, like so many others, would be a short war.[46] From this point he moved slowly and inexorably toward a shrilly chauvinistic position. In 1915 he had already begun to write of Germany's "sacred cultural mission," the defense of which was the "great German task." From here on Natorp, as much as any German intellectual, placed his pen and his reputation in unqualified support of the war effort, and this support did not wane as the military and political situation became more precarious in 1916 and 1917. During the war, he authored more than twenty publications—books, journal articles, and contributions to collections of war propaganda distributed at the front, as well as patriotic songs he had composed.

The most detailed if unfortunate statement of the neo-Kantian attempt to construct a quasi-philosophical justification of German involvement as well as provide an exhortation to its participants, was Natrop's 1918 book entitled *Deutsche Weltberuf* ("German World Vocation").[47] This work represented the most strident statement of the neo-Kantian *Kreigsphilosophie,* as well as a unique foray of the neo-Kantians into the field of metahistory. The development of culture through time, Natorp proposed as his basic axiom, exhibited two principal aspects: spirit (*Geist*) and soul (*Seele*). The terms connoted an idea not uncommon at the time, of a universal spirit of man within which develops the "soul" of each *Volk,* as well as the soul of individuals.[48] The use to which Natorp put these categories was also common among intellectual enthusiasts for the German cause, as idealistic philosophical categories and attributions of national characteristics combined in a predictably banal—and popular—assessment of the war and its causes.

As Germany found itself engaged in a two-front war, so a unique German culture was faced on either side with alien and morally inferior enemies. To the east, despotic Russia tended to a foreign policy of aggressive domination, while holding its people in a state of ignorance and subjugation. The potential depth of the Russian soul was revealed only in its literature, Natorp believed, particularly that of Dostoyevsky.[49] In the other direction, in the England of utilitarianism, parliamentarianism, and democracy, individualism reigned supreme, along with absolute dedication to money, power, and success. This definitive characteristic of the English rendered understandable their present aggressive imperialistic stance, as well as the British effort to remove Germany from its rightful place in the sun. England's closest ally in the undertaking was "the nation, and the people of mediocrity—France." The French rationalistic, as opposed to idealistic, concepts of liberty, equality, and fraternity and their concomitant egoistic political expression revealed the bankruptcy of their ideas and their antihumanist tendencies. The French demanded their freedom, Natorp exclaimed, at the expense of the rest of mankind, more precisely at the moment at the expense of the Germans.[50]

What the war represented to this neo-Kantian philosopher was a struggle between the French "Ideas of 1789," and the German "Ideas of 1914." The former, full of promise at first, had revealed their lack of possibility and now served to advance the cause of antihumanistic cultures. The ideas of 1914 embodied the "unconscious reservoir of idealism" implicit in the German character, which had been the quintessential aspect of the German spirit since Eckhardt. It continued to live in all "true Germans," finding its expression in the "folk songs of peasants, as well as the tomes of philosophers."[51] The quintessential principle of idealism was of course the continual striving toward realization of the good in man and society. History for Natorp was a process of eternal becoming and progress toward the ethical ideal. This he called modestly the "great notion of history as eternal future."[52]

What was the significance of what can most mercifully be dismissed as a "period piece?" As with Cohen's war writing, the "German World Vocation" theses represented an attempt to impose moral sense and purpose in an aspect of human activity by nature inaccessible to these ideas. Brought out in opposition to the war, the neo-Kantian moral principles would have been more internally consistent, if unpopular. From the philosophers' own perspective, this may have been asking too much; in any case the attempt was not made.

Natorp, his fellow Marburg philosophers, and many of their academic colleagues, had for twenty years been viewing German society in the throes of its greatest crisis. Confronted with the enormity of World War I, they had since 1914 warned of the demise of peoples and entire civilizations. Now in 1918, forecasting the deep pessimism that Oswald Spengler was to reflect in the twenties, Natorp saw European civilization entering its dark night of the soul. The great continent stood at the precipice, and its salvation lay, not in a peace represented by mere cessation of struggle, but rather in renewed efforts to establish conditions of genuine peace—inner freedom and a moral existence for all mankind.[53]

At this critical moment Natorp's final clarification of the German vocation was an appeal to what he believed to be the unique embodiment of true humanism. As with their striving to engender "right" thinking and a sense of moral purpose within the socialist movement, so the neo-Kantians brought a fundamental proposition to the war effort: without German idealism there was no possibility of real freedom for man. So finally it had come to this: as one of those doomed to suffer at the rear, Natorp had drawn himself into the thick of the fray. Germany's and mankind's struggle fell upon those who battled in the trenches. It fell also upon those who preserved the classic tradition of Germanic philosophy and culture in this mass and machine age—to Germany's *Kulturträger*.

NOTES

1. George L. Mosse, *The Culture of Western Europe* (New York: Rand McNally, 1961), pp. 213, 214.
2. On this general topic significant studies include: George L. Mosse, *Germans and Jews* (New York: Grosset & Dunlap, 1970); Walter Struve, *Elites against Democracy: Leadership Ideals in Bourgeois Political Thought in Germany, 1890–1933* (Princeton: Princeton University Press, 1973); Hermann Lübbe, *Politische Philosophie in Deutschland* (Basel: Verlag Schwabe, 1963); H. J. Sandkühler (ed.), *Marxismus und Ethik* (Frankfurt: Suhrkamp, 1970); Fritz K. Ringer, *The Decline of the German Mandarins: The German Academic Community, 1890–1933* (Cambridge: Harvard University Press, 1969); H. Stuart Hughes, *Consciousness and Society: The Reorientation of European Social Thought, 1890–1930* (New York: Vintage, 1958).
3. Hermann Cohen (1842–1918) followed the socialist sympathizer and critic of materialism Friedrich Albert Lange to the chair of philosophy at the University of Marburg in 1875, where he taught until leaving in 1912 for the Lehranstalt für die Wissenschaft des Judentums in Berlin. His student Paul Natorp (1854–1924) taught philosophy and pedagogy at Marburg from 1894 until his death. Because of his political activism and publicly declared support for the German Social Democratic party, Karl Vorländer (1860–1928) was denied a university position, teaching instead at a Solingen Gymnasium until the end of World War I, when he joined the University of Münster faculty.
4. Hermann Cohen, *Einleitung mit kritischen Nachtrag zur neunten Auflage der Geschichte des Materialismus von Friedrich Albert Lange in Dritter, erweiterter Auflage* (Leipzig: Friedrich Branstetter, 1914), p. 112.
5. Ibid. Aside from the above cited introduction to F.A. Lange's history of materialism, Cohen's most extensive formulation of his social and political philosophy is found in his ethics. I have used here: Hermann Cohen, *Ethik des reinen Willens*, 2nd rev. ed, (Berlin: Cassirer, 1907).
6. Immanuel Kant, *Groundwork of the Metaphysic of Morals* (New York: Harper & Row, 1964), p. 96.
7. Cohen, *Ethik*, pp. 314 ff.
8. Ibid., p. 312.
9. G.W.F. Hegel, *Hegel's Philosophy of Right* (London: Oxford University Press, 1952), p. 10.
10. Cohen, *Ethik*, p. 331.
11. Cohen, *Einleitung zu Lange*, pp. 115–16; Cohen, *Ethik*, pp. 597–99. On Cohen and the state especially valuable is: Steven S. Schwarzschild, "The Democratic Socialism of Hermann Cohen," *Hebrew Union College Annual*, vol. 27 (1956).
12. Ibid.
13. Karl Vorländer, *Marx und Kant* (Vienna: Deutsche Worte, 1904).
14. Ibid., pp. 24, 25. Vorländer had been advocating this view since the publication of his dissertation (under Cohen) ten years earlier: Karl Vorländer, *Der Formalismus der kantischen Ethik in seiner Notwendigkeit und Fruchtbarkeit* (Marburg: Universitäts Buchdruckerei R. Friedrich, 1893), pp. 6, 15.
15. Vorländer, *Marx und Kant*, pp. 8–11. Friedrich Engels, "Ludwig Feuerbach and the End of Classical German Philosophy." In *Marx and Engels on Religion*, ed. Reinhold Niebuhr (New York: Schocken, 1964), p. 236. Eugene Kamenka, *Marxism and Ethics* (New York: St. Martin's Press, Macmillan Co., 1969), pp. 4, 5.

16. On the epistemology of the neo-Kantians especially perceptive is: Nathan Rotenstreich, *Experience and Its Systematization: Studies in Kant* (The Hague: Martinus Nijhoff, 1972), pp. 178 ff.
17. Kurt Eisner, "Kant," *Kurt Eisner's Gesammelte Schriften,* 2 vols. (Berlin, 1919), vol. 2, p. 168.
18. Eduard Bernstein, *Evolutionary Socialism* (New York: Schocken, 1961), pp. 223, 224.
19. Eduard Bernstein, *Wie ist Wissenschaftlicher Sozialismus Möglich?"* (Berlin, 1901), pp. 32, 33.
20. Ibid.
21. Ibid., pp. 18, 32–35.
22. Bernstein was exiled from Switzerland to London from 1888 to 1901.
23. Karl Vorländer, "Die neukantische Bewegung im Sozialismus," *Kantstudien,* vol. 7 (1902).
24. Ibid., pp. 23 ff.
25. Letter from Karl Kautsky to Eduard Bernstein, September 8, 1899, *International Instituut voor Sociale Geschiedenis* (hereafter cited as *IISG*), Bernstein *Nachlass,* D 804.
26. Franz Mehring, "Die Neukantianer." In *Franz Mehrings Gesammelte Schriften,* 13 vols. (Berlin, 1961), vol. 13, pp. 197, 198; Peter Nettl, *Rosa Luxemburg,* abr. ed. (London: Oxford University Press, 1969), p. 12.
27. August Bebel, "Rezension, Pestalozzis Ideen über Arbeiterbildung und soziale Frage," *Die neue Zeit* 44 (1894), p. 568.
28. Timothy R. Keck, "Kant and Socialism: An Exchange of Letters between Paul Natorp and August Bebel," *Archiv für Sozialgeschichte,* 15 (1975), p. 324.
29. Ibid., pp. 327, 328.
30. Letter from Karl Kautsky to G. Plekhanov, May 22, 1898. In H.J. Steinberg, *Sozialismus und deutsche Sozialdemokratie: Zur Ideologie der Partei vor dem 1. Weltkrieg,* 3rd rev. ed. (Bonn-Bad Godesberg: Neue Gesellschaft GmbH, 1972), p. 102.
31. Karl Kautsky, "Ethik und materialistische Geschichtsauffassung: Ein Versuch." In *Marxismus und Ethik,* ed. H.J. Sandkühler.
32. Ibid., pp. 210–15, 261.
33. Karl Vorländer, *Kant und Marx,* 2nd rev. ed. (Tübingen: JCB Mohr, 1926), pp. 251–54.
34. Carl E. Schorske, *German Social Democracy, 1905–1917: The Development of the Great Schism* (New York: Harper & Row, 1972), p. 24. *Protokoll über die Verhandlungen des Parteitages der Sozialdemokratischen Partei Deutschlands, abgehalten zu Dresden vom 13 bis 20 September 1903* (Berlin, 1903), pp. 380–82.
35. Letter from Karl Vorländer to Eduard Bernstein, September 4, 1899, *IISG,* Bernstein *Nachlass,* D 804.
36. *Protokoll,* pp. 174.
37. Hermann Lübbe, *Politische Philosophie,* pp. 123, 124.
38. See esp.: Hermann Lübbe, "Die philosophischen Ideen von 1914." In Hermann Lübbe, *Politische Philosophie,* pp. 173–238; Klaus Schwabe, "Zur politischen Haltung der deutschen Professoren im ersten Weltkrieg," *Historische Zeitschrift* 193 (1961); Klaus Schwabe, *Wissenschaft und Kriegsmoral* (Göttingen, 1969).
39. Fritz Ringer, *The Decline of the German Mandarins,* pp. 188–89; Lübbe, *Politische Philosophie,* pp. 211 ff.

40. Lübbe, *Politische Philosophie,* pp. 178 ff.
41. Karl Vorländer, "Kant und der Krieg," *Das Forum* (Munich, 1915), vol. 1, pp. 469–72.
42. Letter from Karl Vorländer to Paul Natorp, June 29, 1916, *Universitätsbibliothek Marburg, Archiv Abteilung, Natorp Nachlass,* 831: 532.
43. Hermann Cohen, *Deutschtum und Judentum* (Giessen, 1915).
44. Ibid., pp. 34–40, 43.
45. Letter from Hermann Cohen to Paul Natorp, October 27, 1916. *Universitätsbibliothek Marburg, Archiv Abteilung, Natorp Nachlass,* 831:60.
46. Paul Natorp, "Brief an einen hollandische Theologen," *Frankfurter Zeitung,* September 8, 1914; Paul Natorp, "Ueber den gegenwartigen Krieg: Brief eines deutschen Universitätsprofessors an einen amerikanischen Kollegen," *Kölnische Zeitung,* September 18, 1914.
47. Paul Natorp, *Deutscher Weltberuf: Geschichts-philosophische Richtlinien,* 2 vols. (Jena: Eugen Diederichs Verlag, 1918).
48. Ibid., vol. 2, pp. 36–58.
49. Ibid., vol. 1, pp, 198 ff.
50. Ibid., vol 2, pp. 19–20.
51. Ibid.
52. Ibid., vol. 1, p. 20.
53. Ibid., vol. 1, p. 27.

CHAPTER FOUR

Caftan and Cravat: The *Ostjude* as a Cultural Symbol in the Development of German Anti-Semitism

Steven E. Aschheim

Once as I was strolling through the Inner City, I suddenly encountered an apparition in a black caftan and black hair locks. Is this a Jew? was my first thought. For, to be sure, they had not looked like that in Linz . . . my first question assumed a new form: Is this a German? . . . Wherever I went, I began to see Jews, and the more I saw, the more sharply they became distinguished in my eyes from the rest of humanity. . . . The cleanliness of this people, moral and otherwise, I must say is a point in itself. By their very exterior you could tell that these were no lovers of water, and, to your distress, you often knew it with your eyes closed. Later I often grew sick to my stomach from the smell of these caftan wearers.

Adolf Hitler[1]

When Hitler wrote these words he was appealing to an established cultural tradition bound to have resonance for his German and Austrian readers. The historical memory of the ghetto Jew had never died in Germany. Once German Jewry became emancipated and modernized and no longer seemed to fit this traditional image, East European Jewry — unemancipated and bordering both Austria and Germany — served as a constant reminder of the mysterious and brooding ghetto presence. This geographic element is important[2] for it rendered more difficult German Jewry's (enthusiastically undertaken) attempt to cast off its own preemancipation ghetto past. By their mere existence Eastern Jews kept the stereotype of the ghetto Jew alive. In that sense the post-Enlightenment German perception of the Jew was profoundly affected by the disjunction between emancipated and unemancipated Jewry.[3]

The stereotype of the ghetto Jew was not exclusively the property of "anti-Jewish" forces, nor was the ghetto initially seen as a specifically East European phenomenon. The Enlightenment held that all traditional

Jewry — whether in the East or West — possessed negative moral, religious, and economic traits in need of drastic transformation. These traits were derived from the life experience in that specific mode of Jewish society — the ghetto. While Enlighteners like Christian Wilhelm Dohm in his *Über die Verbesserung der Juden* (1783) were among the first to grasp the issue sociologically and to understand that such traits were in large degree the products of objective conditions — political oppression, social isolation, and economic distortions — all agreed that such traits were undesirable. The ghetto became identified with social pathology, filth, and narrowness in both a physical and spiritual sense. Goethe's classic description of the ghetto's fundamental unpleasantness[4] referred not to Eastern Europe but to the Jewish quarter in Frankfurt.

This rejection of the ghetto was a constant in almost all "modern" discourse on the Jewish problem and was an integral part of the discussion well into the twentieth century. It seemed to coincide with a progressive political outlook. The very notion of a ghetto conjured up images of isolation, compulsion, and outdated particularism. Ghetto life made human reconciliation impossible for it fed on mutual distrust and antagonism.[5] Existing on the fringes, it became identified with lack of spiritual creativity and cultural sterility.[6] Ultimately it served to highlight the distinction between progress and reaction, Enlightenment and obscurantism, even beauty and ugliness.

The fact that progressive forces rejected the ghetto made the same exercise easier for German Jewry. Much of nineteenth-century German Jewish assimilation was a concerted effort to transcend all vestiges of the ghetto and eliminate its influence from both personal and collective Jewish life. Over the course of that century German Jews succeeded in their goal, at least insofar as they dropped the external trappings associated with that rejected past. But this move from tradition to modernity, from "caftan" to "cravat," as dramatic as it was, could not impede the popular memory of the ghetto. East European Jewry with its unemancipated masses infiltrating Germany's space and consciousness, replaced the German ghetto of old and became the embodiment of an alien and hostile culture. By the time mass migrations of East European Jews began in the 1880s, German Jews had become thoroughly acculturated and the notion of the ghetto Jew had become synonymous with the *Ostjude*. (This was an association German Jews themselves had done much to foster:[7] it allowed the displacement of those characteristics negatively labeled as "Jewish" to be externalized onto the unemancipated Eastern ghetto Jew, emphasizing the difference between the modern, assimilated Western Jew and his medieval Eastern counterpart.)

This repudiation of the ghetto constituted something close to a general perception. As George Mosse[8] has pointed out, the nineteenth century stereotype of the Jew was popularized by men who shared this perspective and were in favor of assimilation: this was the very antithesis of racism for it presupposed a full submergence into *Deutschtum* (Germanism). In their writings they portrayed the "good" Jew as the assimilated Jew. The problem lay with the *Urjude* intent on maintaining traditional and unethical ghetto practice, unwilling to change his loyalties and dubious values. Gustav Freytag's famous rendition in *Soll und Haben* (1855) of Veitel Itzig as the stereotypical Jew was based on his observations of just such ghetto Jews, *Ostjuden,* who had penetrated into his city of Breslau. Similarly in the 1864 novel by Wilhelm Raabe, *Die Hungerpastor,* Moses Freudenstein is portrayed as a demonic Jew who has inherited the age-old ghetto hatred of the Christian and is consumed by the ruthless drive for wealth while others starved.

The animus against the *Ostjude* as ghetto Jew was not only expressed in popular literature. In the political arena agitation, using similar imagery, began early. Polish Jews were identified to the Prussian Chamber as habitual criminals and thieves well before the rise of politically organized anti-Semitism.[9] In 1865 a conservative member of the Prussian House argued that Russian and Polish Jewish refugees were increasingly becoming the masters of mobile capital in Prussia.[10] The highly respected Heinrich von Treitschke was speaking to an already familiar theme when, in his 1879 remarks, he saw the migration of *Ostjuden* as a fundamental threat to Germany's national integrity. While accepting the possibility of German Jewish assimilation he argued that "our country is invaded year after year by multitudes of assiduous pant-selling youths from the inexhaustible cradle of Poland, whose children and grandchildren are to be the future rulers of Germany's exchanges and Germany's press. This immigration grows visibly in numbers and the question becomes more and more serious how this alien nation can be assimilated."[11]

It is no coincidence that a major demand of the famous 1881 *Antisemitenpetition,* one of the high points of the early anti-Semitic movement and signed by 250,000 German citizens, was the elimination of immigration of alien Jews.[12] Political anti-Semitism was born in Germany and Austria at the same time as East European Jewry began its westward mass migration. Their entry into Western Europe made the stereotype plausible. In many cases their strange, unkempt appearance confirmed mythical fears of the ghetto. Increasingly their external appearance was seen as a sign of an equally degenerate inner life. The traditional Jew reconfirmed the pristine perception of Jewish impurity and physical cues were vital in this. Over the years "scientific" analyses pondered whether there was an inherent racial Jewish smell or whether it was simply a product of ghetto life or of the specific dietary habits of Eastern Jews who used garlic in their daily diet.[13] Typically the anti-Semitic movement composed mock hymns of praise to the Jewish garlic smell[14] (sung in a pseudo-Yiddish format). It was in this physical dimension, in their instant recognizability, that the *Ostjuden* could become the obvious target for anti-Jewish animus. German children at play would instantly recognize Polish Jewish children, taunt them with cries of "Itzig," and refuse to sit on park benches after them.[15] The *Ostjude* became a yardstick for the unaesthetic. Many people opposed to anti-Semitism almost automatically accepted this. Nietzsche,[16] certainly no Volkish anti-Semite, wrote: "We would no more choose the 'first Christians' to associate with than Polish Jews — not that one required any objection to them: They both do not smell good." Upon exposure to Polish Jews in their own ghetto surroundings Hugo Ganz[17] guiltily admitted to the thought that it would not have been a great loss to the world had such unpleasing-looking creatures never existed at all!

The almost consenual distaste for the *Ostjuden* contributed to the fact that they became the first victims of early anti-Semitic successes. Constant agitation against "alien" Jews was connected to the 1884–87 official expulsions from Prussia of "Polish" citizens. While the order covered all Poles, the evidence is clear that it contained an anti-Semitic element closely linked to the fears the stereotype of the ghetto conjured up.[18] The importance of these expulsions lies in the fact that previously outlawed anti-Semitic demands now became incorporated into state policy, and it was precisely on the question of the "alien" Jew that this change could occur in the first place. Officials denied the anti-Jewish component, but documents demonstrate that Bismarck himself — never a "principled" anti-Semite, his political thinking was too fluid and subtle for that — shared the animus against the ghetto Jew. Certainly he viewed the threat of Jewish immigration from the East with grave concern. At a cabinet meeting in May 1882 he urged that these "undesirable elements" be kept out of Germany. He also ordered that all Jews living off usury be expelled from Oppeln, an area of concentration for Jewish refugees. Thereafter the cabinet initiated special patrols of the Russian border to keep out persons who — in obvious code language — "looked undesirable."[19] These were not even the first expulsions; in Prussia's Polish provinces there was a considerable prior history of governmental measures against Polish Jews going back to the eighteenth century.[20] Still, the measures of the 1880s coincided with organized anti-Semitic agitation, and from then on through World War I there were various local expulsions.[21] Moreover, numerous German universities promulgated regulations banning East European Jewish students.[22]

The antipathy to the *Ostjude* penetrated the highest levels. Bismarck's press secretary Moritz Busch wrote one of the most vicious diatribes on East European Jews; some observers have even suggested that his writing reflected Bismarck's own ideas.[23] Busch's anonymously published *Israel und die Gojim*[24] fully exploited the fear of the ghetto Jew as radically alien and hostile. The *Ostjuden*, he claimed, were streaming into Germany in an unending mass. These were the "real" Jews, strange medieval Semitic types, bringing their criminal ways into Germany, maintaining their primeval hate for all Christians, and waiting to enrich themselves while impoverishing Germans. Like vampires they were coming to suck the lifeblood out of the German national organism in accordance with the ancient Talmudic injunction of hatred for the Christian. The only way to stop these "leeches" was to hermetically seal Germany's borders *(Grenzschluss)*.

As more East European Jews settled in Germany and concentrated in the same residential quarters, the anti-Semitic press was quick to play on fears that the despised ghetto with all its criminality, backwardness, and dirt had been reintroduced into Germany.[25] (Assimilationist Jews did not undermine this perception when they wrote almost identical descriptions of Eastern Jewish ghetto life in Germany. "Is *this* Berlin?" asked one shocked Jewish observer.[26]) The *Ostjude* played a central role in the genesis, mythology, and disposition of modern German anti-Semitism. East European Jews were both symbolically and legally alien; this was a lethal combination. Visible and vulnerable, they made obvious and easy targets.

Let us spell out some of the implications and limits of this analysis. It seems to lay the "blame" for the rise of German anti-Semitism squarely on the shoulders of the *Ostjude*. It accepts the assumption that modern anti-Semitism was derived from an objectively based "clash of cultures." It implies that only the continuing presence of unemancipated Eastern Jewry, lapping the edges of civilized Europe, reinforcing the ghetto stereotype, and constantly infiltrating into the "emancipated" West makes the rise of modern political anti-Semitism comprehensible.[27] Hitler's own juxtaposition of the caftan Jews from the East with the cravat Jews of Linz makes the point clear: while the assimilated Jew was becoming increasingly indistinguishable from other Germans, *Ostjuden* were keeping alive historical stereotypes. This is not only a question of historical analysis — many German Jews in the period under discussion openly insisted that the *Judenfrage* was essentially a product of the East European Jews.[28] Such a view implies that an "assimilationist" strategy would have been successful were it not for continuing Jewish intrusions from the East.

The *Ostjude* played an important role in the development of German anti-Semitism. Yet such an analysis is in need of refinement and modification. While emphasizing a critical element, it sidesteps another equally significant factor: the attack on the "assimilating" and "assimilated" Jew. We need a more differentiated analysis to illuminate the dialectic and sort out the respective places of the "caftan" and "cravat" Jews in the cultural mythology and political practice of German anti-Semitism.

While the image of the ghetto Jew was inherited from centuries of separate Jewish/Christian existence, a new — although related — stereotype of the "emancipated" Jew was created in the nineteenth century. This critique of the modern assimilationist Jew in German popular culture was formulated almost simultaneously with the attempt to assimilate. The stereotype initially employed old notions of the ghetto Jew but placed this within a new context. The dramatic stage was an effective vehicle for the early critique because much of it was based on the use of visual caricature and contrast. In Julius von Voss's play *Die Griechheit* (1807) the Jewess Rahel Joab interests herself in "high culture," avoids all intonations of a Jewish accent, and even shows Catholic inclinations — but betrays her "Jewish being" when it comes to matters of money.[29] This perception was ominous, for von Voss was an avowed advocate of Enlightenment and was in favor of assimilation.

The most biting critique of Jewish assimilation appeared in Karl Alexander Sessa's satire *Unser Verkehr* (1814). In this extremely popular and controversial play[30] Sessa mercilessly satirized the "new" German Jews desperately denying their ghetto origins and seeking to make themselves culturally respectable *(Salonfähig)*. There was little artistic merit in the work, but its vogue attested to the fact that it had captured the comic side of a popular perception. Sessa's critique of the move from the ghetto to emancipated society (which was to be echoed over the next century) was effective precisely because it concentrated on the absurdity (and implied impossibility) of Jewish assimilation. The locus of animosity now shifted to the Jew's spinelessness, hopeless mimicry, lack of respect and character. The new view despised the Jew because he wanted to leave the ghetto, not because he was of it. The assimilating Jew was usurping his historical place, and it was in the attempt to assimilate that the threat was now placed. The Jew previously blamed for being a product of the ghetto was now castigated for his pretensions to transcend it.[31] Even at that early stage Sessa was not the first to popularize the theme. In 1802 C.W.F. Grattenauer's widely read pamphlet *Wider die Juden* appeared. The old contempt for the ghetto Jew was transferred to the "rapacious" Jewish urge for social integration. The Jew was viewed as a philistine and vulgar upstart. The ludicrous Jewish desire to discard Jewishness became itself an object of ridicule. In the early days of assimilation the Jew was increasingly identified with the "philistine."[32]

The satirical critique of cultural assimilation grew more difficult as the century wore on, precisely because German Jews were assimilating so successfully. What had made Grattenauer's and Sessa's work so effective was the hilarious contrast of the genteel salon with "typical" Jewish characteristics. When they wrote, Jews still retained traces of their despised jargon and physical gesticulation associated with the ghetto. In this there lay a genuinely comic side.

The actor Albert Wurm, who had a major role in *Unser Verkehr,* made a career out of his hilarious imitation of the accent and mannerisms of Jewish arrivistes. Wurm performed these imitations not only on the stage but in the private homes of Berlin burghers.[33] Jewish reformers spent much time through 1850 trying desperately to remove these vestiges from their language and gestures.[34]

Assimilation involved the removal of all external badges of distinction (that is why the caftan and side-locks were seen by most German Jews as a deliberate provocation to the non-Jew) and extinguishing Jewish conspicuousness — essentially it was an exercise in social blending. With the rise of the organized anti-Semitic movements in the 1880s these obviously distinguishing elements had disappeared. But even before this where caricature was no longer in place, deadly culture criticism could take over.

Jacob Toury[35] has pointed out that the very formulation of the term *Judenfrage* (the Jewish question) referred to the issue of "emancipated" and "assimilated" Jews. As early as 1821 fears that Jews would dominate the cultural worlds of literature and journalism were voiced. By the 1830s it was clear that the anti-Jewish animus was aimed as much against the "new" Jew as it referred to traditional conceptions. Bruno Bauer's famous *Die Judenfrage* (1843) attacked "new" Jews whose links with traditional Jewry were severed and who were thoroughly acculturated. For Bauer these Jews were indulging in duplicity. Assimilation was impossible, emancipation a chimera, for beneath social surfaces, there was ultimately no difference between the old and new Jews.

Bauer attacked the modern Jew but also radically opposed "traditional" Jews. The negative connection remained intact. But later cultural criticism sometimes found value in the "old" Jews and concentrated its animus against "modern" Jews. Julius Langbehn, the Volkish thinker obsessed with "aestheticizing" German life, viewed the "emancipated" German Jew as the key obstacle to such a vision. This was not a playful matter but rather an issue of life and death in which Germany's future was depicted as dependent upon the extirpation of the assimilated German Jew. Volkish critique of assimilation reached here its most extreme pre–World War I expression. Langbehn distinguished the traditional from the modern Jew. The traditional Jew, he argued,[36] was worthy of respect; he had something in common with a spiritual and moral aristocracy. These were "genuine" Jews who wanted nothing else but to be Jews and, as such, had "character." "Modern" Jews were quite the opposite: they wanted so desperately to become Germans that they had lost all integrity and character. A self-acknowledging Jew was an "authentic" Jew *(rechter Israelit)* and as such acceptable; not so inauthentic *(gefälschten)* Jews, for honor resided only in those who remained true to themselves. The "old" Jew possessed at least a spiritual homeland — the "enlightened" Jew had nothing and was in constant, restless flight. It was against such Jews that Germans had to take a decisive stand.[37]

Langbehn typified one strain of Volkish and anti-Semitic thinking which feared the Jew precisely because he seemed to have lost all resemblance to the ghetto Jews of old and was realizing the promise of assimilation according to those premises of liberal modernity which he and his colleagues were so vitriolically opposing.[38] Such men held that the assimilated Jew was a "poison" for Germany and would have to be treated as such.[39] For folkish thinkers who simultaneously confronted a "new" kind of Jew and a radical uprooting of traditional values and structures, there was a certain bewilderment. For all his distastefulness the ghetto Jew was at least identifiable. The "modern" Jew, on the contrary, was more slippery and elusive. No longer synonymous with a backward and obscurantist past, he now embodied the ruthless drive for constant change. He became a metaphor for "decomposition."

If the rise of organized anti-Semitism coincided with the westward migrations of the Eastern Jewish masses, it also dovetailed with the push to rapid industrialization in Germany and various financial scandals in the capitals of Europe. This identification of modernity and capitalism with explicitly assimilated Jewry was to lead Volkish thinkers like Paul de Lagarde, who in the 1850s accepted the possibility of German Jewish assimilation, into radically hardened positions. From 1881 on he lumped all Jews together. Lagarde was at his most vitriolic when describing the machinations of modern Jewish capitalists. It is in that context that the horrifyingly prescient language of extermination is employed: "With trichinae and bacilli one does not negotiate, nor are trichinae and bacilli subjected to education; they are exterminated as quickly and as thoroughly as possible."[40]

Even for men like Freytag and Raabe, who appeared to clearly distinguish "good" assimilated from "bad" ghetto Jews, the distinction was never clear-cut — rather they merged into one another. Freytag located the danger at the point where the Jew was uprooted from the ghetto and sought his fortune without. Veitel Itzig's parents — rooted in the ghetto — are portrayed as honorable, honest, and loving.[41] Closer examination reveals that it is not the ghetto but the break from it which constitutes part of the new Jewish threat.

Treitschke's acceptance of the possibility of German Jewish assimilation was seriously undermined by a quasi-racial analysis.[42] He argued that while most West European Jewry was assimilable because they came from a more noble "Spanish" background,[43] "we Germans have to deal with Jews of the Polish branch, which bears the deep scars of Christian tyranny. According to experience they are incomparably alien to the European, and especially to the German national character." Treitschke's meaning was clear. An analysis made in terms of "stock" meant that even emancipated

German Jewish citizens had inherited these Polish Jewish characteristics and as such Jewish integration would be made that much more difficult.

Certainly for political activists most closely associated with the drive for *Grenzschluss,* the distinction between Eastern and Western Jews was tenuous at best. One supporter of Treitschke asserted that German Jews would always remain essentially different from Germans even if they were fully cosmeticized and removed the caftan and shaved off their beards.[44] Ominously Moritz Busch (one of the first to advocate the formation of political groupings exclusively dedicated to fighting the Jewish menace) made a distinction between ghetto and assimilated Jews which made the latter, if anything, more dangerous. German Jews, he proclaimed,[45] were merely "Semitic colonies in the West." But they were insidious for they were coiffured and disguised. They had made themselves so "respectable" that it was hard to believe they had any connection with their Polish or Lithuanian counterparts. But this was an illusion, for acculturation had not removed the Jewish *Volkseele.* The identical ancient hatred for the Christian characterized the assimilated Jew. It was precisely their invisibility which made them more dangerous than the ghetto Jews, for this put them into an ideal position to achieve their aims of power and domination unrecognized from within.

From Busch onward anti-Semitic fears focused increasingly on the dangers of the "invisible" assimilated Jew.[46] *Der Stürmer*'s 1938 textbook for schoolchildren *The Poison Mushroom*[47] was merely restating an old theme in its didactic warnings to innocent Aryan youth: The modern Jew, the textbook informed its readers, was like the mushroom. As one often confused the poisonous from the healthy mushroom, similar confusion could occur when trying to identify the Jewish swindler. This sameness of appearance had caused many unwary Aryans to succumb to this illusion and fall prey to *Judenschwindel.* One must always keep one's eyes wide open, for then the disguise could be penetrated, as underneath "the Jew always remained a Jew." This attack went side by side with the hatred for the *Ostjude.* This was a continuing dialectic. The same work — with suitably repellent illustrations — portrayed the infiltration of three hideous stereotypical *Ostjuden* into a spotlessly clean Aryan village. The contrast could not be more marked and there were no problems of recognition.[48]

From the outset Berlin anti-Semites, while they had to be more circumspect with their prescriptions for German Jewish citizens, concentrated their attack equally on "assimilated" Jews and sought to undo many of the successes of Jewish emancipation. The Petition of 1881 was not only addressed to the problem of "alien" Jewish immigration. It also outlined a program for excluding Jews from government posts and teaching jobs in primary schools, limiting their employment in higher education, and restricting appointments of Jews as judges. It even contained the ominous demand for a special Jewish census.[49] Adolph Stoecker's first anti-Semitic speech was addressed to the emancipated Jews of Germany. Entitled "What We Demand of Modern Jewry,"[50] it argued that "Berlin Jews are much richer, much more clever and influential than the Polish Israelites. They control the arteries of money, banking, and trade; they dominate the press and they are flooding the institutions of higher learning." The center of Jewish danger was to be located in modernization and emancipation, in the license German Jews had been given to dominate German culture.

The strength of the attack on the modern emancipated Jew was reflected not only in anti-Semitic tracts. It was mirrored too in the structure of German Jewish self-hatred based upon the stereotype of the "modern" Jew. This may seem obvious but the point has never been made explicit. Pre–World War I documents of German Jewish self-hatred echo Volkish perceptions of the German, more than the East European Jew. Of course these men were never enamored with the caftan Jews but, more centrally, they shared their preoccupations with the folkish critics of "Jewish modernism." Like Stoecker and Langbehn, Walter Rathenau (1867–1922) regarded the restless, rootless parvenu spirit as the most distasteful aspect of contemporary German Jewish behavior. In his tract *Höre Israel* (1897)[51] he stressed the offensive philistinism of German Jews. They tried to become pillars of culture but not even eau de Cologne could wash away their alien nature. They were "loud and self-conscious in their dress, hot-blooded and restless in their manner." Rathenau, like other Volkish thinkers, regarded modern restlessness as spiritually corroding. He viewed "modernity" and "spirituality" as antithetical qualities. This was profoundly paradoxical for Rathenau, an industrialist who was himself an exemplar of the very "modernity" he so despised.[52] A capitalist who despised capitalism, perhaps Rathenau's Jewish problem was rooted in his acceptance of the Volkish analysis of the Jewish role within modernity. His — admittedly short-lived — "return" to Judaism was not based upon a West European model but upon Martin Buber's "spiritual" and "mystic" *Hasidim*. If at all, *Geist* was to be found with the East European and not the Berlin Jew.[53]

Rathenau was by no means exceptional in this regard. The novelist Conrad Alberti (1862–1918) internalized the Volkish critique of the modern Jew even more precisely.[54] For him Judaism had lost all right to exist. The modern Jew was the natural enemy of organic, progressive development. He incarnated the accumulative principle of modern capitalism. Jews liked material things but never performed honest work and lacked basic values. They were responsible for the corruption of German culture. Alberti clearly had little use for the ghetto Jew, but his portrait of the Jew as an unethical parvenu was borrowed directly from the Volkish critique of the "assimilated" Jew. Similarly Otto Weininger (1880–1903) depicted Jews as essentially amoral, cynical, and lacking in warmth in his classic self-hating work *Sex and Character* (1903). These were the same properties anti-Semites attributed to deracinated Jews.

While German Jewish self-haters borrowed their self-images from anti-Semitic portraits of the German Jew, anti-Semites found it more politic to concentrate their fire on the dangers of foreign Jewish immigration. But these attacks often served merely as a pretext for the attack on the local Jew. Hermann Ahlwardt's 1895 proposal to the *Reichstag*[55] that Germany close its borders to "Israelites who are not citizens of the Reich," was a vicious attack on German Jewry and a diatribe on the impossibility of assimilation:

> The Jews have lived here for 700–800 years, but have they become Germans? Have they placed themselves on the soil of labor? They have never dreamed of such a thing; as soon as they arrived they started to cheat and they have been doing that ever since they have been in Germany. . . . The Jew is no German. If you say he was born in Germany, he was nursed by a German wetnurse, he abides by German laws, he has to serve as a soldier . . . then I say that all this is not the critical factor with regard to his nationality; the crucial factor is the race from which he stems. Permit me a rather trite comparison which I have already used elsewhere in my speeches: a horse that is born in a cowshed is far from being a cow.

Ahlwardt's remarks must be seen in the paradoxical context of successful Jewish acculturation: "race" became an effective explanation of "Semitic/Aryan" differences precisely because external differences were now so few. It was no longer a matter of religion, nationality, dress, or language; so many Jews had followed the assimilationist path that the difference now had to be located in internal genetic agents where human will and social amelioration were powerless. "Race" became the center of the Jewish question because among German Jews cultural distance had all but been overcome. It was the threat and perception of radical closeness which ushered in "race theory." This sheds a different light on the notion that anti-Semitism flowed from an objectively based cultural clash. For Western Jews, at least, it was the identity of culture which necessitated the invention of a new principle of differentiation.

While the Volkish picture of the Jew seemed to fit the emancipated and the ghetto Jew — both were characterized by their grasping materialism, lack of ethics and creativity — there were important differences in the stereotype. While the caftan Jew embodied a mysterious past, the cravat Jew symbolized a frightening present. The *Ostjude* was too primitive, the Western Jew too modern. It was the function of racist thinking to resolve this apparent dilemma by uniting the two indivisibly. For most Volkish anti-Semites this was only an apparent dilemma. The "international" image of the Jew had never been eradicated — in spite of repeated German

Jewish attempts at Jewish denationalization and the insistence that Jewry be conceived purely in terms of its "religious" character.[56]

Popular historical memory retained the picture of a kind of primeval Jewish unity which made all Jewish behavior — individual or collective, assimilationist or traditionalist — appear "essentially" Jewish. For those who clung to such an image — that predated the division of Jewry into its emancipated and unemancipated components — Jewish volition was beside the point. Whatever the Jew did (or did not do), his actions could be absorbed into the overall negative picture. This does not mean that modern German anti-Semitism took root entirely outside the realm of social reality and that it was purely the product of the demented fantasies of lunatic fringe thinkers. The myth of the *Ostjude* (who *was* in many ways radically different from West Europeans in appearance and outlook) and that of the "assimilated" Jew (who *was* disproportionately involved with modern institutions most closely associated with liberalism and capitalism) have some foundation in reality. But both racism and the notion of international Jewry (which preceded and then became tied into the racist scheme) were impervious either to empirical refutation or the possibility of Jewish reformation.

This undifferentiated impulse against the Jew ultimately made the distinction between the local German and the *Ostjude* irrelevant. If the political venom was more obviously directed against the ghetto Jew this was for reasons of political prudence, not principle. Disenfranchised immigrants were both visible and vulnerable and less likely to arouse storms of protest. But actions against the *Ostjuden* were seen as the *first* step toward solving the Jewish question;[57] few claimed it would be the last.

Well before the war, German Zionists were warning their fellow Jews that the classic attempt to shake off the *Ostjude* and see him as the source of anti-Semitism was not only morally contemptible but also a critical misunderstanding of the whole basis of modern German hostility to the Jew. They claimed that such a dissociation served to reinforce accusations concerning Jewish lack of character and spinelessness.[58] But these were minority views which only became more plausible in the violent years following World War I. Still they described equally well the post-1870 period. The treatment accorded the *Ostjude* was always a sensitive barometer of the more general attitude toward Jews, and if the attack upon him was easier it could, nevertheless, seldom be distinguished from a potential attack on German Jews.

It should be clear by now that this is not merely an issue of ex post facto historical judgment. German Jews themselves passionately debated these questions at the time. Those inclined toward a liberal assimilationist position held that the penetration of the *Ostjuden* into Western Europe impeded local Jewish assimilation, kept alive the memory of "the Jew," and lent credibility to accusations of ineradicable differences between Jews and their host nations. Those who adhered to a Zionist or national Jewish viewpoint argued that anti-Semitism was attributable to a Jewish loss of national nerve and self-respect. In a letter to the representative body of German Jewry, the *Centralverein,* Albert Einstein, who was deeply moved by the plight of the *Ostjuden,* adopted that position:[59] "More dignity and more independence in our ranks! Not until we dare to regard ourselves as a nation, not until we respect ourselves, can we gain the esteem of others, or rather only then will it come of its own accord!"

Both positions ironically echoed anti-Semitic sources. By emphasizing one strain over the other, each party thought it had found an explanatory key and practical guide to action. Yet as we have tried to show, Volkish thought and anti-Semitic ideology from its beginnings attacked Jewry in all its manifestations. For most, Jewish behavior could make little difference. While some attacked the Jew because he embodied despised ghetto characteristics, others concentrated their venom on the Jew as philistine and destroyer of values, disagreeable because he had sought to shed those same characteristics. Apparently conflicting tendencies existed side by side and it was this welter of ambiguous signals which made both interpretations seem plausible. Behind this lay the fact that the historical image of the Jew had never died in Germany and was available for exploitation in appropriate structural crises. Onto the traditional fear and dislike of the "Talmud and ghetto Jew" was grafted the notion of the "modern Jew," characterless and destructive in intent.

This placed the Jew in an inescapable double bind: if he maintained his prior characteristics he would be labeled a ghetto Jew; if he tried to assimilate this could be construed as a duplicitous exercise in camouflage or as proof of flawed "character." In practice the distinction was never that tight, but operated on a continuum. Racism only formalized and modernized the age-old picture of an ineradicable Jewish unity. In this sense the fear of the caftan Jew and the cravat Jew could be fused. The *Ostjude* was feared as a potential German Jew. Franz Rosenzweig[60] saw this clearly: "The whole German fear of the East European Jew does not refer to him as such, but to him as a potential Western Jew." The Western Jew, on the other hand, was to be feared, according to some anti-Semites, because he had never transcended his "internal" ghetto.[61] Some saw East European Jewry as the demographic reservoir and spiritual backbone of Western Jewish survival.[62] Still others saw inhabitants of the ghetto as foot soldiers marching to the tune of their commanders, the great Western Jewish capitalists.[63] In the minds of anti-Semites — if not Jews themselves — Jewish interdependence was never in doubt.

Yet we cannot leave it at that. It is true that ultimately the anti-Semitic attack was directed as much against the Western as the Eastern Jew. Still

the *Ostjude* always retained his salience as a highly charged and differentiated cultural symbol. This distinctiveness gave the *Ostjude* a special role
in the later disposition of German anti-Semitism. We must now examine
this specific function. The post–World War I attack on the ghetto Jew
served as a barometer of a more general animus, one that prefigured by a
decade the fate of German Jews themselves. No direct link between these
earlier events and subsequent actions can be construed, yet they bear resemblance to, appear almost like an unconscious rehearsal of even more
brutal events to come. In the end the *Ostjude* played a specific and differentiated role which demonstrated the extent of postwar political escalation.

We cannot include here an examination of the complex developments of
anti-Semitism during World War I. Suffice to say that with the German
occupation of Poland and Lithuania, where masses of soldiers were for the
first time exposed to *Ostjuden* in their home surroundings, the stereotype
of the ghetto Jew was concretized and reinforced. The attack on *Ostjuden*
began almost immediately after war was declared. From then on, anti-
Semitic circles warned of the horrible dangers an *Ostjuden* "invasion"
would bring. But again, this does not mean that the animus was directed
against Eastern Jews alone. The political truce — *Burgfrieden* — disal-
lowed the attack on the German Jew, whereas the *Ostjude* was still fair
game. It was only after the infamous *Judenzahlung* that hostility to native
German Jews could be expressed more freely. Certain German Jews saw
the early attack on the *Ostjude* as providing them with some respite. But
prescient observers like the Zionist Julius Berger saw the situation with
remarkable clarity. As early as 1916, he wrote to a friend that "anti-Semitism is growing, growing against the Eastern Jews, growing against the
Western Jews, growing enormously and preparing for a real orgy which
will be celebrated after the war."[64]

Although hostility to all Jews was explicit in 1918–23, political chaos
and economic collapse made the foreign *Ostjuden* an especially suitable
target. Disenfranchised, visible, and vulnerable they bore the brunt of the
ideological and physical attack of a brutalized anti-Semitic movement and
became the first victims of official anti-Semitic policies.[65]

The classic stereotype was constantly invoked as justification for the attack. In a flood of publications their presence in Germany was portrayed as
an invasion, fundamentally endangering German morality, economy, sexuality, politics, and culture. Above all, total economic breakdown gave renewed vigor and plausibility to the Shylock myth — while German workers starved, ghetto Jews were eating off the fat of the land. Hitler[66] was
only one of many agitators to use this as a central theme. And Jewish involvement with the German post–World War I revolutions gave credibility
to increasingly voiced accusations of nihilism and "Talmudic Bolshev-
ism."[67]

Retrospectively, this portrayal of the *Ostjude* by the radical Right must be seen as the point at which the language of dehumanization became almost normative in public discourse. What was previously limited to small circles or said in private, seemed almost to acquire national legitimacy. The *Ostjude* became the constant object of what can only be described as parasitological terminology. Ghetto Jews were by nature "pests," had faces of "animals of prey," and were devoid of human feeling. They were trained in special Talmudic schools to ruthlessly despoil the land and peoples among whom they dwelled.[68] The *Ostjude* was the first to be pictured, publicly and routinely, as withdrawn from the reference points of "humanness" itself. This portrayal of the ghetto Jew foreshadowed a dehumanization that would extend to all European Jews at a more propitious time.

It was not only as object of linguistic extremism that *Osjuden* living in Germany were distinguished from their German Jewish counterparts. Even more ominous were the physical attacks and government actions against *Ostjuden*. Here again were portents of the future. In Berlin, police harassment and raids on the ghetto in the *Scheunenviertel* became almost routine. These were tasks which Berlin police president Ernst — operating under Social Democratic authority — relished.[69] When in December 1919 the Prussian government announced that all "undesirable" *Ostjuden* were to be interned in special camps[70] it appeared that official policy was working with, and not against, the radical Right. To be sure, these camps were only set up in 1921 and then by Democratic interior minister Dominicus and not the Social Democrats. Again there were arbitrary arrests; people were not allowed to stand trial but instead were sent to Stagard and Cottbus camps. Reports soon leaked out that beatings and maltreatment were common in these institutions.[71]

If things looked grim in Prussia, they were worse in Bavaria. *Ostjuden* became the constant focus of the anti-Jewish animus and most political parties included a demand for their immediate expulsion. After much agitation and incidents of physical violence, in 1923 the *Ostjuden* were summarily expelled from Munich and other Bavarian cities.[72] Almost identical attacks on Eastern Jews were made in Austria during the same period.[73] By 1923 the whole process had reached its climax. Aside from the Bavarian expulsions, attacks and harassments were reported throughout Germany — in Beuthen, Königsberg, Nuremberg, Sachsen and elsewhere.[74] The first pogrom in twentieth-century German history took place in Berlin during the month of November. Sustained looting and beating of *Ostjuden,* lasting a number of days, took place in the Jewish quarter, at times with the passive encouragement of authorities.[75]

During 1918–23, *Ostjuden* were singled out as a group and subjected to arbitrary arrests, internment camps, expulsions, beatings, and even a pogrom. Their salience as a cultural symbol had made them the first real victims of a brutalized German anti-Semitism. The attack prefigured what was to happen to German Jewry itself. Many years before the essential dynamic of Nazi bureaucratic methods became evident, the Zionist *Juedische Rundschau* analyzed the Bavarian expulsions as a new kind of anti-Semitism in which the state itself had systematically organized an "administrative pogrom."[76] When in the wake of the Berlin riots the same paper dramatically announced that the achievements of Jewish emancipation in Germany had been shattered and that the hour of fate for German Jewry had arrived,[77] it was seen as overblown rhetoric. Could anyone have known how accurately that description would have fitted the plight of German Jews only one decade later? In this sense the *Ostjude* became a metaphor for all Jews — only more so and ten years earlier.

NOTES

1. *Mein Kampf* (Boston, 1971), pp. 56–57.
2. On this point see Isaac Eisenstein Barzilay, "The Jew in the Literature of the Enlightenment," *Jewish Social Studies* 18 (October 1956), pp. 245–46.
3. This essay is extracted from a larger work which examines some implications of this disjunction for German Jewry and how the *Ostjude* — both "negatively" and "positively" — affected German Jewish development.
4. See Wilhelm Stoffers, *Juden und Ghetto* (Graz, 1939), p. 69.
5. The ghetto was perceived as radically antithetical to all socialist goals. See the classic statement by Karl Kautsky, *Rasse und Judentum* (Stuttgart, 1921).
6. Literary critic Franz Blei was only echoing Enlightenment sensibility when he castigated the ghetto for producing moneylenders but not building cathedrals(!) or creating art, poetry, or music. Jews could not be understood as products of their Biblical heritage but rather as the outcome of isolated ghettos. See "Die Juden." In *Menschliche Betrachtungen zur Politik* (Munich, 1916), pp. 279–80.
7. German Jewish popular literature is full of negative descriptions of East European Jews. The work of Karl Emil Franzos (1848–1904), who popularized the notion that such Jews were "half-Asian," must get special mention.
8. See his path-breaking essays, "Culture, Civilization, and German Anti-Semitism" and "The Image of the Jew in German Popular Literature: Felix Dahn and Gustav Freytag." In *Germans and Jews* (New York, 1970).
9. Quoted in Jacob Toury, *Soziale und politische Geschichte der Juden in Deutschland, 1847–1871* (Düsseldorf, 1977), p. 31. This was claimed in a petition of 1852 by Ballnus of Czichau.
10. Ibid., p. 31.
11. "Unsere Aussichten," *Preussische Jahrbücher* 44 (1879), pp. 559–76. The translation here is from Robert Chazan and Marc Lee Raphael (eds.), *Modern Jewish History: A Source Reader* (New York, 1974), pp. 81–82.
12. See Helmut Neubach, *Die Ausweisungen von Polen und Juden aus Preussen, 1885–86* (Wiesbaden, 1967), p. 10.
13. Among the many examples see Richard Andree, *Zur Volkskunde der Juden* (Leipzig, 1881), pp. 68–69. Also Hans F. Günther, *Rassenkunde des jüdischen Volkes* (Munich, 1930), p. 266.

14. "Ehren—unn Loblied oufn Knoblich. ...." In Eduard Fuchs, *Die Juden in der Karikatur* (Munich, 1921), pp. 282–83.

15. Franz Kafka, among others, was struck by this. See his "Travel Diary: Trip to Weimar and Jungborn, June 28–July 29, 1912." In *The Diaries of Franz Kafka, 1914–1923* (New York, 1976), p. 301.

16. "The Anti-Christ." In Walter Kaufmann (ed.), *The Portable Nietzsche* (New York, 1974), p. 625. The work was originally written in 1888.

17. Quoted in Kurt Aram, *Der Zar und seine Juden* (Berlin, 1914), p. 178.

18. Neubach, pp. 219–20.

19. Fritz Stern, *Gold and Iron* (New York, 1977), p. 526. Berlin Jewry felt similarly and warned the Alliance Israélite that they would break off all relations if it continued to encourage Jewish refugees to proceed through their city.

20. See J. Herzberg, "Die Ostjudenfrage am Ausgange des achtzehnten Jahrhunderts," *Im Deutschen Reich 22* (March-April 1916). See also Edouard Roditi, "Wandering Jews," *Commentary 68* (August 1979), p. 55.

21 See *Allgemeine Zeitung des Judentums 59* (15 February 1895), p. 76. *Juedische Rundschau 11* (8 May 1906), p. 289. *Juedische Rundschau 19* (1 May 1914), p. 189.

22. Not unexpectedly, there was much opposition to East European Jewish students from the German *Studentschaft*. For details on university regulations in Prussia, Bavaria, and Baden see Julius Heilbronner, "Die Aufnahme von Ausländern am deutschen Hochschulen," *K.C. Blätter* (March-April, 1916), esp. pp. 603–6.

23. It is surprising that in his scrupulously documented study of Bleichröder, Bismarck, and the Jewish question, *Gold and Iron,* Fritz Stern mentions Busch's name three times but never alludes to his anti-Semitism. For details on Busch see Paul Massing, *Rehearsal for Destruction* (New York, 1949), pp. 84–85. On the background of Busch's publication and the possibility that it reflected Bismarck's ideas, see Neubach, p. 9.

24. Leipsig, 1880. See esp. p. 175.

25. "Im Ghetto von Berlin" appeared in the *Deutsche Zeitung* and is quoted in *Jeudische Rundschau 12* (1 March 1907), pp. 88–89.

26. Adolph Grabowsky, "Ghettowanderung," *Die Schaubühne* (3 February 1910), p. 124.

27. See for instance the formulation by Leon Poliakov, *Harvest of Hate* (New York, 1979), pp.304–5.

28. This notion that the Jewish question was imported went hand in hand with the opinion that *Ostjuden* were the biggest single obstacle to the successful integration of German Jews. For a symposium overwhemingly inclined to this position see Werner Sombart, *Judentaufen* (Munich, 1912).

29. See Stoffers, pp. 131–32.

30. For commentary on this play and the history of its reception, see Stoffers, pp. 110–21. Also Elizabeth Frenzel, *Judengestalten auf der deutschen Bühne* (Munich, 1940), pp. 86–113.

31. German Jews protested vociferously and attempted to ban performances of the play. To stereotype the ghetto was one thing, to caricature assimilation quite another.

32. Grattenauer had written a similar work much earlier. But his *Ueber die physische und moralische Verfassung der heutigen Juden* of 1791 came too early in the history of assimilation and did not find an echo. For details on this and the Jew as "philistine" see Hannah Arendt, *The Origins of Totalitarianism* (Meridian, 1963), pp. 61–62.

33. See Frenzel, pp. 96 ff. Also Jacob Katz, *Out of the Ghetto* (New York, 1978), p. 86.
34. On one level, assimilation was a concerted attempt at impression management. Anton Ree, *Die Sprachverhältnisse der heutigen Juden im Interesse der Gegenwart, und mit besonderer Rucksicht auf Volkserziehung* (Hamburg, 1844) is a good example. The work consists of an impassioned plea to remove all traces of "Jewish" ways of speaking and gesticulating.
35. Jacob Toury, "'The Jewish Question': A Semantic Approach," *Leo Baeck Institute Yearbook* 11 (1966), esp. pp. 90–94.
36. *Rembrandt als Erzieher* (Leipzig, 1896), p. 43 (originally published in 1890).
37. Ibid., p. 293.
38. For excellent accounts of Volkish antimodernity see George L. Mosse, *The Crisis of German Ideology* (New York, 1964); Fritz Stern, *The Politics of Cultural Despair* (University of California Press, 1974).
39. Langbehn, p. 292.
40. Quoted in Stern, *The Politics of Cultural Despair,* p. 63.
41. *Debit and Credit* (London, 1858), p. 66.
42. Treitschke, p. 81.
43. This was all very confused and compounded by a semantic irony. German Jews were not considered part of the Polish branch but vice versa. Both Polish and German Jews were known as *Ashkenazi* (i.e., German) Jews. In that sense the *Ostjude* was a German Jew!
44. Wilhelm Ender, "Zur Judenfrage." In Walter Boehlich, *Der Berliner Antisemitismusstreit* (Sammlung Insel, 1965), pp. 106–7.
45. Busch, esp. 228, 273, 304–12.
46. Often this was done to emphasize that the exclusive attack on *Ostjuden* was misfounded. As Otto Diebhart put it, the real threat was at home where the rush of intermarriages with assimilated Jews constituted "inner" Judaization. See "Die Ostjudenfrage (Zionismus und Grenzschluss): Eine Erwiderung," *Politische-Anthropologische Monatschrift* 14 (1915–16), pp. 582–90.
47. *Der Giftpilz* (Nuremberg, 1938)
48. After listing their "criminal" natures, the commentator asks: "Und sie wollen auch Menschen sein?" (And they also want to be people?)
49. Massing, pp. 39–40.
50. The speech was delivered in September 1879. It is reprinted in Massing, pp. 278–87.
51. Published under the pseudonym W. Hartenau, *Die Zukunft* 18 (6 March 1897).
52. See the insightful review by James Joll, "The Contradictory Capitalist," *Times Literary Supplement* (25 August 1978).
53. See *Martin Buber Briefwechsel, 1918/1938* 2 (Heidelberg, 1973). Letter 261 to Harry Graf Kessler, 16 January 1928, p. 300.
54. Conrad Alberti, "Judentum und Antisemitismus," *Die Gesellschaft* 5 (1889).
55. Ibid., pp. 300–305.
56. Hannah Arendt, p. 28, has argued that the anti-Semitic conception of Jewry as an international "family closely knit by blood ties, had something in common with the Jews' own picture of themselves." But for some German Jewish assimilationists of the nineteenth and twentieth century this does not hold. Indeed, they argued that practically nothing linked them with *Ostjuden*.
57. Neubach, p. 220. The words were those of Reichstag member Pickenbach.

58. See for instance Gustav Krojanker, "Wille und Kampf," *Juedische Rundschau* (11 September 1912), p. 351.
59. Letter of 3 April 1920. See Ronald W. Clark, *Einstein: The Life and Times* (New York, 1971), p. 461.
60. Nahum N. Glatzer (ed.), *Franz Rosenzweig: His Life and Thought* (New York, 1953), p. 37. Letter of 7 June, 1916.
61. See Adolf Bartels, *Die Berechtigung des Antisemitismus* (Berlin, n.d.).
62. See Alfred Piech, "Slawentum und Judentum," *Deutschlands Erneurung* 3 (no. 2, 1919), p. 102.
63. Alfred Roth, *Judentum und Bolschewismus — Enthüllungen aus jüdischen Geheimakten. Ein Mahn — und Warnruf in letzter Stunde* (Hamburg, 1920).
64. Letter to Helene Hanna Cohn of 26 September 1916. (Jerusalem, Central Zionist Archives, Z3/716).
65. Good accounts of this period can be found in Werner E. Mosse (ed.), *Deutsches Judentum in Krieg und Revolution, 1916–1923* (Tübingen, 1971).
66. See his speech of 12 April 1922: "Die 'Hetzer' der Wahrheit!" In *Adolf Hitler's Reden*, ed. Ernst Boepple (Munich, 1933), p. 12. Identical accusations were made in Austria. See "Das Judentum in Osterreich," *Deutschlands Erneurung* (no. 10, 1920), p. 619.
67. Typical of this strain was Reinhold Wille, "Der Stern Judas," *Deutsche Zeitung* 24 (13 March 1919).
68. *Die Hammer* exemplified this tendency most clearly. See the excerpt in "Die Hetze gegen die Ostjuden," *Mitteilungen aus dem Verein zur Abwehr des Antisemitismus* 30 (10 January 1920), p. 3.
69. For good accounts see C.Z. Klötzel, "Razzia," *Neue Juedische Monatschefte* 4 (no. 11–12, March 1920); "Jagd auf Juden," *Jeudische Rundschau* 25 (no. 15, 24 February 1920), p. 99.
70. See Werner Jochmann, "Die Ausbreitung des Antisemitismus." In Werner E. Mosse, pp. 505–6.
71. "The Torture of Eastern Jews in Stagard," *Der Ostjude* 2 (no. 22, 3 April 1921). This was the only journal of *Ostjuden* in Germany and appeared in Yiddish. See also *Die Juedische Arbeiterstimme* 1 (no. 6, 1 June 1921).
72. "Judenaustreibung aus Bayern," *Juedische Rundschau* 28 (no. 94, 2 November 1923), pp. 547–48.
73. See *Allgemeine Zeitung des Judentums* 84 (no. 26, 25 June, 1920), p. 291.
74. See "Die Hauptversammlung des Reichsbunds jüdischer Frontsoldaten, 21–22 Oktober 1923," *Der Schild* 2 (No. 18, November 1923).
75. For a description of this pogrom see Ulrich Dunker, *Der Reichsbund jüdischer Frontsoldaten, 1919–1938* (Düsseldorf, 1977), pp. 49–56.
76. "Judenaustreibung aus Bayern," *Juedische Rundschau* 28 (no. 94, 2 November 1923), pp. 547–48.
77. "Die Schicksalsstunde des deutschen Judentums," *Juedische Rundschau* 28 (no. 96, 9 November 1923), p. 557.

CHAPTER FIVE

Myth and Symbol in Georges Sorel

David Gross

Every student of modern political symbolism must sooner or later confront the work of Georges Sorel (1847–1922). As one of the more engaging minds of his generation, Sorel made a number of original and important observations about the nature of symbolic images and their relationship to political action. These observations are not always easy to uncover, since they are scattered throughout an enormous range of work, some of it dealing with topics as seemingly remote from the subject as the history of Christianity, modern economics, the methodology of the sciences, or the trial of Socrates.[1] Often Sorel's most interesting ideas are mentioned only in passing, or else developed in a fragmentary and unsatisfactory manner. At other times he disdains to follow step-by-step the logic of his own thought, saying that what he writes is entirely "personal and individual," and consequently there is no need to be concerned with the transitions between things "because they nearly always come under the heading of commonplaces."[2]

Despite these many difficulties Sorel's work easily repays careful study. This is especially true with regard to what may well be the most innovative aspect of his *oeuvre:* his study of the psychology of political motivation, including the numerous irrational, spontaneous elements that affect all human behavior. Sorel was one of the first to explore this area with any degree of sophistication, and his conclusions had notable consequences.

In the following pages the focus of attention will be on one part of Sorel's "psychology of political motivation": the place that myths and symbols must occupy in modern political movements and in modern life in general. Three aspects of this topic need to be investigated in some detail: first, how it came about that myths and symbols moved into a central, pivotal position in Sorel's thought; second, what he meant by these terms and what he expected to achieve by utilizing them; and third, what significant differences, if any, exist between the concepts of mythology and symbolism as found in Sorel, and these same concepts found later in fascism and national socialism. To pursue each of these issues, it is important to grasp the cultural and intellectual context out of which Sorel emerged. This will help explain why he felt compelled to enter into the study of myths and symbols in the first place.

The more one looks at the period in Europe roughly between 1870 and 1914, the more this age seems to represent a decisive turning point in Western consciousness. It was at this time that a "crisis of certainty" gripped many of Europe's leading intellectuals, artists, and writers. The aftereffects of this crisis have remained with us. What began to be asserted during this period was the following, put here in the most condensed terms. (1) There is no objective, verifiable structure to existence. (2) There is no *telos* operating in the universe, including inevitable progress. (3) There is no essence behind appearance, but rather only appearances referring to other appearances ad infinitum. With only appearances, and nothing solid behind or within them, everything becomes arbitrary—hence a collapse of signification itself. (4) On the social and scientific level there are no facts, only interpretations. (5) On the personal level there are nothing but masks hiding other masks which lie still deeper inside a fiction called the "self." (6) In all areas of life there is no ultimate eternal truth. In earlier times, truth usually meant the identity of an idea or concept with reality, but since reality itself was now being called into question, there was no way to measure the truth of anything. This line of reasoning represented a profound development in modern thought which had become fairly widespread by the end of the nineteenth century. Before this time most thinkers assumed there was a truth: they simply disagreed about the best methods of reaching it (by reason, feeling, intuition, etc.). By 1900 many influential thinkers had come to doubt whether the word *truth* had any meaning at all. Moreover, if there were no truths, perhaps there were no values either.

In this context the whole "appearance vs. reality" problem emerged strongly in all areas of European culture: in literature (Hofmannsthal, Musil, Strindberg, Gide, Huysmans, D'Annunzio), in art (impressionism, expressionism, futurism), and in philosophy (Nietzsche, Bergson, Husserl). Oscar Wilde put it this way: "Try as we may, we cannot get behind the appearance of things to reality. And the terrible reality may be, that there is no reality in things apart from their experiences."[3] Nietzsche pushed matters still further by suggesting the even more frightening prospect of no anchorage whatever: "We have abolished the true world [reality]: what has remained? The world of appearances perhaps? . . . Oh, no! With the true world we have also abolished the apparent one!"[4] These concerns led to one of the central dilemmas of the period: if there are no fixed truths or values, how then should one live? Some, like the fin de siècle dandies, answered this question by saying that one should live wholly in appearances, since this is all there is. Others urged hedonism, or the life of pure sensation, where as many pulsations as possible are crammed into every moment. Still others argued that one should live "as if" there were ascertainable truths, even though there were none, since this was the only way to give life meaning.

Sorel was aware of these and other solutions to the dilemma of his age—and rejected most of them. Each seemed built upon the assumption that truth was undiscernible; and each was an alternative to this state of affairs, a way of being-in-the-world without any grounding in an ultimate reality. Sorel denied the premise of this argument. The truth of an idea or value could be determined, though not by the usual methods of studying its "inherent worth" or measuring it against some putative "objective reality," which Sorel admitted did not exist.[5] Rather, the truth of something was discovered solely by looking at its effects. A thing is true if, subjectively speaking, it has true or useful consequences, and a thing has value if its results are valuable for the individual.[6]

An idea can be judged good or bad exclusively in terms of the results it produces in those who hold it and believe in it. He seemed to have three criteria to determine whether an idea was true, i.e. beneficial: if it made the individual who embraced it more creative; if it increased an individual's character or moral consciousness; and above all if it led to action — a combative, engaged orientation toward life. For Sorel life is action, and ideas must be valued by the degree to which they lead to praxis, or produce life-enhancing qualities. In all this there is some amount of determinable truth from Sorel's point of view, but it lies entirely in its efficacy and advantageous consequences. Sorel very adroitly managed to shift the whole question of truth to a new level and thereby overcome the pervasive appearance/reality dualism that obsessed so many of his contemporaries. The point was not to distinguish, as Yeats put it, the "dancer" (reality) from the "dance" (appearance), but to investigate the completely different area of how the dance is received by those observing it. If it increases an individual viewer's creative energy, if it drives him toward more intense participation in life, then the dance possesses "truth" regardless of the supposedly objective qualities of the performance. All that is important about anything resides in its consequences.

Once Sorel hit upon this instrumental notion of truth, he felt that he had solved a problem that continued to transfix many other thinkers of his generation. He no longer had to remain incapacitated by the crisis of certainty, but could transcend it and move on to more important matters. One of these was what he considered the deplorable moral and spiritual condition of his age. It was sunk in a miasma of decadence, mediocrity, and corruption. No one was shriller in condemning the general tone of European civilization around 1900 than Sorel. Everywhere he saw attitudes which revolted him. The leading ideas of his age appeared to encourage self-indulgence, resignation, degeneration. Since he judged the consequences of these ideas to be uniformly pernicious—the decadence he saw around him seemed incontrovertible, for its effects were everywhere[7]—the ideas that produced them had also to be judged pernicious.

The major blame for this condition was placed at the feet of the bourgeoisie. To Sorel the dominant class in Europe had become desiccated by too much rationality, or what he called, following Vico, the "barbarism of reflection."[8] Furthermore, it generally lived "without morals," and had gradually given up certain important "habits of liberty" with which it was once acquainted.[9] The result was a total loss of virtue and honor, a drastic decline in the "heroic" qualities which Sorel believed the bourgeoisie once possessed. But something more was involved. Since this class also controlled the dominant political, economic, and cultural institutions of the period, the corruption unavoidably spread out beyond the class itself and became firmly embedded in the very fabric of modern society. When the middle class became decadent, so did the whole world of institutionalized values it created. There was therefore the added danger that other classes would be dragged down with the bourgeoisie unless something drastic were done to remedy the situation.

What was needed, Sorel thought, was the infusion of a new sense of morality into modern life. As a French moralist of the type extending back to Pascal and Rousseau, Sorel defined the central problems of the age in ethical terms. Therefore the principal solutions also had to be ethical. According to Sorel, the bourgeoisie lost its morality because it ceased to have convictions or believe in anything "indemonstrable." This took the mystery and elevation out of life, and the bourgeoisie lost contact with the energizing ideals that any group must have to be great or ethical. Without ideals or strong beliefs, there can be no inward force capable of stimulating creativity, morality, or the impetus to act—the three qualities Sorel identified with his instrumental view of truth. This loss of belief had happened before in history, in ancient Greece around the time of Socrates,[10] and in Christian Europe after the "age of the martyrs."[11] In the face of this kind of spiritual enervation the only hope lay in a revitalization or restoration of heroic ideals. Only in this way could a dynamic quality be restored to daily life. Even more important, only such energizing ideals could animate the inner state of the soul, out of which might come a more vigorous social ethic. It was a matter of indifference to Sorel what the ideals might happen to be. All that mattered was that they produce vigorous moral sentiments. "It is not a question of knowing what is the best morality, but only of determining if there exists a *mechanism capable of guaranteeing the development of morality.*"[12] Much of Sorel's thought was taken up with precisely these two questions: how to reconstruct morality now that it had broken down, and what "agent" to rely on in order to bring this about.

Sorel's reasoning unfolded in the following sequence: The only way out of decadence was to support some group which is in society but not of it — a group able to believe in something again—for only such a group could find its way to a new ethic. Sorel was resolute in his claim to defend any social element that could accomplish this. The working class seemed the most likely group in contemporary life with the potential to remoralize society. But, Sorel added, this was true only if the proletariat was rescued from the bourgeoisie, which was trying to make it decadent, and from parliamentary socialists like Jaurès who wanted to lure the proletariat into a dependence upon the state. Only by forming independent syndicates or *bourses du travail* could workers acquire the initiative and autonomy from bourgeois values that would be necessary to reinstate virtue. Still, even determining that the proletariat offered the greatest possibility for a revaluation of values, Sorel felt that it could not originate action toward this end without outside help.[13] The workers needed to be spurred into action, since only by doing, rather than talking or theorizing (another middle-class fault!), does a new morality get embodied in practice. Consequently, the way to motivate the workers was through myths or "mobilizing ideas" which would decisively move them into action. Even if it could be shown that these myths were objectively untrue, they might still be effectively true if they had significant consequences—if they set the working class in motion and helped it bring about a transforming ethic. These myths had to be embodied in symbols and images of great power. Otherwise the impact of a myth was not successfully communicated. The pivot of Sorel's theory turned on these last points: the effective use of both myths and symbols vis à vis the working class. We shall now take a closer look at what he intended to achieve by means of each of these.

What is a myth? For Sorel a myth is an emotionally charged artificial construct or interpretation which, though perhaps inaccurate or absurd, reaches people at a deeply unconscious level and inspires them to action. Being an "imaginary picture" rooted in and inseparable from the sentiments it evokes, a myth is always mysterious. It can never be cognitively understood because it operates in some prereflexive area of the mind where intuition and beliefs are also stimulated. Even more mysteriously, a myth is frequently the objectification of the convictions of a group, that is, an expression, in the form of images, of the goals and aspirations of an entire collectivity.[14] For these reasons it is too amorphous and volatile, too filled with "indeterminate nuances" ever to be accessible to scientific investigation. A myth cannot be broken down into its component parts, or subjected to face-value statements as to whether it is true or false, valid or invalid, since only its consequences can ultimately reveal that. It follows that a myth, because it is not a description but only an action-image, cannot be criticized. It is for all practical purposes irrefutable, just as a belief (as opposed to a fact) is irrefutable, since the power of a myth rests on faith, which does not lend itself to rational analysis.[15]

Myths are composed of a "body of images" which elicit a "mass of sentiments" that are then "grasped by intuition alone, before any considered analyses are made."[16] By their very nature they are indemonstrable, standing outside the realm of verification. But, Sorel insisted, this is why they are tremendously forceful constructions. People want and need to believe in things that are beyond confirmation.[17] Because myths "seize the imagination with an extraordinary tenacity," they provoke emotions and qualities of sacrifice and struggle without which nothing great or heroic has ever been achieved. Even if they are exaggerations or misrepresentations, myths are, precisely for this reason, more true than exact descriptions because they tap a vital part of the psyche which would otherwise never be activated.[18]

Yet for Sorel myths are not the same as lies. Nor do they carry connotations which would link them with propaganda or ideology as these terms are usually understood today. It is essential to Sorel that these are not cynically manufactured and imposed upon the masses but that they are already present, in latent form, within the mass itself, and need only be drawn out to become real forces in people's lives. Well before Jung's discussion of archetypes, there is some hint here of myths being anchored to predispositions within a collective unconscious. When myths work effectively they stir up, in Sorel's words, the "quickening fire . . . hidden under the ashes," making "the flames leap up."[19] Myths actuate sentiments never touched by ratiocination. The more successfully they hit responsive chords inside individuals, the more people are likely to become aware of their deepest needs and desires. And, Sorel conjectured, the more this awareness grows, the more they will be willing to struggle against decadence and *for* a new morality. This is why myths became so essential to Sorel's social philosophy. Without them there would be no movement and hence no moral change.

Just as for Sorel the value of a thing lay in its consequences, the same was true with myths. A myth was pronounced good (effective) if it yielded some or all of the following results. First, it had to arouse qualities of enthusiasm and inspriation, intensity and passion, since these were in danger of disappeairng in periods of decline. Sorel thought that decadent ages like his own were more inclined to encourage utopias than myths. Utopias, in his view, always lacked the fire, the emotion, and the energizing power of myths since they were merely intellectual constructs, rationally formulated for some distant future, and therefore generally conducive to passivity rather than activism in the present.

Second, a myth had to engender an inclination toward action. Sorel was convinced that if people did not project an entirely "artificial world" out in front of them, and then let it affect their motivation, they would never act to "attain durable results."[20] According to Sorel there would probably have been no French Revolution if "enchanting pictures" of what might occur had not been prompted in people's minds beforehand. Sorel remained certain that the greatest value myths can have is to trigger action in those who adhere to them. "We do nothing great without warmly coloured and clearly defined images, which absorb the whole of our attention."[21]

Third, to be beneficial a myth had to produce freedom. By Sorel's reasoning, freedom developed in an individual when he acquired a more holistic or inclusive sense of himself, thereby making it possible to act from within and freely, since freedom was equated with self-direction. Sorel cited Bergson in this respect: "To act freely is to recover possession of oneself."[22] But myths help recover the fuller, unconscious, irrational side of the self. Consequently they necessarily lead toward freedom—and freedom means more than simply wanting something, it also implies training the will to pursue what one wants. An individual is most free when he wills. If he ceases to will, all his efforts begin to "fade away into rhapsodies" and he sinks into lethargy and mediocrity.[23] Myths can prevent this by focusing emotions and mobilizing will. They can keep people agitated and constantly attuned to an inner drive for the ideal. Even more, they can awaken in the depths of the soul a "sentiment of the sublime."[24] To cultivate such a sentiment under the guidance of a firm inward motivation would be the essence of freedom.

Fourth, a myth had to simplify the world, make it clear and transparent again, so that equivocation would be impossible and nothing could be left in a state of indecision.[25] It was especially important for myths to identify enemies so that an unbridgeable gulf could be established between two sides, as happened between Christians and pagans in the late Roman era. Sorel insisted on the necessity of this cleavage. Not only did it set up battle lines and promote the martial spirit so crucial for an unconditional war against the status quo; it also permitted one's own side to be portrayed as oppressed or unjustly abused, thereby provoking an active mood of resistance which always brings out the noblest elements of character. Like Proudhon, Sorel believed that only by resisting something, by fighting and struggling against it, were extraordinary accomplishments possible. Even the artist needed the physical resistance of his material in order to give it form. It was the same with myths. They distinctly point out who or what is to be opposed, so that monumental energies can be generated to fight against them.

Finally, a myth had to stimulate creativity, either in an individual or in whole groups. Because it so sharply cuts through the veneer of civilization and stirs up primitive residues within the mind, a myth can elicit an entire range of perceptions and feelings that would otherwise never be tapped. In Sorel's view, myths heighten the imaginary and even mystical quality of experience which appeared to be eroding under the impact of rational, bourgeois values. A myth, in contrast to the normal habits of mind, releases internal energies which are more "barbaric" (in Vico's sense), but also more creative, poetic, and revitalizing. However, a myth has not done enough when it merely arouses an "inner turmoil" no matter how creative; it fulfills its function only when it turns this inner turmoil in the direction of action bent on moral and spiritual liberation.[26]

In these five positive results of myths, all the qualities mentioned earlier which made something "true" for Sorel were present: morality, action, and creativity. To the extent that a myth encouraged each of these, it was a valid myth. To the extent that it did not, it was invalid. This latter type Sorel called "illusions." An illusion could have different origins. It could, for example, be an "artifice for dissimulating" purposely devised by a ruling group to manipulate other elements of society.[27] Illusions here became, in Sorel's words, "multiple fantasies" or "conventional falsehoods" which might roughly correspond with Marx's notion of false consciousness. Or an illusion could simply be an outdated myth which had become unserviceable because, with its loss of ability to evoke moral responses, it had assumed a co-optive and "morbid" influence on the population. Whatever its origin, an illusion performed a function almost exactly opposite that of a myth. When it had a "stranglehold on men's minds," as Sorel believed it did for most people during his own age, it produced passivity, immorality, and a stultifying frame of mind. This side of Sorel's work has never been closely studied, but it provides an interesting and important counterpoint to his more familiar ideas about myth.

If one accepts Sorel's definition of what a myth is and what it should achieve, there is still the question of how a myth is embodied or made manifest. Sorel's answer: by means of symbols. A myth cannot be conveyed except by being depicted in some striking form which appeals to the imagination and emotions. Thus, Sorel's discussion of mythology led him directly into a discussion of symbolism as well. Though Sorel nowhere specifically defined a symbol, it is obvious that his meaning was the traditional one. A symbol is, as Mosse has summarized it, a "visible, concrete objectification" of a myth, a myth made operative.[28] Symbolism occurs when one word or thing, perhaps not meaningful in itself, represents something else (or a whole line of emotional associations and wider meanings), and is therefore more dynamically charged because of these emotional associations.[29] When Sorel talked about symbols in relation to myths, he usually implied that symbols were forms which expressed a mythical content; in this sense they were treated as outward signs representing an inward message. At other times he implied that the symbols were themselves the content, or the form and content compressed into one, so that myths and symbols were intimately fused and analytically inseparable. In either case, a symbol was always understood to be an image, but an image with a double existence. It was present both in the mind of the believer and in an external manifestation which captured an awareness already in the psyche. This is why Sorel could speak of symbols that exalted deep-seated "psychological qualities," or enkindled latent awarenesses which were then drawn out of the unconscious, not implanted there.[30]

But by linking symbols with images Sorel did not always have artistic metaphors in mind. More often he seemed to think that not art but the spoken word was most effective in arousing "warmly coloured images" which incite people to act. The written word was played down. Except for Marx's *Das Kapital,* which Sorel found full of "social poetry" and moving apocalyptic images,[31] written language seemed to be associated with linear thinking, rationality, logic, and calculated expression. Writing was by nature "cunning" and analytical, the natural medium of intellectuals. Speaking was seen as evocative and inspiring, the appropriate medium for those who want action rather than thought. Sorel considered direct verbal communication the most conducive means for stirring others to movement because it "act[s] on the feelings in a mysterious way and easily establish[es] a current of sympathy between people."[32] The fact that the spoken word, not art forms or texts, was singled out as the primary agency for conveying or inducing symbols is important. It underscores how much Sorel thought symbols ultimately reside in the believer's psyche. He discussed no fixed embodiments of symbolic awareness in signs, emblems, or posters beyond the fleeting words of an inspiring speaker.

For Sorel, history supplied important examples of successful myths and symbols. The ancient Greek mind, for instance, was moved by Homeric myths and images mystically in tune with the Greek character and therefore eliciting its best qualities to epic achievements. Christianity had a myth of the Second Coming, beautifully captured in the symbolic evocation of the Apocalypse. Even though this image of the future was untrue, since the Second Coming never came, it was nevertheless effectively true because it aroused great courage and conviction in those who believed, and in the long run led to significant moral progress.[33] The French Revolution also evoked a number of highly effective myths and symbols. According to Sorel, the armies of the revolution fought with a ferocity unknown in the *ancien régime* because the symbols they responded to prompted a fervent "will-to-victory."

The age in which Sorel wrote was the early twentieth century. All the old myths and symbols seemed to have lost their efficacy. Precisely because, in Sorel's opinion, so much of Europe had stopped believing in anything, it had fallen into decadence and mediocrity. It was living by illusions rather than myths. However, there appeared to be one sector of the population that still revealed qualities of will, drive, idealism, and morality however buried or hidden they might be. If this sector could be set in motion to actualize its values, Europe would perhaps experience the moral revitalization which Sorel so greatly desired. The group Sorel had in mind was the proletariat. To perform its proper role, it had to be aroused to action by suitable myths. According to Sorel, the myth which most corresponded to the "working-class mind," and had the potential for "dominating [it] in an absolute manner," was the myth of the general strike.[34]

Since this is the concept for which Sorel is best known, there is no need to repeat what has been analyzed elsewhere.[35] It is sufficient to touch briefly on those aspects of the general strike which relate to the above discussion of myth and symbol. The myth of the general strike was for Sorel a kind of updated version of the Apocalypse. It was a vision of an approaching Dies Irae in which the whole bourgeois world would collapse under the impact of a mass proletarian strike. As a vision the myth acquired a compelling force because it was the projection of the collective "will to deliverance" of the entire proletariat, and not because it was the creation of a handful of syndicalist intellectuals.

To be effective as a myth, the general strike had to be pictured in vivid, catastrophic images. This meant that its inevitably violent nature had to be accented. Yet for Sorel the violence did not necessarily have to be carried out in practice. He appears to have been repelled by certain forms of violence such as terrorism, which one might be engaged in for impure motives, or sabotage, which he viewed as a blow against the objectification of some unknown worker's labor—labor that needed to be respected rather than destroyed.[36] When Sorel spoke of violence he usually meant the state of "battle readiness" which talk of violence usually brings. Being prepared to use violence, he believed, was often more effective than actual use of it, and the effectiveness or utility of an idea was always Sorel's primary concern. If violence were resorted to, Sorel set several conditions for its proper use. For instance, it would have to be done gratuitously, "without hatred and without the spirit of revenge."[37] It could not be exercised for material gain or the "profits of conquest," since this would reflect the value system of the bourgeoisie which violence was to overcome.[38] It had to be implemented with reserve, and in light of the high moral aspirations of the proletariat, violence only becomes "purified" when fused with the most exalted ethical intentions. Sorel seemed to think that proletarian violence would not get out of hand and become brutality because of the intensity and spiritual beauty of the workers who perpetrated it. They would always be responsible people, basically in possession of themselves, proud, confident, and disciplined due to the sense of rigor and self-control they learned as producers in their workplaces. From them, violence was always very beautiful and heroic, and it always produced the right effects of inspiring fear in the enemy. It simultaneously promoted class solidarity, determination to act, and primordial creative energies, which Sorel lyrically associated with that "torment of the infinite" which the timorous middle class had long since lost.[39]

For Sorel the general strike, embellished with frightful images of violence, did not have to be achieved in order to bring about the results he intended. Its efficacy as a myth rested solely on the action-inducing qualities it engendered among those who merely *believed* it would come about. This was the whole purpose of myth as opposed to illusion. It set people in motion to accomplish the moral revolution Sorel wanted to see in modern society. The general strike appeared to be the last viable myth that could successfully mobilize people to reappraise values. It alone could provide the motivation and "epic state of mind" out of which the proletariat could forge a new moral order.

This was Sorel's most pressing concern. It even appears at times that he availed himself of the proletariat not so much because he valued it as a class, but because of what he thought it could do for the renovation of morals. When, around 1908–13, Sorel became disillusioned with the syndicates and doubted that they would be "instruments of moralization" as he had once hoped,[40] he momentarily abandoned the working class as an agent of revolution and searched for other groups which might perform the same role. By the end of his life, he returned with somewhat less enthusiasm to the proletariat as the only sector of society still able to ethically refashion a decadent world.

Though Sorel must certainly be treated as a man of the Left, it is undeniable that he had some influence on extremist elements within the European Right. For a time the Camelots du Roi, a youth group tied to Maurras's Action Française, were attracted to him, and a curious association called the Cercle Proudhon was formed (1912) to bring together radical syndicalist and royalist elements on the basis of some of Sorel's ideas. Mussolini, too, was reputed to have been influenced by Sorel's views on myth and violence, though here the ties seem somewhat more dubious.[41] It is no wonder, then, that in the 1930s some of Sorel's remaining syndicalist followers often found themselves in the embarrassing position of defending their mentor from charges of being one of the progenitors of fascism.

Since a connection between Sorel and the far Right has consistently been made, it would be useful to investigate this link in more detail. Here there is space to do this only in the realm of myth and symbols. What follows is a brief comparison of Sorel's treatment of both these concepts with their treatment in fascism and national socialism. No effort at establishing a causal link between Sorel's ideas and the radical Right can be attempted here, nor is there any pretense at systematic analysis. Taking note of similarities and significant differences between Sorel's mythology and imagery and that found in fascism and national socialism, one may get a better sense of the dividing line that separates this theorist of proletarian violence from the theorists and practitioners of fascist violence.

First, some similarities. Sorel, fascism, and national socialism all attacked the status quo for its venality and decadence, and called for moral regeneration. All were antiparliamentarian, since they wanted to create a mood of solidarity outside bourgeois institutions. At the same time they were antiliberal, since liberalism seemed cowardly, weak-minded, "feminine." Sorel and the extreme Right were also repulsed by the alleged hedonism and materialism of modern life, and wanted to see a return to a more austere, rigorous, and self-disciplined lifestyle. Consequently each defended old middle-class, as opposed to modern bourgeois, values. Despite much talk about heroism, vitality, and the epic state of mind, one often finds underneath such rhetoric an emphasis on simple domestic virtues: family closeness, chastity, honesty, industry. In Sorel as well as in fascism and national socialism there was a strong idealization of some group as the embodiment of virtue. For Sorel it was the proletariat, which he characterized as pure in heart, rich in sentiment, resolute, noble, decisive, hostile to shallow rationality, and in possession of a superior "moral culture."[42] In national socialism the *Volk* was idealized, usually in terms very similar to Sorel's working class. Similarly, Sorel and the Right placed tremendous importance on the power of ideas to affect life, agreeing, as Sorel expressed it, that "ethics springs from aspiration." Both also believed, perhaps contradictorily, that the value of ideas lies in their effects, and that "truth" must be judged by results. Even myths and symbols were dealt with pragmatically, their operational function always foremost.

Both for Sorel and the far Right there was a fascination with the psychology of motivation. It seemed imperative to understand what makes people act, so that the masses or the proletariat could be set in motion. This meant exploring the subjective and nonlogical side of human behavior (which the Left at the time usually failed to do), since it was thought that emotion and sentiment held the key to the secrets of motivation. Once Sorel and the fascists grasped the role that instincts and subconscious drives play in collective psychology, both went on to utilize myths and symbols to stimulate purposive behavior. They sought to activate archaic residues by means of forceful images which often centered on suggestions that combat, struggle, the glory of war, and "barbaric simplicity" would restore vigor and vitality to life. Finally, both Sorel and the Right implied that ultimately just being in movement may be more important than arriving at a goal. The ferment of movement provides everything that is needed: action, morality, energy, creative turmoil. If the goal was reduced to the process, the process in turn was frequently reduced to a psychological disposition or a state of mind. The fascists often described their movements, not in terms of ideologies but of "attitudes" ("Our movement," said Primo de Rivera, "is not a manner of thinking; it is a manner of being.)"[43] The same was true of Sorel. In a revealing article on the ethics of socialism he wrote: "Little does it matter whether communism is realized sooner or later . . . . The essential thing is our ability to render account of our own conduct. What is called the final goal exists only for our *internal* life."[44]

These are the considerable similarities between Sorel and the radical Right; but they are offset by notable differences. Sorel always called for a *real* social revolution, not simply a "spiritual" one as the fascist ideologues did. At least in theory, he wanted bourgeois institutions (including capitalism) abolished and power turned over to the proletariat. Also unlike the extreme Right, Sorel was not hostile to modernity. He accepted the configurations of modern industrial society and leveled no attack on urbanization, the machine, or the technological depersonalization of man. Similarly, there was no *Führerprinzip* in Sorel. "Anonymous heroes" might be needed to evoke mythological thinking in the proletariat, but their role would fade as the myths took hold and became self-generating.[45] With fascism and national socialism it was different. The myths were intended to create a mystical symbiosis between leader and led, so that the leader was not to disappear but remain to guide and discipline the masses by manipulating symbols. Hitler never relinquished his role as leader, unless it was to tie the masses to symbolic rituals rather than to himself, since these would perpetuate the political system after he was gone.[46] Mussolini also learned how to direct popular energies to himself as leader, and then through this role to attach them to the state. Sorel was opposed on principle to leader figures and states. In this case, the radical Right learned more from Gustave LeBon than from Sorel, for it was LeBon who spoke of a leader mystique, the mobilization of crowds, and the manipulation of mass contagion.[47] All of this was foreign to Sorel's thought.

The attitude toward symbolism was markedly different in Sorel and the extreme Right. For Sorel symbols were internal psychic images (or external signs used to activate these images) which he had no interest in institutionalizing. In Sorel there was no focus on emblems, cultic rites, processions, holy flames, Thing convocations, and the like, so central to national socialism. There was also no nature mysticism, no concern with cosmic forces to be tapped, no blood and soil imagery. Neither was there any visual stereotyping of the Jew, since anti-Semitism was never a major issue for Sorel. (There was a streak of anti-Semitism in him, but it derived from Proudhon and Renan rather than Drumont; not the Jews as such, but the decadent nouveaux riches and their retainers, were defined as the real enemies of the working class.)

Like the fascist and nazi Right, Sorel placed great importance on the function of speech in symbol formation. He strongly believed that it was primarily through the spoken word that myths become activated. Hitler understood this well, and so did Mussolini, with his ritual balcony dialogues recalling the liturgy of the Christian Responsa.[48] But Sorel viewed the relationship between words and symbols very differently than either of them. In his opinion language always had to be ethical; even when an orator spoke before large crowds he was obliged to remain within the constraints of his moral attitude toward the world. It was otherwise with someone like Hitler. In *Mein Kampf* he unabashedly described how a speaker needs to manipulate his audience with propaganda and highly charged "verbal images" which appeal to the susceptibilities of the "narrow-minded" masses whose "powers of assimilation . . . are extremely restricted."[49] This kind of cynicism would have been wholly unacceptable to Sorel. But even more than this, the effect of a Hitler speech was not so much in what was said, ethical or not, as in *how* it was said. As Mosse has described it, there was an undulating rhythm and cadence to Hitler's speeches: the rhetorical question, followed by an unambiguous statement, with plenty of room for people to join in with exclamations at the right places.[50] The liturgical context in which words were spoken was also essential to Hitler—as for example at the Nuremberg rallies where the total impact was made by the visual and acoustical power of the setting, not the specific and easily forgotten message of Hitler's speech. This was a far cry from Sorel's stress on ethical words or his "body of images" which were supposed to strike a chord in the workers' hearts without manipulation.

Finally, there was a significant difference between Sorel and the far Right on the question of myth. Though myths performed the same function for both—they mobilized people—in practice they operated in divergent ways and were designed to achieve opposite results. For Sorel and the nazis, for example, one of the points of a myth was to simplify the world into opposing camps by encouraging a Manichean perception of reality. But to Sorel the approaching battle of virtue against vice would be waged between the proletariat and the bourgeoisie, not between Aryans and Jews. The intent of a myth like the general strike was to arouse "ardent sentiments of revolt" leading to a catastrophic class war and victory for the proletariat. In nazi mythology the effect was altogether different since myths were calculated to elicit at least three kinds of responses, none of which Sorel could approve. The first was self-abandonment, or the loss of one's individuality to the group (while Sorel, by contrast, wanted myths to spark autonomy, independence, and self-activity). The second was patriotism. Most nazi myths celebrated the joys of conformity and the excitement of belonging to a superior racial group. Consequently, tribal symbolism prevailed wherein the *Volk* worshipped itself—hence the stress on national festivals, monuments, and racial and traditional imagery drawn from the German past. Sorel's myths were antipatriotic; he was not interested in consolidating national identities but in demolishing them.[51] The third response was hatred of an enemy. In Nazi ideology the enemy was defined in racial terms. It was always the Jews, or the dark-haired *Tschandalas,* or the "dwarfed Sodomites," or the ape-like "creatures of darkness" who had to be overcome by the blond, Nordic "god-men."[52] Though Sorel had his enemy, the venal middle class, he never stereotyped it in this way, but rather treated it as a somewhat impotent adversary. The real issue for him was not the nature of an external enemy, but the more pressing internal task of creating proletarian self-consciousness.

In retrospect, Sorel's concept of myth may seem inherently dangerous, even if it was not identical with the mythology of fascism or national socialism. There are legitimate grounds for this position. But it should also be remembered that historical events since Sorel's time have made one think that any interest in myth or its psychological underpinnings must necessarily have fascist overtones. This has closed off discussion of areas which need further exploration from different points of view. There are many features of Sorel's thought which are wholly unattractive. Some of these might be mentioned in passing: his pronounced antidemocratic strain, his overzealous attack on reason, his rigid Huguenot puritanism, his excessive fascination (like Péguy's) with *mystique* over *politique,* his contempt for peace and humanitarianism, his moral absolutism bordering on dogmatism, his often mindless defense of violence without regard for the perils of collective mythology, and his simplistic division of the world into two hostile camps, with no sensitivity for nuances. Without justifying these numerous misjudgments and dubious positions, Sorel still deserves credit for being one of the first on the Left to try and grasp the psychological mainsprings of action without having recourse to the crude economism and positivism of Second International Marxism. It is this side of his thought which has been given most attention in this essay.

During his own lifetime Sorel's influence was minimal on orthodox syndicalist and socialist circles of Western Europe. Victor Griffuelhes, the anarcho-syndicalist secretary of the French Confédération Générale du Travail, was once asked if he read Sorel and he replied: "I read Dumas."[53] The Italian Marxist Arturo Labriola also spoke for many socialists when he voiced the following criticism of Sorel: "Myths, fables, and revelations are precisely the opposite of socialism, which proposes to teach individuals as such to fashion for themselves their own lives, and in thus constructing their lives, to see within themselves as in clear, transparent water."[54] In the work of some contemporary Marxists of the younger generation—Georg Lukács, Antonio Gramsci, Walter Benjamin, among others—the traces of Sorel are much in evidence in certain aspects of their thought. This topic has yet to be thoroughly investigated. Despite various differences, one thing this younger generation could agree on was that a comprehensive understanding of human behavior could not be attained without understanding the role that myths, symbols, and emotions play in motivating people to act. This was what Sorel grasped at the turn of the century.

NOTES

1. See, for example, the following works by Sorel: *La Ruine du monde antique* (Paris, 1902); *Introduction à l'économie moderne* (Paris, 1903); *Le Procès de Socrate* (Paris, 1889).
2. Georges Sorel, *Reflections on Violence,* trans. T.E. Hulme (New York, 1961), p. 28.
3. Oscar Wilde, cited in Thomas Mann, *Last Essays,* trans. Richard Winston and Clara Winston (London, 1959), p. 157.
4. Friedrich Nietzsche, *Götzen-Dammerung.* In *Werke in zwei Bänden,* vol. 2, ed. Karl Schlechta (Munich, 1967), p. 341.
5. Sorel frequently spoke of reality being "fluid," "inexplicable," or merely "a hypothesis." In *Les Illusions du progrès* (Paris, 1908), for example, he claimed that reality is a "fundamental mystery" which is "protected by obscurity" (p. 2).
6. This notion resembles the pragmatism of William James, but Sorel developed this approach to truth before his discovery of the American philosopher. For Sorel's later views on pragmatism, see his *De l'utilité du pragmatisme* (Paris, 1921).
7. See Jean Wanner, *Georges Sorel et la décadence* (Lausanne, 1943), pp. 39–55.
8. Sorel, *Reflections on Violence,* p. 88; id., *Matériaux d'une théorie du prolétariat* (Paris, 1919), pp. 145–51, passim.
9. See Sorel, *Reflections on Violence,* pp. 80–98, 249.
10. For Sorel's critique of Socrates (which in many respects resembled Nietzsche's, whose work Sorel did not then know), see his *Procès de Socrate,* esp. pp. 170–72, 375 ff. Sorel attacked Socrates for being an urban middle class intellectual whose strict rationalism destroyed the religious, heroic, and rural-warrior orientation which once made Greece thrive. Since pure rationalism cannot inspire either morality or faith, post-Socratic Greece fell into decadence.
11. Sorel, *Ruine du monde antique,* pp. 1–28.
12. Sorel, *Matériaux d'une théorie du prolétariat,* p. 127 (Sorel's italics).
13. Sorel never adequately explained why he believed this. Perhaps it was his deep-seated pessimism about most aspects of human nature. But ironically he was optimistic as well, since he did have confidence in the working class once they were *in movement.* The key problem of much of Sorel's most interesting work was how to set them in movement to begin with.
14. Sorel, *Reflections on Violence,* p. 50.
15. Sorel, *Matériaux d'une théorie du prolétariat,* pp. 61–68.
16. Sorel, *Reflections on Violence,* p. 122.
17. "According to a law embedded in our nature, we want to have something indemonstrable to believe in." Georges Sorel, *Procès de Socrate,* pp. 145–46.

18. Sorel, *Reflections on Violence*, pp. 183–84, 240.
19. Ibid., p. 30.
20. Sorel, *Matériaux d'une théorie du prolétariat*, p. 138; id., "Critical Essays in Marxism." In *From Georges Sorel: Essays in Socialism and Philosophy*, ed. John L. Stanley (New York, 1976), p. 117.
21. Sorel, *Reflections on Violence*, p. 148.
22. Ibid., pp. 47–48.
23. Ibid., p. 45.
24. Georges Sorel, cited in Irving Louis Horowitz, *Radicalism and the Revolt against Reason: The Social Theories of Georges Sorel* (Carbondale, Ill., 1961), p. 82.
25. Sorel, *Reflections on Violence*, p. 122.
26. Horowitz, *Radicalism and the Revolt against Reason*, p. 49.
27. Georges Sorel, "Vues sur les problèmes de la philosophie," *Revue de la Métaphysique et du Monde* (September 1910), p. 616; see Richard Humphrey, *Georges Sorel: Prophet without Honor* (Cambridge, Mass., 1951), p. 122.
28. George L. Mosse, *The Nationalization of the Masses* (New York, 1975), p. 7.
29. Edward Sapir, "Symbolism." In *Encyclopedia of the Social Sciences*, vol. 14 (New York, 1934), p. 495.
30. Sorel, *Matériaux d'une théorie du prolétariat*, pp. 7, 188–89.
31. Ibid., p. 189.
32. Sorel, *Reflections on Violence*, p. 28.
33. Ibid., pp. 35, 182 ff.
34. Ibid., p. 129.
35. The best short discussion of the general strike can be found in the following works: Horowitz, *Radicalism and the Revolt against Reason*, pp. 78–89, 127–40; Humphrey, *Georges Sorel*, pp. 186–203; Jacques Rennes, *Georges Sorel et le syndicalisme révolutionnaire* (Paris, 1936), pp. 156–79; Helmut Berding, *Rationalismus und Mythos: Geschichtsauffassung und politische Theorie bei Georges Sorel* (Munich, 1969), pp. 102–17.
36. See Isiah Berlin, "Georges Sorel." In *Against the Current: Essays in the History of Ideas* (New York, 1980), p. 314. Sorel also strongly attacked: (1) *brutality*, which he defined as an unnecessary excess of violence, or rather as a form of violence that had lost touch with the moral ends it was supposed to serve; and (2) *force*, which he invariably associated with the state, which used it as an instrument of control and domination. Force was always exercised by a ruling class to stabilize a status quo, whereas violence was a proletarian tool for destabilization.
37. Sorel, *Reflections on Violence*, p. 115.
38. Ibid., pp. 164–65, 167, 275.
39. Ibid., p. 46.
40. Sorel, *Matériaux d'une théorie du prolétariat*, p. 129.
41. In an inteview given in 1932, he claimed that Sorel was his intellectual "master," though for a long time before this he rarely referred to him and in fact called Marx "the magnificent philosopher of working-class violence." See James H. Meisel, *The Genesis of Georges Sorel* (Ann Arbor, 1951), p. 219; Ernst Nolte, *Three Faces of Fascism*, trans. Leila Vennewitz (New York, 1966), p. 153.
42. Sorel, *Reflections on Violence*, pp. 122, 127, 129; id., *Matériaux d'une théorie du prolétariat*, p. 125.

43. José Antonio Primo de Rivera, "What the Falange Wants." In *Varieties of Fascism,* ed. Eugen Weber (Princeton, 1964), p. 177.

44. Sorel, cited in Meisel, *The Genesis of Georges Sorel,* p. 120. See Sorel's "The Ethics of Socialism." In *From Georges Sorel,* ed. Stanley, pp. 94–110.

45. Only when Sorel temporarily gave up on syndicalism (ca. 1908–13) did he begin to toy with the notion of charismatic leadership. This was not typical, but it was in this context that he hailed (in 1912) the young Mussolini as a modern-day condottiere, "the only energetic man capable of redressing the weaknesses of government." See Scott H. Lytle, "Georges Sorel: Apostle of Fanaticism." In *Modern France: Problems of the Third and Fourth Republics,* ed. Edward Mead Earle (Princeton, 1951), p. 288.

46. Mosse, *Nationalization of the Masses,* p. 200.

47. See Gustave LeBon, *The Crowd* (New York, 1966), pp. 1–71.

48. George L. Mosse, *Nazism: A Historical and Comparative Analysis of National Socialism* (New Brunswick, 1978), pp. 34, 37. Marxism, by contrast, remained highly textual, building on a corpus of works that had to be interpreted.

49. Hitler, cited in Werner Betz, "The National Socialist Vocabulary." In *The Third Reich,* ed. by the International Council for Philosophy and Humanistic Studies (New York, 1975), p. 784. See also Jean Pierre Faye, *Langages totalitaires* (Paris, 1972).

50. Mosse, *Nationalization of the Masses,* p. 201.

51. Sorel, *Reflections on Violence,* p. 117.

52. For an excellent short discussion of this aspect of nazi mythology see Jost Hermand, "The Distorted Vision: Pre-Fascist Mythology at the Turn of the Century." In *Myth and Reason: A Symposium,* ed. Walter D. Wetzels (Austin, 1973), pp. 101–26.

53. Edouard Dolléans, *Histoire du mouvement ouvrier,* vol. 2 (Paris, 1948), pp. 126–27.

54. Arturo Labriola, cited in David Roberts, *The Syndicalist Tradition and Italian Fascism* (Chapel Hill, N.C., 1979), p. 78.

PART II

Science, Myth, and Ideology

CHAPTER SIX

Feminism, Fertility, and Eugenics in Victorian and Edwardian England

Richard Allen Soloway

English eugenics before World War I was caught in a dilemma it never succesfully resolved. Originally conceived by Francis Galton as a new science of human heredity in the 1860s, it became in the twentieth century, with its founder's blessings, a pressure group for social, political, and economic reform. Galton's close friend and disciple, the eminent statistician Karl Pearson, vigorously resisted the trend to convert eugenics into an activist movement. He feared that if it became embroiled in highly emotional, complex, class-oriented issues, its fragile credibility in the scientific community would be quickly undermined. The popularization of Darwinian evolution was a case in point. The later Victorians and their Edwardian offspring readily adopted simplistic derivations of biological determinism to explain a multitude of contemporary problems ranging from the persistence of poverty to the impulse for imperial expansion.

Eugenics, the science of "good breeding," as Galton described it, was itself a direct offshoot of Darwinism.[1] It drew much of its support from evolutionary-minded scientists, physicians, academics, and other well-educated professionals attracted by the possibility of improving the quality of the race by the manipulation of human heredity. Though Pearson argued that decades of pure research should precede any eugenic recommendations, many of his contemporaries, including the elderly and impatient Galton, believed that enough was already known in the early twentieth century about the inheritance of physical, mental, and personality characteristics to warrant their inclusion in the formulation of new political and social policies and strategies. To further this goal, the Eugenics Education Society was founded in 1907 as the first "scientific" organization dedicated to applying the laws of hereditary probability, extracted from the biometrical calculations of Galton and Pearson, or the rediscovered genetic experiments of Gregor Mendel, to the resolution of existing and future problems confronting the race.

The "woman question" was one of the most divisive contemporary issues to which eugenists tried to apply their uncertain hereditarian calculus. Despite their confidence in the efficacy of biosocial causality, they proved to be as perplexed and uncertain about the implications of female emancipation as was the educated public at large. The eugenic response to feminist demands points up the confusion and potential danger of trying to explain social and political phenomena in biological terms. It is a legacy of social Darwinism which has persisted throughout the century. In the case of eugenics, science, as Pearson warned, was quickly compromised. It became an agent of class and ideology reflecting the culture-bound values, biases, preconceptions, and anxieties of emotionally committed partisan interests.

The appearance of eugenics in the last thirty years of the nineteenth century paralleled the expansion of women's claims for greater legal, political, economic, and educational equality. The militancy of the suffragettes after 1905 coincided with the initial efforts of eugenists to take the offensive on behalf of "race betterment" and establish an organization to challenge the environmental assumptions of misguided liberal social reformers whose collectivist proposals ignored the primacy of nature over nurture. Although eugenists buttressed their arguments with biostatistical data and volumes of scientific testimony, they never lost sight of the biological imperative of "race-motherhood" which, in the final analysis, delineated the role of the modern woman in an evolving society.

No obstacle was more difficult for feminists to overcome than this pervasive belief in a biological imperative. It decreed that the female had been created or had evolved for the primary purpose of reproduction and nurture. Her physical and mental characteristics were inevitably determined by these demanding functions. Consequently, her activities, opportunities, and aspirations were also prescribed by her paramount maternal obligations. Few people questioned the existence of a natural "separation of spheres" between the sexes, clearly marked by innate and distinct qualities which determined specific roles and a necessary division of labor.[2] To do so meant not only challenging deep-seated beliefs rooted in popular perceptions of reality, but also calling into doubt a great deal of theological and scientific evidence.

Physicians, particularly obstetricians and gynecologists, who presumably knew best, were especially vocal in their disapproval of women attempting to push beyond the boundaries of biologically determined gender spheres. The psychic and somatic penalties for such a transgression ranged from minor disorders to masculinizing sterility, certifiable lunacy, or terminal cancer.[3] These alarming prognoses were frequently reinforced by neo-Darwinist colleagues and other scientists who saw in female emancipation serious implications for the future evolution of the race.

The "woman question" was only one of a number of perceived threats to the continued progress of Britain's imperial civilization. Reactions to feminist demands became caught up in a growing national preoccupation, evident since the 1890s, with racial decadence, cultural degeneration, and political and economic decline. Fears that British world ascendancy had peaked were initially stimulated by the "Great Depression" of the 1880s and imposing challenges from such new international competitors as Germany and the United States. They were reinforced by the military's bungling performance during the Boer War. Balfour's government was forced in 1902 to order an inquiry into the possibility of race deterioration, one of several official and unofficial investigations of a similar nature undertaken before World War I.[4] Lamentations about "race suicide" punctuated the gloomier forecasts of decline and fall, and doubts about Britain's "racial vigor" underlay much of the talk about national efficiency heard in more moderate, elevated circles. When, as was increasingly the case, challenges to British preeminence were analyzed in the context of social Darwinism, the question of adaptation and fitness took on ominous significance.

Eugenics, with its interest in the comparative genetic capacity of individuals and classes to adjust to the demands of the modern world, flourished in such a climate. It gave scientific credibility to many current anxieties and articulated the concerns of an educated, professional middle class worried about preserving its prosperity and status in an era of unpredictable changes and rapidly rising costs to support what it perceived to be a growing multitude of "incapables."[5] The key to continued predominance in the new age, eugenics proclaimed, was the adoption of scientific "race culture" based upon an empirical assessment of the inherited physical and mental qualities of the populace.

Though the total membership of the elitist Eugenics Education Society barely exceeded 1,600 before World War I, it included a number of prominent scientists, physicians, academics, barristers, and other people in the professions. More importantly, eugenic beliefs about human inheritance were pervasive in the Edwardian years, especially in those educated, middle-class circles whose successful members presumably embodied most of the physical, psychological, and behavioral attributes eugenists were certain reflected superior breeding. Whether the continued transmission of racially desirable qualities was compatible with feminist ambitions was of particular importance to such people, since it was assumed that middle-class women would be in the best position to take advantage of expanded opportunities.

Critics of the suffragists had long observed that a disproportionate number of feminists were middle-class spinsters or, if married, the mothers of very small families. It seemed to suggest that celibacy or diminished fertility was a cause of female dissatisfaction and that both would surely increase if greater liberties were extended to that sex. As the Victorians knew, a substantial minority of women were destined for spinsterhood in any event. Their surplus numbers precluded their finding a suitable husband and fulfilling their natural maternal function. A confusion of the "spheres," antisuffragists reasoned, would only compound the problem and stimulate a greater flight from maternity. This argument became much more compelling in the 1890s and opening decade of the new century as people became aware of a rapid decline in the birth rate.[6] Throughout much of the nineteenth century, fertility had averaged 34 births per thousand of the population reaching a recorded peak of 36.3 in 1876. By 1901 it had fallen to 28.5 and to around 24 at the outbreak of the war in 1914. During the same period the average number of children born to women of child-bearing age also dropped by a third.[7]

Complaints about the demise of the large Victorian family proliferated in the Edwardian era, accompanied by countless warnings that the diminished birth rate was "a national calamity seriously threatening the future welfare of our race."[8] Though a determined minority insisted that the decline was a consequence of diminished fecundity resulting from higher cerebral evolution ("individuation") predicted by Herbert Spencer in the 1860s, more pessimistic analysts interpreted it as a sign of waning racial vitality or degeneration, similar to that which prostrated Rome in its imperial twilight.[9] Most agreed with the conclusions of the prestigious National Birth-Rate Commission, established in 1913, that the striking trend toward smaller families was not a consequence of depleted biological capacity but the result of the rapid spread of neo-Malthusian contraceptive practices since the famous trial of Charles Bradlaugh and Annie Besant in 1877. The adoption of birth control as it was described after 1914 was primarily in response to mounting economic pressures and changing religious and moral values.[10]

Of even greater concern than the decline in the birth rate was its differential socioeconomic characteristics. The Victorians assumed that the fertility of working-class women was higher than that of their social betters, but the difference was not particularly striking or alarming. By the 1890s, the unrelenting drop in the birth rate stimulated more precise differential calculations. The most widely quoted figures were those of Karl Pearson. His growing interest in eugenics and the statistical probability of inheritance (biometrics) led him to project in 1897 that if current reproductive trends continued, half of the next generation of Englishmen would be produced by no more than one-fifth or one-quarter of the present generation of married couples. Since that minority was generally poor and uneducated, Pearson warned that "any correlation between inheritable (physical or social) characteristics and fertility must thus sensibly influence the next generation."[11]

Pearson's estimates were quickly adopted in the next decade by analysts and critics of the declining birth rate. His general conclusions were substantiated and defined by a series of studies comparing fertility in various London districts and in other parts of the country.[12] In every test correlation, one such enquiry concluded in 1906, "the wives in the districts of least prosperity and culture have the largest families, and the morally and socially lowest classes in the community are those which are reproducing themselves with the greatest rapidity."[13]

The unique *Fertility of Marriage Census* taken in 1911 was in large measure prompted by the many questions surrounding the declining birth rate and its alarming differential aspects. Although the final report was delayed until 1923, some of the evidence was released before the war. Comparisons of all occupational groups in the country not only verified the inverse correlation of fertility with social status, but to the dismay of the eugenically minded, revealed that the 1.8 offspring recorded for married couples in the educated, professional classes was less than half the number born to the wives of semiskilled and unskilled laborers.[14] Despite the superintendent of statistics, T.H.C. Stevenson's attempts to avoid invidious class comparisons, there was no escaping the conclusion that in recent years "our population has been recruited . . . under conditions fundamentally different from those of the immediately preceding and probably of any previous period." The change had "much significance from the eugenic point of view." Like many of his generation, Stevenson, though not a member of the Eugenics Education Society, was clearly eugenist in his social perceptions. It led him to reason that "if the more successful classes may be assumed to be in bulk better equipped than others with the qualities adapted to command success, the failure of this stock to maintain itself in proportion to the rest of the nation is evidently undesirable from the national point of view."[15]

The central goal of the Eugenics Education Society was the reversal of this unfortunate trend by promoting Galton's dream of identifying "all influences that improve the inborn qualities of a race" and bringing as many of them "as can be reasonably employed to cause the useful classes in the community to contribute *more* than their proportion to the next generation." In practice this meant the encouragement of early marriages and large families for couples of obvious hereditary fitness or high "civic worth."[16] Positive eugenics, as the promotion of selective nuptiality and procreation was described, was calculated to match and even exceed the fertility of the less desirable stocks whose questionable physical, moral, intellectual, and behavioral characteristics were presumed to be largely inheritable. The key to its success, all eugenists agreed, was the inculcation of an elevated concept of "race motherhood" among the fittest classes. Whether it was compatible with feminist demands for expanded opportunities beyond the domestic sphere was another problem on which there was much less accord.

The eugenic campaign for "race culture" appeared to many feminists to be intrinsically hostile to women's rights. Not only were eugenists openly critical of the trend toward collectivist social reforms and greater democracy, but the physicians and scientists who adorned the hierarchy of the Eugenics Education Society represented professions assumed to be opposed to greater female emancipation. Eugenists' responses, like those of active antisuffragists, varied considerably. Many "antis" over the years supported such feminist goals as the Women's Property Acts, higher education, expanded economic opportunities, and more liberal divorce laws, even when they balked at extending the vote.[17] Eugenists were no less diverse in their reaction to particular feminist issues, but invariably evaluated their position in the context of a woman's unique role in the reproduction and nurturing of the race.

They were not interested in women in general, only in those exceptional representatives of the sex whose superior, inheritable qualities might not be passed on to future generations if they strayed too far from their biologically prescribed path. Eugenists knew that these were often the same strong-willed, energetic, intelligent middle- and upper-class women who populated the suffragist ranks and whose low marriage rate or small families were continually cited as irrefutable evidence that the women's movement was a revolt against domesticity and maternity. Whatever impact it might have on the health of individual rebels was secondary to the threat it posed to the genetic composition of future generations.

Though eugenists were certain that the desirable qualities of race motherhood could be isolated and scientifically analyzed, they were hopelessly imprecise and invariably traditional in delineating the maternal hereditary contribution made to superior offspring. Despite a variety of biometric studies proving that nature was overwhelmingly more important than nurture, whenever eugenic scientists discussed the role of the race mother, they dwelt upon the "innate nurturing instincts" evident in her gentleness, intuition, sensitivity, and emotional insight.[18] At no time did they attempt to explain how these special virtues were biologically associated with the reproduction of genetically valuable progeny.

Galton had himself set the pattern a generation earlier in his extensive studies of eminent men in various walks of life. His reliance upon published genealogical and biographical sources which concentrated almost exclusively on male lineage, precluded his finding much information about the possible maternal contribution to hereditary talent. Galton recognized this limitation, but nevertheless concluded that eminent men derived most of their ability from the male rather than the female side of their descent.[19] In numerically plotting the degrees of transmission of talent through the ancestry of great worthies in law, science, religion, the military, music, the arts, and even some sports, the father of eugenics could find a woman's hereditary influence demonstrably important only for clergymen and, to a lesser extent, judges. Statistically, it seemed obvious to Galton that the popular notion that notable men had remarkable mothers was scientifically insupportable.[20]

One explanation for the more modest role of female heredity, Galton suggested, was the lower marriage rate of the aunts, sisters, and daughters of prominent males. Women of talent and intellect often had elevated expectations, which reduced the circle of men whom they found attractive. Similarly, since such women were usually "dogmatic and self-assertive" or "shy and peculiar," they frightened potential suitors away.[21] Galton never denied that many heritable characteristics, especially "temper" and "disposition," were probably passed through the female line, but he always suspected that the feminine contribution to heredity was of lesser value. In his examination of extinct peerages and other distinguished families, he noted a disproportionate number of marriages to infertile heiresses who were obviously the last representatives of genetically weakened families incapable of siring male heirs.[22] The burden of failure was by inference maternal rather than paternal. Among the results of Galton's pioneering anthropometric measurements in the 1880s and early 1890s was the additional discovery that women were not only physically inferior to men, but in contrast to what many believed, their sensory acuity and, as a consequence, their intellectual ability were less developed than previously thought.[23]

Galton's measured doubts about female capacity carried the authority of his distinguished reputation. His quantified observations, though often based upon the flimsiest evidence, were like pronouncements of eminent physicians given added credence by their scientific validation of popular perceptions of sex roles. At the same time, the concurrent growth of the women's movement and social Darwinism inevitably meant that feminist demands were increasingly evaluated in evolutionary and hereditary terms. Karl Pearson, in his struggle to separate scientific from popular eugenics, was wary of much of the so-callled objective evidence his neo-Darwinist contemporaries tacked on to their preconceptions about female emancipation. He distrusted the emotionalism on both sides of the issue, doubting that the passionate invocation of the writings of Mary Wolstonecraft or John Stuart Mill was any more helpful than the unproven prognoses of self-serving, antifeminist gynecologists and their evolutionist allies.[24]

As a Fabian socialist in the 1880s, Pearson had questioned whether a woman would be able to contribute her fair share of labor to a socialist society if she remained ill-educated and economically dependent. Yet the effect her emancipation would have on the future of the race was a legitimate concern requiring serious scientific investigation based upon unprejudiced data not yet available.[25] Even before he turned his considerable mathematical talents to the cause of Galtonian eugenics in the early 1890s, Pearson was trying to formulate accurate statistical procedures for measuring the hereditary contribution of each sex. Though he personally doubted the existence of any "rigid natural law of feminine inferiority" and suspected that a woman's "physique and intellect" were to a considerable extent environmentally determined, the evidence was at best uncertain and contradictory.[26] Anticipating the work of Havelock Ellis, who was to become an important spokesman for eugenics a few years later, Pearson cited the need for a real "science of sexualogy" before the arguments for or against women's rights could be convincingly resolved.[27]

Pearson's innovative calculations of statistical probability and correlation coefficients made him highly suspicious of individual case studies cited by doctors, psychologists, and sexologists to substantiate their generalizations. It was impossible to determine how representative such cases were of the female sex in general. Only the accumulation and analysis of extensive data based upon a wide, scientifically determined sample would permit an accurate correlation, for example, of the relationship between childbearing and intellectual and political activity. With some 20 percent of English women unmarried, Pearson reasoned, it was important to know if there were statistically significant physical and mental differences between mothers and childless women.

The real issue of female emancipation was not the extension of the franchise as suffragists would have us believe, Pearson argued. Even if women were biologically and intellectually inferior, he insisted, these liabilities ought not to deny them the ballot any more than they prevented weak and slow-witted men from comprising a large proportion of the democratic electorate. Other questions were far more important: whether female children inherited parental capacity to the same degree as male children; whether the prolonged study associated with advanced education had "ill effects on women's childbearing efficiency" as critics charged; or whether the "physical degradation of the race" or its improvement was likely to follow a dramatic change in traditional relations between the sexes. Until reliable answers were forthcoming, it was premature to pontificate upon a woman's rights, "which are after all, only a vague description of what may be the fittest position for her, the sphere of her maximum usefulness in the developed society of the future."[28]

Pearson's preliminary correlative studies in the 1890s led him to question a number of popular and scientific assumptions about the natural characteristics of men and women. Contrary to what Darwin, Galton, and other evolutionists believed, Pearson found that in the aggregate women were slightly more variable and consequently physiologically more complex than men.[29] He informed Galton privately that a survey of nearly six thousand male and female correlations indicated that fertility seemed to be equally inherited in both the male and female lines, implying that his friend's theory about heiresses and sterility might have to be revised.[30] Statistics also suggested "that *the hereditary influence of the female is inversely proportional to her fertility*" and therefore more evident in smaller families. "Is there," he wondered, "a sort of quantitative limit to the amount of 'self' which a fertile animal can put into the world . . . [which] may be a check to the influence of reproductive selection . . . ?[31]

The more he pondered the statistics of hereditary probability, the more Pearson was struck by the absence of truly talented families in contemporary Britain. This was of constant concern to eugenists in the early years of the new century. Many of them were, like Pearson, liberal imperialists wedded to the promotion of "national efficiency" as a way of meeting the multiple challenges of the age. They complained repeatedly about the lack of real ability in the country, especially when compared to the intellectual, economic, and political giants who had led Great Britain to world preeminence only a few decades earlier. The extent of female culpability was uncertain, though numerous antifeminists blamed the problem on the flight from maternity by emancipated women. Disciples of Herbert Spencer suggested that it was not merely a question of modern, middle-class women being unwilling to produce gifted children but of their ability to do so in an advanced, highly evolved civilization.

Though Galton had shown some sympathy for Spencer's famous theory of individuation and genesis, he was eventually persuaded by Pearson and other eugenists that there was no scientific evidence of a "diminution of reproductive power" and a rise in "absolute sterility" among well-bred, intelligent women. Spencer's evocative image of "flat-chested girls who survive their high-pressure education" only to be unable to bear and nurture well-developed infants clashed with the basic eugenic assumption that men and women who possessed racially desirable qualities would be able to breed a sufficient quantity of offspring to elevate the level of the race.[32] The problem for eugenics was not one of reproductive capacity but of identifying the fittest stock and persuading them to mate early and often. The later age at which middle- and upper-class men — presumably the largest repository of genetic treasure — married, if at all, was already a major cause of concern, and explained, as social analysts and unhappy spinsters had long observed, the surplus of racially promising but unwed genteel women in the country.

From the eugenic standpoint, female emancipation threatened to compound the racial evils of prolonged celibacy. Galton, no friend of feminism, harkened back to the disastrous effects of medieval celibacy on the reproduction of talented men and women. Pearson, though sympathetic to the women's cause, agreed that it was a "momentous social issue" involving the future of Britain's imperial destiny. There is a real possibility, he wrote, that "the best women will be too highly developed to submit to childbearing; in other words the continuation of the species will be left to the coarser and less intellectual."[33]

When in 1901 the octogenarian Galton decided that his countrymen were ready to consider seriously the eugenic doctrines he had set aside a decade earlier, he gave as one of his reasons mounting public concern about the differential characteristics of the falling birthrate. He noted in particular the pronounced tendency among cultured women to defer marriage or to raise very small families.[34] Never militantly antifeminist, Galton had nevertheless feared that the achievement of feminist goals would divert the best women from their reproductive obligations and make them sexually less attractive to men. Though in 1893 he resigned from the Royal Geographical Society when it denied election to fifteen well-qualified women, it was not an endorsement of feminist aspirations but an acknowledgement of rare merit.[35] Galton grudgingly accepted the establishment of women's colleges at Oxford and his own alma mater, Cambridge, but he always doubted the intrinsic intellectual ability and emotional and physical stamina of female students and never relented in his opposition to granting them university degrees.[36]

Galton's point of view was widely endorsed in the scientific and academic community as well as within the eugenics movement. It was by no means universally accepted and led to a good deal of ambivalence and conflict within eugenic ranks before World War I. Pearson, who was impressed by the mathematical talents of the young women he encountered at University College, London, tried for years to convince the skeptical Galton that popular and scientific doubts about the mental capacity and vigor of educated women were unfounded. Although the female sex was supposed to lack much aptitude for the abstruse science of mathematics, he reminded his elderly friend in 1908, five of the fourteen people attached to the Eugenics Laboratory endowed by Galton four years earlier were women.[37] Not only was their work as good if not better than that of the men, but one of them, Ethel Elderton, was the "real heart of the laboratory." Not suprisingly then, he admonished Galton, "they were a little tried . . . when your name appeared as on the Committee of the Anti-Suffrage Society!"[38] With characteristic courtesy Galton declined to point out that the five women in question were all unmarried and were therefore depriving future generations of whatever special talents they might possess.

Pearson was no less concerned about the low marriage and birthrate of such eugenically qualified candidates for race motherhood. He was persuaded that differential nuptial and fertility patterns were not caused by advanced education, wider professional opportunities, or political aspirations. Rather, they reflected changing values and perspectives as well as economic goals and social strategies among those classes where the hereditary incidence of "civic worth," as eugenists increasingly described the qualities they admired, were most prevalent. In 1890 Eleanor Mildred Sidgwick, principal of Newnham College, Cambridge, had statistically demonstrated that college-educated women were no less healthy, less married, or less fertile than their sisters or first cousins who had not enjoyed the advantages of additional learning. Both groups married much less often and had fewer children than women further down the social scale, a phenomenon, Mrs. Sidgwick concluded, which was a consequence of class rather than education.[39]

Later studies made the same point, but feminists and antifeminists alike selected data that reinforced their own preconceptions. The eugenics movement was no exception. When in 1904 Galton delivered a provocative address on "Eugenics: Its Definition, Scope, and Aims" to the newly formed Sociological Society, a number of listeners were immediately struck by the potential of eugenics to stimulate "the resumption of a lost power of race-motherhood," which had of late shown frightening signs of "partial paralysis." Concern about the differential decline in the birthrate and the more strident demands of female militants combined in the charge that the fair sex had "lost that discerning guidance of eugenic instinct and that inerrancy of eugenic preference" which in previous generations gave us "the highest types of man yet developed."[40]

It seemed to such critics that the turning point had come in the 1860s and 1870s when the rise in feminist activity coincided with the beginning of the fall in fertility. Despite feminist organizations having scrupulously avoided any association with the contentious issue of birth control, their leaders were suspected of being crypto–neo-Malthusians by those who charged that female emancipation was incompatible with motherhood and a sound family life.[41] W.C.D. Whetham, the outspoken Cambridge University physicist and agronomist, was particularly vocal on this point. As a member of the Eugenics Education Society Council from 1909 to 1915, Whetham, along with is wife Catherine, represented the most antifeminist sector of that organization. They were distressed that their own contribution of six children to the racial coffers was rarely matched by Whetham's academic colleagues who, like the artistocracy and professional middle classes in general, were unable to average a third of that number. The Whethams were certain that by "withdrawing its women from the home and . . . throwing them into the competitive struggle for existence or the political organization of the country" the fittest classes were leading the nation down a path of self-destruction traversed by many great civilizations in the past.[42]

Not all Galton's antifeminist disciples questioned the ability of the female sex to pursue successfully higher education and a more varied, challenging way of life. But at what price? Whetham drew a familiar economic analogy in which men were valued as income to be used and spent freely by each generation. Women, by contrast, were likened to capital to be spent sparingly and husbanded carefully for the future.[43] Eugenic arguments were frequently laced with similar references to the law of the conservation of energy. R. Murray Leslie in 1911 added a new Law of Consonance, which decreed that "a woman should only develop intellectually along lines that are consonant with the natural development of her capacity for race creativeness."[44]

Leslie, a physician, had no doubts that the educated "new women" in the arts, sciences, and the professions were perfectly capable of succeeding, but to do so they would have to remain single or defer marriage and childbearing to a later age. This would curtail the number of children available for effective "race culture" and increase the risk of defective offspring frequently borne by older women.[45] Eugenic studies indicated that the most talented children were likely to be the third to the sixth, but they were no longer being produced by couples of high genetic potential, Leslie complained.[46] Another eugenist physician, Arabella Kenealy, thought the situtation was already so severe that "the refined . . . highly organized, but neurotic and over-taxed mothers of our cultured classes" were bearing children "of the crude, rough hewn, unintelligent peasant type." To Kenealy the advanced woman, "all nerves and restless activity . . . highly civilised . . . highly educated and fastidious," was for all her recent achievements "notoriously deficient in mother power."[47]

While eugenists found much in the Edwardian era to suggest that the seeds of decadence were already sown, most believed it was still possible to avoid a harvest of regressive hybrids. If the nation's leaders would but examine the evidence and support eugenic education and legislation, race decay was by no means inevitable. This meant that eugenics, as Galton proposed, must become the religion of the twentieth century with its precepts, dogma, and values permeating every area of British life.[48] No one was better qualified for implementing the new gospel of "race betterment" than the "well-bred woman" whose energies had unfortunately been diverted in other directions in recent years. She still had the opportunity to produce "the finest race the world has ever seen," Leslie promised, if she would only differentiate the fit from the unfit and marry accordingly.[49]

Few eugenists disputed such a strategy of race renewal, but a number of them questioned whether female emancipation was in fact inimical to their goal. The feminist movement, they noted, had never eschewed domesticity despite the much-publicized ravings of a few man-hating suffragettes. More typical was Mrs. Sidgwick who, in proving that a college education was not the cause of low marriage and fertility rates, regretted the statistics and maintained that marriage and motherhood was the natural career for even the most learned of her sex.[50]

A significant minority of opinion in both the feminist and eugenist camps insisted that their respective interests were not only compatible but logically lent themselves to some type of alliance.[51] The Eugenics Laboratory, under Pearson's direction, was after all a microcosm of female professional achievement. Half the membership of the Eugenics Education Society and a quarter of its officers and council members were women. Forty percent of the total were, like many other women of their class, unmarried, and a number of them were active in the moderate wing of the suffrage campaign. They were frequently the wives and daughters of successful professional men, and in endorsing the eugenic goals of higher fertility among women like themselves, they were often unwilling to be undereducated or permanently disenfranchised to achieve that racially beneficent end.[52]

Naturalists as eminent as Alfred Russel Wallace were cited to support their position. Even before the appearance of organized eugenics Wallace, the codiscoverer of evolution, postulated in 1890 that natural selection might actually be enhanced by the triumph of women's rights. Impressed by his reading of the American Edward Bellamy's utopia, *Looking Backward,* he reasoned that in a truly equitable society where women were economically independent, intellectually active, and full participants in public life, they would meet a much wider range of able men from whom to select their husbands. Where marriage was based upon mutual attraction, ability, and esteem, women would be in a position to spurn the idle, selfish, diseased, intellectual weaklings whom they were often currently forced to wed. Wallace thought that in light of Galton's recent discoveries about hereditary probability, the possiblities of raising the average of the race from such selective marriages were inestimable.[53]

A decade later the same argument was explicitly linked by feminists to eugenics. "Eugenia Newmarch," writing in *The Englishwoman* in 1910, promised that the new woman would be instinctively attracted to the best sort of man and would choose him for her husband rather than the dullard or wastrel who had nothing but wealth or family connections to recommend him. Emancipated women, she argued, were devoted to the improvement of the race and "eminently fitted" to promote it through eugenic marriages. Sensitive to the familiar charge that the struggle for women's rights was an unnatural revolt against domestic obligations, eugenically alert feminists assured their accusers that they did not condemn the institution of marriage, only the drudgery, torpidity, and oppressiveness of stultifying alliances of convenience and dependency.[54]

Many feminist sympathizers, including Wallace, who proclaimed the racial advantages of wider sexual selection implicit in the triumph of female emancipation, accepted a later marriage age as an inevitable consequence of women expanding their education and experience. They were confident that the quality of the fewer children born to these deferred but more selective unions would offset any numerical disadvantages. The eugenic disciples of social Darwinism in the early twentieth century were much less optimistic as they compared the plummeting birthrate of their own class to the higher fertility of the "less fit." Few of them believed any longer that natural selection could function in modern societies where the reproduction and survival of the lower classes was subsidized by the state to the financial, and, inevitably, racial detriment of the middle and upper classes. The deferral of marriage and childbearing by the ablest women *was* what frightened eugenists and other class-conscious analysts of the declining birthrate in the years before World War I.

One solution, rejected by the Eugenics Education Society, was the promotion of birth control among the poor as a way of bringing their excessive fertility into balance with that of their betters. Neo-Malthusians had been complaining for decades that the menacing growth of collectivism and socialism had seriously undermined the effectiveness of natural selection to the obvious detriment of the race. The widespread adoption of birth control practices, they promised, had the dual advantage of curtailing the alarming fertility of the genetically deficient, while permitting eugenically preferable couples to marry earlier and space the arrival of their valued offspring. Enlightened, ambitious, new women could, by rationally planning their families, pursue a life of individual satisfaction while enjoying the natural pleasures of compatible domesticity and race-enhancing motherhood.

The Malthusian League, since its establishment in 1877, had struggled with little success to convince the varous feminist organizations that true emancipation would never be possible until women had control over their own fertility.[55] With the emergence of eugenics in the early twentieth century, neo-Malthusians saw an obvious alliance.[56] Alice Vickery Drysdale, an ardent feminist physician and wife of the Malthusian League's first president, argued with Galton, Pearson, and other eugenists in the Sociological Society in 1905 that the success of their new science ultimately depended upon the economic and physiological independence of able women. Unless women were confident of the control of their own lives, starting with their own bodies, she insisted, "their individuality . . . could not exercise that natural selective power in the choice of a mate, which was probably a main factor in the . . . evolution of the race."[57]

The new Sociological Society had enough difficulties defining its role and purpose without taking on the contentious, emotional, and still rather salacious subject of birth control. Despite a concerted effort by Drysdale and her son Charles to persuade the fledgling Eugenics Education Society to take up their cause, it proved equally unreceptive. Like the suffragist organizations, the Eugenics Education Society considered the issue an offensive diversion which could only lower the level of its campaign and embroil it in unneeded controversy.

Before the war the eugenics movement was strongly committed to *positive* race culture. Both Galton and Pearson consistently rejected birth control as a useful form of *negative* eugenics calculated to reduce the dangerous fertility of the lower classes. They were convinced that in practice it would not be adopted by the thoughtless and ignorant poor but by the rational, prudent, educated classes whose families were already too small.[58] Their assessment, supported by the class fertility correlations published by the Eugenics Laboratory and verified by the 1911 Census, appeared irrefutable. Though birth control arguments made some headway in eugenic circles before 1914, they repeatedly ran into a wall of statistics enumerating the dangers of differential procreation.[59]

In spurning birth control as a viable form of negative eugenics, several of the Eugenic Education Society's most prominent spokesmen nevertheless endorsed the contention that greater female independence and self-control could indeed stimulate positive eugenic selection. The young Edinburgh physician Caleb Saleeby, perhaps the society's most effective propagandist, and the prominent London barrister Montague Crackanthorpe, its president until 1911, shared this view. Both openly supported the enfranchisement of women, confident it would make the recipients of the vote aware of the problems of the modern world and conscientious about fulfilling their responsibilities. At the same time they were concerned that the prolonged and increasingly bitter struggle for the ballot was diverting talented middle- and upper-class women from their more important biological obligations.[60]

Crackanthorpe knew that many of his eugenist colleagues, including his long-time friend and neighbor Galton himself, agreed with the assertion of the psychologist William McDougall that emancipated women would never find maternity and domestic life satisfying.[61] Whether true or not, Crackanthorpe argued: "Woman is now wide awake, her long slumber ended. To put her to sleep again is beyond human power." There was no turning back, he insisted; if the full implications were uncertain, that was true of almost everything in the new century. While many of his younger contemporaries feared the worst, the septuagenarian Crackanthorpe was optimistic about the future and the role the new woman would play in determining the destiny of the race. She would decline "to give to her children for father the degenerate, the drunkard, the physically or mentally unfit." Consequently, despite dire prognoses to the contrary, the women's movement posed no danger to the home or race. Political enfranchisement, which women already enjoyed at the local level, was really a minor issue blown out of proportion by the anxieties of the age, the shrewd Crackanthrope contended. It should be resolved as quickly as possible so women could concentrate on satisfying their obligations as wives, mothers, and now citizens.[62]

By the standards of the day Crackanthrope and Saleeby represented the most progressive wing of the eugenics movement. They were not only openly supportive of votes for women, but, in contrast to most other eugenists, they believed the Eugenics Education Society should consider the possible advantages of birth control in the advancement of the race. Yet in their defense of female rights, neither of them contemplated that intelligent, educated, independent women, having achieved their goals, would consider them serious alternatives to marriage and motherhood. Both Crackanthorpe and Saleeby thought that once women were enfranchised they would probably defer from exercising the vote and participating in affairs of state until after their children were grown. Charles Frederick D'-Arcy, the bishop of Down and Connor and a vice president of the Eugenics Education Society, made one of several recommendations to the council before the war that it petition the government to limit any extension of the franchise to mothers of at least four children.[63] The council, while sympathetic, thought that so exclusionary a measure might create more conflicts than it would resolve.

Eugenists trying to reconcile the undeniable requirements of race motherhood with the inevitability of enfranchisement, in the end fell back on their confidence in education and the compelling logic and scientific validity of their new-found eugenic faith. The best women, a number of whose outstanding representatives graced the rolls of the Eugenics Education Society, would somehow be drawn to the rational renewal of the race. In spite of all that might occur in the troubled years ahead, Saleeby promised in 1911, woman is still "Nature's supreme organ of the future . . . . Her body is holy, for it is the temple of life to come."[64] Ultimately the ancient biological imperative would prevail, illuminated by the new light of eugenics.

When science seemed uncertain, advocates of "eugenic feminism," as Saleeby described it, reverted to a mystical law of dimishing returns. There was a critical point of individual freedom beyond which the ablest women could not go without "deserting the ranks of motherhood and leaving the blood of inferior women to constitute half of all future generations."[65] The suffragist Mabel Atkinson suggested in 1910 that the crisis had been passed, and that modern feminists, in contrast to the first generation of reformers, tended more often to be married. She offered no evidence, but felt there was every reason to believe that the extension of equal rights would accelerate the trend. Even the early feminists wanted children, she claimed, but not as sexual slaves. As women's opportunities have expanded, more of them have wed. Once enfranchised, Atkinson promised, they would prove invaluable in the design of legislation and policies to encourage the fitter classes to marry.[66]

Although the percentage of middle-class women marrying increased steadily in the twentieth century, in 1910, Atkinson, like most eugenic feminists, assumed it as an act of faith. If the principles of positive eugenics were sound, it logically followed that as the better stocks became aware of their hereditary responsibilities the number of racially promising marriages would expand. This had been Galton's dream from the earliest stages of his statistical enquiries into the probabilities of inherited talent. In his first article on the subject, in 1865, he envisioned a utopia in which a system of competitive exams for girls and boys was employed to identify "every important quality of mind and body." The marriage of those with superior health, vigor, beauty, intelligence, and disposition would be endowed by the state, and the costs of rearing and educating their "extraordinarily talented issue" would be cheerfully subsidized by public authorities.[67]

Confident that careful genealogical studies coupled to anthropometric data would identify the most valuable men and women, Galton in subsequent years proposed a variety of schemes to advertise the results. These ranged from "racial diplomas" for outstanding university graduates to "certificates of eugenic fitness" endorsed by physicians, clergymen, teachers, and other authorities in a position to observe and test the physical, moral and mental attributes of potential candidates for race parenthood.[68] To facilitate the task, he recommended the maintenance of elaborate family albums, and when the Eugenics Education Society was founded, he hoped it would become a central repository for information gathered by local associations of "Eugenes" — people of above average physique, intellect, and character devoted to mutual aid and to helping "worthy couples" marry.[69]

While he anticipated that the state would eventually assume these tasks, Galton appreciated the difficulties of its doing so in a democratic society. Instead, for the time being, he proposed that individual and community benefactors subsidize the marriages and progeny of the "well born." It might "become a point of honour and as much an avowed object,'" he suggested in 1901, "for noble families to gather fine specimens of humanity around them as it is to procure and maintain fine breeds of cattle, etc., which are costly, but repay in satisfaction." On various occasions he called attention to the enormous sums annually contributed to public charities and recommended that such generosity could be better directed toward the endowment of "natural gifts" and the "national efficiency" of future generations.[70]

When in 1906 Galton drew up a design for "eugenic certificates" to be awarded worthy candidates for racial subsidies, he singled out educated men between the ages of twenty-three and thirty as the most likely recipients. Women, he claimed, presented "a different problem," as they had so few demonstrable attributes beyond their family pedigree.[71] Though he expected a eugenically promising woman to select her mate from the pool of certified men, her race potential would have to be extracted from male genealogy where "hereditary family qualities, including those of fertility and pre-potency" were amply demonstrated. If a girl came from a family of pronounced masculine ability and numerous male heirs, she was a likely candidate for race motherhood.[72] Few eugenists doubted Galton's assurances that in general the ability in the nation lay "in the higher of our classes" whose persistent achievements over generations ruled out the importance of "environmental [social and economic] advantages."[73] Whether the talent of these classes was as masculine-centered as Galton believed was increasingly a subject of dispute.

There were continual arguments among eugenists about the inheritability of particular characteristics and defects. Some were more sensitive than others to the accusation of their critics that they were antidemocratic elitists who employed dubious scientific evidence to support class prejudices and thwart needed social reforms. The rediscovery of Mendelian genetics at the turn of the century raised serious doubts about the biometric foundations of eugenics and illustrated, even to eugenists, how little was known about human heredity.[74] These doubts were quickly brought to bear on the "woman question," for it was immediately obvious that if Mendel was correct the genetic contribution of women to the furtherance of the race might be much greater than statistical correlations indicated.

Havelock Ellis, for example, responding to Galton's proposal for "eugenic certificates," suggested that women were far more important to race culture than previously believed. The likelihood that hereditary characteristics were transmitted equally from both sexes meant that documents of race worthiness were valuable for men and women as "testaments of natural ability." Those who held them, he wrote, would be "Nature's aristocrats, to whom the future of the race might be safely left without further question."[75] At the same time Ellis approved of the certificates as an ideal, he doubted there would be any "spontaneous demand on the part of the public" for them.[76]

Other eugenists who embraced Mendelism, such as Saleeby, were less restrained in their criticism of the biometrical or statistical approach to the study of human heredity. Among its many defects none was more obvious than a serious undervaluation of female genetic capacity. Saleeby, who led the fight against biometrics within the Eugenics Education Society, was sensitive to Galton's feelings but nevertheless complained in 1909 of the distorted concentration upon male ancestry in most eugenic studies.[77] Modern genetics clearly proved that inherited qualities not only came from both parents, but that the chances were one in four that a child would be endowed with a given character from either of them. Alert to the practical applications of science to public affairs, Saleeby reasoned that since females could also inherit parental traits as well as males, the denial of the vote to women cut off an enormous amount of inbred talent from political life.[78]

The recognition that daughters might be as generously endowed with diverse abilities as sons led to a spirited debate within eugenic circles about "racial efficiency." At present, Saleeby noted, the only outlet for a woman's talent was its transmission to male offspring.[79] During the British Association meetings of 1909, a distinguished chemist acknowledged that although it was now clear that a woman could inherit an aptitude for science equal to that of a man, she ought not to develop her gift but marry early and pass it on to her sons.[80] To a nation supposedly starved for ability, such a solution raised difficult questions about the best use of the country's racial resources. While sympathetic to the imperative demands of race motherhood, eugenic feminists were uncertain whether emancipated women, aware of their newly discovered biological equality, would be content to channel it into traditional roles. The future of the race, they warned, could depend upon a sound, scientific resolution of this likely conflict.

To biometricians like Karl Pearson, already stung by the serious challenge of Mendelian genetics to his statistical methods, the widespread confusion of eugenics with such contentious, popular issues as the woman question threatened to undermine whatever credibility eugenics had in the scientific community.[81] He had always disapproved of Galton's eagerness to publicize the preliminary investigations undertaken by the Eugenics Laboratory and insisted that years of biometric enquiries should precede public speculation and recommendations for practical application. Though Pearson was himself guilty of running too far ahead of his data on occasions, he tried repeatedly to warn eugenic enthusiasts, including Galton, that their only hope of eventually influencing public policy was to achieve scientific recognition as a serious research discipline.[82]

Pearson was therefore strongly opposed to the creation of the Eugenics Education Society in 1907. He refused to join, tried in vain to dissuade Galton from lending his prestigious name to the group, and always refused to permit any ties between the Eugenics Laboratory and the Eugenics Education Society. Despite its impressive roster of scientists and physicians, Pearson believed that the organization's appearance was premature. The study of human heredity was still in its infancy, he argued, and the claims of many popularizers bordered on quackery.[83] Eugenics was clearly in danger of becoming a fashionable pseudoscience when raffish eccentrics like George Bernard Shaw began demanding freedom for genetically superior men and women "to breed the race without being hampered by the mass of irrelevant conditions implied in the institution of marriage."[84] The vision in *Man and Superman* of a robust, cheerful, "eupeptic British country squire" coupling temporarily with a clever, intellectual, "highly civilised Jewess" to reproduce an extraordinary son provoked the kind of hilarity Pearson feared could ruin eugenics.[85]

Before World War I at least, Pearson's warnings went unheeded. Eugenics remained divided between a small number of advocates of pure research and a majority who were certain that enough was already known about human heredity to justify policies of race culture. Whether biometry or Mendelian genetics eventually proved correct was of secondary importance to the latter. Neither hereditary mechanism challenged the dominance of nature over nurture which supported the eugenic conviction that the future of the empire depended not on ruinously expensive social welfare schemes but on the revitalization of individualism. In this sense eugenics was a reaction to the collectivist, some claimed socialist, tendencies of the age which portended a leveling, dependent mediocrity when what was needed to compete in the twentieth century was independent leadership by accomplished individuals in all walks of life.

What most worried eugenists, in contrast to other pessimistic analysts of the declining birth rate, was not the greater populousness of such rivals as Germany, the United States, and even Japan, but their apparent race efficiency. The personal quality of Britain's competitors as reflected in business acumen, scientific and technological invention, military organization, political vitality, and a general accommodation to the realities of the new era seemed to be keeping pace with their expanding numbers and appetites. The triumph of biometrics or genetics was less important than their confirmation of the heritability of those physical, mental, and behavioral characteristics eugenists wished to see replicated.

Eugenic feminists and antifeminists alike knew that this was only possible if the most promising women agreed to arrange their individual priorities to conform to the collective needs of the race. Whether this meant traditional marriages of convenience and dependency with men of good stock or emancipated marriages contracted freely on the basis of equality, mutual respect, and compatibility, the outcome had to be the same — full cradles in the nurseries of the fit. The other alternative, no marriage at all, was racially unacceptable. Whatever the scientific basis of eugenics, nothing was to alter the preconceptions that created it in the first place.

World War I and the extension of franchise to women in 1918 brought an end to the suffragist turmoil of the Edwardian years. It also effectively destroyed the illusion that a sufficient number of race mothers could be persuaded to rear families large enough to offset the higher fertility of the genetically less desirable classes. In spite of a variety of proposals from the Eugenics Education Society to encourage middle- and upper-class warriors to marry and sire as many children as possible before facing the risks of battle, eugenists saw the birth rate of the fit, like that of the nation as a whole, fall to new lows. It was a trend that continued, despite minor fluctuations, until after World War II.[86]

The eugenic campaign had reached its peak in 1914. The fears and anxieties about race decadence which had given eugenics much of its impetus and provided it with an attentive audience rapidly diminished. The British not only proved to be more vigorous and adaptable than their enemies, as well as most of their allies, in the Great War, but the extension of democratic politics and the rapid rise of Labor in the 1920s precluded eugenics playing much of a role in planning for the future.

Eugenists had always been uncertain as to what that role should be. They failed to resolve the basic question of whether theirs was a natural or a social science. This ambivalence left eugenics open to any number of possible interpretations by an educated sector of the middle class eager to explain the inequities of society while justifying their own essential role in it. On one level eugenics as a science of heredity was exceedingly complex, beyond the comprehension of much of the public that embraced its precepts. On the level of a social science, it was, like social Darwinism, remarkably clear, even simple, and could be easily adapted to a variety of existing perceptions of contemporary issues. More basically, eugenics explained and reinforced strong class assumptions about "good breeding" prevalent in British society long before Galton or anyone else tried to isolate the determining factors in human heredity.

That was part of its appeal. At the same time, eugenics made old preconceptions and values appear new, dynamic, and scientifically credible. In this sense it succeeded far more as a popular, respectable way of expressing class prejudices about social, economic, and political change than it ever did as a legitimate science. As the prewar debate over the woman question demonstrates, eugenists of sharply different persuasion had little difficulty in finding what they believed to be scientific evidence to sustain their varying arguments. In the final analysis, all their evidence supported the same conclusion: female emancipation, whether disastrous, desirable, or inevitable, must not interfere with the reproduction of numerous progeny similar to themselves. It is doubtful that their judgment would have been any different if eugenics, instead of entering the arena of public controversy, had remained confined to the laboratory.

NOTES

1. Francis Galton, *Inquiries into Human Faculty and Its Development* (London, 1883), pp. 24–25.
2. Brian Harrison, *Separate Spheres: The Opposition to Women's Suffrage in Britain, 1867–1928* (London, 1978), p. 56.
3. John N. Burstyn, "Education and Sex: The Medical Case against Higher Education for Women in England, 1870-1900." In *Proceedings of the American Philosophical Society* 117 (no. 2, April 1973), pp. 79–89. For examples of the persistence of these views into the Edwardian years see T.S. Clouston, "The Psychological Dangers to Women in Modern Social Developments." In *The Position of Women* (London, 1911), pp. 111–12; *British Medical Journal* 1 (March 5, 26, 1904), pp. 578, 757; Almroth E. Wright, *The Unexpurgated Case against Woman Suffrage* (London, 1913).
4. Great Britain, Parliamentary Papers, *Inter-Departmental Committee on Physical Deterioration,* 3 vols., XXXII (1904), Cd. 2175, 2210, 2186. Also *Report of the Royal Commission on Physical Training* (Scotland), 2 vols., XXX (1903), Cd. 1507, 1508. In 1903 the Worshipful Company of Drapers began a series of grants to Karl Pearson's biometric laboratory for "Studies in National Deterioration" which were continued when the laboratory merged a few years later with the Francis Galton Laboratory for National Eugenics, established in 1904 at the University of London.
5. For an analysis of the early eugenics movement as professional middle-class ideology see Donald A. MacKenzie, "Eugenics in Britain," *Social Studies of Science* 6 (1976), pp. 499–532.
6. For a comprehensive analysis of class marriage differentials see *Census of England and Wales 1911: Fertility of Marriage* 13, pt. 2 (London, 1923), pp. lxxviii–lxxx, ci–civ.
7. B.R. Mitchell and Phyllis Deane, *Abstract of British Historical Statistics* (Cambridge, 1962), p. 6. See also Arthur Newsholme and T.H.C. Stevenson, "The Decline of Human Fertility in the U.K. and Other Countries as Shown by Corrected Birth Rates," *Journal of the Royal Statistical Society* 69 (1906), pp. 34–87; *Parl. Ps., Registrar-General 82nd Report* 11 (1920), Cmd. 1017, Table 3, p. 5.
8. Sidney Webb, *The Decline in the Birth-Rate* (London, Fabian Society Tract 131, 1907); Arthur Newsholme, *The Declining Birth-Rate: Its National and International Significance* (London, 1911); Ethel M. Elderton, *Report on the English Birth-Rate,* pt. 1, *England North of the Humber,* Eugenics Laboratory Memoirs 19 and 20 (Cambridge, 1914). See also *The Daily Mail,* August 10, 1903; *The Lancet* 1 (March 11, 1905), p. 652.
9. Herbert Spencer, *The Principles of Biology,* 2 vols. (London, 1864–67), vol. 2, pp. 427–31.
10. The National Birth-Rate Commission was established under the auspices of the eminently respectable National Council of Public Morals and was particularly concerned about the threat the declining birth rate might hold for the future of sound, moral domestic life in Britain. The commission consisted of sixty-six dignitaries including eight peers, three M.P.s, the heads of two Cambridge colleges, two medical editors, seven bishops, the leaders of the Free Churches, General William Booth, Beatrice Webb and, for the working classes, James Ramsay MacDonald. See The National Birth-Rate Commission, *The Declining Birth-Rate: Its Causes and Effects. Being the Report of*

and the Chief Evidence Taken by the National Birth-Rate Commission Instituted, with Official Recognition, by the National Council of Public Morals — for the Promotion of Race Regeneration — Spiritual, Moral, and Physical (London, 1916), pp. 20–21. For the rise of neo-Malthusianism see Rosanna Ledbetter, *A History of the Mathusian League, 1877–1927* (Columbus, 1976).

11. Karl Pearson, "Reproductive Selection." In *The Chances of Death and Other Studies in Evolution,* 2 vols. (London, 1897), vol. 1, pp. 78–80.

12. See for example David Heron, *On the Relation of Fertility in Man to Social Status, and on the changes in this Relation that Have Taken Place during the Last Fifty Years.* Drapers Company Research Memoirs, Studies in National Deterioration, no. 1 (London, 1906); Elderton, *Report.*

13. Heron, *On the Relation,* p. 20.

14. *Census* (1911), pt. 2, pp. cxix–cxxi.

15. Ibid., pp. xciv, xci.

16. Francis Galton, "Eugenics: Its Definition, Scope, and Aims." In *Sociological Papers* 1, 1904 (London, 1905), pp. 47–50. In the early twentieth century the expression "civic worth" was increasingly used in place of "genius" or "talent." It was considered to be the goal of good breeding but much more complex and comprehensive than Galton's original concept of hereditary ability. "Civic worth" emphasized the individual contribution to both society and the race. See Caleb Saleeby, *The Methods of Race Regeneration* (New York, 1911), pp. 17–19.

17. Harrison, *Separate Spheres,* p. 56.

18. See for example *Sociological Papers,* 1, pp. 76–77.

19. Francis Galton, *Hereditary Genius: An Inquiry into Its Laws and Consequences* (London, 1869), pp. 328–29.

20. Ibid., pp. 36–62, 329. See also *English Men of Science: Their Nature and Nurture* (London, 1874).

21. Galton, *Hereditary Genius,* p. 329.

22. Ibid., pp. 131–40. Charles Darwin, Galton's cousin, noted his theory in *The Descent of Man* (London, 1871), pt. 1, ch. 4.

23. D.W. Forrest, *Francis Galton: The Life and Work of a Victorian Genius* (New York, 1974), pp. 226–27.

24. Karl Pearson, "The Woman's Question." In *The Ethic of Freethought and Other Addressses and Essays,* 2nd ed. rev. (London, 1901), p. 356.

25. Ibid., pp. 356–57.

26. "Socialism and Sex" in ibid., p. 425.

27. "Woman's Question," p. 355.

28. Ibid., pp. 355–59.

29. Pearson to Galton, October 7, 1896, *Francis Galton Papers,* University College London Archives, file 293/B.

30. Ibid., December 27, 1896.

31. Ibid., August 29, 1896.

32. See *The Lancet* 2 (September 10, 1910), pp. 815–17. For a typical late Victorian view see John Thorburn, *Female Education from a Physiological Point of View: A Lecture, Introductory to the Summer Course on Obstetric Medicine* (Manchester, 1884), p. 11.

33. Pearson, "Woman's Question," pp. 374, 377–78; Galton, *Hereditary Genius,* pt. 1, p. 164.

34. Francis Galton, "The Possible Improvement of the Human Breed under the Existing Conditions of Law and Sentiment." In *Annual Report of the Board of Regents of the Smithsonian Institution . . . for the Year Ending June 30, 1901* (Washington, 1902), p. 535.
35. Forrest, *Galton,* pp. 225–26.
36. William Bateson to Galton, May 2, 1897, *Galton Papers,* f. 198.
37. Galton in 1904 gave money to the University of London to establish a Eugenics Record Office which in 1906 was merged with Pearson's Biometric Laboratory. The following year it was renamed "The Francis Galton Laboratory for the Study of National Eugenics" and left a substantial endowment by Galton at his death in 1911. See Lyndsay A. Farrall, *The Origins and Growth of the English Eugenics Movement, 1865–1925.* Ph.D. disseration, Indiana University, 1970, ch. 4.
38. Pearson to Galton, December 15, 1908, *Galton Papers,* f. 293/J.
39. Mrs. Henry Sidgwick, *Health Statistics of Women Students of Cambridge and Oxford and of Their Sisters* (Cambridge, 1890).
40. Having failed to persuade the Anthropological Institute to embrace his new science, Galton hoped that the newly established Sociological Society would be more receptive to innovative ideas for social improvements. See Karl Pearson, *The Life, Letters, and Labours of Francis Galton,* 3 vols. (Cambridge, 1914–30), vol. 3, p. 226. Also *Sociological Papers* 1, pp. 76–78.
41. J.A. Banks and Olive Banks, *Feminism and Family Planning in Victorian England*(New York, 1972), pp. 90 ff.
42. W.C.D. Whetham and C.D. Whetham, "The Extinction of the Upper Classes," *The Nineteenth Century* 66 (July 1909), p. 106.
43. W.C.D. Whetham and C.D. Whetham, *The Family and the Nation: A Study in Natural Inheritance and Social Responsibility* (London, 1909), pp. 198–99.
44. *Eugenics Review* 2 (no. 4, January 1911), p. 290.
45. Ibid., pp. 284–85.
46. Ibid., p. 293.
47. Ibid. 3 (no. 1, April 1911), p. 44.
48. Galton, "Possible Improvement," p. 534; "Eugenics: Its Definition," pp. 12-13.
49. *Eugenics Review* 2 (January 1911), pp. 294-95.
50. Mrs. Henry Sidgwick, *University Education for Women: Presidential Address Delivered to the Education Society, Manchester University, on 21st November 1912* (Manchester, 1913), p. 18.
51. See *Sociological Review* 3 (no. 1, January 1910), pp. 51–52.
52. Nearly two-thirds of the society's membership was located in London, while the remaining one-third was affiliated with one of seven branches of the central organization.
53. Alfred R. Wallace, "Human Selection," *Fortnightly Review* 48 (1890), pp. 333–37.
54. *The Englishwoman* (no. 28, 1910), pp. 36–38.
55. See for example *The Malthusian* (no. 67, September 1884), p. 546; 27 (no. 11, November 1903), p. 65; 31 (no. 3, March 1907), pp. 20-21.
56. See Richard A. Soloway, "Neo-Malthusians, Eugenists, and the Declining Birth-Rate in England, 1900-1918," *Albion* (Spring 1979), pp. 264–86.
57. *Sociological Papers,* 2, 1905 (London, 1905), pp. 21-22.

58. Galton, *Inquiries,* pp. 207–10; id., *Hereditary Genius,* pp. 356–57; Pearson, "Socialism and Sex," pp. 423–24.
59. See for example Ethel Elderton et al., *On the Correlation of Fertility with Social Value: A Cooperative Study* (London, Eugenics Laboratory Memoirs 18, 1913).
60. Caleb W. Saleeby, *Woman and Womanhood: A Search for Principles* (London, 1911), pp. 22–23.
61. *Sociological Papers* 3, 1906 (London, 1906), p. 71.
62. Montague Crackanthorpe, *Population and Progress* (London, 1907), pp. 116–17.
63. Eugenics Education Society, *Minute Book* 2 (June 17, 1914), London, Eugenics Society Library.
64. Saleeby, *Woman,* pp. 25, 47; id., *Parenthood and Race Culture: An Outline of Eugenics* (London, 1909), p. 106.
65. Saleeby, *Woman,* pp. 14–16.
66. *Sociological Review* 3 (January 1910), pp. 54–56.
67. Galton, "Hereditary Talent and Character," *Macmillan's Magazine* 12 (June 1865), pt. 1, pp. 164–65.
68. See for example "Possible Improvement," pp. 532–33; *Sociological Papers* 2, p. 17.
69. Francis Galton, "Hereditary Improvement," *Fraser's Magazine* 7 (January 1873), pp. 124–25; id., *Nature* 78 (October 22, 1908), p. 647.
70. Galton, "Possible Improvement," pp. 536-37; id., *Nature* (October 22, 1908), p. 647.
71. *Galton Papers,* f. 138/4, 138/10.
72. Galton, "Possible Improvement," pp. 532–33.
73. Ibid., p. 527.
74. See William Bateson, *Mendel's Principles of Heredity* (Cambridge, 1902).
75. Havelock Ellis, "Eugenics and St. Valentine," *Nineteenth Century* 59 (1906) p. 784.
76. Ellis to Galton, April 1, 1907, *Galton Papers,* f. 239.
77. Saleeby, *Parenthood,* pp. 175–76.
78. *Westminster Review* 172 (August 1909), pp. 186–88.
79. Ibid.
80. *Sociological Review* 3 (no. 1, January 1910), p. 51.
81. P. Froggart and N.C. Nevin, "The Law of Ancestral Heredity and the Mendelian-Ancestrian Controversy in England, 1889–1906," *Journal of Medical Genetics* 8 (1971), pp. 1–36; Lyndsay Farrall, "Controversy and Conflict in Science: A Case Study — The English Biometric School and Mendel's Laws," *Social Studies of Science* 5 (1975), pp. 269–301.
82. Pearson, *Life of Galton,* vol. 3, pp. 296–97.
83. See Pearson to Galton, October 14, 1908, *Galton Papers,* f. 293/J.
84. Sociological Papers 1, p. 75.
85. George Bernard Shaw, *Man and Superman* (1903). The Revolutionist's Handbook, pt. 2.
86. For the Eugenics Education Society's war-time campaign see Soloway, "Neo-Malthusians," pp. 280–82.

CHAPTER SEVEN

Darwinism and the Working Class in Wilhelmian Germany

Alfred H. Kelly

Historians are fond of saying—usually as an aside—that important ideas eventually "trickle down" to the masses. That they rarely follow the trickles is an indication not only of the state of the historical craft, but also of the difficulties and imponderables inherent in such a pursuit. Reading popular authors and assessing their impact is often neither rewarding nor easy. But when analyzing Marxism, it is essential that those trickles of popularizationbe followed. For if the masses are cast in a central role as historical actors, we must know what they read and thought to understand why they acted (or failed to act) as they did. Massive tomes on learned socialist theoreticians, whom the masses neither read nor understood, are likely to be misleading. The most we could infer from such works is that the workingman's view of socialism was a dim, oversimplified reflection of sophisticated ideology—akind of clichéd Kautskyism or thirdhand Marxism.

In the case of the German working class before World War I, this impression would be false; here the patterns of popularization were more subtle and devious. As Marxism trickled down to the German working class, it did not simply become more diluted and vapid. Its character changed radically because it mixed with another momentous system of ideas—Darwinism. By the time Marxism reached a popular level, it had ceased to be recognizable and had become vague Darwinian monism. The reason for this metamorphosis is fairly simple. Whereas Marxist political and economic theory was difficult and abstruse and good popularizers were scarce, Darwinism was relatively simple, and good popularizers abounded. Above all, there were Ernst Haeckel and Wilhelm Bölsche, both devoting their careers to making Darwinism an easily understandable and comprehensive philosophy of life, a *Weltanschauung*. As this term suggests, popular Darwinism was not confined to biology; it made monopolistic, religious-like claims of the sort that threatened the integrity of other belief systems. Marxism as a theory of change made similar claims to totality. One of the two had to yield to the other. To put it in Darwinian terms, Darwinism and Marxism were closely related and therefore competing species of ideas in the popular arena; but Darwinism was fitter, so it survived, while Marxism perished. If the image is a bit overdrawn, the outcome is still clear: the German workingman saw his future in Darwinian terms. He was a natural evolutionist rather than a political revolutionist.

This popular substitution of Darwin for Marx was preceded on a high theoretical level by a subtle infusion of Darwinian terminology into Marxist ideology. The outlines of this infusion are well known and need only be alluded to briefly. At Marx's funeral in 1883, Friedrich Engels could think of no higher praise for his departed friend than to compare him to Darwin. "Just as Darwin discovered the law of evolution in organic nature," Engels said, "so Marx discovered the law of evolution in human history."[1] Marx probably would have been proud of the company Engels placed him in. Although he found Darwin philosophically crude, Marx admired the biologist and was quick to sense that Darwinism would set the intellectual style of the age.[2] Evolution, struggle, nature—these concepts were "scientific" and by 1870 were on the lips of every educated layman.[3] Why not exploit the situation? Thus Marx acquiesced when, as early as the 1870s, Engels began a Darwinization of Marxism. Whereas he professed to share Marx's distinctions between natural and human history, Engels turned Marxism into a kind of scientism. The future became for him a necessity of natural Darwinian law rather than a consequence of the dialectical historical process. Engels inserted Darwin into the place Hegel had held in Marxist analysis. In so doing he neutralized the very dialectical materialism he so avidly propounded and muddled the meaning of the transformation to a socialist future. As George Lichtheim has aptly put it, Marxist thought in the years 1840–80 moved "from Hegel to Haeckel."[4]

Lichtheim suggests that the scientism or Darwinism that permeated social democracy was a necessary adaptation "to the rather modest intellectual requirements of the labour movement."[5] This seems to imply that the party knowingly transmitted to the masses a distorted Darwinized Marxism, believing it to be the only popularly understandable Marxism. Actually, the effects on the masses were more indirect: the workers tended to bypass Marx (or popularizations of him) and go directly to popular Darwinism; and because of their philosophical leanings (or confusion), party leaders usually acquiesced. There is a wealth of evidence on workers' reading habits showing that they were far more interested in science than in economics or politics. And science usually meant Darwinism, the workingman's favorite subject. Popular Darwinism in Germany had always had an antiestablishment tone. It was no coincidence that when the future socialist leader August Bebel was in prison in the early 1870s, his reading list included Darwin's *Origin,* Haeckel's *Natural History,* Büchner's *Force and Matter,* and Liebig's *Chemical Letters.*[6] These reading interests would set the tone for succeeding generations. Many, even liberals like Rudolf Virchow, feared that Darwinism could "lead to" socialism and ought to be kept out of the public arena. ("What a foolish idea seems to prevail in Germany on the connection between Socialism and Evolution through Natural Selection," Darwin mused.[7]) The fact that Darwinism was successfully excluded from schools only served to enhance its attractive, forbidden aura. It is also probable that the ban on much socialist literature during the formative years of the movement in the 1880s had much to do with focusing workers' attention away from Marxism. Science (or culture generally) was "safer" and could serve as a substitute radicalism.[8]

The pattern of interest in Darwin rather than Marx was clearly established by the 1890s and persisted throughout the next generation. As Paul Göhre, a young theologian who worked in a machine factory in Chemnitz, reported in 1891, workers knew little of socialist theory, but they were fascinated by the popular scientific, "materialistic" literature.[9] Göhre's impressions are confirmed by all available surveys of workers' libraries. With the exception of Bebel's *Die Frau und der Sozialismus (Woman and Socialism,* 1879), popular Darwinism dominated worker nonfiction reading. As *Die Neue Zeit* reported in 1894 (on the basis of statistics from a Social Democratic club in a South German city), political literature was just not in demand. After Bebel, the most popular nonfiction authors were Arnold Dodel, Oswald Köhler, and Edward Aveling—all Darwin popularizers. *Die Neue Zeit* speculated that the lack of political interest was due to the workers already having the political brochures.[10]

The most impressive reading survey at the turn of the century casts doubt on this explanation. In 1899 A.H.T. Pfannkuche placed an ad in *Die Neue Zeit* asking librarians of workers' libraries to send him lists of the most popular books. Pfannkuche published the results the next year in a short book entitled *Was liest der deutsche Arbeiter?* (*What Does the German Worker Read?*) Although Bebel's *Woman and Socialism* headed the list of nonfiction, four of the top ten books in this category were of the genre Darwiniana. Workers were also very fond of bourgeois family magazines like *Gartenlaube;* for their fiction reading, they preferred Zola above all others, as well as *Die Neue Welt,* which came with most socialist newspapers as an entertainment supplement.[11] Typically, librarians lamented their patrons' lack of political interests. Pfannkuche concluded that the number of political and economic titles was actually inflated because librarians pushed the "right kind" of books.[12] Many were probably returned unread.[13] It was wrong to argue, he said, that workers' political curiosity was already satisfied by party newspapers, for these papers also followed science. The fascination with science was deep and genuine — what concerned workers most could be summarized by the title of Dodel's popular book, *Moses or Darwin?*[14]

The same patterns emerge from other surveys after 1900. Questionnaires distributed to workers taking evening courses in Berlin during 1904–08 showed "knowledge of nature" as their main interest, with economics and politics lagging far behind.[15] Adolf Levenstein, who did a sociological survey of workers in metals, textiles, and mining during 1907–11, found that workers usually listed popular science books as their favorite reading, the names Bölsche and Haeckel appearing repeatedly.[16] Further, *Der Bibliothekar,* a monthly magazine for workers' libraries, is a gold mine of statistical reports from these institutions. Everywhere the story was the same: workers liked exciting fiction and science. Except for *Woman and Socialism,* books on economics and politics remained largely unread. Haeckel, Bölsche, Rudolf Bommeli, Aveling, Köhler, even Darwin himself—these were the nonfiction authors in demand. Zola, Edward Bellamy, the German classics, and cheap escape literature (E. Marlitt, Karl May, and the like) remained the fiction favorites.[17] These interests were stable and persistent, lasting beyond World War I. A questionnaire distributed to Leipzig workers taking evening courses in the early 1920s revealed that Bölsche was by far the favorite nonfiction author.[18]

Workingmen's memoirs, of which there are several dozen for the period before World War I, are another source of information on reading habits. Rarely do the memoirs mention Marx or even Kautsky. More typically the road to political awareness (if there is any) goes via popular science. Moritz Bromme, whose recently reissued *Lebensgeschichte eines modernen Fabrikarbeiters (Life Story of a Modern Factory Worker,* 1905) is probably the best known worker memoir, reports reading among others Darwin, Bebel, Karl Vogt, and Bommeli.[19] Nikolaus Osterroth, a clay miner, tells eloquently of the great impression Dodel's *Moses or Darwin?* made on him;[20] while Wenzel Holek, a Czech worker who learned German to read Darwinian literature, boasted that his personal collection contained volumes by Vogt, Ludwig Büchner, Lassalle, Haeckel, and Bölsche. Holek recommended Bölsche as a starting point for workers studying science. He once loaned a fellow worker (who had been a little puzzled by Haeckel) a copy of Bölsche's *Vom Bazillus zum Affenmenschen (From Bacillus to Ape-Man,* 1900). "That pleased him; he understood it," Holek recalls.[21] Nor are these reading lists isolated cases; they typify many others.

While one should not generalize too much from workers' memoirs, they are at least typical of a small articulate minority of self-educated workingmen. Just how large this literate minority was can only be roughly determined. The mere fact that in 1914 only 2,156,014 books were checked out of workers' libraries in all of Germany suggests the minority status of reading workers.[22] Workers' memoirs are filled with complaints that most fellow workers are ignorant and unread. Bromme, who worked in a machine factory in Gera, refers to himself and his small circle of reading friends as "we enlightened," and suggests that they were the only ones who read anything better than trash.[23] Wives and mothers may have been one inhibiting influence, for women were usually more closely tied to traditional values and frequently regarded serious reading as unchristian or impractical.[24] There is even some limited evidence that interest in serious reading was declining in the generation before World War I. Data from the woodworkers' library in Berlin for the period 1890–1913 show a dramatic drop in the relative interest in science in favor of escape fiction.[25] It is also suggestive that after the war Bölsche was most popular among older workers.[26]

But this is not the whole story. In some areas workers made up as much as half the patrons of city libraries.[27] The year 1906, for example, witnessed 400,000 workers taking some 1,600,000 books from public libraries in big cities.[28] The high circulation figures (several hundred thousand in the cases of Haeckel, Bölsche, Bebel, Zola, and Bellamy), combined with low prices of many editions, suggest that some workers owned a small personal library. Many workers were avid readers of the party or union papers, *Die Neue Welt,* and the various calendars for working-class homes. In 1900 Social Democratic newspapers had a total circulation of about 400,000;[29] by the eve of the war, about 1,000,000.[30] And for each copy there were probably four or five readers. Most workers at least claimed to be readers. In the survey by Levenstein mentioned above, only 4.5 percent of the metalworkers, 13.6 percent of the textile workers, and 26 percent of the miners admitted to not having read a book.[31]

Given the great diversity of the working class, it is very difficult to make generalizations about reading habits. Still, a few patterns emerge: the more skilled a worker, the more he read, printers being the most avid readers. Big-city workers read more than small-town workers, and those in the western part of the country more than those in the east. Women workers read a lot of cheap fiction but almost no serious books. Reading for all groups tended to increase in the winter and in bad economic times.[32] In 1891 Göhre estimated that intellectually aware workers in the machine factory where he worked comprised about 4 percent of the total. The rest he dismissed as ignorant.[33] Levenstein, writing twenty years later, was a bit more generous. On the basis of some 5,000 detailed questionnaires, he estimated that the "intellectual strata" of workers was 5.9 percent and the "mass strata" 64.1 percent. The rest fell somewhere in between. But there were great variations: whereas Silesian miners were 88 percent "mass" and only 1.2 percent "intellectual," Berlin metalworkers were only 24.6 percent "mass" and 14.7 percent "intellectual."[34]

In sum, there was a small but still significant minority of self-educated workingmen who knew their popular Darwinism. Reading the memoirs of these men, one is struck by their passionate belief in the efficacy of scientific knowledge as an agent of social change; reading was the central non-work experience of their lives. These serious readers were numerous enough to have been present in many, if not most, work places, and their influence as local informal opinion leaders was probably far beyond their numbers. If we can judge from the memoirs, they were treated with respect and seen as a source of authority. (Some were called "Herr Professor" by their comrades![35]) Many lower-echelon party and union functionaries as well as minor socialist journalists had risen from the ranks of the literate working class. Unlike the middle-class socialist intellectuals, these men had genuine ties to the workers and were more likely to influence (and vice versa) the vague, inarticulate opinions and desires of the "mass strata."[36] To understand the impact of socialism on the working masses it is therefore essential to appreciate the view of reality afforded by the Darwinian books which the articulate minority so eagerly read. As we shall see, the average workingman's *Weltanschauung* was a close replica of the content of these books.

Bebel's *Woman and Socialism,* the single most widely read nonfiction book among workers, was in the form of a popular anthropological tract. Bebel's aim was to make socialism comprehensible to the masses, a task that would elude Kautsky. Yet unlike Kautsky in his *Erfurt Program,* Bebel began not with an economic analysis of capitalist society but with man's (or woman's) primitive past. Elsewhere Bebel insisted on a clear distinction between natural and historical law;[37] but in *Woman and Socialism* that distinction was blurred, and history was firmly rooted in natural evolution. Change was an eternal part of human history, part of the whole animal world to which man belonged. Bebel largely ignored Marx, not to speak of dialectical, historical change; nor was there much talk of how socialist transformation would occur. The most obvious inference was that socialism was like any other stage in the world's natural history. Political and economic change to socialism had a *natural* justification. Under capitalism, said Bebel, class structure inhibited natural selection; those at the top were protected from competition and those at the bottom had no real chance. Only socialism could restore the natural balance: "The point in question, then, is, so to arrange social conditions that every human being will be given an opportunity for the untrammeled development of his nature, that the laws of development and adaptation—called Darwinism after Darwin—may be consciously and expediently applied to all human beings. But that will only be possible under socialism."[38] Bebel's analysis of capitalism (similar to Kautsky's) was really tacked onto the anthropology, splitting the book clumsily into two poorly related parts. Given what we know of working-class reading habits, it is fair to ask just how many readers even got through the later, more tedious sections of the book.

Turning to Darwinian literature as such, two names stand out: Bölsche and Haeckel. It might seem odd at first that Ernst Haeckel should find so much favor among workingmen. Haeckel was a vehement opponent of social democracy; he believed that, if anything, Darwinism was aristocratic. There are even traces of eugenic thought in some of his works. But it is all too easy to exaggerate the importance of Haeckel's political convictions. In his *Die Welträtsel (The Riddle of the Universe,* 1899),[39] the book through which most workers knew Haeckel, he stayed clear of politics almost entirely. Instead of a clear political line, what came through was an attack on so-called reactionary forces that conspire to suppress scientific enlightenment. Haeckel was most scornful of the Christian churches and schools, and here the workingman could empathize, for this seemed like an attack on fundamental and oppressive social institutions. The church, Haeckel contended, had enslaved people with an ignorant dualism that posited a bogus spiritual man apart from nature, thus preventing man from attaining his true rational potential. For Haeckel, Darwin showed the way to liberation by breaking the shackles of dualistic philosophy. The theory of evolution proved that all of nature—including man—was interrelated. Going beyond Darwin's modest claims, Haeckel then erected a Darwinian monism based on a material unity of the universe. Everything, including the "spiritual" activity of man, could be reduced to material causes and effects.

According to Haeckel's monism, the future of man was just a minuscule part of the future of materialistic nature. It sounds like a grim vision, but unlike the harsh materialism of the 1850s, Haeckel's materialism had a "silver lining" of romantic natural philosophy. His universe of matter was, like Gustav Fechner's, alive and permeated with soul or feeling. If the Christian God had been buried under a heap of invective, the God of nature (Goethe's *Gott-Natur*) stepped in to replace him. Science led directly to pantheism, said Haeckel. As men once went to church to worship, now they needed only to go out into the beauty of nature. Equipped with the marvelous techniques of science, all could experience the unraveling of the riddles of the universe.

Since for Haeckel there was no life after death, the monistic religion of science was totally this-worldly. Evolution was the guide to a higher rational consciousness. The future was uncertain, but there was hope. Through his very group struggle for existence, man had evolved natural protective feelings toward his own species. These feelings were the natural basis of a monistic ethics which, as Haeckel acknowledged, was no different from the Christian ethics. But now man's moral progress was rooted in an evolutionary understanding of nature. The monist knew *why* he must pursue truth, goodness, and beauty. Haeckel brandished an aggressive, even intolerant rationality against all the supposed forces of superstition. It was probably this negative side of Haeckel, the vicious polemics against already suspect institutions, that so endeared him to working-class readers. Reading Haeckel one gained the impression that Darwin was mankind's greatest liberator.

The appeal of Wilhelm Bölsche, the other great master of popular Darwinism, was more subtle and gentle—though no less powerful. A school dropout, Bölsche had begun his career in the 1880s as a novelist and literary critic.[40] Like many of the young literati in Berlin, he was deeply affected by the poverty and ignorance he saw around him. He began to travel in socialist circles, giving science lectures to workingmen and fighting on the side of his friend Bruno Wille for a workers' free theater. His hero was Darwin, but he was troubled by the failure of science to create a spiritually satisfying modern *Weltanschauung.* Bölsche's autobiographical novel *Die Mittagsgottin (The Noon Goddess),*[41] serialized in *Die Neue Welt* in 1892, embodied this inner struggle. The novel's protagonist, a young science writer and social activist, is driven by a sense of spiritual emptiness to abandon science and the urban struggle. He finds solace with a group of spiritualists in an idyllic castle in the Spreewald. As the foundation of his Darwinian scientific *Weltanschauung* is eroded by spiritualism, so too is his sense of social commitment. But when his spiritualist lover turns out to be a clever fake, the hero returns to the city and the arms of his working-class fiancée. Science is vindicated, and the focus of human endeavor is seen as the here and now struggle for social justice.

By its vague identification of science with progress and justice, the novel unwittingly dramatizes the failure of Darwinism to translate into a coherent political program. When Bölsche talked about finding a new *Weltanschauung,* he was really looking for a new religion. And like Haeckel, he found it by marrying Darwinism to the old idealistic nature philosophy of the early nineteenth century. But whereas Haeckel equivocated (or was just plain muddleheaded!), Bölsche openly repudiated materialism. Far from being a materialistic doctrine, Darwinism, he contended, confirmed the pan-psychic idealism of the romantics. All life and nonlife forms—there being no clear distinction between the two—were related on a great evolutionary scale; mind was present everywhere. Even the process of natural selection revealed mind and purpose because it was driving the universe toward greater harmony and beauty. The key element of Bölsche's view was love, the primeval attracting force of the universe and the "engine" of evolution. Bölsche's most famous book was significantly titled *Das Liebesleben in der Natur (Love Life in Nature,* 1898-1902).[42] In it he traced the evolution of love from the sexual orgies of day flies to love's spiritual manifestations in man's art, ethics, and religion.

This "erotic monism," as it might be called, flowed like a great river not only through *Liebesleben* but also through dozens of his other books whose total circulation ran into the millions—far exceeding that of Haeckel's *Welträtsel*.[43] Like Haeckel, Bölsche saw Darwinian monism as the new creed, transcending Christianity; but Bölsche had no scorn for Christianity, which he regarded as merely obsolete. To him science was a modern reformulation of the Bible. Adam became the symbolic primeval bacillus, while the teachings of Jesus paralleled the evolution of love as a protective natural principle. Evolutionary science was like a "Third Testament"—avision of a future of universal love binding mankind. Struggle he downplayed to a transitional, incomplete stage of evolution. Wrapped as it was in a package of piquant sexuality and lurid, effusive prose, this was a heady brew — a grandoise optimism saved from absurdity only by Bölsche's sincerity and sound factual base.

Neither Haeckel nor Bölsche offered the workingman any concrete hopes. They each tied man's future to the interminably slow process of natural evolution. Even Bölsche, who was sympathetic to socialism, could grasp it only as another expression of Darwinism.[44] At most he thought of socialism as the popularization of knowledge.[45] Both he and Haeckel were really envisioning a worldly alternative to heaven: a future of secularized Christian love. But by enclosing man in the process of natural evolution, they effectively shut off discussion of how any real transition to a cooperative future might come about. This was typical of Darwin popularizers; they had forged their views in opposition to Christian theology, not capitalist class structure. Aveling, Bommeli, Dodel, Köhler, and Büchner all believed that science, especially Darwinism, was intentionally being kept from the people to protect oppressive institutions. Once enlightenment was spread to the masses, justice could not be far behind. This was noble sentiment, but largely devoid of any political meaning. When Dodel in his *Moses or Darwin?* spoke of Darwinism's promise of "realizable and desirable happiness of all mankind during our lifetime, not beyond the grave,"[46] it was significant that he had reached the last page of the book. He had nowhere to go with such a claim.

Popular Darwinism was spread not only by scientific tracts; it also found its way into popular fiction, Zola's works being prime examples. Gripped by evolutionary thought, Zola saw man as primarily a biological being, a pawn of heredity and environment. This view is most strikingly evident in *Germinal*,[47] a book always near the top of the German workingman's list of favorite fiction. Étienne, the hero of *Germinal* who leads the great strike of coal miners in northern France, is an avid student of Darwin, or rather popular Darwinian tracts. The idea of struggle fills him with a religious-like fervor that overshadows his intellectual endeavors to understand the socialism of the First International. For Étienne the survival of the fittest means the ultimate triumph of the robust proletariat over the effete bourgeoisie. When the strike collapses and the men of the International are discredited, Étienne still retains his faith in revolution, but not for economic reasons. He believes that new, vigorous blood will naturally and inevitably overwhelm degeneracy. As Étienne leaves the scene at the end of the novel, the miners are back at work underground, but all around him nature is bursting out in the first flush of eternally recurrent spring. Here again hope for the working man springs not from historical action but from nature.

Nor was a reading of Edward Bellamy's utopian novel *Looking Backward* (1888)—probably the best-loved novel among working people—likely to promote revolutionary consciousness. Translated as *Im Jahre 2000,* the novel appeared in serial form in many socialist newspapers. It tells the story of a middle-class Bostonian, Julian West, who wakes up in the year 2000 after sleeping since 1887. During the hero's 113-year sleep, industrial society managed to solve all its social and economic problems. The state is now a gigantic co-op with all needs perfectly and harmoniously met. After a period of pleasurable social service, each individual is totally free to pursue personal interests. West's hosts explain that the great transition came about peacefully and naturally; all saw it coming and agreed on its desirability—no class conflict here.

Bellamy leaves the reader in the dark about the specifics of historical change. According to his postscript, the forecast is "in accordance with the principles of evolution,"[48] which entail a shift from a "bad Darwinian" society to a "good Darwinian" society. In 1887 society was a cruel free-for-all, demeaning man, stifling real opportunity. Now, in the year 2000, the Darwinian struggle has narrowed to a purely sexual selection and works toward the ultimate refinement of the race. All marry for love (a great boon to sustaining romantic interest in the story). The invisible hand of biological evolution, rather than historical action, has liberated man, and there is really nothing to do but to wait passively for the future to happen. Kautsky was quick to see that Bellamy's evolutionary vision lifted the burden of struggle from the proletariat. In his review of *Looking Backward* for *Die Neue Zeit,* he took Bellamy to task for his un-Marxist view of history and failure to deal with class struggle. Yet Kautsky proceeded to recommend the book highly because its entertaining view of a noncapitalist future would stimulate the working-class reader to further study. The worker would see through Bellamy's limitations, Kautsky predicted.[49]

Kautsky's wavering typified the Social Democratic party's inconsistency on the question of popular evolutionary literature. In spite of the obvious threat to revolutionary consciousness posed by such literature, the SPD actually did much to promote it. As early as 1876, the very first issue of the new entertainment magazine *Die Neue Welt* carried an article on Darwinism, contrasting it to the Bible and to teachings in schools. Later in the same year, the magazine also carried a picture of Darwin and an article on the origin of man.[50] Then in 1886 the first volume of the party's own low-priced *Internationale Bibliothek* was a Darwinian book, *Die Darwinsche Theorie* by Edward Aveling. Three more such books followed in the same series.[51] *Die Neue Zeit* (originally conceived as a popular monthly, though it never achieved that goal) also paid close attention to Darwinism. At the founding of the journal in 1883, Kautsky wrote that Darwinism would be central to the journal's political message. "The name itself is already a program," he said of Darwin.[52] Although Kautsky himself later decided that Darwinism and socialism had nothing to do with each other, *Die Neue Zeit* continued to follow popular science. Bölsche's *Liebesleben* was very favorably received, though the reviewer was a bit taken aback by the "tone of an uncle in the nursery."[53] Even Haeckel's *Welträtsel* found a sympathetic reception in the pages of *Die Neue Zeit*. Franz Mehring, the party's chief cultural critic, acknowledged that Haeckel was no friend of social democracy. But he went on to praise Haeckel for unwittingly rendering service to the proletariat. Haeckel was a good educator of the masses, Mehring said, even though his naturalistic materialism lacked a historical dimension.[54] The implication was that the proletarian reader could make the conceptual leap from natural to human history—adubious assumption, especially considering the relative difficulty of Haeckel's writing.

Other socialist publishers were equally keen to cater to the working-class taste for Darwinism. In 1908, *Vorwärts Verlag* put out Eduard David's *Referentenführer,* a list of recommended books to acquire political consciousness. Typically, David had high praise for Bölsche in particular.[55] A similar pattern is evident in a brochure put out by *Verlag der Leipziger Buchdruckerei* in 1914 as a guide for workers who wanted to acquire their own inexpensive libraries. The basic twenty-six-book, fifty-mark collection included five popular science works.[56] One of these, Grottewitz's guide for Sunday afternoon nature walks for workers (originally published by *Vorwärts Verlag* in 1905) contained a revealing introduction by Bölsche. Alienation from nature, Bölsche argued, was the great crisis of the time, and so an emotional yet informed "feeling for nature" was the closest thing to liberation for the modern worker. In effect, what Bölsche was doing— with tacit party sanction—was locating the origins of the worker's problems in the city itself rather than in class oppression. The worker would recover his lost humanity by returning to and comprehending nature, not by changing society politically. For Bölsche there was a golden future, but the key to it was held by Darwin, not Marx.[57]

Not everyone wanted or could afford a fifty-mark book collection (about two to three weeks' wages for the average worker). But almost every serious social democratic household could subscribe to one of the various workers' calendars. Among the little inspirational messages ("Golden Words") in the pages of these calendars, quotations from Darwin popularizers like Büchner and Haeckel were as frequent as those from Marx, Lassalle, or Engels. *Die Neue Welt Kalender* for 1909, for example, advised its readers that the theory of evolution "fills us with a happy confidence, insofar as it lets us hope that all the irrationality, injustice, and inadequacy that we find everywhere, but especially in our social order, will not continue forever; rather these are only steps in the development to higher, more complete forms of human community."[58] This is pure Bölsche, the apolitical optimism of popular Darwinism that would form the core of the workers' view of progress. And the calendars were not alone. By the eve of the war, the circulation of the easily readable *Die Neue Welt* had soared to 550,000, bringing a flood of popular science into working-class homes every week.[59]

The party's promotion among the masses of such evolutionary non-Marxist thought was a reflection of its larger failure to develop real alternatives to bourgeois culture. In theory, knowledge was supposed to be directly revolutionary. "Knowledge is power, power is knowledge,"[60] Liebknecht had asserted back in 1872. But a glance through the pages of *Die Neue Welt* is enough to belie these fighting words; it differed hardly at all from the "bourgeois" *Gartenlaube*. The simple fact was that the party was living off the progressive elements of bourgeois culture, of which popular Darwinism was an integral part.[61] That this was true not only in the case of popular Darwinism, but also in the case of naturalist literature and workers' education generally, reveals how broad the party's cultural problem really was.[62] On the one side were party regulars who wanted direct politicization through art and education ("dramatized Marx," one naturalist scoffed[63]); on the other were bourgeois radicals, often on the fringe of the party, who wanted to use art and education for the cultural elevation of the masses. The schism in the free theater movement in Berlin was a typical symptom of this divisiveness. In 1892 party regulars forced the expulsion of the *Freie Volksbühne's* founders, Bruno Wille and Bölsche, because under them the theater had offered mere educational entertainment rather than revolutionary agitation.[64] (Wille too was an avid Darwinist.) The same question came up again at the 1896 SPD Congress. *Die Neue Welt's* editor, Edgar Steiger, came under attack for printing so much naturalist literature. It was not only offensive in a family magazine but also unrevolutionary, some delegates said. Steiger's reply was significant: he argued that naturalism dissected reality with the tools of Darwinian materialism that all socialists accepted.[65] With Bebel's support, Steiger kept his job. It was no accident that Bölsche, the apostle of Darwinism, was on the side of cultural uplift rather than agitation. He believed that the enlightenment of the proletariat would eventually bear its own fruits—though what they would be was never too clear.

However much some in the party might deplore the "mere education" that popular Darwinism represented or the nonrevolutionary thought it implied, they seemed unwilling and powerless to stop it. Engels protested that *Die Neue Welt* was a bore, that science never scared anyone,[66] but the number of science articles merely increased, while references to Marx were almost impossible to find. Every issue of *Vorwärts* was filled with ads for workers' education, often including courses on evolution. Aveling called the workers' educational organizations "temples" of evolution.[67] Bölsche and others lectured and showed their slides to packed assemblies of workers.[68] Those involved in workers' education felt a special need to cover science because it was so slighted in the regular schools.[69] A typical cycle of lectures, aimed at both general and political education, was sponsored by the Berlin lithographers in 1911. Before turning to history and economics, the lectures considered "The Wonder of the Cosmos" and "From Primeval Animals to Man," hooking society onto nature. Well-known scientists shared the platform with prominent socialists, including both Eduard Bernstein and Rosa Luxemburg.[70]

The problem was that the theoretical relationship between Darwinism and Marxism was so complex that there was no practical way that the distinction could be made to the masses. Even those like Engels, Kautsky, and Bebel, usually careful to distinguish between Darwin's natural history and Marx's human history, were neither consistent nor really aware of how much their own thought was imbued with Darwinism. When Ludwig Woltmann told the party congress in 1899 that Darwinian evolution was familiar to the masses and thus ought to replace the difficult notion of dialectics, he was advocating what had already taken place in practice.[71] And why not? After all, most popular Darwinism taught rationality, struggle, the inevitability of change, and, above all, scepticism of Christianity—all virtues in the eyes of socialists. Breaking the church's hold on the worker's mind and heart was a prerequisite for the success of socialism. With the prestige of science running so high at the end of the nineteenth century, it seemed to make good practical sense—at least in the short run—to exploit the workingman's interest in evolution.

Those who wanted to link science directly to politics had a nearly impossible task. An amusing and revealing example of such an attempt is an 1897 article in *Die Neue Welt* on the canals of Mars, then thought to be artificial. The author remarked that these stupendous engineering achievements required an intelligence and technology far in advance of man's—which was only natural since Mars was older and life there had had more time to evolve. He then told his working-class readers that until capitalism was abolished, man would have no chance to catch up with the Martians.[72] Clearly they were already socialists! The clumsiness of the whole image points to the difficulty of enlisting science in the class struggle. Lenin himself might extol Haeckel's *Welträtsel* as a "weapon in the class struggle";[73] but revolutionary socialism paid a high price for this weapon. Science was imperious; it would not simply lend its prestige to socialism without bringing along a dangerously independent world view. Thus the sifting of Marxism through a Darwinian filter in the process of popularization meant that mass consciousness was inevitably different from what the party might have wished.

There is little evidence that the SPD imparted any real understanding of economics and politics to the masses before 1914. Max Weber was probably right when he remarked in 1895 that politically the workers were "far less mature than left-wing journalists would make them believe they are."[74] The caution and expediency of socialist politicians at the top of the party were reflected at the bottom by an almost complete lack of revolutionary consciousness. As mentioned, workers' memoirs rarely discussed Marx or the possibility of revolution; more frequently they paid tribute to Bellamy's influence.[75] Even those who later became party functionaries or journalists admitted that it took them years before they had any understanding of socialist theory.[76] When Levenstein did his poll in 1907–11, he found a very low state of class consciousness. Only a small minority told Levenstein that they ever thought about political or organizational questions.[77] When asked what they would do with more time, their favorite answer was not party or union work, but self-education.[78] Workers were more interested in nature than politics; they liked to walk in the woods, and their dream of what they would do with more money was to build a little house in the country.[79] Earning more money was more important to them than the victory of socialism![80] Their values differed little from those of the middle class.[81] And those who share society's values are more likely to want to join it than overthrow it.

The above analysis of workers' reading suggests that the wide diffusion of popular Darwinism may have played an important role in shaping these values. Marxism was tedious and difficult (even in simplified forms), and the conspicuous failure of its popularization left an intellectual and emotional vacuum which Darwinism rushed in to fill. Reading was only one of many influences on the workingman, but it is nonetheless striking to note how closely his values paralleled those of Darwinian literature. Obviously popular Darwinism struck a resonant chord in workers' experiences. The world as the worker saw it was indeed a *Kampf ums Dasein*, a struggle for jobs and money; a struggle just to live through a sixty-hour week or keep up with the brutal demands of piecework. No doubt the worker could also experience exploitation on a daily basis, but it was hard to integrate this experience into the complex theoretical system of Marxism. The advantage of the Darwinian *Kampf ums Dasein* was that it was not only concrete but also comprehensible within the relatively simple theoretical scheme of evolution. In Darwinism it was easy to move back and forth between mundane reality and theory; in Marxism only the very sophisticated could do so. Granted, most workers said they were social democrats, but they meant it in a Darwinian rather than a Marxist way. Many had come to socialism via a destruction of their Christianity prompted by Darwinism. For them the gripping question had been (as Dodel had it) "Moses or Darwin?"—not " Moses or Marx?" Having chosen Darwin, they often went no further, being either unaware of Marx or unable to distinguish him from Darwin. Their *Weltanschauung* remained grounded in the familiar anti-Christian evolutionary monism.[82] Socialism, which countless workers referred to as a religion or a "new gospel," became a peculiar mixture of science and emotional commitment to a brighter future.[83] Marxist socialism already had a pseudoreligious strain; the infusion of popular Darwinism could only deepen and broaden that strain.

When the workingman spoke of the future, he used the emotional yet naturalistic language of popular Darwinism. Here Levenstein is an invaluable source, for he encouraged the workers to give their philosophy in their own words. Many wrote sizable essays, sometimes inarticulate, sometimes eloquent, frequently both. One metalworker wrote movingly: "Oh, I think so deeply, but writing, that I can't do."[84] Levenstein found that hopes for the future were almost invariably vague—dignity, justice, love, brotherhood, and the like. But all was in "the foggy-gray distance," as one young miner put it.[85] Another was content to die in a "social democratic sense!"[86] But the future did not seem to be graspable for these men. It was not a tangible result of progress, but a formless cosmic development. It would inevitably, as that almost magic word had it, "evolve." "Everything evolves," as one miner put it.[87] And therein lay the hope. Not a few had succumbed to the despair of a hard life, but another young miner spoke for the many who still had hope: "Yes, it will get better because the whole of evolution is pointed toward something great, to the realization of a higher stage of culture when we will finally separate from the animal kingdom."[88] Here speaks the marriage of Marx and Darwin.

Not only did nature give hope for the future, but it was also an object of worship in the present. Most workers denied to Levenstein that they believed in God, but it is clear that they meant the Christian God.[89] They referred repeatedly to the God in nature so beloved by Haeckel and especially Bölsche. "I believe in Nature," remarked one metalworker.[90] "I profess the monistic world view," said another.[91] These men saw the purity and promise of nature as an antidote to the misery and ugliness of city life. Their views were romantic and arcadian (not surprising perhaps, since the rural life was not too far in the past for many—just far enough to be enveloped in an idealized glow). Somehow evolution would bring that little house in the country for their descendants. That such views persisted into the 1920s is a tribute to the power of popular Darwinism. Gertrud Hermes's study of the workers taking workingmen's courses in Leipzig in the early 1920s reveals continuing faith in Darwinian science as a substitute religion: "The core of their world of thought is the theory of evolution. It is the beginning and end of the workers' natural philosophy; it recurs in the most varied forms as a leitmotif in their testimonies,"[92] says Hermes. Their faith in the future, she adds, comes not from Marx, but from Darwin, as befits a group whose favorite nonfiction author was Bölsche. Similarly, Paul Piechowski, who surveyed Berlin workers in 1927, found that when workers were asked their *Weltanschauung,* they would often reply "Darwinism," "pantheism," or "monism."[93] He concluded from his questionnaires that a "scientific pantheism meets us at every turn: God-Nature."[94]

This deification of Darwinian nature inevitably had a debilitating effect on revolutionary consciousness. Darwinism offered no political solution to the proletariat's problems. It could just as easily be used to support bourgeois society as to undermine it. But even if interpreted as a theory of radical change, Darwinism tended to obscure the role of praxis in the Marxist revolutionary equation. Seen from a Darwinian perspective, the proletariat no longer worked in tandem with inexorable historical forces to create its own destiny. The focus of change was shifted away from human relationships (and thus out of human control) onto nature at large. Man's development, in this Darwinian view, was no longer a result of class struggle, but only a small facet of an ever-improving universe. Once human history was subsumed by cosmic evolution, the vision of a greater future receded into oblivion and the will to revolutionary action atrophied. This is not to suggest that popular Darwinism blocked the understanding of economic exploitation or class interests, only that it interfered with a full understanding of the meaning of socialist liberation.

It is tempting to suggest that the monistic evolutionism of Darwin popularizers translated directly into evolutionary socialism. But this would be misleading. There was no clear lineup of forces in the SPD on the meaning and importance of Darwinism. The economic and political questions raised by Bernstein and other revisionists were largely irrelevant to the continued mass interest in Darwinism. Revisionism's retreat from historical necessity was more likely to open the way to Kantian ethics than to Darwinian natural necessity. The wide and deep diffusion of popular Darwinism tended to work in favor of moderating forces within German social democracy. As did the exigencies of parliamentary politics, popular Darwinism helped to push the party in the direction of an idealistic radical democracy.

Playwright Karl Sternheim dramatized this point well in his play *Tabula Rasa* (1916), which treats Darwinian monism as a force that makes socialism bourgeois. In the play Sternheim contrasts a revolutionary firebrand with a humanitarian, moderate socialist as the two compete for the sympathies of workers in a glass factory. The latter, Artur, is an avid Bölsche fan; he regards Bölsche as a kind of demigod and prophet of the coming age. Reading *Liebesleben* (with his fiancée) he exclaims: "If anything could be dearer to me than the ideal of social democracy, it would be monism."[95] Artur pleads for the establishment of a huge workers' library that would help raise everyone up to the bourgeois level. Artur's political philosophy seems to be the only logical application of Bölschean principles to the social struggle. Change will come, "but not by violence, rather by the peaceful path of evolution. The citizen with equal rights will take over the place of the privileged. Social democracy does not destroy the present society and reduce all its members to the proletariat; rather it raises the worker from the position of a proletarian into that of a citizen and universalizes the bourgeoisie."[96] Here indeed is the ultimate blow to the revolution: the transformation of evolution into upward mobility. Perhaps Sternheim overstated his case, but the point is sound. It was no accident that those articulate workingmen who wrote memoirs were typically Majority Socialists after the war.[97] The heavy dose of bourgeois culture that these men had absorbed while educating themselves took its toll on their radicalism.

Darwinian monism was a poor ally of revolutionary Marxism. On a theoretical level the two did not mix well; indeed the monism of the sort peddled by Haeckel and Bölsche precluded Marxism, if only for the obvious reason that monism was by definition undialectical. But there were other, more practical obstacles to an alliance. However much popular Darwinism might resemble socialism on the surface, it resisted conversion to a political ideology. It was really just as easy for the Right to stake out a claim in Darwinian territory as for the Left. The closest Darwinian monists could get to even pseudopolitical organizational forms were the Ethical Culture and Free Thought movements. Both advocated a rational culture based on secular humanism, and both aroused the suspicion of socialists. If Darwinism had an ideological role to play on the Left, it was as a weapon against antiscientific, antimodern opponents of the progressive bourgeoisie. To the extent that socialism still had a vested interest in the outcome of this battle, Darwinism was a needed ally. But to the extent that socialism had to go beyond this battle, Darwinian views among the masses could only be an ideological drag.

NOTES

1. Quoted by Gertrude Himmelfarb, *Darwin and the Darwinian Revolution* (London, 1959), p. 349.

2. It was long believed that Marx had tried to dedicate either the second volume or the English translation of *Kapital* to Darwin and that Darwin had refused because he did not want to be publicly associated with atheism. It has recently been shown that the Darwin letter on which this inference was based was not to Marx but to Edward Aveling who wanted to dedicate his *The Student's Darwin* to Darwin. See Lewis S. Feuer, "The Case of the 'Darwin-Marx' Letter: A Study in Socio-Literary Detection," *Encounter* 51 (no. 4 October 1978), pp. 62–78.

3. The phrase *Kampf ums Dasein* appeared in the 1871 edition of Georg Buchmann's *Geflügelte Worte,* a popular guide to "educated" conversation.

4. George Lichtheim, *Marxism: An Historical and Critical Study* (New York/ Washington, 1961), p. 244. On the relationship between Marxism and Darwinism see also Dieter Groh, "Marx, Engels und Darwin: Naturgesetzliche Entwicklung oder Revolution?" *Politische Vierteljahresschrift* 8 (1967), pp. 544–59; Erhard Lucas, "Marx' and Engels' Auseinandersetzung mit Darwin," *International Review of Social History* 9 (1964), pp. 433–69; Hans-Josef Steinberg, *Sozialismus und deutsche Sozialdemokratie: Zur Ideologie der Partei vor dem 1. Weltkrieg,* 3rd ed. (Bonn/Bad Godesberg, 1972), pp. 43–60.

5. Lichtheim, p. 243.

6. August Bebel, *Aus Meinem Leben,* 3 vols. (Stuttgart, 1911), vol. 2, pp. 263–64.

7. Francis Darwin (ed.), *The Life and Letters of Charles Darwin,* 2 vols. (New York, 1896), vol. 2, p. 413.

8. Wilhelm Bock, *Im Dienst der Freiheit: Freud und Leid aus sechs Jahrzehnten Kampf und Aufstieg* (Berlin, 1927), p. 35; Wilhelm Keil, *Erlebnisse eines Sozialdemokraten,* 2 vols. (Stuttgart, 1947), vol. 1, pp. 79–80.

9. Paul Göhre, *Drei Monate Fabrikarbeiter und Handwerkbursche* (Leipzig, 1891), p. 212.

10. J.S. and E.F., "Was lesen die organisierten Arbeiter in Deutschland?" *Die Neue Zeit* 13 (no. 1, 1894–95), p. 154.

11. A.H.T. Pfannkuche, *Was liest der deutsche Arbeiter?* (Tübingen/Leipzig, 1900), foldout appendix.

12. Ibid., p. 59.

13. Wilhelm Nitschke, "Wie und nach welcher Richtung entwickelt sich das Lesebedürfnis der Arbeiterschaft?" *Sozialistische Monatschefte* 19 (no. 1, 1913), p. 366. Friedrich Stampfer recalls taking Katusky's *Erfurt Program* out of a workers' library. The first twenty pages were well worn, but the rest of the book was untouched. See Stampfer's *Erfahrungen und Erkenntnisse: Aufzeichnungen aus meinem Leben* (Cologne, 1957), p. 14.

14. Pfannkuche, pp. 8, 9, 60. A survey done in Leipzig at the same time yielded the same favorite authors. See Konrad Haenisch, "Was lesen die Arbeiter?" *Die Neue Zeit* 18 (no. 2, 1899–1900), pp. 691–96.

15. E. Graf, "Die Bildung der Berliner Arbeiter," *Zentralblatt für Volksbildungswesen* 9 (1909), p. 22.

16. Adolf Levenstein, *Die Arbeiterfrage* (Munich, 1912), pp. 388–403.

17. See for example the article "Statistisches über die Bildung Berliner Arbeiter," *Der Bibliothekar* 2 (1910), pp. 168–69. See also Deubner, "Das Lesebedürfnis der gewerblichen Arbeiter," *Concordia* 19 (1912), p. 260. In Vienna the story was the same; only 2-3 percent of all books lent were socialist literature; the figures are cited by Günther Roth in his article "Die kulturelle Bestrebungen der Sozialdemokratie im kaiserlichen Deutschland." In *Moderne deutsche Sozialgeschichte,* ed. Hans-Ulrich Wehler (Cologne/Berlin, 1966), p. 361.

18. Gertrud Hermes, *Die geistige Gestalt des marxistischen Arbeiters* (Tübingen, 1926), pp. 317–23.

19. Moritz Bromme, *Lebensgeschichte eines modernen Fabrikarbeiters* (Frankfurt, 1971), p. 287.

20. Nikolaus Osterroth, *Vom Beter zum Kämpfer* (Berlin, 1920), p. 149.

21. Wenzel Holek, *Vom Handwerker zum Jugenderzieher* (Jena, 1921), p. 103.

22. Manfred Häckel, "Arbeiterbewegung und Literatur," *100 Jahre Reclams Universal Bibliothek, 1867–1967* (Leipzig, 1967), p. 395.

23. Bromme, p. 287. See also Otto Buchwitz, *50 Jahre Funktionär der deutscher Arbeiterbewegung* (Berlin, 1949), p. 47; August Winnig, *Frührot: Ein Buch von Heimat und Jugend* (Stuttgart, 1924), p. 310.

24. Bromme, p. 287; Bruno Bürgel, *Vom Arbeiter zum Astronomen: Der Aufstieg eines Lebenskämpfers* (Berlin, 1950), p. 42. Also Günther Roth, *The Social Democrats in Imperial Germany* (Totowa, N.J., 1963), p. 218. Adelheid Popp tells of the astonishment she aroused by her serious reading. See Adelheid Popp, *The Autobiography of a Working Woman,* trans. F.C. Harvey, intro. by August Bebel, (London, 1912), p. 102.

25. Nitschke, p. 366. It is possible that the high percentage of escape fiction reflects the desires of the workers' wives and daughters. See Roth, "Die kulturelle Bestrebungen," p. 361. A recent study of workers' readings suggests that the decline in serious reading was general throughout Germany. See Dieter Langewiesche and Klaus Schönhoven, "Arbeiterbibliotheken und Arbeiterlektüre im Wilhelminischen Deutschland," *Archiv für Sozialgeschichte* 16 (1976), pp. 166 ff.

26. Hermes, pp. 317–23.

27. Deubner, p. 259. Pfannkuche estimated that the workers made up 25 percent of the *Volksbibliothek* clientele. Pfannkuche, p. 10.

28. Langewiesche and Schönhoven, p. 151.

29. Friedrich Apitzsch, "Die Deutsche Tagespresse unter dem Einfluss des Sozialistengesetzes" (Diss., Leipzig, 1928), pp. 100–101.

30. Roth, *Social Democrats,* p. 247.

31. Levenstein, pp. 382–405.

32. Pfannkuche, p. 19; Deubner, p. 259; Levenstein, pp. 388–403; Langewiesche and Schönhoven, pp. 137 ff.

33. Göhre, p. 111.

34. Levenstein, p. 13.

35. Bürgel, p. 36; Count Stenbock-Fermor, *My Experiences as a Miner,* trans. Frances, Countess of Warwick (London/New York, 1930), p. 67.

36. When discussing the Levenstein survey, Barrington Moore, Jr. makes the same case. See his book *Injustice: The Social Basis of Obedience and Revolt* (White Plains, N.Y., 1978), p. 195.

37. See Bebel's review of Ludwig Woltmann's *Die Darwinsche Theorie und der Sozialismus* in *Die Neue Zeit* 17 (no. 1, 1898–99), pp. 484–89.

38. August Bebel, *Woman and Socialism,* trans. Meta L. Stern-Hebe (New York, 1910), p. 249.

39. The following discussion is based largely on Haeckel's *The Riddle of the Universe at the Close of the Nineteenth Century,* trans. Joseph McCabe (New York/London, 1900).

40. This and other information on Bölsche comes from my dissertation *Between Poetry and Science: Wilhelm Bölsche as Scientific Popularizer* (University of Wisconsin, 1975).

41. Wilhelm Bölsche, *Die Mittagsgottin: Ein Roman aus dem Geisteskampf der Gegenwart,* 3 vols. (Stuttgart, 1891).

42. Bölsche, *Das Liebesleben in der Natur: Eine Entwicklungsgeschichte der Liebe,* 3 vols. (Florence/Leipzig, 1898–1902).

43. Almost all of Bölsche's seventeen little books in the *Kosmos Bändchen* series sold more than 100,000 copies. The first of this series, *Die Abstammung des Menschen* (Stuttgart, 1904), sold 140,000 copies and was widely read by workingmen. Haeckel's *Welträtsel* sold about 460,000 copies by 1927.

44. Bölsche, "Sozialismus und Darwinismus," *Der Sozialistische Akademiker* 2 (1896), p. 269.

45. Kelly, p. 115.

46. Arnold Dodel, *Moses or Darwin?* trans. Frederick Dodel (New York, 1891), p. 345.

47. Emile Zola, *Germinal,*.trans. L.W. Tancock (Baltimore, 1934).

48. Edward Bellamy, *Looking Backward, 2000–1887* (New York, 1951), p. 272.

49. Karl Kautsky, "Die jüngste Zukunftsroman," *Die Neue Zeit* 7 (1889), pp. 268–76.

50. See *Die Neue Welt* 1 (1876), pp. 5–8, 40–42, 141.

51. In series 1, two out of the ten volumes were on popular Darwinism; in series 2, two out of four.

52. Quoted by Steinberg, p. 51.

53. *Die Neue Zeit* 21 (1902), pp. 699–700.

54. Franz Mehring, "Die Welträtsel," *Die Neue Zeit* 18(1899–1900), pp. 417–21.

55. Eduard David, *Referentenführer* (Berlin, 1908), p. 19.

56. Häckel, pp. 398–99.

57. Bölsche, "Zur Erinnerung an Curt Grottewitz," foreword to Curt Grottewitz, *Sonntage eines Grosstädters in der Natur* (Berlin, 1905).

58. Quoted by Steinberg, p. 141.

59. See the article "Die Neue Welt." In *Lexikon Sozialistischer Deutscher Literatur* (Leipzig, 1973), pp. 380–82.

60. This was the title of his speech at the opening ceremonies of the *Dresdener Arbeiterbildungs-Verein.*

61. At the end of 1899 the *Berliner Illustrierte Zeitung* surveyed its largely middle-class readership about their opinions on the outgoing century. The readers voted Darwin's *Origin* as the most influential book written in the century. They considered Darwin the third greatest thinker of the century, after von Moltke (!) and Kant. See Friedrich Luft (ed.), *Facsimile Querschnitt durch die Berliner Illustrierte Zeitung* (Munich, 1965), pp. 46 ff.

62. For a good analysis of the relationship of radical intellectuals to the SPD, see Vernon L. Lidtke, "Naturalism and Socialism in Germany," *American Historical Review* 79 (no. 1 February 1974), pp. 14–37.

63. Ibid., p. 25.

64. Kelly, pp. 109–112.

65. *Protokoll über die Verhandlungen des Parteitages der Sozialdemokratischen Partei Deutschlands, abgehalten zu Gotha vom 11. bis 16. Oktober 1896* (Berlin, 1896), pp. 78–85.

66. *Lexicon Sozialistischer Deutscher Literatur,* p. 381.

67. Edward Aveling, *Die Darwinsche Theorie* (Stuttgart, 1887), p. 71.

68. Many workers recall taking such courses. See for example Joseph Joos, *Krisis in der Sozialdemokratie* (Mönchen-Gladbach, 1911), p. 120; Franz Bergg, *Ein Proletarierleben,* ed. Nikolaus Wetter (Frankfurt, 1913), p. 56; Keil, pp. 79–80.

69. See Zadek's remarks in support of the Berliner Arbeiterbildungsschule in *Vorwärts* (no. 56, supplement 2, March 8, 1894).
70. Langewiesche and Schönhoven, p. 146.
71. *Hannover Protokoll* (Berlin, 1899), p. 148.
72. Th. Overbeck, "Erde und Mars," *Die Neue Welt* (1897), pp. 284–86.
73. V.I. Lenin, "Materialismus und Emperiokritizismus." In *Werke* (Berlin, 1962), vol. 14, p. 353.
74. Quoted by Eda Sagarra, *Tradition and Revolution: German Literature and Society, 1830–1890* (New York, 1971), p. 263.
75. Wolfgang Emmerich (ed.), *Proletarische Lebensläufe: Autobiographische Dokumente zur Entstehung der Zweiten Kultur in Deutschland* (Hamburg, 1974), vol. 1, p. 304. On Bellamy's influence see Bürgel, p. 50; Keil, pp. 104–5.
76. Popp, p. 87; Carl Severing, *Mein Lebensgang: Vom Schlösser zum Minister,* 2 vols. (Cologne, 1950), vol. 1, p. 34; Alfons Petzold, *Aus dem Leben und der Werkstätte eines Werdenden* (Vienna/Leipzig, 1913), p. 56. Men like Otto Buchwitz, for whom class-consciousness came early and easily, were the exception. See Buchwitz, pp. 25–29. In *Mein Kampf* Hitler claimed that not one worker in a thousand understood anything of Marx's *Kapital*. See his *Mein Kampf* (Boston, 1971), p. 372. This may not have been a bad guess. Friedrich Stampfer estimated that in 1885 in his industrial town of Brunn there were only a few dozen men (out of a population of 80,000) who knew anything about Marx. See Stampfer, p. 10.
77. Levenstein, pp. 115, 123, 130.
78. Ibid., pp. 187, 198, 212.
79. Ibid., p. 213.
80. Ibid., pp. 213–42.
81. Moore makes the same point, but makes no attempt to link it to the influence of Darwinism. Moore, pp. 216–17.
82. Bürgel, p. 49; Osterroth, p. 149; Karl Scheffler, quoted by Hermann Bertlein, *Jugendleben und Soziales Bildungsschichksal* (Hannover, 1966), p. 175. The same theme appears repeatedly in the testimonies given to Levenstein in *Die Arbeiterfrage,* as well as in his *Aus der Tiefe. Arbeiterbriefe: Beiträge zur Seelenanalyse moderner Arbeiter* (Berlin, 1909). Likewise, Fritz Bolle, who worked on construction sites in the early 1930s, recalls that discussions with the old "gelernte Sozialisten" always started from the assumption that Marx and Darwin were the same. See Bolle, "Darwinismus und Zeitgeist," *Zeitschrift für Religions- und Geistesgeschichte* 14 (1962), p. 150.
83. Ernst Preczang, *Rückblick* (unpublished), quoted by Emmerich, pp. 288–89; Otto Krille, *Unter dem Joch: Die Geschichte einer Jugend,* ed. Ursula Münchow (Berlin, 1975), p. 96; Severing, vol. 1, p. 34; Keil, pp. 79–80. Also, throughout Levenstein, *Die Arbeiterfrage.*
84. Levenstein, *Arbeiterfrage,* p. 381.
85. Ibid., p. 288.
86. Ibid., p. 215.
87. Ibid., p. 297.
88. Ibid., p. 291.
89. Ibid., pp. 336, 343, 353.
90. Ibid., p. 348.
91. Ibid., p. 349.
92. Hermes, p. 159.

93. Paul Piechowski, *Proletarischer Glaube: Die religiöse Gedankenwelt der organisierten deutschen Arbeiterschaft nach sozialistischen und kommunistischen Selbstzeugnissen* (Berlin, 1927), p. 188.

94. Ibid., p. 123.

95. Karl Sternheim, *Tabula Rasa*. In *Dramen* (Berlin, 1964), vol. 2, p. 231.

96. Ibid., p. 188.

97. Emmerich, p. 25.

CHAPTER EIGHT

Science and Religion in Early Modern Europe

H.G. Koenigsberger

Ever since Max Weber pointed to the development of modern science as one of the characteristic features of European civilization,[1] historians have proposed a variety of reasons for this phenomenon.[2] These proposals have included attempts to trace connections between certain Protestant religious doctrines and the "scientific revolution" of the seventeenth century — in analogy to Weber's own attempts to derive the capitalist spirit from the Protestant ethic.[3] I do not intend to enter the controversies about these or other current theories but rather to propose a hitherto neglected aspect of the development of modern science. It is meant as an addition to a composite picture and not a criticism or rejection of any of its generally accepted or debated components.

Some years ago I attempted to show by a kind of inversion of Weber's approach that as religious sensibilities declined in Europe from the Renaissance onward, there appeared a new psychological need, a kind of emotional void, which came to be filled primarily by music. This happened not so much by a direct opposition between music and religion, but rather through the longstanding alliance between them which allowed music to play an increasingly important and eventually preponderant emotional role in the European psyche. Non-European societies witnessed no similar decline of religious sensibilities, or at least not until much later. They missed one important psychological stimulus for the specifically elaborate development of music which Weber had detected in Europe.[4]

I want to argue a parallel case for religion and science. I shall take the phenomenon of secularization of European civilization for granted. This phenomenon started slowly in the later Middle Ages and the Renaissance and proceeded more and more rapidly and noticeably in the seventeenth century and from then onward. At that stage it was a phenomenon primarily of the educated classes, and much more than in the case of religion and music, we are here concerned with a small intellectual minority. This fact will allow us to take the role of theology in intellectual life as a rough measure of religious sensibilities. At least for intellectuals, secularization meant the emancipation of systematic thinking from the control of theology and theologians. This involved the gradual relegation of theology to a more or less exclusive concern with doctrine and morals. This happened simultaneously with a strong emotional and intellectual revulsion against the theologians' concentration on doctrinal controversies, for the bitter results of such controversies were only too apparent. Traditionally, young intellectuals in search of wisdom had chosen to be theologians, almost as a matter of course. Now it seemed to many of them that theology had become too narrow and sometimes even dangerous and destructive, while natural philosophy appeared as an intellectually more promising and emotionally more satisfying pursuit.

Historically, this shift in the choice of an intellectual career was somewhat masked by the available career structure for highly gifted young men. Jobs for pure scientists were few, and universities in both Catholic and Protestant countries continued to be controlled by the churches. It was often necessary to become a clergyman, whatever one's primary interests. There was no necessary contradiction. At least until the eighteenth century, very few of those interested in science were antireligious, but increasingly it was the pursuit of science which became the central interest of an important group of European intellectuals. For most of these men religion had not become unimportant, let alone an object of hostility. They approached religion by a long journey through natural philosophy, and this journey came to absorb more of their interests and energies. By the eighteenth and certainly the nineteenth century, natural philosophy had become for many of its most distinguished practitioners virtually self-justifying — a psychologically satisfying substitute for the former pursuit of religion, theology, and personal salvation — even while many scientists were unaware of this substitution and would not have admitted it. This phenomenon played an important part in that very distinctive European achievement — the development of modern science.

In the later Middle Ages there was hardly any conflict between religion and natural science. Such conflict would have been almost unthinkable, for the most important religious and philosophical traditions of the time emphasized the basic harmony of the total created world, the world of ideas as well as the physical universe. This could be seen in different ways and with different emphases. From Plato came the argument that the world had to contain all possible kinds of things, and this later developed into the idea of a "Great Chain of Being."[5] From Aristotle came a coherent hierarchical model of the physical world. Both ideas had been Christianized without great difficulty, for they did not contradict the biblical teaching of God's creation of the world and everyting in it.

A number of tricky philosophical and theological problems could arise when the implications of the different traditions were pursued. But the conflicts between different schools of philosophy and theology were not usually seen as arising out of any antithesis between a scientific and theological approach. Even the Ockhamists' denial of the possibility of a rational understanding of divine creation did not produce such a conflict. On the contrary, the Ockhamists and Nominalists who believed in the validity of experience, as well as of revelation, were often the keenest students of the physical world. With very little exaggeration, the Platonist Nicholas of Cusa wrote in 1440: "All our greatest philosophers and theologians unanimously assert that the visible universe is a faithful reflection of the invisible, and that from creatures we can rise to a knowledge of the Creator, 'in a mirror and in a dark manner,' as it were."[6]

Cusa himself then went on to propound a revolutionary new view of the universe that contradicted the Aristotelian model in which the Earth was the fixed center of the universe. While Cusa arrived at his conclusions partly by mathematical reasoning, he started not from systematic observation of natural phenomena, as a modern scientist would and as Aristotle had done, but from a theological premise: God is the absolute maximum and minimum, and this means that God is totality. He is the sum of all things, although not in their own form but in his. Thus, by analogy, the reality of line is in the dimensionless point, and the reality of motion is in rest, its absolute minimum, and this is parallel to the relation between God and the Universe. In God all opposites coincide. In God the center and circumference of a circle or sphere are identical. Therefore the Earth cannot be at the center of the universe nor can the universe be finite, because center and circumference can exist only in God. Equally, the Earth cannot be at rest, for only God can be at rest.

Only at this point, having established his indefinite and essentially relativistic universe on theological principles, Cusa introduces observation into his argument to explain our apparently contradictory observational experience. How is it that we see the dome of the heavens above us, as we do, unless we stand at its center? We do, answers Cusa, but so would an observer standing on another planet or on a star or anywhere else in the universe.[7] As to the movement of the apparently stationary earth.

> it is only by reference to something fixed that we detect the movement of anything. How would a person know that a ship was in movement, if, from the ship in the middle of the river, the banks were invisible to him and he was ignorant of the fact that water flows? Therein we have the reason why every man, whether he be on earth, in the sun, or on another planet, always has the

impression that all other things are in movement whilst he himself is in a sort of immovable center; he will certainly always choose poles which will vary accordingly as his place of existence is the sun, the earth, the moon, Mars, etc. In consequence, there will be a *machina mundi* whose center, so to speak, is everywhere, whose circumference is nowhere, for God is its circumference and center and He is everywhere and nowhere.[8]

It is possible to see the origins of Cusa's concept of the crucial importance of the place of an observer in the contemporary development of the theory of perspective in drawing and of projection in cartography. Cusa was the first to apply the principles of artists and mapmakers to cosmology in conjunction with a theological approach.[9] It was a classic case of studying the "two books" in conjunction, the book of God's word — the Bible — and the book of nature — God's creation — and arriving at startling conclusions in both theology and cosmology. There is not the slightest hint of conflict. The idea that Cusa was a pantheist with heretical views derived from his scientific ideas was a complete misunderstanding. The church never doubted his theological orthodoxy.

Cusa's cosmology was largely ignored, both by his contemporaries and for the next 150 years, until Giordano Bruno. The reason is probably that Cusa's argumentation was hard to follow and that, for all the esteem accorded to his theological and political work, his theory of the universe did not address itself to current intellectual problems. Even after Bruno, since cosmology was then set on a very different path, Cusa's view was regarded as something of a curiosity until the development of relativity theory led to a reappraisal of his astonishing argumentation.

By the first half of the sixteenth century, large areas of traditional late-medieval scientific beliefs were coming under attack. Much of this was due to the discovery and publication of hitherto unknown texts of the ancients which contradicted Aristotle or Galen. Some of it was the result of a more critical attitude toward established authority, even a delight in cocking a snook at its great names, coupled with a typically Renaissance assurance of one's own merits. Paracelsus certainly had no doubts about these: "What asses will you appear when Theophrastus [Paracelsus] will be prince of this realm [of true knowledge]? How will it seem to you when you will have to accept my philosophy and you will shit on your Pliny and Aristotle and piss on your Albertus [Magnus], Thomas [Aquinas], Scotus, etc., and when you will say: they lie beautifully and subtly . . . . How will it seem to you when I shall mess up your heaven and the [constellation of the] Dragon shall gobble up your Avicenna adn your Galen?"[10] A physician had to be knowledgeable in three fields — philosophy, astronomy, and alchemy. The professors of the great medical schools of Paris, Montpellier, Salerno, Vienna, Wittenberg, knew nothing of any of these, for this profession depends not on the Holy Ghost but on "the light of nature . . . . The Holy

Ghost teaches us faith, but natural matters belong to nature and therefore must be learnt from nature."[11]

Setting up "the light of nature" in opposition to the Holy Ghost was a significant shift in heuristic method, but for Paracelsus it meant neither a rejection of religious inspiration nor even the banishment of religion from the study of medicine. He drew no clear line between religion and science, astrology and astronomy, or between his religious and natural philosophy. His aim seems to have been to use the "light of nature" to test and confirm his mystical religious beliefs.[12] His style was reminiscent of the contemporary religious reformers. Some called him the "Medical Luther," although he rejected this clearly dangerous title. He was quite capable of inventing his own titles. But the enormous enthusiasm he evoked among his students was due, just as in Luther's case, not only to the attraction of his own teaching, but also to the eternal delight university students take in the deflation of pompous authority.

Scientists much less flamboyant than Paracelsus found themselves equally critical of established views backed by theological authority. The Belgian anatomist Vesalius was appalled by established theories of the brain propounded by scholastic philosophers:

> If by accurate and painstaking examination of the parts of the brain and from an observation of the other parts of the body, the use of which is obvious even to one little practised in dissection, some analogy were traceable, or if I could reach any probable conclusion, I would set it out, if I could do so without injury to our Most Holy Religion. For who — Oh Immortal God — can fail to be astonished at the host of contemporary philosophers and even theologians who detract ridiculously from the divine and most wonderful contrivance (*admirabili machinae*) of man's brain. For they fabricate, like a Prometheus out of their own dreams — dreams blaspheming the Founder (*Conditor*) of the human fabric — some image of the brain, while they refuse to see that structure which the Maker of Nature has wrought, with incredible foresight, to accommodate to the actions of the body. Putting before themselves the image which they have formed, which abounds in so many incongruent (*inartificiosis*) monstrosities, little do they heed — oh shame! — the impiety into which they lure the tender minds which they instruct, when these, no longer mere students, yearn to search out Nature's craftsmanship, and many with their own hands pry into [the parts of] man and of other creatures which are handed into their power.

When he was a student at Louvain, Vesalius continued, the lecturer who taught Aristotle's *De Anima* was "a theologian by profession and therefore, like the other instructors at that Academy, ready to mingle his own pious views with those of the philosophers" and taught that the brain was equipped with three ventricles each with specific functions. Not only was this an absurd view, Vesalius maintained, but it was likely to mislead those not yet confirmed in religion. It would lead them to ascribe "every power of reason and even a rational soul" to animals, the structure of whose brains corresponded to that of the human brain. All this was the result of "the inventions of those who never look into our Maker's ingenuity in the building of the human body."[13]

There is nothing irreligious here; quite the contrary. But Vesalius, unlike Cusa and unlike his contemporary anatomist Servetus, does not start from theological propositions but, like Paracelsus, insists on the need for starting with the investigation of nature. This method, he maintains, will lead the young and inexperienced student to true religious belief. The reverse method, which was the traditional one and which "mingled pious views with philosophy," was most likely to lead to false religious beliefs. It was not an approach which, as Vesalius was well aware, would recommend itself to the church.

Yet the church was slow to react to such views. It was more concerned with theological heresy. In this respect the Catholic church and the Protestant churches acted very similarly, as Servetus found to his cost. Paracelsus had a genius for offending the establishment as a whole and was outstanding even in an age which expected and appreciated academic invective. But the burning of a copy of Avicenna during a student's rag day, shocking as it was to the university authorities of Basel, did not have the same implications as Luther's burning of a papal bull of excommunication. Paracelsus, Vesalius, and other scientists with original ideas and methods were in trouble mainly with their enraged professional colleagues. They had no intention of breaking with the church and were not regarded as having done so. By contrast, Servetus was accused of heresy, both by Catholic authorities and by Calvin, for his denial of the trinity and his rejection of infant baptism. His medical theory of the lesser circulation of the blood through the lungs was not mentioned in any of his indictments,[14] even though it was closely connected with his religious beliefs. Servetus identified man's rational soul with the animal spirits of the blood, spirits which were held to consist of an invisible but fine material substance. Such an identification was theologically unorthodox and, in Servetus's case, certainly heretical,[15] but neither Catholic nor Protestant authorities were prepared to do anything about it.

Only from the last quarter of the sixteenth century were the implications of unorthodox scientific beliefs for religious orthodoxy being systematically thought out. This is not surprising. Orthodox doctrine had seemingly now been definitely settled at the Council of Trent. Religious controversy had become full-scale confrontation. It had also become involved with all sorts of political and social ambitions, struggles, and fears. In France and in the Netherlands, it had escalated into civil wars with foreign intervention, fought à outrance. Every aspect of life and thought tended to become enmeshed with this all-pervading religious controversey. The churches, both Catholic and Protestant, could not afford to allow any field of human activity to escape from their influence, and thus perhaps become a center for the opposing forces, which both sides equated with Satan and which were an objective threat to their survival. Where the churches differed was less in this basic attitude than in the powers of control they were able to wield either directly or through political authorities.

Many creative thinkers, artists, and musicians were perfectly willing to exercise their talents in the services of their own side and to allow all their activities to be judged by the criterion of religious orthodoxy, but not all were willing to go as far as they were asked. Painters, sculptors, and musicians, all had their brushes with church authorities, perhaps worst of all in some Calvinist parts of Europe. Inevitably, those who used words were most directly affected by this situation: philosophers, writers on politics and history, and scientists. They did not see their problem as one of dividedloyalties, for most thought of themselves as good Catholics or Protestants. They saw it as a question of the autonomy of their own art or profession or, more precisely, of the autonomy of their own professional judgment as against the interference and misinterpretations of theologians. Often scientists rather than theologians were the first to raise the question of the religious implications of their work, to forestall accusations of unorthodoxy. This they did by using one or both of two types of argument. The first was a straightforward defense of the orthodoxy of their views and the implications of their conclusions. This type of argument presented no problems for the church. It could be judged in each individual case on its merits. The second type of argument turned out to be much more important. This was the attempt by the scientist to fence off altogether his work from interference by drawing dividing lines between the realm of religion and that of natural philosophy or knowledge of nature.

But was this possible? Was there not an inescapable overlap between these fields? And even if it were possible to draw a line, who was to draw it, the scientist or the theologian? To the theologians, Catholic and Protestant, the answer was clear. Religion was the ultimate measure of everything. Theology was the queen of the sciences and all others were her handmaidens. Scientists rarely disputed these views openly. But in practice, it was often only too clear that theologians did not know what they were talking about and that only scientists could draw the line. Gradually, they pushed this line outward, including increasing territory within the realm of science and even making alarming forays into the very core of the theological position, the study of the nature of God and his relation to creation. The very term by which such inquiries were described, *natural philosophy*, implied all the ambiguities of this changing balance.

Nowhere is this development clearer than in the history of astronomy and cosmology. There are good reasons for this. Many of the images and metaphors of the central doctrines of Christianity were astronomical and cosmological. God, the Bible tells us, created the earth and the heavens and all that is in them. The heavens, the stars in their splendor and perfection, and ultimately God himself were above us. All that was below was of the earth, subject to change, decay, and sin but yet the center of creation, for God had created man in his image and everything else for the sake of man.

When Copernicus displaced the Earth from the center of the cosmos and reduced it to the status of one of six planets revolving around the Sun, he was fully aware of the shattering implications of what he was doing. Only at the end of his life was he finally persuaded to publish his theories. It is possible that Copernicus knew of Nicolas of Cusa's attack on traditional astronomy and of Greek views which posited the rotation of the Earth.[16] Whether he did or not, Copernicus had done something very different from Cusa. Cusa had shown that, logically, the Earth could not be at the center of an infinite universe and that, since only God could be regarded as at rest, the Earth was bound to be in motion. But he had made no attempt to suggest, let alone calculate, what sort of motion this might be. This was precisely what Copernicus did, which made his theory a much more formidable problem for the churches than Cusa's apparently rather abstract speculations. It explains why Copernicus's Protestant theologian editor, Andreas Osiander, was so anxious to claim that Copernicus's theory was only a hypothesis, a mathematical model. It is now generally accepted that Copernicus fully believed that his heliocentric model represented reality. But although *De revolutionibus orbium coelestium* was widely read and even taught in some universities, both Catholic and Protestant, it did not at first stir up any serious opposition. The controversies started in the changed intellectual climate of the post-Tridentine church at a time when Tycho Brahe's observations were beginning to cast serious doubts on the Aristotelian model of the physical universe.

The first great open clash between religion and science owed a great deal to the personality of Galileo Galilei — just as the Reformation owed a great deal to the personality of Martin Luther. Kepler was as convinced a Copernican as his Italian colleague, and while he ran into plenty of opposition in Germany, he managed to avoid serious trouble with the churches. It was Kepler who urged Galileo to publish his Copernican arguments as early as 1597.[17] This is significant, for the educated European public was becoming passionately interested in astronomy and cosmology. When in January 1605 Galileo lectured on the *nova* of the previous year, his normal lecture room in the University of Padua proved too small, and he had to adjourn to the university's Great Hall.[18] His book *Sidereus Nuncius (The Message [or Messenger] of the Stars)*, in which he published his first telescopic findings, was so eagerly awaited that Henry Wotton, the English ambassador in Venice, wrote about it to the Earl of Salisbury on the very day of its publication, 13 March 1610:

> I send herewith unto his Majesty the strangest piece of news (as I may justly call it) that he hath ever yet received from any part of the world; which is the annexed book of the Mathematical Professor at Padua, who by the help of an optical instrument . . . hath discovered four new planets rolling about the sphere of Jupiter, etc. . . . So upon the whole subject he hath first overthrown all former astronomy . . . and next all astrology. For the virtue of these new planets must needs vary the judicial part, and why may there not be more? . . . By the next ship your Lordship shall receive from me one of the above instruments, as it is bettered by this man.[19]

Galileo's book became an immediate best-seller in Europe, and it became fashionable to buy telescopes.

It was in this excited atmosphere that the theological implications of Copernicanism began to be debated and not only, as had been mainly the case hitherto, its radical destruction of the academically accepted Aristotelian world view and its apparent offense to common sense. Galileo himself was fully aware of these implications, more than church authorities who disapproved of the sniping against Galileo by individuals and uninformed clerics. The great debate was triggered neither by church authorities nor by Galileo himself, but by Benedetto Castelli, an enthusiastic pupil and follower of Galileo, defending his master at a dinner party at the Medici court at Florence against the needling of other learned guests and the doubts expressed by the pious mother of the grand duke, the Grand Duchess Christina. Castelli was convinced he had won the argument and reported triumphantly to Galileo:

> Madame [the grand duchess] began, after some questions about myself, to argue the Holy Scripture against me. Thereupon, after having made suitable disclaimers, I commenced to play the theologian with such assurance and dignity that it would have done you good to hear me. Don Antonio [de Medici] assisted me, giving me such heart that instead of being dismayed by the majesty of Their Highnesses I carried things off like a paladin. I quite won over the Grand Duke and his Arch-duchess . . . . Only Madame Christina remained against me, but from her manner I judged that she did this only to hear my replies. Professor Boscaglia [a philosopher who, earlier on at the dinner party, had raised doubts about the motion of the earth] said never a word.[20]

It was probably not just Castelli's indiscretion of "playing the theologian" which now set the debate on the religious orthodoxy of the Copernican system in motion. The incident shows that such a debate was no longer avoidable. Certainly Galileo was now convinced of this. He wrote first a long letter to Castelli detailing his own views, and in 1615 he expanded and refined his arguments in the famous *Letter to Madame Christina of Lor-*

raine Grand Duchess of Tuscany. It was the most detailed and sophisticated statement yet of the relationship between natural sciences and the teachings of the Bible. Significantly, it was written by a devout Catholic who wished to preserve the church from making the terrible blunder of linking its dogma to a mistaken theory of the physical world.

Galileo started with an apologia. It was not he, he argued, who "had placed these things in the sky with my own hands in order to upset nature and overturn the sciences."[21] As to Copernicus, he did not discuss matters of faith but drew his conclusions from mathematical demonstrations based on exact observations. But these conclusions were condemned by people who quoted the Bible, the church fathers, and the councils.[22] The Bible Galileo said, could never speak untruth, but its true meaning must be understood and "in discussions of physical problems, we ought to begin not from the authority of scriptural passages but from sense experiences and necessary demonstrations."[23] Not only that, but "having arrived at any certainties in physics, we ought to utilise these as the most appropriate aids in the true exposition of the Bible."[24] Finally, and this was the longest part of his argument, Galileo tried to show that much of what the Bible said could not be interpreted literally. In the case quoted most often by anti-Copernicans, Joshua's bidding the sun to stand still, Galileo had some mathematical fun, demonstrating that in the Ptolemaic system this would have made the day shorter rather than longer.[25] Of course, the Holy Ghost who dictated the Bible did not get these things wrong, but it "sometimes wished to veil itself under words of different meaning, whether for our exercise of for some purpose unknown to me."[26]

Like Luther in his *Address to the Christian Nobility of the German Nation*, Galileo objected to the walls with which the Catholic church had surrounded itself to keep out free criticism. Where Luther relied on his reading of the Bible and on his God-given conscience, Galileo relied on his observation of nature and on his God-given reason. To the church establishment and its conventional and traditionalist theologians, the two were almost equally objectionable, for both struck at the central tenet of the church that it alone was the arbiter of truth. Unlike Luther, Galileo had no intention of reforming the church or its doctrine, except in the very specific matter of cosmology. He could not foresee that his path to truth would appear to later generations as a much surer path than the traditional religious path or, if not to ultimate truth, at least to an understanding of the universe and man's position in it. Here the church had probably a surer instinct than Galileo. But it was an instinct rather than a fully reasoned position. Galileo's whole way of thinking and reasoning was different from the religious thinking with which most churchmen were familiar. In the same year, 1615, in which Galileo wrote his letter to the Grand Duchess Christina, Cardinal Bellarmine wrote *The Mind's Ascent to God by a Ladder of*

Created Things. This was a work in a well-established tradition in which the author leads the soul upward in fifteen steps along the "great chain of being," from the contemplation of the solid and immovable earth, "the very first foundation of the whole world,"[27] through the four elements, to the heavens, the sun, moon, and stars, and then to the angels and to God himself. Aristotelian cosmology and mystic contemplation reinforce each other: "God, the Creator of all things, places his tabernacle in the sun, as being a most noble creature" and "he willed that the heaven itself should be the palace of the sun in which it might freely take its course."[28] Bellarmine saw God in physical as well as spiritual terms. But how were these physical terms to be described, apart from the use of epithets like "great" and "immense"? Bellarmine quotes the psalmist that the sun "rejoiceth as a giant to run his course."[29] This could be measured: "I myself was once desirous of learning what space of time the sun would take in setting. At the beginning of its setting I began to read the psalm *'Miserere mei Deus':* and I had scarcely read it twice through when the whole sun had set." Since the diameter of the Earth is 7,000 miles and the Sun is much larger than the Earth, "it must traverse a distance much greater than 7,000 miles" and therefore "every one but he who is stupid or a dunce must admire the infinite power of the Creator."[30]

Bellarmine was perfectly happy to use scientific observations and arguments, and he shared with Copernicus and Kepler a view of the Sun derived most probably from hermetism. But the intellectual level of their, and Galileo's, scientific arguments was already a world apart from that of the cardinal. Of this difference, Bellarmine seems to have been quite unaware. To Paolo Antonio Foscarini, a theologian who had sent him a treatise supporting the Copernican view, he wrote courteously but half-dismissively: "Since you ask for my opinion, I shall give it to you briefly, as you have little time for reading and I for writing" — and then proceeded to give an entirely conventional reply about the interpretation of the Bible by the common agreement of the Holy Fathers, the wisdom of Solomon, and the falseness of the argument that to an observer aboard a ship it appears that the beach moves away. The Copernican theory might well save appearances, but that "is not the same thing as to demonstrate that in fact the sun is in the center and the earth in the heavens."[31] Bellarmine was still thinking in Aristotelian terms, for he imagined that Copernicus had simply interchanged the positions of the Sun and Earth and had therefore transplanted the latter into one of the celestial spheres. Just as in the case of Cardinal Cajetan's meeting with Luther in 1518, so a hundred years later the best minds in the Catholic church were unwilling to spend the time and mental effort to try to understand the new views presented to them. They were content to leave this exercise to mediocre and self-serving pedants — with disastrous results for the church.

Galileo had tried to draw a dividing line between religious knowledge and scientific investigation. He also claimed that a correct interpretation of the Bible (which he, not the professional theologians, provided) would confirm the basic unity of science and religion. Some of his contemporaries were prepared to go much further in dividing the two fields. Bacon held to the traditional belief that nature showed the power and wisdom of God. But he was emphatic that this was as far as one could go: "If any man shall think, by view and inquiry into these sensible and material things, to attain to any light for the revealing of the nature or will of God, he shall dangerously abuse himself."[32] The reverse was also true:

> The corruption of philosophy by superstition and an admixture of theology is far more widely spread, and does the greatest harm . . . . Yet in this vanity some of the moderns have with extreme levity indulged so far as to attempt to found a system of natural philosophy on the first chapter of Genesis, on the book of Job, and other parts of the sacred writings, seeking for the dead among the living; which also makes the inhibition or repression of it the more important, because from this unwholesome mixture of human and divine there arises not only a fantastic philosophy but also a heretical religion. Very meet it is therefore that we be sober-minded, and give to faith that only which is faith's.[33]

Such a formulation swept aside both Galileo and Cardinal Bellarmine, and it is not surprising that it was published in a Protestant country, outside the reach of the Inquisition. Yet Bacon, like Bellarmine, was anxious to repress heresy, and his fear was of the radical reformers, those who judged everything by the special illumination they claimed to have received from the Holy Ghost.[34] We are still a long way from freedom of thought, even in England. Bacon's distinction between our possible knowledge of God and of nature was intended to safeguard the true religion, just as much as scientific inquiry, from dangerous attacks. It was also not always as categorical as he insisted it was. He maintained the traditional view of nature as the "second book" in which to study the greatness of God, and he held that the end of such study was love and charity and practical use.[35] Because he insisted on such pious ends for the study of nature, he gave it an enormous moral boost while shielding it from interference by theologians. It was not so much Bacon's contemporaries but the generation of the mid–seventeeth century that was to find Bacon's philosophy most congenial.

If Bacon had greatly contributed to the practical division between science and religion while proclaiming their common end, he had done so by turning his eyes away from the issues which had exercised Galileo and his opponents. This he was able to do, not least because he was not a mathematical scientist, in fact not a scientist at all. All he was putting forward was a method for the study of nature. He could therefore afford not to commit himself to a specific theory of cosmology or any other specific scientific theory. The issues raised by Galileo, implied in scientific theories, would not simply go away by denying their existence as Bacon had at least implicitly done. Inevitably they became a part of an even wider and more fundamental philosophical debate within an international scientific-philosophical community that was just beginning to emerge into self-consciousness in Western Europe.

The historical background of this emerging community was the religious wars and the revulsion they caused. The story is well known: the rise of political parties which placed political unity and stability above religious unity and orthodoxy, the spread of precepts of reason of state and neo-Stoicism, and above all, the growing attraction of a philosophical scepticism of which Montaigne was the most famous exponent. None of these was overtly and intentionally antireligious, but all in one way or another devalued religion as the principal criterion of political and intellectual activity.

The most fundamental breach with traditional religion and the authority and teaching of the Christian churches was made by a mathematician: Descartes, as he tells us in his *Discours de la méthode,* "revered theology" and would not "dare to submit it to the feebleness of my reasoning."[36] Yet he rejected all received and established philosophy by carrying the doubts of the skeptics to the ultimate extreme of questioning the existence not only of the universe but of God. Claiming to use the methods of mathematicians of accepting as certainty only what was self-evident, he found such self-evident certainty only in his own consciousness, his activity of doubting everything and hence of thinking: *cogito ergo sum.* Only when Descartes had established his own "being," he derived the existence of God and thence of the universe from a specific aspect of his consciousness, the recognition of a perfection which he did not possess and which a perfect being, God, must therefore have given him.[37] In terms of human knowledge but not of creation, Descartes had established the priority of his own consciousness to the possibility of awareness of God's existence. Descartes had turned the tables on the atheists and skeptics and used their very doubts to establish God more firmly. He claimed he was constructing his new philosophy only for himself and did not advise everyone to follow his example. He would retain the religion in which, by the grace of God, he had been brought up.[38] He maintained that the laws of the material universe were established by God and that mathematical and other "eternal" truths depended on God and could not exist without him.[39]

This was all very well, but it did not mask what had really happened. Descartes did expect to convince others of his views. If he hesitated before publishing them, it was not because he was not convinced of their correctness, but from a not unjustified fear of how the authorities, ecclesiastical and lay, would react to them. Their reaction was hostile. Descartes had not just drawn lines between scientific and religious knowledge as Galileo and, in a sense, Bacon had done. He had made an image of God and the soul of man, on the one hand, and of the material universe, on the other, which did not depend on the Scriptures and revelation. It is no wonder he found himself at odds, not only with the Catholic church, but also with Calvinist authorities in Holland. Fortunately the latter did not dispose of the coercive powers of the Inquisition.

Both Bacon and Descartes had elevated God above the cosmological controversies with which the traditional Catholic world picture had encumbered religious belief. By doing so they had also placed him outside most principal intellectual and emotional endeavors.[40] These would now be increasingly concentrated on the investigation of nature, with the aim of controlling it for the benefit of mankind. On this worthy and Christian principle both Bacon and Descartes were agreed. Descartes, viewing the human body as a machine and passions as arising from the body, even argued that his physics would provide a "certain foundation of morals"[41] and of the control of morality.

It was not long before Descartes's contemporaries realized that his "clockwork universe" with its absolute division between mind and matter would open the door to atheism. This was not Descartes's intention, nor did atheism necessarily follow from his philosophy. What did follow was a shift in interest among many of the most gifted minds in Europe. Bacon had excluded the Bible from scientists' arguments, and Descartes had gone further and excluded it from the arguments both of moralists and those looking for first causes. The full effects of this shift took time to work themselves out. But from then on the churches were on the defensive. They had lost the battle fought against Galileo and the Copernicans for the defense of their position as supreme arbiters of the validity of all human ideas about the universe. The basis of their arguments, the absolute validity of Scripture as the word of God and its interpretation through the traditional science of theology, had been sidestepped by arguments which claimed an equally religious validity but which were based on the scientific investigation of the natural world.

The loss to theology was tremendous. Having been excluded from a vast intellectual field over which it had ruled benignly but autocratically for many centuries, it lost its attractiveness to young men wishing to embark on intellectual inquiry. The personal piety of most of these men is not in doubt, but natural philosophy had now become their primary interest. The religious and philosophical debates of the late seventeenth and early eighteenth centuries were concerned with the consequences of this new position.

Not everyone was prepared to go as far as Descartes in accepting the need to create a completely new metaphysical basis for the understanding of natural phenomena. Pierre Gassendi accepted a traditional religious metaphysics of the first causes of the world. But having allowed God to create atoms and the laws of their movement, he then excluded him from any further interference in, or influence on, the physical world. The task of physics was to determine the nature of the laws and movements of the atoms. This would allow the building of a coherent and systematic hypothesis on the nature of the universe. It was not the absolute truth which only God could comprehend, but it was the best man could in his limitation understand, and it did not conflict with God's truth.[42] For Gassendi the free philosophical study of nature lead to the greatest tranquility of the mind (*animi tranquilitas*) and hence to the greatest felicity (*summa foelicitas*).[43] The consolations of philosophy to the human mind was an old and, for Christians, entirely respectable topos. What was new in the seventeenth century was its exclusive interpretation in terms of the study of the natural sciences.

This happened even to some of those most anxious to uphold the primacy of religion. Nicolas Malebranche, youngest son of a distinguished robe family and destined for the church, found little to excite him in the traditional curriculum for Catholic intellectuals — the study of the Bible in its original languages, the history of the church, and scholastic philosophy. At the age of twenty-six, if we are to believe Fontenelle's funeral oration, he came across Descartes' *Traité de l'homme* and "was struck as if by a completely new light."[44] From then on he set himself to harmonize Cartesian philosophy with Christianity in a system in which he equated God with reason.[45] "Geometry and physics were the steps which led him to metaphysics and theology," says Fontenelle.[46] Malbranche had devoted followers, but there were many theologians whom he could not convince, and his life was a succession of controversies with such diverse and mutually inimical opponents as the Jesuits and Jansenist theologian Antoine Arnauld. The Catholic church, unable any longer to present a credible Aristotelian-Ptolemaic front, was equally unable to construct another generally acceptable view of the world which took account of the new scientific discoveries. Increasingly this intellectual initiative passed to scientists and natural philosophers.

It was this initiative which Leibniz took, to defend religion against atheism and to bring about a reunion of the churches on the basis of a true religion, which was to be a Christian faith based on scientific understanding of the harmony of the world which God in his divine goodness, omnipotence, and omniscience had created.[47] For this purpose (as well as dealing with the metaphysical problems involved in the Cartesian attempts to account for physical phenomena in purely mathematical terms), Leibniz reintroduced final causes, or metaphysics, into scientific investigations from which Cartesians had banished them. If, for instance, several bodies move with relation to each other, it is not possible by considering these bodies alone to determine to which one of them motion or rest can be attributed. What is needed is an investigation of force, a concept not found in the Cartesian categories of extension and motion. "It appears more and more clear," Leibniz concluded,[48]

> that although all the particular phenomena of nature can be explained mathematically or mechanically by those who understand them, yet nevertheless, the general principles of corporeal nature and even of mechanics are metaphysical rather than geometric, and belong rather to certain indivisible forms or natures as the causes of the appearances, than to the corporeal mass or to extension. This reflection is able to reconcile the mechanical philosophy of the moderns with the circumspection of those intelligent and well-meaning persons who, with a certain justice, fear that we are becoming too far removed from immaterial beings and that we are thus prejudicing piety.

What is this metaphysics? For Leibniz it was the laws of reason, and these had ultimate validity. Descartes had said that these laws were true because God had willed them so. Leibniz reversed this position: God willed these laws because they were true, because truth must be contained in God's nature, and he must therefore will it.[49] If the eternal laws depended on God's caprice, we could not be sure that he was not a demon or, indeed, the Devil. God's will is therefore identical with reason, and reason is, at least in principle, apprehensible to man.

This was an essentially Greek position, as against the Hebraic stress on God's inscrutable will, which was the basis of traditional Christian teaching. Since man must assume as a rational, as well as religious principle that God is good, it followed for Leibniz that the world God had created was bound to be the best possible world:

> It follows from the supreme perfection of God that in producing the universe He chose the best possible plan, containing the greatest order, the best arranged situation, place and time; the greatest effect produced by the simplest means; the most power, the most knowledge, the most happiness and goodness in created things of which the universe admitted. For as all possible things have a claim to existence in the understanding of God in proportion to their perfections, the result of all these claims must be the most perfect actual world which is possible. Otherwise, it would not be possible to explain why things have happened as they have rather than otherwise.[50]

Perhaps not to offend orthodox Christians, Leibniz claimed that this choice among an infinite number of sets of possible worlds demonstrated God's freedom. It has been shown convincingly that, on Leibniz's premises, God could not have made a real choice but was bound to have chosen as he did by virtue of the eternal truths which did not depend on him.[51]

All this meant that even though man might not know all contingent truths, ultimately the universe was governed by reason and eternal truths accessible to him. The study of science and natural philosophy would become the basis of any valid theology. In the preface to his *Theodicée* Leibniz wrote: "We see that Jesus-Christ . . . wanted God to be the object not only of our fear and of our veneration, but still more of our love and our tenderness . . . . To love [Divinity], it is enough to envision its perfections, which is easily done because we find its ideas within ourselves."[52]

It is not surprising that Arnauld, on first encountering Leibniz' ideas, reacted sharply: "The Catholic Church would prohibit his entertaining them . . . . Would it not be better for him to leave these metaphysical speculations which can be of utility neither to himself nor to others, in order to apply himself seriously to the most important matter he can ever undertake, namely to assure his salvation by entering into the Church."[53] But almost at once Arnauld succumbed to the fascination of Leibniz' intellect and engaged in lengthy correspondence with him, although he could never quite get over his unease.[54] Voltaire was to make savage fun of Leibnizians in his *Micromegas* and in *Candide.*[55] But Leibniz' influence on his contemporaries was real enough and if it could not rival that of Descartes, it too tended to reinforce the role of scientific inquiry in both philosophical and religious speculation. Although the truth of nature could never indicate the whole truth of God, it still was the most accessible and certain pathway of human knowledge.

Leibniz had attempted to provide an intellectual escape from the religious passions of the century by the construction of a rational and scientific religious metaphysics. In England, where religious passions had flourished during the Civil War and Commonwealth period in great profusion and variety, many intellectuals turned to science and natural philosophy. The principles of Bacon's scientific method with their apparently clear-cut division between the study of God and the study of nature were particularly congenial to the founders of the Royal Society. Thomas Sprat, the historian of the Royal Society, is explicit on this question of motivation. Those who studied "experimental philosophy," — science — could expect little material advantage from their studies.[56] However,

> for such a candid and unpassionate company, as that was, and for such a gloomy season, what could have been a fitter subject to pitch upon, then [sic] *Natural Philosophy?* To have been always tossing about some *Theological question,* would have been, to have made that their private diversion, the excess of which they themselves dislik'd in the publick: To have been eternally musing on Civil business, and the distresses of their Country, was too melancholy a reflexion: It was *Nature* alone which could pleasantly entertain them, in that estate.

In this contemplation of nature men could "differ without animosity" and "without any danger of a Civil War."[57]

Here, as with Gassendi, the motivation for natural philosophy, especially in an age of social and political upheaval, anxiety, and passion was tranquility of mind. Where the medieval intellectual in similar circumstances had retreated into a monastery and studied theology and philosophy, the mid–seventeenth-century intellectual retreated into an "invisible college" of like-minded men "to assemble in a private house, to reason freely upon the works of nature: to pass Conjectures and propose problems, on any Mathematical, or Philosophical Matter, which comes in their way."[58] It was, of course, a religious undertaking. Speaking of the help which the Royal Society would be prepared to give in setting up the *Académie des Sciences* in Paris, Sprat spoke of two common aims for similar institutions all over Europe to fight the common enemy of Christendom, the Turk: "The other also against powerful and barbarous Foes, that have not been fully subdu'd almost these six thousand years, *Ignorance and False Opinions*."[59]

Membership in the Royal Society would not depend on religion or nationality, "for they openly profess, not to lay the Foundation of an English, Scotch, Irish, Popish, or Protestant Philosophy; but a Philosophy of Mankind."[60] The study of the works of God, the job of the natural philosopher, Sprat argued, is an excellent grounding for the contemplation of man's redemption. Work on man's body, especially the study of the spirits of the blood, will even lead to 'near-guesses' about the actions of man's soul."[61] Yet the analogy of the retreat of the seventeenth-century natural philosopher with the retreat of the medieval monk must not be overdone. The founders of the Royal Society, for whom and with whose advice Sprat wrote his *History*, had very practical aims in mind, as well as the peace of mind to be achieved by the pursuit of natural philosophy. Like Bacon, they thought in terms of practical usefulness to mankind of scientific inquiry and of the moral and social value of such pursuits, keeping men from corrupting habits.[62] Henry Oldenburg, secretary of the Royal Society, wrote to his fellow member John Winthrop, governor of the Massachusetts Bay Company: "I doubt not but the savage Indians themselves, when they shall see the Christians addicted, as to piety and virtue, so to all sorts of ingenuities, pleasing Experiments, usefull Inventions and Practices, will thereby insensibly and the more cheerfully subject themselves to you."[63]

It was hoped that the religious tolerance which members of the Royal Society professed would benefit the Church of England. It would remain quite safe, Sprat claimed, in a "Rational Age" and with the "subversion of old opinions about Nature." Both the Anglican church and the Royal Society derived from a reformation, "the one having compass'd it in Religion, the other purposing it in Philosophy."[64] There was even an element of millenarianism in this attitude, which gave men an added incentive to pursue natural philosophy, for at some point, it was argued, God would give man complete mastery over nature. Naturally, this would be likely to happen in England where the true, rational Protestant religion as believed by the latitudinarian wing of the Anglican church would triumph. For it was the latitudinarian Anglicans, as we now know, who were the leading spirits in the foundation of the Royal Society.[65]

The Royal Society represented, at least in the minds of many of its founders and early members, a deliberate attempt to reconstruct the unity of religion and science which Copernicanism had shattered. Characteristically, Robert Boyle held, just as Galileo had done, that the Bible and science did not contradict each other. Equally characteristically, he argued the need for careful biblical scholarship to make this evident.[66] Here was the key to the new attitude. The initiative had passed from the church and from theologians to scientists and scholars. It was by their efforts that God's providential design for man would be laid bare. It promised both material and spiritual satisfaction beyond even the individual felicity of the peaceful investigation of nature.[67]

It is in this context that we have to see the towering and still enigmatic and controversial figure of Isaac Newton.[68] At least since E.A. Burtt's classic *The Metaphysical Foundations of Modern Science* of 1924, it has become clear that Newton can no longer be simply regarded as the great early exponent of modern positivistic science as was held in the nineteenth century.[69] On the contrary, the ultimate aim of his investigations seems to have been nothing less than a complete knowledge of God and his creation. This knowledge had been revealed and was known to the ancient Babylonians, Egyptians, and pre-Socratic Greeks and to Noah and Moses. But they or their successors had been corrupted and the knowledge had been lost. It was the task of modern philosophers, and especially of Newton himself, to retrieve it.[70]

Newton set about doing this by his scientific investigations, which he conducted through mathematics and/or in the best Baconian tradition of inductive argument from observation and experiment. It was in this activity that he rejected metaphysical hypotheses. But equally important was unraveling the truths God had hidden, not in the physical universe, but in the more obscure parts of the Old Testament, the Revelation of St. John, and in other ancient writings and prophesies. In Newton's eyes all these truths belonged together, were a part of God's providential design. No doubt this design was mysterious, but it was penetrable:

> The main business of natural philosophy is to argue from phenomena without feigning hypotheses, and to deduce causes from effects, till we come to the very first cause, which certainly is not mechanical, and not only to unfold

the mechanism of the world, but chiefly to resolve these and such like questions . . . and though every true step made in this philosophy brings us not immediately to the knowledge of the first cause, yet it brings us nearer to it, and on that account is to be highly valued."[71]

Thus Newton is his *Queries* to his *Opticks*. He made the same point in the *General Scholium* in the second edition of his *Principia:*

This Being [God] governs all things, not as a Soul of the World but as Lord over all. The Supreme God is a Being eternal, infinite, absolutely perfect; but a being, however perfect, without dominion, cannot be said to be Lord God . . . . We know him only by his most wise and excellent contrivances of things, and final causes; we admire him for his perfections but we reverence and adore him on account of his dominion; for we adore him as his servants; and a God without dominion, providence, and final causes, is nothing else but Fate and Nature . . . . And thus much concerning God; to discourse of whom from the appearances of things does certainly belong to natural philosophy.[72]

For Newton the universe was not only the creation of God, but it also constituted his true purpose, apprehensible by man through natural philosophy. Such a view, while theologically unorthodox, was not irreligious, nor did it oppose science to religion. God remained essential to Newton's world view, not only as creator of the universe but as a constant replenisher and adjuster of its motive forces which, without such continual intervention, would have run down. Nevertheless, the balance between science and religion, in the common territory of the explanation of the physical universe, had now shifted still further in favor of science, or rather, of natural philosophy.

In 1718, for instance, there appeared in London a translation of a Dutch defense of Christianity in which the author claimed he could convince the "atheists and infidels," i.e. the Spinozists, of the authority of the Scriptures by "*the right Use of the Contemplation of the World.*" "The Methods we have made use of to prove the same," he wrote, "are only taken from the *modern Observations* and *probable Discoveries in Natural Philosophy,* without laying down any bare Hypotheses, since in the Things of natural knowledge, we have no farther Foundation for Arguments than we can produce Experiments."[73] He went on to claim that "the Manner of *proving the Divinity of the Holy Scripture from Natural Phenomena or Appearances*" was a totally new method.[74]

And so, at least in this formulation, it was. In traditional belief the study of "the second book," i.e. nature, revealed to man the existence and greatness of God. But the first book, the Bible, had not depended on such study. The word of God had always stood by itself, without need of further proof. "In the beginning was the Word, and the Word was with God and the Word was God" (St. John I.1.). The most that Galileo had claimed was that the study of nature could, in certain specific cases, help in the interpretation of the true meaning of passages in the Scriptures which dealt with natural phenomena. But now, because the "atheists" had thrown doubt on the divine nature of the Bible, it was claimed that the study of the "second book," i.e. natural science, could provide the best proof of the divinity of the Scriptures. In this spirit the Newtonian propagandist Desagulier warmly welcomed the Dutch work. The translation would do even more good than the original, he wrote to the translator in a letter published in the English edition, for it had left out arguments the author drew "from the Modern Philosophy for Reveal'd Religion; the weakness of which latter might give those Free-Thinkers occasion to triumph, who would be struck dumb by Convictions from the former."[75]

The intellectuals of the Anglican church were happy to use the Newtonian world picture with its emphasis on God's providence in a material universe composed of lifeless and inert matter, to fortify their own liberal Protestant theology and conservative social philosophy.[76] But Newtonianism was also used by the contemporary free thinker to support a materialist philosophy in which God and nature were equated and matter became the source of life and change and order. In this view Newton's concept of gravity became a force inherent in matter.[77] These were forerunners of the more famous eighteenth-century atheists La Mettrie and the Baron d'-Holbach.But atheism was not the predominant belief of the Enlightenment. In general the alliance between science and religion held. Voltaire, the great apostle of Newtonianism, was convinced of its necessity: "We know nothing of first principles," he wrote to Prince Frederick William of Prussia, in 1770.

> It is surely very presumptuous to define God, the angels, spirits, and to pretend to know precisely why God made the world, when we do not know why we can move our arms at our pleasure. Doubt is not a pleasant condition, but certainty is an absurd one. What is most repellent in the *System of Nature* [of d'Holbach] — after the recipe for making eels from flour — is the audacity with which it decides that there is no God, without even having tried to prove the impossibility . . . *Si dieu n'existait pas, il faudrait l'inventer.* But all nature cries aloud that He does exist: that there *is* a supreme intelligence, an immense power, an admirable order, and everything teaches us our own dependence on it.[78]

Voltaire was a great deal more humble about man's ability to penetrate first causes, or God's purpose, than Newton or Leibniz had been. But while specific religious beliefs and the metaphysical bases of science were coming to seem increasingly doubtful, the positive laws of science itself, the practical results of scientific enquiry in a Newtonian universe assumed to be accessible to human reason appeared much more promising. "Nothing is more necessary," d'Alembert wrote in his *Preliminary Discourse to the*

Encyclopedia of Diderot, "than a revealed religion, which may instruct us concerning so many diverse objects. Designed to serve as a supplement to natural knowledge, it shows us part of what was hidden, but it restricts itself to the things which are absolutely necessary for us to know. The rest is closed to us and apparently will be forever. A few truths to be believed, a small number of precepts to be practiced: such are the essentials to which revealed religion is reduced."[79] The rest of his *Discourse* d'Alembert devoted to the sciences and the arts.

Some twenty-five years ago, the distinguished scientist and sinologist Joseph Needham suggested that one of the differences between the histories of science in Europe and in China was the development in Europe of the concept of the laws of nature.[80] This concept had appeared in rudimentary form among the Greeks and was fully developed during the sixteenth and seventeenth centuries. Its essence and importance in the history of science was its positing of a suprarational divine creator and law-giver whose creation was subject to law and hence discoverable and comprehensible by rational methods. In China the prevailing philosophical schools did not develop the analogy between human law and nature. "Universal harmony," Needham writes, "comes about not by the celestial fiat of some King of Kings, but by the spontaneous co-operation of all beings in the universe brought about by their following the internal necessities of their own natures . . . . Nature shows a ceaselesness and regularity, yes, but it is not a commanded ceaselessness and regularity."[81] The Chinese did not regard human reason and logic as capable of achieving a full understanding of nature. In the last two hundred years, Western philosophy of science has come closer to the Chinese view, with the laws of nature being regarded as statistical regularities rather than prescriptions imposed on matter by a creator. "The problem," Needham says, "is whether the recongition of such statistical regularities and their mathematical expression could have been reached by any other road than that which Western science actually travelled."[82]

Granting the importance of the connection between Western religious and scientific thinking — Was it not also the decline of religious sensibilities in the early modern period which gave scientific inquiry an added emotional attraction to European intellectuals? While such inquiry generally remained strictly Christian — whether Catholic or Protestant — it tended to expand into areas formerly the fields of purely religious thought. In these areas it had great advantages over religion. It could give answers philosophically more satisfactory; it could promise results that would bring practical benefits to mankind; and, perhaps psychologically most important, its disputes could avoid the murderous consequences of theological disputes. Science, the handmaiden (*ancilla*) of theology and revealed religion, had not exactly asserted itself over its former mistress, but had set up house on its own. Many of Europe's most gifted intellects, while still paying occasional visits to the house of the old mistress, found the house of the new one engrossing and came to spend most of their time and energy in it.

NOTES

An earlier version of this paper was read in German at the 32. Deutscher Historikertag in Hamburg on October 6, 1978. I would like to thank Peter Winch, Margaret C. Jacob, and Dorothy Koenigsberger for reading the typescript of this paper and for their helpful criticisms and suggestions.

1. M. Weber, "Die protestantische Ethik und der Geist des Kapitalismus," *Gesammelte Aufsätze zur Religionssoziologie,* vol. 1, (Tübingen, 1934), p. 2.
2. P.M. Rattansi, "The Social Interpretation of Science in the Seventeenth Century." In P. Mathias (ed.), *Science and Society, 1600–1900* (Cambridge, 1972); A.R. Hall, "On the Historical Singularity of the Scientific Revolution." In J.H. Elliott and H.G. Koenigsberger (eds.), *The Diversity of History: Essays in Honour of Sir Herbert Butterfield* (London and Ithaca, 1970); and bibliographical references in these two articles.
3. Cf. R.K. Merton, "Science, Technology, and Society in Seventeenth-century England," *Osiris* 4 (1938); also as a book (New York, 1970); R. Hooykaas, *Religion and the Rise of Modern Science* (Edinburgh and London, 1972).
4. H.G. Koenigsberger, "Music and Religion in Modern European History." In Elliott and Koenigsberger, *The Diversity of History.*
5. A.O. Lovejoy, *The Great Chain of Being* (New York, 1960), pp. 50 passim.
6. Nicolas Cusanus, *Of Learned Ignorance,* tr. G. Heron (London, 1954), bk. 1, ch. 11, p. 25.
7. Ibid., bk. 2, ch. 12, esp. p. 110.
8. Ibid., bk. 2, ch. 12, p. 111.
9. For a detailed discussion of Cusanus and his epistemological and scientific thinking, see Dorothy Koenigsberger, *Renaissance Man and Creative Thinking: A History of Concepts of Harmony, 1400-1700* (Hassocks, 1979), ch. 3.
10. *Theophrastus Paracelsus Werke,* ed. W.E. Peuckert, vol. 1 (Basel and Stuttgart, 1965), p. 501.
11. Ibid., p. 512.
12. W. Pagel, *Paracelsus* (Basel and New York, 1958), pp. 349–50.
13. *Vesalius on the Brain,* ed. and trans. C. Singer (Oxford, 1952), pp. 4–6; from A. Vesalius, *De humani corporis fabrica,* bk. 7, ch. 1.
14. R.H. Bainton, *Hunted Heretic: The Life and Death of Michael Servetus, 1511–53* (Boston, 1960), pp. 207–9.
15. Ibid., pp. 124–27. D.P. Walker, "Francis Bacon and Spiritus." In *Science, Medicine, and Society in the Renaissance: Essays in Honour of Walter Pagel,* ed. A.G. Debus, vol. 2 (New York, 1972).
16. R. Klibansky, "Copernic et Nicolas de Cues." In *Léonard de Vinci et l'expérience scientifique au XVIe siècle.* Colloques internationaux du Centre National de la Recherche Scientifique, Sciences Humaines. (Paris, 1953), pp. 230–31.
17. Kepler to Galileo, 13 October 1597. In *Johannes Kepler Gesammelte Werke,* ed. M. Caspar, vol. 13 (Munich, 1945), p, 145.
18. M. Nicolson, *Science and Imagination* (Ithaca, 1956), p. 8.

19. Logan Pearsall Smith, *Life and Letters of Sir Henry Wotton* (Oxford, 1907), vol. 1, pp. 487–88. Also quoted in M. Nicolson, *Science and Imagination,* pp. 35–36.
20. Castelli to Galileo, 14 December 1613. In *Le Opere di Galileo Galilei,* vol. 11 (Florence, 1934), pp. 605–6. Trans. and quoted in Stillman Drake, *Discoveries and Opinions of Galileo* (Garden City, N.Y., 1957), pp. 151–52. The grand duke was Cosimo II(1609–21). His wife was the Arch-Duchess Maria Maddalena of Austria (d. 1631).
21. *Opere,* vol. 5, p. 309 (Drake, *Discoveries,* p. 175).
22. *Opere,* vol. 5, p. 314 (Drake, p. 179).
23. *Opere,* vol. 5, p. 316 (Drake, p. 182).
24. *Opere,* vol. 5, p. 317 (Drake, p. 183).
25. *Opere,* vol. 5, pp. 343–44 (Drake pp. 211–12).
26. *Opere,* vol. 5, p. 332 (Drake, p. 199).
27. *Roberti Bellarmini De ascensione mentis in Deum per scalas rerum creatarum,* ed. F.X. Dieringer (Cologne, 1850), gradus tertius, ch. 1, p. 61.
28. Ibid., gr. sept., ch. 1, pp. 157–58.
29. Ibid., gr. sept., ch. 2, p. 161 (Psalm 19).
30. "Ego ipse volens curiose aliquando cognoscere, quanto temporis spatio sol totus occumberet in mari, coepi ad initium occasus ejus legere psalmum *Miserere mei Deus;* ex vix totum bis legeram, cum jam sol totus occubuisset." Ibid., pp. 162–63.
31. Bellarmine to Foscarini, 12 April 1615. In G. Galilei, *Opere,* vol. 12, pp. 171–72 (Drake, *Discoveries,* pp. 162–64).
32. Bacon, *Works,* vol. 3, p. 218. Quoted in C. Hill, *Intellectual Origins of the EnglishRevolution* (London, 1972), p. 91.
33. Bacon, *Novum Organum,* 1, 65.
34. Rattansi, "The Social Interpretation of Science," p. 15.
35. Hill, *Intellectual Origins,* pp. 91–92; R. McRae, *The Problem of the Unity of the Sciences: Bacon to Kant* (Toronto, 1961), p. 37.
36. R. Descartes, *Discours de la méthode pour bien conduire sa raison et chercher la vérité dans les sciences* (Leiden, 1637/Manchester, 1941), p. 9.
37. Ibid., pt. 4. A.J. Krailsheimer, *Studies in Self-Interest from Descartes to La Bruyère* (Oxford, 1962), pp. 38–39.
38. Descartes, *Discours,* pt. 2, 3.
39. Descartes to Mersenne, 15 April, 6 May 1630. In Descartes, *Oeuvres,* ed. Adam and Tannery, vol. 1, pp. 145, 149.
40. I would like to thank Dorothy Koenigsberger for drawing my attention to this effect of both Bacon's and Descartes' teachings.
41. Descartes to Chanut, 15 June 1646. In *Oeuvres,* vol. 4, p. 441. Quoted in McRae, *Unity of the Sciences,* p. 59.
42. R. Tack, *Untersuchungen zum Philosophie- und Wissenschaftsbegriff bei Pierre Gassendi, (1592-1655)* (Meisenheim am Glan, 1974), pp. 108–10, 152, 155–56.
43. Ibid., p. 127, 140–41.
44. B. de Fontenelle, "Éloge du P. Malebranche." In *Oeuvres,* vol. 1 (Paris, 1825), p. 321.
45. E.g. in his *Entretiens sur la métaphysique,* 6. In *Oeuvres de Malebranche,* ed. A. Robinet, vol. 12 (Paris, 1965), pp. 145–56.
46. Fontenelle, "Éloge du P. Malebranche," p. 338.

47. R.W. Meyer, *Leibnitz and the Seventeenth Century Revolution*, trans. J.P. Stern (Cambridge, 1952), p. 145.

48. G.W. von Leibniz, *Discourse on Metaphysics*. In *Basic Writings*, trans. G.R. Montgomery (La Salle, Ill., 1962), p. 33.

49. "However, we must not imagine, as some do, that eternal truths, being dependent on God, are arbitrary and dependent on His will, as Descartes seems to have held." *La Monadologie*, 46. In *Oeuvres Philosophiques de Leibniz*, ed. P. Janet (Paris, 1866), vol. 2, p. 601. Also quoted in Meyer, *Leibnitz*, p. 151, n. 421.

50. Leibniz, *Principles of Nature and of Grace Founded on Reason* (1714), trans. M. Morris and G.H.R. Parkinson. In *Leibniz Philosphical Works*, ed. G.H.R. Parkinson, par. 10, p. 200. *Oeuvres*, 2, p. 613.

51. Lovejoy, *The Great Chain of Being*, pp. 166 ff.

52. Leibniz, *Essais de Théodicée. Oeuvres* (1866), 2, pp. 3–4.

53. A. Arnaud to Ernst von Hessen-Rheinfels, 13 March 1686, ibid., vol. 1, p. 581.

54. Id., 31 August 1687, ibid., p. 667.

55. Voltaire, *Micromegas: Histoire Philosophique. Oeuvres complètes*, vol. 44 (Kehl, 1785), pp. 176 ff.

56. T. Sprat, *The History of the Royal Society* (London, 1667), ed. J.I. Cope and H.W. Jones (St. Louis/London, 1959), p. 27.

57. Ibid., pp. 55–56. Cf. also p. 344. Sprat's italics.

58. Ibid., p. 56.

59. Ibid., p. 57.

60. Ibid., p. 63.

61. Ibid., p. 83.

62. Ibid., pp. 342–45. J.R. Jacob, *Robert Boyle and the English Revolution* (New York, 1977), pp. 154–55.

63. Quoted, ibid., p. 155.

64. Sprat, *Royal Society*, pp. 370–71.

65. J.R. Jacob, *Robert Boyle*, pp. 154–59.

66. Ibid., p. 123.

67. Cf. also Margaret C. Jacob, *The Newtonians and the English Revolution, 1689-1720* (Ithaca, 1976), pp. 135–37.

68. For recent work on Newton, cf. C.R.S. Westfall, "The Changing World of the Newtonian Industry," *Journal of the History of Ideas* 37 (March 1976).

69. It seems as if Reiner Tack still sees Newton in this way. *Untersuchungen*, p. 226.

70. J.E. McGuire and P.M. Rattansi, "Newton and the 'Pipes of Pan,' " *Notes and Records of the Royal Society of London* 21 (no. 2, December 1966), pp. 122–23 and passim. F.E. Manuel, *The Religion of Isaac Newton* (Oxford, 1974), pp. 42 ff.

71. *Queries* to Newton's *Opticks*, pp. 334 ff, quoted in E.A. Burtt, *The Metaphysical Foundations of Modern Science*, 2nd ed. (Garden City, 1932), p. 260. Cf. also J.M. Keynes, "Newton, the Man." In *Essays in Biography*, ed. G. Keynes (New York, 1963), p. 314: "He regarded the universe as a cryptogram set out by the Almighty — just as he himself wrapt the discovery of the calculus in a cryptogram when he communicated with Leibnitz."

72. Newton, *Mathematical Principles of Natural Philosophy*, 2nd ed., ed. F. Cajori (Berkeley, 1934), p. 545. Also quoted in Burtt, *Metaphysical Foundations*, p. 294.

73. B. Nieuwentyt, *The Religious Philosopher,* trans. John Chamberlayne (London, 1718), vol. 1, p. 1. Nieuwentyt's italics. I wish to thank Margaret C. Jacob for drawing my attention to this source.
74. Ibid., p. II.
75. Ibid. The pages of Desagulier's letter to John Chamberlayne are unnumbered.
76. Jacob, *The Newtonians,* passim.
77. Margaret C. Jacob, "Newtonianism and the Origins of the Enlightenment," *Eighteenth Century Studies* 11 (no. 1, Fall 1977).
78. *Voltaire's Correspondence,* ed. T. Besterman, vol. 77 (Geneva, 1962), pp. 119–20.
79. D'Alembert, *Preliminary Discourse to the Encyclopedia of Diderot,* trans. R.N. Schwab (Indianapolis and New York, 1963), p. 26.
80. J. Needham, "Human Law and the Laws of Nature." In *The Grand Titration: Science and Society in East and West* (London, 1969), pp. 299–331.
81. Ibid., p. 323.
82. Ibid., p. 330.

PART III

Political Discourse and Cultural Symbols

CHAPTER NINE

Popular Theater and Socialism in Late–Nineteenth-Century France

Joan Wallach Scott

On July 14, 1895, the socialist municipal councilors of France, who were assembled in Paris for their third congress, adjourned deliberations to attend the theater. The plays they saw were not standard Parisian fare. The spectacle was described as "social theater," an alternative to, indeed a transcendence of, bourgeois theater. The plays were written by socialists, and they carried a message, which at once reflected the outlook of the spectators and bound them more closely in their common enterprise. The published account of the congress contained this report of the evening: "The members of the congress, many of whom were accompanied by their family and friends, as well as a large number of socialist militants . . . experienced at the performance of these two beautiful productions, a sensation superior to [mere] artistic enjoyment, which flowed from the communion of socialist ideas and socialist hearts."[1]

The members of the congress sponsoring the plays were men who had been elected to municipal councils on socialist slates. Since the municipal elections of 1892, socialists of various tendencies — Guesdists, Broussists, Allemanists — but of local origin and with important local ties, had represented a majority in some sixty communes.[2] Socialist mayors and councilors presided over municipal affairs in the textile center of Roubaix, in the metal and mining towns of Montluçon, Commentry, and Carmaux, in the cities of Narbonne and Marseille, and in a host of smaller towns. In many more communes they represented a significant and vocal minority. In 1892, 1893, and again in July 1895, these socialist councilors convened a national congress at which they discussed issues of mutual concern, debated tactics, coordinated certain activities, and offered one another moral, if not always ideological support.[3]

In 1895 the timing of the congress had created some controversy in the planning committee and among the assembled delegates. The conference was planned for July 12-15 and thus would be in session on July 14, the national holiday which commemorated the fall of the Bastille, the beginning of the first French Revolution. Although the delegates represented different and competing strands of French socialism, they were united in the belief that the true French Revolution, the social revolution, had not yet happened. Their election as municipal councilors, their activities in socialist-run cities, their annual meetings, and their campaigns on behalf of striking workers and socialist candidates for Parliament, were all meant to bring closer the day of the triumphant social revolution.

The question facing the delegates was not whether to hold the conference during these July days but whether to interrupt their proceedings on the 14th to observe the national holiday. The debate echoed positions argued among socialists since 1880 when the Third Republic had proclaimed July 14 the highest national holiday. Those insisting on business-as-usual were Guesdists who reminded their comrades that since 1890 the working class had taken May 1 as its own holiday. July 14 was a bourgeois holiday, sponsored by an oppressive state that corrupted republican principles. Those who dissented from the social purposes and politics of this state ought therefore to ignore the holiday. Among the delegates were representatives of the municipality of Carmaux who, in protest against the killing of a young Parisian worker by police, had forbidden July 14 celebrations in their town in 1893.[4]

Despite the apparent logic of the Guesdist argument, those who urged that the congress celebrate Bastille Day ultimately prevailed. But rather than dispute their opponents' interpretation of the holiday, they invoked practicality and history. Although it had become official only in 1880, the celebration of July 14 had a longer history, they reminded the congress, one inextricably linked to the revolutionary tradition. For years opponents of monarchs and emperors had commemorated the holiday clandestinely. Even now the festivities had enormous popular appeal. If military parades and the presentation of flags celebrated the power of the state in the morning, in the evening street dances and fireworks evoked the memory of crowds of sans-culottes storming the fortress of reaction and tyranny, demanding liberty and justice for all.

The holiday legitimized the importance of revolutionary action by the popular classes. In addition, supporters of observance of the holiday argued that the bourgeois revolution was the forerunner of the socialist revolution. The holiday, therefore, must not be rejected but appropriated. Just as bourgeois institutions such as schools and municipal councils could be qualitatively transformed when socialists controlled them, so Bastille Day, celebrated by this congress, could become a symbol of the unfulfilled revolution, of the aspirations of the French working class.[5]

The congress decided to hold a holiday of its own on July 14 by attending social theater. The decision reflected the predominance of non-Guesdist socialists at the congress and in the municipalities, and foreshadowed the formal withdrawl from future congresses of this sort by members of Guesde's Parti Ouvrier Français. It would be a mistake to read the history of socialism in the municipalities or indeed of French socialism generally in this period simply in terms of this debate. Doctrinal and tactical differences separated Guesdists from the followers of Brousse and Allemane. Their views about local socialism differed fundamentally. While Brousse argued that the capture of city halls would cumulatively build socialism, Guesde insisted that electoral triumphs at the local level were only exercises in preparation for the seizure of state power. Socialist municipalities, however many existed, would never add up to a socialist state. If Brousse's view was quantitative, Guesde's insisted that there was a qualitative difference between municipal socialism and social revolution.[6]

In practice, at the local level, there were important similarities in the actions and outlooks of socialists by the 1890's. Their approach to elections was similar: all endorsed the ballot as a weapon of class struggle. Once elected they undertook similar actions to improve the living conditions of their working-class constituencies, to build and support institutions which organized and mobilized collective action, and foster and develop socialist attitudes among the inhabitants of the cities and towns they controlled. Socialist attitudes were loosely defined and all-encompassing in the 1890s. If at the national level leaders were preoccupied with theoretical and strategic differences among themselves, at the local level populations acted as if these differnces did not exist. Socialist organizers commented to national congresses that doctrinal divisions did not interest provincial constituencies. The appeal of socialism, they reported, did not rest on ideological subtlety.[7] Nor were local populations responsive to repeated efforts by Guesde to substitute new holidays for old. They turned out for May 1 demonstrations, but that did not preclude celebrating July 14. The municipality of Carmaux tried to ban July 14 celebrations in 1893 and 1896 but encountered resistance each time.[8] Even within the Guesdist camp local leaders were accustomed to celebrations, albeit socialist celebrations, on the day of the national holiday. So it was not at all unusual that despite the debate, Guesdists at the congress joined their comrades on July 14, 1895, at the social theater.

It was customary on the 14th for urban populations to go to the theater. In Paris lines formed at the Opera on the evening of the 13th to get free tickets for performances.[9] The plays presented were usually historical dramas, marking the great moments of the French past. The socialist alternative theater took the customary form of July 14 festivities and infused it with new meaning. Theater was an appropriate choice for the socialists' alternative celebration. They could not stage a parade to compete with the state's display of military power. Even if they could have assembled a sufficiently impressive "army" of workers, it would not have symbolized the socialists' self-definition. In addition, securing legal authorization to march through the streets of Paris would have been nearly impossible. Neither was there any point in tampering with the boisterous street demonstrations on the evening of the 14th, since these expressed and endorsed the popular revolution. Theater, on the other hand, served the socialists' purpose. It was festive yet educational, and could explicitly convey their point of view. Some socialists argued that theater was the ideal socialist art form for the education, liberation, and transformation of the working class. Theater could not only convey a message but could weld an audience into a collectivity and prepare them for, if not push them to, action.[10]

The plays performed in the social theater were representative of what might be deemed a socialist repertoire of the 1890s. It was a varied collection, consisting of different themes and written by an array of authors, from self-taught militants to acknowledged playwrights. The Guesdists created "dramatic sections" and encouraged their followers to write and present plays as an effective means of propaganda.[11] Independents, like the Communard and poet Clovis Hugues (the first Socialist ever elected to the legislature — from Marseille in 1881) were also celebrated in working-class circles as playwrights. When socialist municipalities sponsored social theater, as they did increasingly in the 1890s, they had a wide range of similar types of plays from which to choose. Social theater was a typical example of propaganda activity. The similarities of form and purpose of the plays were far more important than the particular ideological persuasion of the individual playwrights or of the municipal councilors in the towns where they were performed. They reflected the broad-based appeal which characterized the efforts of local socialist organizers in this period.

For the celebration of July 14, 1895, two plays were performed, which the Congress record called masterpieces. One, by Clovis Hugues, was called *Le Mauvais Larron (The Bad Thief)*.[12] The other, entitled *La Pâque Socialiste (The Socialist Passover)*, was written by Emile Veyrin.[13] No record survives to explain why these particular plays were selected. Perhaps it was simply because both were new and thought to be in vogue at the time. There is no doubt that they were representative of the 1890s genre of social theater.

Emile Veyrin's play was a long, five-act production. Hugues's was a brief poetic tableau vivant. I shall focus on the Veyrin play because it permits a more extensive discussion of the themes and form of plays of this genre and because it became one of the most popular and frequently performed of the 1890s socialist plays.[14]

La Pâque Socialiste takes place in Rouen. The central characters are not workers. They are Gilbert Lemoine, the owner of a textile factory, and his half-sister Micheline. As the play opens Gilbert, dressed in mourning, ponders his father's death-bed confession which acknowledged the existence of an illegitimate daughter. He summons the girl, who works in his factory as a payroll cashier, and announces that she is his sister and that he is sharing his inheritance with her. Gilbert questions Micheline about her ideas, and she declares that she is a socialist and that she learned her socialism from the teachings of the Gospel.[15] He reveals his plan to make his workers the heirs to his factory and his fortune.[16] They then discuss their shared commitment to humanity and their hatred of egoism.

In the scenes that follow Lemoine confronts the egoists, his fellow bosses. He refuses to go along with their plan to close their factories to avert major losses during a slump in the industry. He prefers, he says, to follow the example of the more enlightened manufacturers in Mulhouse. The calculating, inhumane capitalist, Rousselot, warns him that his action will lead to his ruin. In acts 2 and 3, Lemoine admits he is ruined and declares himself bankrupt. Micheline offers to save the business by contributing her inheritance. But Lemoine's creditors and the other employers have him arrested for fraud. His crime was having given Micheline money, an action they declare was meant to conceal his real assets. The legal technicalities permit capitalist justice to punish Lemoine for violating all the rules of the system. In despair Gilbert raises a pistol to his temple, murmuring "death will stop the proceedings." Micheline throws herself into her brother's arms and prevents his suicide. "You do not have the right to desert the struggle." "But," he counters, "what if I am sent to prison"? Her reply: "You will be a martyr. It is necessary."[17]

Act 4 is called "Le Repas symbolique" ("The Symbolic Meal"). It begins with the "bad" capitalist, Rousselot, boasting of his paternalism to a group of unemployed weavers. They reply that his charity is insufficient and demeaning. The foreman of Lemoine's factory, Ardouin, arrives with the news that work is available. There follows an exchange between Ardouin and Rousselot during which the foreman calls the factory owner "an enemy of the working class." Rousselot leaves. Ardouin then gives details of the reopening of the factory. Micheline has turned over her capital to the workers, and they promise to run the factory themselves, pay off her brother's debts, and redeem his name.[18] Micheline arrives and elaborates the reasons for her action. The workers gather around, and she distributes bread and wine while instructing them in collectivist morality. She speaks and the workers, in chorus, repeat her last lines. Then she stands on a stool and sheds her cloak revealing a long, white dress, like a "ray of sunlight." She raises her arms and continues the lesson, speaking of the new day to come, the day of "social redemption." Each description of the new society ends with the phrase, "An idea runs across the centuries," repeated by the workers. Micheline promises the arrival "as soon as possible" of "the day of the rehabilitation of the just." The group repeats the phrase. The choral repetition continues:

> *Micheline:* Day of the liberation of the wage-earner!
> *All:* Day of the liberation of the wage-earner!
> *Micheline:* Day of fraternal settlement!
> *All:* Day of fraternal settlement!
> *Micheline:* Day of social redemption!
> *All:* Day of social redemption!
> *Micheline:* Awaited day! Sacred day!
> *All:* Sacred day![19]

The workers echo Micheline in ever louder voices. Then all is silent for several minutes. The curtain falls slowly on a tableau vivant of an immobile group, eyes and hands raised to Micheline.

In the fifth act Gilbert, just released from prison, arrives at the factory which is now clearly a prosperous enterprise. He is pale, thin, ragged, and walks with difficulty, a broken man. He had had no news during his eighteen months in prison and is now without bread or hope. He comes upon a group of workers about to unveil a statue of their benefactor handing tools to a worker. "Capital to labor" is written on the base. As he rests against the statue, one of the workers asks Gilbert to pass him his tools. Gilbert and the worker replicate the tableau of the statue. Another worker asks them to hold the pose and in astonishment remarks that there is a striking similarity between the live figures and the statue. Gilbert's identity is then revealed. He is overcome with emotion. He utters his last words of advice and collapses, dead, at the foot of the monument.[20]

Micheline arrives too late to wish her brother farewell. But she quickly dries her tears. Though sadness tempts us to sit and cry, she says, "life goes on; duty does not stop."[21] Her attention is then drawn to a group of strikers from the other factories. They have been attacked by police and in revenge are pursuing Rousselot with knives, sticks, and stones, calling for his death. Micheline forces the demonstrators to stop, telling them not to stain their hands with blood. Invoking the message of Christ, she reminds them, "on the battlefield of progress, victory belongs not to those who kill, but to those who die." She tells Rousselot to leave, calling him a "vile exploiter." "Your reign is finished," she warns him, "and your days are numbered." Rousselot departs.[22]

In the final scene Micheline urges the starving strikers not to despair. When they turn to Ardouin and the Lemoine workers for help, however, Ardouin refuses. To Micheline's disappointment the foreman condemns the strikers and insists that his group must be practical and defend its own interest. "Our money is our own," he says. She replies that he is an egoist. "Have you become bourgeois yourselves"? she asks angrily.[23] Then she stoops to kiss her dead brother's forehead, turns to the ragged strikers, and orders them to follow her. She raises her arms and, with long strides, leads the miserable band to an indeterminate future as the final curtain falls.

The major themes of the play are represented in the two tableaux vivants. The first (act 4) centers around Micheline, an inspirational figure who articulates and incarnates the dream of the future new society. The second (act 5) involves Gilbert. It depicts the passage of history, the transfer of the ownership of the means of production from capitalist to worker. (At the end of this act Gilbert, having fulfilled his historic mission, dies.) The tableaux visually symbolize what the characters have articulated verbally in earlier acts. The play is about the transforming power of ideas in history. Micheline symbolizes the idea, the dream which Veyrin depicts as the leading force for social change. "It is often forgotten," she says early in the play," "that each time humanity has advanced a stage, a dream has led the way."[24] And, of course, she literally leads all the action in the play.

The dream is about cooperation and social justice. As the workers partake of the bread and wine at the symbolic meal they promise to care for the sick, the young and the old, those who cannot work but deserve a fair share. They promise to treat equally women who are "weaker by nature" and must devote some time to maternal duties. They agree to share everything and to abolish hierarchical rewards. And they assure each person "a place at the family table."[25] The dream is eternal, passed on from generation to generation, having been articulated by Christ and others "across the centuries." ("An idea runs across the centuries" is the refrain of the symbolic meal.) But the dream can also be realized now. Its realization will bring about an end to human suffering and oppression. The dream inspires people to act to end wage labor, to bring about brotherhood, fraternity, social justice, and social redemption. "The great crucified one [humanity] will detach itself from the cross; it will redeem itself."[26]

The inspirational aspect of Micheline's dream distinguishes it from the religion extolled by Rousselot. The boss's Christianity preaches submission in his life and reward in the next. The priest, he declares, is the right arm of the bourgeois order because his message engenders resignation in the people. (The army, which imposes obedience, is the left arm.) For Micheline, the Gospel's teachings bear no resemblance to the doctrines of organized religion. On the contrary, her message arouses the masses to action. It is subversive of the established order. The Christian humanitarian vision resurrected in a female figure in a nineteenth-century context is socialism.

The socialism Micheline preaches involves cooperation, social justice, and class struggle, but not class warfare. Early in the play she warns Gilbert that his failure to move in step with history will unleash a "social war which will last a long time and spill torrents of tears and blood . . . . To avoid this war is the highest of missions."[27] Later, when she prevents the strikers from killing Rousselot, she tells them it is better to die than to kill. "Let [others] present themselves at the tribunal of posterity with blood-stained hands."[28] This viewpoint was decidedly Christian in its emphasis on martyrdom and sacrifice, but it was also shared by most socialists in the 1890s. Only anarchists explicitly urged violence. Guesde insisted after 1891 that ballots, not bullets, were weapons of class struggle. And Engels wrote, in his 1892 introduction to Marx's *Class Struggles in France,* that the time of street-fighting and barricades had passed. In addition, the opposition to bloodshed had a longer history on the French Left. Throughout the nineteenth century its spokesmen sought to distinguish the revolution they wanted from the second year of the Jacobin Terror, and they appealed to images of the "revolutionary from Nazareth" to justify their position.

The creation of socialism in this play comes from Gilbert's forward-looking action and, to some extent, from the workers' willingness to follow Micheline's plan. But the specific actions required are not entirely clear. No real program is set forth. Gilbert represents less human design than historical inevitability. His counterpart, Rousselot, stands for the corrupt old order. Individualism and class interest alone motivate his action. He is told over and over again that his days are numbered and that his time has come. "Representative of a departing world, disappear into the night," commands Micheline. And the stage directions have Rousselot leave with bowed head.[29] Gilbert is a transitional figure, an enlightened bourgeois whose sensibility makes him empathize with his workers. It is not paternalism that leads him to characterize his employees as his children and to specify in his will that the factory they inherit will be called "Lemoine et ses fils." The action represents an interpretation of the direction of history. The workers are the next generation, a new stage of social and economic development. He is their father, as capitalism is the progenitor of socialism.

The play's message is contained in the two tableaux and in the relationship between Gilbert and Micheline. (She is the natural daughter of a working-class mother and a capitalist father. Gilbert is unmarried and has no children of his own. Neither can produce offspring entirely in his or her image.) She strengthens his will and gives him courage to act. Without her, he would have committed suicide, and his sensibility would have remained a personal, individual feeling. Without her, too, the workers would have been unprepared to assume collective responsibility for the factory and for one another. The dream inspires and gives larger significance to individual action. It at once infuses history with meaning and interprets it. That is why Micheline's tableau precedes Gilbert's. The tableaux juxtaposed depict the inevitable passage from capitalism to socialism, informed by the inspirational and directional force of the eternal ideas of human love and social justice.

The play makes eclectic use of many themes. The most striking and initially perplexing is the repeated use of biblical symbolism. Its title, "The Socialist Passover," refers to the emergence from slavery of the Jews. Micheline is Moses leading her people to freedom. The symbolic meal is a Passover celebration, and it also recalls Easter, Christ, and the Last Supper. It is tempting to read his play entirely as a form of Christian allegory. Gilbert is the Christ figure; Micheline his apostle. His sacrifice and death make possible the rebirth of humanity, the creation of a new order. In this reading the symbolic meal in act 4 is the Last Supper; the bread and wine, the eucharist. Gilbert's appearance at the factory in act 5 recalls Christ's Easter-morning reappearance. But the story in Veyrin's play is not so neat. Micheline, not Gilbert, is the central figure, leading all the action. It is she who presides at the symbolic meal, distributes the bread and wine, and instructs the workers. It is she who makes possible the creation of the cooperative factory and she who will presumably end the suffering of the unemployed strikers. In a sense Micheline usurps Gilbert's role. Her actions proclaim (but do not entirely create) the new order and make his death necessary. If Gilbert is Christ, Micheline is at once his apostle and his reincarnation. But if she is a reincarnation, why does she assume her role before he dies? The answer is that she is not strictly speaking his reincarnation but that she displaces him.

Micheline is a usurper in other ways as well. She is an illegitimate child recognized by her brother and given her share of the inheritance as if she were legitimate. Yet the circumstances of her birth and absence of her father's written will, always make her status questionable. Micheline is Gilbert's younger sister, yet she usurps his role as head of the family business by deciding how to use the family capital. She is a woman directing the actions of men; a woman leading her people to freedom; a female distributing the bread and wine customarily distributed by Christ or his diciples or priests — all, of course, male. The miracle she performs is one of transformation and redemption, but the transformation is social and economic, and the redemption is not individual but collective. The collectivity is not humanity but the working class. The bread and wine invoke the mystery of the Mass, the transformation into Christ's body and blood. Micheline's words as she distributes bread and wine are about redemption and a sacred day. The sense of magical transformation associated with the eucharist remains, but it is redefined in socialist terms. The symbolic meal enacts a socialist sacrament.

Micheline is not an entirely religious figure. She does evoke images of Mary. She is virginal and pure in her white dress. But Micheline also represents a secular figure, one long associated with the efforts of revolutionaries, of those intent on transforming the social and political order. She was clearly meant to evoke thoughts of Marianne, whose name was synonymous with the Republic. Marianne's roots lie in the French Revolution's Festivals of Reason. Then, actresses were called upon to depict symbolically the triumph of Reason. The choice of women to represent the abstract ideas of reason, liberty, justice, equality, and even fraternity may have followed in part from the gender in French (and Latin) of the words themselves — all of them are feminine. (*La raison, la liberté, la justice, l'égalité,* even *la fraternité.*) The literal depiction of the idea required a female figure. Once female, of course, the figure elicited gender-specific responses. In addition, these female figures had explicit pagan references, to Minerva, to nature, and to earth. They were the Enlightenment's deliberate counters to religious imagery. During the revolution, one Jacobin "catechism" appealed to "La Liberté, fille unique de l'Être Suprême."[30]

According to the only source I have been able to find on this subject, the name Marianne was, in the 1790s, the slang expression in Montpellier for women of easy virtue, many of whom were actresses. Critics of the revolution dubbed the republic "une Marianne." In a wonderful inversion of its original deragotory use, the name lived on, chosen in the 1840s and 1850s as the secret password of underground republican societies: "Do you know Marianne?" "Oh, yes, I know her."[31] By the 1850s Marianne embodied the ideals and hopes of the suppressed republican movement. Maurice Agulhon, who has written an important book on Marianne's history, cites a letter to her from the 1850s by Felix Pyat. "For us, proscribed Republicans, without hearth or place to go, without a home or a country, you are everything; refuge, city, home, our family, our mother, our lover, our faith, our hope, the idol to whom we sacrifice . . . the ideal for which we live and die content."[32]

According to Agulhon, Marianne was captured and tamed by the bourgeois governments of the Third Republic and stripped of her revolutionary garb in public monuments. (Her red Phrygian cap was exchanged for a crown of laurels, her sword for a torch, like the one in the hand of the Statue of Liberty.) The official Marianne of the Third Republic was ossified in marble and plaster busts and represented the established order. She remained in the working-class tradition, however, as a symbol of revolt and resistance to oppression, a rebel against the establishment, enshrined in songs and tableaux vivants.[33]

In this play Micheline is the revolutionary Marianne. She usurps both Christian and Republican traditions and prepares the workers in the play and in the audience for the transition to socialism. The story is ultimately secular. It is about history, the power of ideas, and the necessity for human action. It uses biblical imagery in the service of socialism. How did Micheline prepare the audience for action? No specific plan or program was offered and violence was discouraged. From one perspective this play can be read as a reformist tract, preaching restraint by workers in view of the historical inevitability of socialism. But that would be too literal a reading, indeed a misreading of the play's purpose and of the reasons for its enormous popularity.

Although *La Pâque Socialiste* offered no specific program, its ending left open a number of possible interpretations. Does Micheline lead the ragged workers to another cooperative experiment? Perhaps, but has not her experience with the Lemoine workers shown the limits of such action? Socialism in one factory did not create a social revolution. One could conclude that employer paternalism never leads to socialism. Perhaps then the answer lies in larger-scale organization, some kind of political revolution. Perhaps the lesson is that there can be no peaceful transition to socialism, that individual acts of violence (such as those advocated by anarchists and atempted by the strikers against Rousselot) may not be efficacious, but that organized class struggle would succeed. Different groups clearly could draw different lessons from the play's uncertain ending, and undoubtedly they did. By leaving open the next step (also making clear that the Lemoine workers were "egoists"), the play could stimulate the elaboration of plans of action to realize socialism. That action in the name of socialism was necessary was a clear message of the play. The order of the tableaux indicated that commitment to socialism preceded, indeed brought about, the end of capitalism. Micheline's usurpation suggested the need for active intervention in the historical process, even if specific actions were not spelled out. The effect was not programmatic, but it was energizing.

The play created in the audience a collective faith in socialism, a disposition to endorse programs and undertake actions designed to bring about social revolution. It did this primarily through the figure of Micheline. Micheline embodied an idea "across the centuries" and an ideal which persevered despite disappointment and defeat. She clearly pointed the way to an as yet unrealized social salvation. Her presence testified to the vitality of the socialist idea and the socialist movement and called forth the faith necessary for the triumph of socialism (the same kind of faith in Christ that in Catholic theology will bring final salvation). Micheline's faith was unshaken by setbacks or failure. The actions of the Lemoine workers did not defeat her belief in the future or her determination to act. Veyrin showed his audience that the failure of a strike or cooperative or union— regular occurrences in the experiences of the French working-class movement — did not mean that socialism would fail. The final scene of the play bolstered the audience against failure, tried to make them accept it, expect it, and go on in spite of it. The audience was meant to admire Micheline's persistence, to follow her example and her teachings whenever the opportunity arose, and most of all to believe in her power and enduring goodness.

The fact that Micheline was female gave additional symbolic force to the socialist idea she represented. Her motives were pure, unsullied by the politics and ambition associated with men's activities. There were no ulterior, selfish motives involved in Micheline's leadership, as there could be no such motives for any women, since they were not considered political beings and were denied formal citizenship under French law. Micheline did not seek power; she sought to improve the welfare of others. Her intervention was unambiguous, simple, and clear. Socialism in its unselfish purity was to capitalism and its egoism, what women were to men in the political realm.[34]

Veyrin's tableau of Micheline evoked all the secular feelings about Marianne articulated in Pyat's letter. The play could also draw on religious ideas of the kind elicited in the Mass and by dramatic depictions of sacred themes. This religious drama was associated with traditions of medieval popular allegory and was performed still in this period by rural populations in Easter passion plays and Saints' Day processions. For peasant audiences or urban workers who had emigrated recently from rural areas, religious symbolism was familiar and salient. The figure of Micheline conjured up images of Mary as well as of Marianne. These images brought forth in the audience certain familiar responses — secular and sacred — of belief, love, and faith, redirected to Micheline and thus to socialism.

As a maternal figure Micheline's role had additional force. She was not a romantic figure exciting individualistic passions. She connoted collective, familiar concepts. In the first act, she describes herself as the mother of "a big family."[35] Her selflessness and dedication to others were the basis of solidarity and survival — of Gilbert, of the Lemoine factory workers, and by implication of the ragged mass which follows her at the end of the play. The figure of Micheline was an idealized version of the mother in working-class families. Whether or not she earned wages, the mother in these families was seen as the cornerstone of the family, the person whose ingenuity and selflessness held together *the* unit upon which individual material and emotional sustenance depended. Micheline represented ideas about mothers embedded in working-class culture in this period and articulated repeatedly in autobiographies, songs, and memoirs.[36] Positive ideas associated with family life were translated into positive attitudes about class identification (membership in "the big family") and socialism. Mary, Marianne, and mother; religion, republicanism, and family. The varied and familiar strands of French popular experience were woven into a new cloth. They were used to legitimize socialism and to make it both the recipient and the source of a positive response, an abiding faith.

That response was underlined by the device of choral repetition at the end of act 4. As the workers in the play chanted in reply to Micheline, the audience was undoubtedly meant to join in. Accounts of performances of

La Pâque Socialiste describe variations on the tableau. Micheline carried a red flag in one presentation and the chorus sang the "International," surely a spur to audience participation.[37] The involvement of the audience welded that collective faith in socialism, that "communion of socialist ideas and socialist hearts," the creation of which was the ultimate purpose of the play.[38] Veyrin's play reveals an approach to popular audiences characteristic of the socialist movement in this period and evident at the local level, most clearly in socialist municipalities. The approach is best described as one which appealed to, understood, and valued popular tradition. Organizers, propagandists, and playwrights spoke to the concrete experiences and traditions of a local population and articulated or translated them into socialist terms.

The appeal to familiar local experience was used by politicians like Henri Ghesquière, a Guesdist, amateur playwright, and eventually the mayor of Lille, the textile city where he had been born, the son of textile workers. During the 1890s, Ghesquière led a cortège of militants from Lille each Sunday to a neighboring town. The group sang songs, read poems, and staged tableaux. Then Ghesquière lectured on the specific benefits of socialism and enlisted new members in cooperatives and in the party.[39] In a similar vein, glassworker leaders in Carmaux and elsewhere organized unions that reflected and sought to bolster craft hierarchies. They interpreted the struggle of skilled craftsmen to protect their privileged position as an aspect of class struggle and in the process they translated a trade-specific craft consciousness into class consciousness.[40] The socialist municipal council in Roubaix distributed milk and clothing to poor children in the city after 1892, distinguishing its actions of "social justice" from the paternalistic charity of previous Radical-Republican adminstrations.[41] The effort in all cases was one of translation. It involved articulating local problems in more general class terms and redefining old solutions — universal ideas of love and justice — as socialism.

The use of allegory and symbolic forms to achieve this effect in the literary and artistic sphere was advocated by certain proponents of "social art." Bernard Lazare argued in 1896 that revolutionary art required revolutionary forms. Symbolism, he insisted, freed human sensibility because it was dynamic and opened a myriad of imaginative possibilities.

> [The symbol] is not solely an end, but a beginning; not only the end of one process, but the commencement of another; it lives its own specific life and it contains a thousand lives, it is a phenomenon, but it is also a symbol, not a hieroglyph, but a living symbol.[42]

In contrast to realism which was materialistic and reflected existing society, symbolism was able to imagine an entirely new reality. It helped prepare the future.

> The artist . . . must prepare today the new morality, he must elicit from old ideas and sentiments new feelings — those which will reign in the new society. This new society is being prepared . . . by large economic and social forces. The work of the writer and the artist, the work of *art social,* is to make contemporary men understand other forms of beauty; in so doing they prepare them to inhabit the city of tomorrow.[43]

Lazare and others in the social art movement believed that the ideas they espoused were accessible to ordinary people. They also assumed that the sentiments they awakened were positive and malleable. The artists' job was to free human sensibility from restrictive forms, to extend the limits of imagination and, in Lazare's words, "to elicit from old ideas and sentiments new feelings."

Veyrin's *La Pâque Socialiste* followed Lazare's prescription, though it is impossible to establish whether there was any direct contact between them. Veyrin not only appealed to "old sentiments," but also used forms familiar to popular audiences. Melodrama had enormous popular appeal in serialized newspaper stories and in dramatic presentations. The tableaux were in a tradition of popular allegory associated with passion plays, carnivals, puppet shows, and mime performances. These often used a familiar story and played with its meanings and implications. Puppet shows in northern French textile towns during the nineteenth century took Bible stories and turned them into secular satires.[44] At least since 1789, groups on the Left had depicted Christ as a revolutionary and used women as Christ figures in the same subversive manner as Veyrin used Micheline.[45] Veyrin not only touched the emotions of his audience with familiar symbols, he used a form of inverting received meanings that was understood and well known by popular audiences.

The use of allegory and popular tradition marks the play as a product of the socialism of the 1890s. In its local aspect, 1890s socialism can be characterized as an effort to incorporate and translate popular traditions and experiences. The translators' skill lay in their familiarity with local populations. National organizations of trade unionists and socialists were founded in this period, and increasingly there were efforts to coordinate and centralize local activities. The strength and appeal of the movements, however, stemmed not from centralization but from loose organization and close ties between local leaders and their followers.

The characteristics of 1890s socialism emerge more clearly when contrasted with the socialism of the early twentieth century. Socialists in this later period became increasingly concerned with eliminating influences that might interfere with clear commitment to specific doctrines and organizations. After the unification of socialist tendencies into a single party in 1905, the flexibility of earlier years ended. The activities of local affiliates were increasingly controlled by the national headquarters. Charles Sowerwine describes the change clearly: "Equivocation became impossible: either one was a member of the party through its duly constituted organs or one was not."[46] The corollary was an emphasis on the unequivocal understanding of socialist teachings, on the creation of strictly socialist traditions of the kind advocated unsuccesfully by Guesde in the 1880s and 1890s.

In socialist theater, allegory gave way to realism, the theory of which was articulated in a 1903 article on "people's theater" by Romain Rolland. Rolland was not an official socialist spokesman; but his article states that position clearly. Rolland was concerned in his essay and in the plays he wrote in this period with creating theater that would inspire and enlighten the working class. The goal was to entertain, to stimulate the masses to act heroically, and to provide "a guiding light to the intelligence." Rolland advocated the creation of people's theater as a means of developing taste and intellect in the masses. He wrote: "It is the duty of those who love the people to develop their taste."[47] Heroic figures were necessary because "the people like to be led."[48] Romantic drama was dangerous, as was "obscure symbolism," because "the people are easily moved without asking the reason," and they will embrace "pseudo-religious or psuedo-humanitarian" themes without understanding why.[49] The point was to remove these themes entirely because their effect was unpredictable; the associations they evoked were out of the playwright's control.

In his own writings Rolland chose historical drama as the best vehicle for the effect he sought. Although he cautioned against preaching "lifeless lessons of moral pedagogy," he tried carefully to control the message an audience received from a play.[50] In discussing Wagner's *Die Meistersinger,* Rolland noted that Hans Sachs offered an example of the "profound and serene conscience of the people." The play might be a model of people's theater but for its music and its "abnormal sentimental complications, its excessive eroticism, its metaphysics."[51] Rolland's own plays (*Danton* and *July Fourteenth*) brought an explicit message about heroism, the virtues of struggle, and the triumph of good. The preface to *July Fourteenth,* which celebrated "the artistic and civic ideals of the Committee on Public Safety," stated the author's purpose:

> To revive the forces of the Revolution, to awaken once more the heroism and the faith of the nation when it was in the midst of the republican struggle, in order that the work interrupted in 1794 might be taken up and completed.[52]

Rolland described the dramatist as a "congenial travelling companion" for the people. He was alert, jovial, heroic if need be, on whose arm they may lean, on whose good humour they may count to make them forget the fatigue of the journey. It is the duty of this companion to take the people straight to their destination — without, of course, neglecting to teach them to observe along the road.[53]

For both Rolland and Veyrin, the theater was a means of educating the people. But there were important differences between them indicative of different approaches to their constituencies of socialists in the 1890s and in the first decades of the twentieth century. In the 1890s socialists sought to expand the meaning of socialism, to make popular groups with diverse traditions recognize that they were already socialists. Veyrin's play drew on religious and republican themes and showed how they could be translated into socialist themes. The evocation of a variety of ideas and emotions was deliberate. The point was that they could all be redefined as socialist. By 1905 the emphasis on inclusiveness and translation had declined; socialists concentrated on more careful and exclusive definitions. The emergence of a national, unified party created a standard of formal membership and belief. And the Dreyfus affair, local experiences with the power of the clergy and rightists to defeat socialist candidates, and deterioration of relations between Radicals and Socialists by 1908, began to convince Socialists of the need to destroy rather than to use older traditions.

After 1905, centralization made possible the implementation of some of Guesde's earlier goals. Attempts to create new holidays never succeeded (and were abandoned after 1914), but Guesde's view of the political purposes of artistic endeavors became increasingly prevalent. For Guesde as for Rolland, theater *was* politics; the message had to be unambiguous and programmatic. For Veyrin and other socialist playwrights like him in the 1890s, theater served the socialist cause, but it supplemented rather than duplicated other political efforts.[54] Veyrin "prepared the new morality" by conjuring up familiar images and associating them with socialism. He created the "communion of socialist hearts" which was then organized and directed in its actions by politicians, by the socialist mayors and municipal councilors who dried their eyes and appluaded on July 14, 1895, and left the theater to take up the work they did not expect a playwright to do.

NOTES

Research for this study was conducted in Paris during the summer of 1978 under a grant from the American Council of Learned Societies. An early version was presented at the Columbia University seminar on the History of the Working Class. The comments of the members of that seminar were extremely useful, but I am particularly grateful for the suggestions and criticisms of Anson Rabinbach and Sean Wilentz. On a later version, William Reddy was an important critic.

Arno Mayer and Debra Silverman offered good advice, which I have tried to follow: The work was written during my year (1978-79) as a member of the School of Social Science of the Institute for Advanced Study, Princeton, New Jersey. The comments of my colleagues at the Institute, Karen Blu, Lionel Gossman, Albert Hirschman, Margaret Jacob, Keith Moxey and Quentin Skinner helped me clarify the argument. Stephen Gudeman offered crucial insights, and William Sewell, Jr. gave me ideas and encouragement when I most needed them. In offering this work to the Festschrift for George Mosse, I honor the activities of a teacher and friend. I have a particular debt to acknowledge as well. One of the important qualities necessary for the survival and success of any graduate student, but particularly of a female graduate student, is a sense of humor. That was the lesson I learned early in my graduate career at the University of Wisconsin thanks to George Mosse.

1. Troisième Congrès des Conseillers Municipaux Socialistes, Paris, 12-15 July, 1895, p. 16.
2. The best tally of the results of the election of 1892 estimates that the total number of councils won by socialists was about sixty. The Guesdists captured twenty-three municipal councils, including those of Roubaix, Montluçon, Narbonne, Caudry, and Carmaux. The Allemanists captured twenty communes in the Ardennes region. The affiliates of the Comité Central Révolutionnaire held seventeen communes in the department of the Cher particularly. The Possibilists won in St. Ouen; the Independents in Toulon. See Michael J. Mc-Quillen, "The Development of Municipal Socialism in France, 1880–1914." Ph.D. dissertation, University of Virginia, 1973.
3. Congrès des Conseillers Municipaux Socialistes: I, September 1892, St. Ouen; II, July 1893, St. Denis; III, July 1895, Paris. See also Archives Nationales (hereafter AN), series F^7 12494 and accounts in *La Revue Socialiste*.
4. Rosemonde Sanson, *Les 14 juillet, fête et conscience nationale, 1789-1975* (Paris, 1976), p. 60.
5. "Our fathers conquered liberty," the independent Benôit Malon had written several years earlier, "it is for us to establish it on [foundations of] social equality and universal fraternity." In contrast was Guesde's position of 1880: "As long as the worker July 14 has not tumbled these capitalist bastilles [the factories], as long as the class that holds them in garrison has not been forced to capitulate . . . the people will have nothing to celebrate." Sanson, pp. 57–8, 61.
6. Paul Brousse, *La Propriété collective et les services publiques* (Paris, 1883); Jules Guesde, *Services publiques et socialisme* (Paris, 1883), and "Liberté communale et collectivisme," speech to the Chamber of Deputies, 20 November 1894, published in *Quatre Ans de lutte de classe à la Chambre,* vol. 1 (Paris, 1901), pp. 97–166.
7. Paule Mink, "Le Mouvement social dans le Midi," in *Almanach de la question sociale,* 1892, pp. 140–42. Cited in Charles Sowerwine, *Les Femmes et le socialisme: un siècle d' historie* (Paris, 1978), p. 71, n. 14, p. 36, n. 58.
8. Archives Nationales. BB[18] 2040.
9. "In Paris, in front of the Opera . . . a line formed: one recognized workers in their blouses, women . . . clerks in suits, and the poor who, the next day will sell their tickets for several *sous*." Sanson, p. 93.
10. Jean Jaurès, "Le Théâtre social," *Revue d'Art Dramatique* (December 1900), pp. 1065–77; "Enquête sur la question sociale au théâtre," *Revue d'Art Dramatique* (January-March 1898), especially p. 251.

11. Claude Willard, *Le Mouvement Socialiste en France (1893-1905): Les Guesd-istes* (Paris, 1965), p. 138.
12. Clovis Hugues, *Le Mauvais Larron: vision dramatique en un tableau* (Paris, 1895). Hugues was born in 1851 in the Vaucluse and died in Paris in 1907.
13. Emile Veyrin, *La Pâque Socialiste* (Paris, 1894; reissued 1905 — citations are to the 1905 edition). Veyrin's dates are 1850–1904. In nineteenth-century French usage La Pâque designated the Jewish festival of Passover while Les Pâques denoted the Christian Easter.
14. One historian refers to it as "the favorite war horse" of socialist theater. Eugenia W. Herbert, *The Artist and Social Reform: France and Belgium, 1885–1898* (New Haven, 1961), p. 37.
15. Veyrin, p. 6.
16. There is some evidence that this was practiced in nineteenth-century France, usually by employers on the verge of bankruptcy. The play may be making explicit comment on the ultimate futility of this kind of action for securing social reform or social change. I am grateful to Edward Fox for this point.
17. Veyrin, p. 36.
18. Ibid., pp. 39–40.
19. Ibid., pp. 45–46.
20. Ibid., p. 53.
21. Ibid., p. 54.
22. Ibid., p. 56.
23. Ibid., p. 58
24. Ibid., p. 11.
25. Ibid., p. 42.
26. Ibid., p. 45.
27. Ibid., p. 11.
28. Ibid., p. 56.
29. Ibid., p. 56.
30. Frank Paul Bowman, *Le Christ romantique* (Geneva, 1973) p. 54. See also Eric Hobsbawm, "Sexe, symboles, vêtements et socialisme." *Actes de la recherche en sciences sociales,* September 1978, pp. 2–18.
31. *Oxford Companion to French Literature* (Oxford: Clarendon, 1959), p. 453.
32. Maurice Agulhon, "Esquisse pour une archéologie de la République: l'allégorie civique féminine," *Annales, E.S.C.* 28 (1973), p. 12; *Marianne au combat: l'imagerie et la symbologie républicaines de 1789 à 1880* (Paris: Flammarion, 1979).
33. In Etienne Pedron's *Le Combat social,* a tableau appears in the third act. "Marianne brandishes a red flag, crushes beneath her feet representatives of the bourgeois order (police, magistrate, bureaucrats), while the chorus sings the 'International' and the rays of the sun of justice appear on the horizon." Agulhon, p. 26, citing Willard, *Les Guesdistes,* pp. 139, 639. Agulhon points out that despite the Guesdist desire to detach the workers from official republican imagery such as Marianne, Pedron, a Guesdist, and others like him continued to use this kind of feminine allegory. Micheline was not a Joan of Arc figure. Joan was a warrior who supported the king and the state. In this period she was not part either of the republican or the socialist imagery.
34. I am grateful to William Reddy for this point and for the one in the preceding paragraph.
35. Veyrin, p. 7.
36. Louise A. Tilly and Joan W. Scott, *Women, Work, and Family* (New York

1978), pp. 143, 210–13.

37. *Le Reveil des travailleurs de l'Aube,* 5-12 June 1897, p. 2.

38. The purpose of *La Pâque Socialiste* and of the other socialist allegories of the 1890s genre was similar to the Indonesian *ludruk,* described as "proletarian plays," by anthropologist James Peacock: "Ludruk stories do not achieve their major impact by serving as ethical, theological, or legal charters for action . . . . Rather, ludruk stories affect participants by seducing them into experiencing certain types of social action, empathizing with certain goals, means, and dramatic forms, and so developing within themselves dispositions to favor these goals and means." James L. Peacock, *Rites of Modernization: Symbolic and Social Aspects of Indonesian Proletarian Drama* (Chicago, 1968), p. 244.

39. Robert P. Baker, "Socialism in the Nord, 1880–1914: A Regional View of the French Socialist Movement," *International Review of Social History 12* (1967), p. 366.

40. Joan Wallach Scott, *The Glassworkers of Carmaux: French Craftsmen and Political Action in a Nineteenth Century City* (Cambridge, Mass., 1974).

41. M.F. Chabrouillaud, "L'Oeuvre des municipalités socialistes, Roubaix." *Le Mouvement Socialiste,* 1 May 1900; Gustave Siauve, *Roubaix Socialiste ou 4 ans de gestion municipale ouvrière (1892-1896)* (Lille, 1896).

42. B. Lazare, *L'Écrivain et l'art social* (Paris, 1896), pp. 29–30. I am grateful to Debra Silverman for introducing me to this aspect of the topic and for sharing with me her collection of materials on social art.

43. Ibid., p. 31. "The fact alone of bringing forth a beautiful work, in the full sovereignty of one's spirit, constitutes an act of revolt and denies all social fictions . . . . It seems to me . . . that good literature is an outstanding form of propaganda by the deed," Pierre Quillard, 1893. Quoted in Herbert, p. 128.

44. William Reddy, "The Batteur and the Informer's Eye: A Labor Dispute of the French Second Empire," *History Workshop Journal* 7 (Spring 1979), pp. 30–44. See also Peter Burke, *Popular Culture in Early Modern Europe* (1978); Maurice Albert, *Les Théâtres des boulevards, 1789–1848* (Paris, 1902); Natalie Z. Davis, *Society and Culture in Early Modern France* (Stanford, Calif., 1975).

45. Bowman, 106–15.

46. Sowerwine, p. 86.

47. Romain Rolland, *The People's Theater,* trans. B.H. Clark (New York, 1918), pp. 93–94, 97, 113. This appeared also in *Les Cahiers de la Quinzaine,* November 1903. See also "Le Théâtre du peuple et le Drame du peuple," *Revue d'Art Dramatique* (December 1900), pp. 1102-04.

48. Ibid., pp. 22–23.

49. Ibid., pp. 29, 113.

50. Ibid., p. 106

51. Ibid., p. 43

52. Ibid., p. 89.

53. Ibid., p. 105. On Roland, see David James Fisher, "Romain Rolland and the Ideology and Aesthetics of French People's Theater," *Theatre Quarterly* 9 (Spring 1979), pp. 83–103. See also the special issue of *Theatre Quarterly* 6 (1976), "People's Theatre in France since 1870."

54. Debate about the political functions of theater was not confined to France. For a discussion of expressionism and revolutionary theater in Germany see the suggestive piece by Anson Rabinbach, "Passage to Politics: Ernst Fischer as Critic, Writer, and Dramatist in the 1920s," *Modern Austrian Literature* 8 (1975), pp. 168–89.

CHAPTER TEN

Dashed Hopes: On the Painting of the Wars of Liberation

Jost Hermand

Translated by James D. Steakley

There are few phenomena in German history as subject to dispute as the patriotic spirit which developed in the years 1806–13 and contributed decisively to the outbreak of the so-called Wars of Liberation. It stands as one of the most impassioned manifestations of that German nationalism, if not chauvinism, which was later to bring such suffering upon the world. This has led to the disparagement of the spirit of those patriots who believed at the time that they were struggling for a noble cause. In light of our experiences with German chauvinism, a negative assessment of their outlook may seem justified. Yet such a perspective distorts an objective historical view of the situation and contributes little to our understanding of an era and ideology.

The nationalism of the Wars of Liberation is a highly complex phenomenon: it exhibits on the one hand distinctly chauvinistic traits, but it is also borne by the longing (on the part of its better representatives) for a unified nation-state and manifests antidynastic, even bourgeois-democratic features. This latter component must not be overlooked. It expresses the legitimate hope of a "belated nation" for a national, cultural, and economic union to overcome that "German misère" known until 1806 as the "Holy Roman Empire of the German Nation." It would be improper to examine the chauvinism without the democratism (or vice versa) which placed itself in the service of the spiritual preparation for the Wars of Liberation. The two are inextricably bound and should not be treated separately.

The way in which this dubious symbiosis of democratic and chauvinistic elements came about cannot be explained without brief reference to German history of the preceding decades. We must begin with the basic presuppositions of the German Enlightenment and the emerging national feeling it contained, for the chauvinism which flared up in 1806–13 and the confrontation with France it entailed are rooted far back in the eighteenth century. In nationalistic blindness, such early figures as Klopstock and the "Göttingen Grove" had simply equated the German character with loyalty, nobility, uprightness, inspiration, and virtue, while pillorying everything French as frivolous, cold, cynical, vicious, and superficial. Behind this open chauvinism lay — consciously or unconsciously—arepublican ideal. This bourgeois hatred of the French manifested class hatred for the French-speaking princes and aristocrats who attempted to imitate in Germany the governmental and personal style of Louis XIV. Between 1750 and 1789, only the haute or reform bourgeoisie, more interested in economic enrichment and personal freedom of movement than national unity, had a fairly positive relationship to France, which appeared to them as a more "advanced" country. With the outbreak of the French Revolution the German Jacobins—who appealed to a petit-bourgeois, radical following— had a hard time, since a deep hatred of the French had taken root in this class and could not be eliminated overnight. When the revolution later moved into the phase of the so-called Reign of Terror, these circles immediately abandoned their Jacobin enthusiasm, hailing Napoleon—like the haute bourgeoisie—as the tamer of the "leaderless" mob and the executor of certain "usable" ideas of the French Revolution.

In 1805–09, when the same Napoleon who had just been celebrated as the tamer and executor of the French Revolution trod on German soil as an imperialistic conqueror, the Germans had to reorient themselves ideologically. This "liberating act of coercion" totally jumbled all heretofore existing factions. One's political stance was decided by where one stood on Napoleon. This led to a split into sociologically and ideologically distinct camps: (1) the princes and aristocrats, (2) the haute bourgeoisie, which remained reform-minded, and (3) the petite bourgeoisie and peasantry. There were also antagonisms within these classes, which is not surprising in light of the contradictions of the political situation.

The German princes were far from united in their attitude toward Napoleon. Those he had elevated in terms of rank, such as the princes of the Confederation of the Rhine or the kings of Bavaria and Wurtemberg, were more inclined to collaborate with him than those who had lost part or all of their land by his territorial consolidation acts. All these princes were nonetheless united, even in this era, by a deep-seated fear of the prospect of a unified German state which could sweep them from their thrones. This is why they cleverly supported the nationalism which flared up in 1806–13, hoping to reconsolidate their own power by eliminating foreign rule, but quickly and brutally suppressing nationalism as soon as it could become dangerous to themselves.

The haute bourgeoisie also clung to its older Enlightenment ideals during this period and welcomed Napoleon as the creator of the Civil Code, which promised increasing liberalization of economic conditions and civil law reform. Beyond that, it honored Napoleon as the entirely self-reliant genius, the social upstart whom they could admire openly because of their own social-climber mentality. Here at last was a man who had not yielded to the ruling dynasties but had made himself into a dynast—and in the process came to serve as an ideal object of identification for every conceivable type of parvenu feelings.

The petit-bourgeois and peasant classes either persisted in the traditional subject mentality during these years—showing loyalty to the dynasties—or linked up with rebellious circles of patriots, who kept alive the old Teutonic cult of virtue and hatred of the French informed by the Klopstockian sentimentalism of the eighteenth century. Under the pressure of the French occupation, the forces which had heretofore let off steam only in poetry were now quick to take on political forms. The result was a rich pamphlet literature in which—alongside moral disdain for everything French—the old antidynastic class hatred of the enlighteners of the 1770s and 1780s could still be felt. They linked the Pietistic concept of an "inner fatherland" with its political counterpart, the "outer fatherland." In much the same way, religion and patriotism, democratic and national strivings were once again intertwined under Napoleon: the "Community of the Pious" (in contrast to the purely rational orientation of the French) was simply equated with the German Volkish community.

Within these circles it is impossible to draw a clear line between pure democrats, longing for a German republic, and pure chauvinists, committed to the idea of a Romantic Volk united under a strong arm from above. Pure democrats, originally recruited in the second half of the eighteenth century from the Rousseauian "storm and stress," the radical late Enlightenment, and German Jacobinism, had largely disappeared after the fall of Robespierre. Pure chauvinists—the kind that would later step forward in response to Bismarck's strategy of unity—can scarcely be said to have existed in the first decades of the nineteenth century. Those recognizable as true rebels in the years 1806–13 were mostly patriots with both chauvinistic and democratic attitudes—i.e. simultaneously wanted to eliminate French foreign domination and German particularism. In this way they sought to create a basis of support for further political, social, and cultural reforms in Germany.

The works of the German patriots in the anti-Napoleonic wars could therefore be used (or abused) later for the most varied purposes. The reactionary tendency—already emerging in the framework of the Imperial Succession party at the Frankfurt National Assembly, then consolidating in the general triumph of Bismarck, and continuing to be felt in the war enthusiasm of 1914 and in fascism—generally bases its interpretation of the era of the Wars of Liberation and its underlying mentality on the purely nationalistic, even chauvinistic components. The figure of Blücher as the most decisive conqueror of Napoleon, increasingly takes on the features of Bismarck or Hitler in the course of time. The progressive tendency, which first burst forth in the patriotic democratism of the pre-1848 era, interprets the Wars of Liberation as Germany's first progressive mass movement, even a "seminsurrectionary war" against the princes, as Friedrich Engels put it at one point.[1] This interpretation was later adopted by the Social Democrats, the liberals and leftists of the Weimar Republic, and finally in the GDR. This tendency singles out those documents which manifest democratic features from the legacy of the Wars of Liberation. Yet this perspective is just as skewed as the purely reactionary one. The various anthologies which treat this era have tended to employ one of the two perspectives, thereby missing the dialectic which contemporaries were already trying to capture in such concepts as "Christian-Germanic" or "German-Democratic."

The same ambiguity prevails in the patriotic art of the Wars of Liberation. This phenomenon has previously been granted only a marginal role in the development of the national-democratic mentality of this period. Some have even doubted whether it is worthwhile to speak of an "art of the era of the Wars of Liberation." I believe that it is—but first it would be necessary to rediscover the buried artistic documents to get an authentic image of this movement. Apart from Carl Maria von Weber's settings of Theodor Körner's *Lyre and Sword (Leier und Schwert)*, the music of this era has been preserved only in a few student songs. We know somewhat more about the patriotic literature of these years, especially those lyric calls to battle written as an expression of patriotic enthusiasm by such men as Ernst Moritz Arndt, Theodor Körner, Friedrich Rückert, and Max von Schenkendorf—who influenced the form and vocabulary of German political poetry well into the nineteenth century.[2] Less well known are the dramas of the Wars of Liberation, mostly written after the fact. Apart from a few plays of agitation and propaganda against Napoleon (August von Kotzebue), the field of drama was dominated by the "Festival Plays on the Victorious End of the Wars of Liberation" ("Festspiele zur siegreichen Beendigung der Befreiungskriege")—Johann Wolfgang von Goethe, Matthäus von Collin, Caroline Pichler.[3] By serving to reconsolidate princely legitimacy, the latter are unequivocally reactionary.

The visual arts of this period are even less well known, although they manifest a range of interesting forms and motifs. The reasons for this unfamiliarity are readily understood. While the poems of an Arndt or Körner, mostly set to music, could easily pass from person to person, it was far more difficult to disseminate the pictorial expression of an anti-French or anti-Napoleonic outlook. It was far more subject to censorship and could therefore pass from hand to hand only in relatively primitive forms (as a pictorial broadsheet, drawing, cheap woodcut). Visual artists—ignoring for the moment a few exceptions—were far more out of touch with the spirit of the times than young writers and students. Most had little formal education and were artists still working as craftsmen. Even when they became involved with the patriotic movement, princely and French censorship wiped out any possibility of exhibiting works with undisguised national-democratic motifs. Most painters of the Wars of Liberation therefore employed highly symbolic, coded, allusive motifs which scarcely allowed for unambiguous political allegorization. This is especially true of the period prior to 1813, when censorship was particularly oppressive; but it also applies to the period after 1815, when the princes regained firm control and ruthlessly suppressed any further nationalist stirrings. A welcome occasion for this was provided by the murder of Kotzebue by the nationalistic student Carl Sand, leading in 1819 to the "Carlsbad Decrees" which put an end to any notions of a nation-state. Free expression was open to the painters of this era only in 1813, 1814, and 1815. Small wonder that they have remained so unknown up to the present.

These paintings have not yet been examined in any thorough, comprehensive manner. They are treated only in a few scattered essays written in a purely nationalistic vein and generally confining themselves to a preliminary motif analysis.[4] This is not surprising, since much of the work was either ignored from the outset or else eliminated, forgotten, or destroyed in the course of the nineteenth century once princely reaction set in.[5] This is especially true of painting's national-democratic variant, which attempted to bring out the "liberating" component of this war instead of glorifying the local dynasty or its generals.

Let us begin with paintings from the period prior to 1813, which could express their Germanic-mindedness only in coded form. What predominates at the outset is a Germanizing tendency, taking its inspiration from Wilhelm Heinrich Wackenroder's *Heartfelt Utterances of an Art-Loving Monk (Herzensergiessungen eines kunstliebenden Klosterbruders*—1797) and Ludwig Tieck's *The Rovings of Franz Sternbald (Franz Sternbalds Wanderungen*—1798), and moving to a Düreresque–Old German *ars sacra*. These currents led in 1808 to the founding in Vienna of the so-called St. Luke League (Lukasbund), which—despite its partiality toward the Old German—soon departed for Rome, where it turned to altar painting in a Nazarene, pre-Raphaelite style and was consequently lost for the further development of a specifically German art.

The tendency which came to the fore in the patriotic painting of the following years was—as in the political literature of this period—the North German, Pietist-Protestant, Klopstockian, Christian-Germanic. As the chief mode of expressing its national-democratic outlook, this tendency turned less to Old German altar painting (although this was not entirely eschewed) than to German landscape painting. There had been a few eighteenth-century predecessors of this type of landscape painting, such as the Rhine landscapes by Christian Georg Schütz, the pictures of the Alps by Ferdinand Kobell and Caspar Wolf, or the Klopstockian oak forests and Harz landscapes by Pascha Johann Friedrich Weitsch, who had ties to the "Göttingen Grove" and was "Old German-minded."[6] But German landscape painting now experienced its decisive breakthrough, particularly in the paintings by Caspar David Friedrich, one of the most impassioned advocates of the War of Liberation mentality.[7]

Friedrich became so upset about the defeat of Prussia in 1806 that he was confined to bed for weeks.[8] After recovering, he dedicated himself all the more strongly to an encoded yet obvious propaganda of national-democratic ideas. He almost always selected landscape painting, in which he gave preference to motifs from Rügen, the sandstone highlands along the Elbe, the Baltic coast, and the Riesengebirge, often embellishing these elements with hidden symbols or emblems. He frequently employed both a Christian and a national death-and-resurrection theme, clearly shown in his five major works in the succeeding years: *Dolmen by the Sea (Hünengrab am Meer*—1806–07), *Dolmen in the Snow (Hünengrab im Schnee*—1807), *Cross in the Mountains (Kreuz im Gebirge),* also called the *Tetschen Altar (Tetschener Altar*—1807–08), *The Monk by the Sea (Der Mönch am Meer*—1808–09), and *Abbey in the Oakwood (Abtei im Eichwald*—1809). What all these paintings have in common is a "neo-German, religious-patriotic" element, as it was put contemptuously by Goethe and Heinrich Meyer; their classicist-aristocratic standpoint granted validity only to the idealized Italianate landscape.[9] It would therefore be equally wrong to place sole emphasis upon either the Christian or the patriotic components.[10] In conjuring up a death-and-resurrection mood in the struggle against Napoleon, the foreign antichrist, all these works are specifically "Christian-Germanic." This mood is evoked by all those elements felt by Friedrich and other patriots of these years to be symbols of a typically "German" outlook: the Germanic, Nordic, Ossianic, Medieval, Gothic, Old German, Hutten-Luther-Düreresque. In all these things they saw guarantors and memorials of dormant German power and strength, which now had to be aroused for the struggle against foreign domination. The tomb of Christ or dolmen, the cross on Golgotha or the Iron Cross, the pillars and cross-ribbed vaults of Gothic churches or the trunks and branches of German oaks: within this framework, all elements become interchangeable or mutually reinforcing.

The overall impression made by these paintings is the predominance of eminently native elements. Be it dolmens, half-dead oaks, or Gothic ruins:

over and over we see not only the painted objects (however realistically reproduced) but also that Germany now in ruins from which a new life will
someday regrow. This is especially true of Friedrich's dolmens and oak
groves, which make the connection to the history of the fatherland particularly obvious. The intensity with which the oak was then held to be the very
essence of the German character is apparent not only in these pictures but
also in the poems of Arndt, Körner, Rückert, and Schenkendorf.[11] In those
years even the Gothic motifs, which we now associate more with the
French, still had a specifically national flavor. In contrast to the classicist-
Renaissance style of the Romance peoples, the Gothic was regarded as a
German, even a Germanic style. Patriotic-minded circles saw the rounded
arches of all Romanesque styles as an expression of mere practicality,
while the Gothic was regarded as a natural, organic style which uniquely
manifested the German longing both for the boundless and for a close kinship with nature. This is evidenced not just in Friedrich's paintings but also
by those Gothic dream castles painted between 1809 and 1814 by Karl
Friedrich Schinkel—which clearly pursue a bourgeois-German goal in opposition to aristocratic-classicist taste. While Napoleon, the courts, and the
nobility paid homage almost exclusively to the ceremonial and authoritarian Empire style, men such as Friedrich and Schinkel preferred Gothic as
the anticeremonial and accordingly bourgeois-libertarian style. In short,
even the Gothic was to them not just an artistic style but also a political
program.[12]

Friedrich's best-known picture of these years, the *Cross in the Mountains* or the *Tetschen Altar,* must also be seen in this light. This German
landscape of forest and rocks with a lonely cross jutting into the sky is set
in a neo-Gothic, altar-like frame designed by Friedrich himself. The meaning of this picture must have been entirely unmistakable to anyone of patriotic persuasion. The German dominates here down to the last detail. The
Gothic pillars are intended to convey the effect of tree trunks, the trees and
rocks are clearly presented as German trees and rocks, the rising sun behind the cross symbolizes the hope for an ideological dawning—everything
appears in the familiar German-Christian perspective. In the center of the
predella is a wide-open eye in an aureola of rays, challenging the viewer
downright apodictically: "Whoever has eyes to see, let him see!" This picture, which caused a considerable stir when first exhibited in 1808,[13] makes
it plain just how "neo-German, religious-patriotic" to the core Friedrich's
art is. The desire for freedom and the fear of God, Pietism and patriotism,
the Gothic and the modern enter into an indissoluble synthesis. By simultaneously mourning the sacrificial death of Christ and the fall of the Reich,
this picture represents the fatherland in both a religious and an Old Ger-
man-Düreresque sense. It stands as one of the most effective Germaniza-
tions of the old death-and-resurrection theme. As in many of the

patriotically inflamed songs of these years, at issue here too are "God! Freedom! Fatherland!" What bursts through is a desire for freedom based on the principle of a revolutionary return to a better past. Whereas the French Revolution had been understood as a return in at least some areas to republican concepts of antiquity, the restoration of Old German-Christian conditions is demanded here. Friedrich and those who shared his outlook saw the struggle against Napoleon as the strengthening of a free, morally pure, religiously cleansed Germanness oriented in a Pietistic-nativist way upon Jesus and Hermann the Cheruskan, the two martyrs on the altar of the inner and outer fatherland. A bourgeois consciousness of nation and self is thus expressed. On the basis of Christian-Germanic virtue, even a pronounced moral stringency and inner spiritualization, it seeks at least moral, if not political superiority to the foreign and aristocratic, felt to be the very essence of frivolity and godlessness. Friedrich enthusiastically joined the ranks of those who wanted to contribute something by their artistic works to the "inner fortification of Germany."[14]

Only after the outbreak of the anti-Napoleonic wars did it become possible to give free rein to this patriotic outlook. Feelings which had been smoldering under the surface could now be expressed more openly. This outlook was so widespread that it now held ever larger segments of the populace spellbound. From this point on, these feelings could no longer be contained. Tens of thousands wanted to shake off the oppressive yoke of the French and enter a war which they hoped would bring freedom not just to Germany but also to them.

Friedrich's enthusiasm for the patriotic, which he shared with many of his Dresden friends (especially the painters Gerhard von Kügelgen and Friedrich Georg Kersting), must also have reached its peak at this time. He enthused for Scharnhorst, had long conversations with Arndt when he came through Dresden in 1813, and supported Kersting (his junior by ten years) in his decision to join the Lützow Fusiliers— as did Körner, Hartmann, and Friesen.[15] Here Kersting acquitted himself so well that he quickly advanced to officer and received the Iron Cross. When the French occupied Dresden in 1813, Friedrich temporarily removed to the sandstone highlands of the Elbe. After Dresden was freed, he returned and wrote the only verses of his life which are still preserved. Characteristically, these are a series of "epitaphs" for the graves of fallen freedom fighters and a few "prayers" under the title After the Liberation of Dresden from the French (Nach der Befreiung Dresdens von den Franzosen),[16] which turns once again on the—by now thoroughly familiar—theme of death and resurrection.

The pictures created by Friedrich in 1813 and 1814 tend in the same direction. On July 20, 1813, he added the patriotic legend: "Arm yourselves for a new battle, men of Germania, hail to your weapons!" to a study of spruce trees. But the pictures of the following year make a more muted impression, since the First Peace of Paris (1814) already made it clear that the princes, not the peoples, would emerge as the victors from this war. Even Friedrich's *French Rifleman in the Forest (Chasseur im Walde—1814)*, which has been interpreted as a "political allegory" on the "defeat of the Napoleonic army in the wintry expanses of Russia,"[17] does not make a particularly triumphant impression. What comes to predominate in Friedrich's pictures during the following years is more a mood of mourning for the fallen than of joy about the victory achieved. In his oeuvre we repeatedly encounter emotionally charged grave motifs, which manifest mourning over the dashed hopes for a real war of liberation. Consider his picture *Graves of Fallen Freedom Fighters (Gräber gefallener Freiheitskrieger—1814)*, in which four gravestones can be seen in a rocky ravine. They bear the following inscriptions: "Arminius"; "Peace unto Your Grave/Savior in Our Need"; "Noble Youth, Redeemer of the Fatherland"; and "Who Fell Nobly for Freedom and Justice, F.A.K.," which Kurt Karl Eberlein has linked to Friesen, Hartmann, and Körner.[18] Of a similar nature is the *Grave of Arminius (Grab des Arminius—1814)*, which again shows a sarcophagus in a rocky ravine, this time bearing the inscription: "May your loyalty and invincibility as a warrior be an eternal example to us." In 1814, Prince Repnin-Wolkonsky—closely associated with Freiherr vom Stein—organized an exhibit in Dresden at which the *Grave of Arminius* and *French Rifleman in the Forest* were shown. The *Dresdener Anzeiger* on August 5 praised this exhibition of "patriotic pictures."

In these years, Friedrich was scarcely able to realize his grander patriotic projects. He and Arndt, for example, conceived of a memorial to the fallen Scharnhorst, but support was not forthcoming. In a letter to Arndt dated March 12, 1814, Friedrich wrote about this: "I am not at all surprised that no memorials are being erected, neither to mark the great cause of the Volk nor to the magnanimous deeds of individual German men. As long as we remain manservants to the princes, nothing grand of this sort will ever happen. When the Volk has no voice, neither is the Volk allowed to feel and honor itself." In the autumn of 1814, Friedrich instead painted a picture with the title *Imaginary City with a Scharnhorst Memorial (Erdachte Stadt mit einem Scharnhorstdenkmal)*. It bore the inscription "To the Reviver and Preparer of German Honor and Freedom, the Calm, Pious, Courageous Scharnhorst," but like many of his specifically "nativist" paintings is presumed lost.

Despite all the great expectations and political hopes pinned upon the renewal of a genuinely popular, national, and free German art,[19] the "painting of the Wars of Liberation" is only a short, if significant episode in the history of German art. Admittedly there is Friedrich, widely regarded as the most significant German painter of the nineteenth century and for whom the anti-Napoleonic war was the central experience of his life. But could anyone else be associated with this tendency, which expected far more from the Wars of Liberation than just the liberation from Napoleon?

There are few painters other than Friedrich and Schinkel active in the area of Christian-Germanic, Gothic, or national-democratic, heightened landscape painting. This made use of hidden symbols and emblems, aiming primarily at the group of already knowledgeable, the initiated. Those painters who held patriotic views and attempted to give them artistic expression in the years following 1813 generally turned to a far more obvious, illustrative manner. There were those who outfitted their figures with specifically Germanic attributes (oakleaf garlands, Bronze Age jewelry, fur clothing, spears), continuing with the classicist Germanic motifs of the Füger and Angelika Kaufmann schools. Examples of this approach can be seen in the paintings by Gerhard von Kügelgen and Ludwig Ferdinand Schnorr von Carolsfeld, men who—while never denying their classicist training—were willingly swept along by the atmosphere of the Wars of Liberation to a passionate patriotism.

These Teutonizing painters were an extremely isolated phenomenon. The majority of patriotic-spirited painters and graphic artists set about presenting their "national motifs" in a far more realistic manner. They applied themselves to portraits of men who had contributed something to the ideological and military preparation for war—such as Freiherr vom Stein, Scharnhorst, Gneisenau, Blücher, Fichte, Schleiermacher, Andreas Hofer, Lützow, Schill, the bookdealer Palm, the publishers Reimer and Perthes, poets such as Arndt and Körner. Also favored in 1813 and 1814 were self-portraits, in which artists portrayed themselves as war-time volunteers. Kersting's self-portrait as a Lützow Fuselier or Adam Weise's as a young infantryman come to mind. This tendency also takes pleasure in depicting movingly patriotic family scenes. Heinrich Anton Dähling's *Departure of Two Volunteer Riflemen from Their Parents (Abschied zweier freiwilliger Jäger von ihren Eltern*—1813) and Peter Krafft's *The Departure of the Militiaman (Der Abschied des Landwehrmannes*—1813) could be cited as examples. These are pictures in which the mothers and wives mostly look on sadly, while the fathers either attempt to bolster the patriotic sentiment of their defiantly gazing sons with great gestures or simply drop their hands for a short, fervent prayer.

Scenes of the folk or any expression of the mass or "semiinsurrectionary" character of this war are rare or almost entirely lacking. The few motifs which can be linked to such an outlook include the anti-French revolt of the Tyrolean peasants under Andreas Hofer or the glowing patriotism of the Lützow Fusiliers, Schill's Volunteer Corps, and the Prussian local militia. But even in this area most works either are lost or were apparently never painted. In the few cases where paintings or graphics of this kind have been preserved, one senses the lack of a specifically "libertarian" element. In his *The Tyrolean Militia (Der Tiroler Landsturm*—1813), for example, Josef Anton Koch—one of the thoroughly progressive painters of this tendency—transfigures only the heroic figure of Hofer (and that in connection with a fanaticized monk who thrusts a crucifix and a sword into the air), while the Volk is granted only the perspective of gazing up admiringly. The specifically anti-French tendency of this picture is expressed only in the figure of the fallen French rifleman, on whom one of the particularly nasty-looking peasants has set his foot.

With that the store of motifs in the national-democratic tendency is already exhausted. All that remains are pictures dominated by a legitimizing view of these events—pictures which confine themselves to the portrayal of military or princely battle commanders and victoriously returning "heroes." This can be seen in Prussia in pictures such as Carl Wilhelm Colbe's *Marshall Blücher (Marschall Blücher*—1814), Eduard Kaiser's *Blücher in the Battle of Waterloo (Blücher in der Schlacht bei Waterloo* —1815), Franz Krüger's *Gneisenau in the Circle of His Officers (Gneisenau im Kreise seiner Offiziere*—1819), and Simon Meister's *Blücher on Horseback (Blücher zu Pferde*—1823); in Austria, there are such pictures as *Archduke Karl in the Battle at Aspern (Erzherzog Karl in der Schlacht zu Aspern*—1815) by Peter Krafft and the numerous portrayals of Kaiser Franz I. Almost all these pictures are linked to the baroque-feudalistic tradition of large-format equestrian images, which direct the gaze of the viewer almost exclusively to the superhuman figure of the towering *imperator* or *triumphator,* while the Volk appears as a secondary concern, an executive organ, on the margin.

What predominates in these works is not the longing for freedom but the official demonstration of power, dominion, of dynastic grandeur which seeks to employ all the means of princely representation (splendid uniforms, shining swords, glittering medals, well-groomed horses) to legitimize its own historical stature. The Wars of Liberation appear here not as a national liberation struggle but as a dynastic-military affair whose outcome is determined by kings and generals alone. Instead of patriotic-spirited youths or Volkish masses, what dominates is the overwhelming figure of the individual: the monarch or his appointed field marshall. The capstone of this outlook is given by Heinrich Olivier's picture, *The Holy Alliance (Die heilige Allianz*—1817), in which the Russian czar, Austrian kaiser, and Prussian king are portrayed as a triumvirate installed by God. An additional religious-legitimist luster is thus given to the restoration of the *ancien régime,* which received its political seal at the Congress of Vienna.

What is almost always lacking in the pictures of this tendency is the Volk

Yet how could this Volk possibly appear, given that the events of 1814 and, after the battle of Belle Alliance in 1815, the Congress of Vienna had definitively condemned it to its previous position as subject? Shortly after 1815 a disturbingly bifurcated development becomes apparent: legitimist-oriented painters depict only kings and generals (or resort to a Biedermeier idyll), while the national democrats devote all their energies to the work of mourning, which has a distinctly defeatist quality. Even such an inflamed patriot as Kersting paints only two pictures of mourning in 1815: the picture *On Outpost Duty (Auf Vorposten),* a portrayal of Körner, Friesen, and Hartmann, who fell in this war, and the picture *The Wreathmaker (Die Kranzwinderin),* in which a girl dressed in white binds a wreath of honor dedicated to the heroes just mentioned, whose names are carved on the oaks in the background.

Friedrich also increasingly devoted himself to this national work of mourning from 1815 on. If he had briefly reached a certain fame before 1814, almost no one was interested in him any longer. After the long years of French occupation and the Wars of Liberation, patrons and collectors were again interested in more cheerful or at least more idyllic motifs. After 1815, these circles could no longer be enthused by gnarled oaks, defiantly towering rocks, Gothic ruins, or gloomy cemetery scenes. Friedrich's work in the following years stands in the shadow cast by somber melancholy, but the vision of another, more libertarian Germany gleams through again and again. It is expressed most hopefully in that Gothic dream cathedral he portrayed in 1818 as a vision hovering in the sky. But it is also expressed in his famous *Abbey in the Oakwood* (1817), which assembles virtually every emblem of the national-religious hopelessness in one picture: Gothic ruins, split crosses, the funeral procession of the monks, weathered oaks, and icy coldness. Yet at the altar stands a Protestant clergyman with a white collar and clerical tabs, seeming to embody the future in an anachronistic, paradoxical way.[20]

All these pictures reveal Friedrich stubbornly clinging to his earlier ideals. There is not only mourning here, but hope as well—which brings us back to the death-and-resurrection theme. The mourning becomes more intense, and the hope more ethereal, but both are still present with equal strength. Even after 1815, Friedrich ventures to make direct political allusions in some pictures. This includes the "Old German costume" worn by almost all of his figures starting in 1816.[21] This costume was not at all welcomed by the authorities and was even officially banned in some states and cities (such as Dresden) after 1819. When Friedrich was asked by Karl Förster on April 18, 1820, what the figures wearing Old German attire in his *Two Men Contemplating the Moon (Zwei Männer in Betrachtung des Mondes—*1819) were actually doing, Friedrich answered laconically: "They're engaging in subversive activity."[22] Even more openly, he wrote to his brother Adolf on May 13, 1820, that the princes would like best of all to transform everyone into patient donkeys which would only be "permitted to scream ia-ia!" (a pun on "heehaw" and "yes"). The picture *Hutten's Grave (Huttens Grab*—1823) pursues the same tendency and attacks the Biedermeier temper of the times particularly sharply. This picture shows a mourning fraternity member with a cap, a hiking staff, a sword, and the costume of the Wars of Liberation standing in the middle of the Gothic church ruins of Oybin. He is bent over the grave, which not only bears the name "Hutten," but also the very revealing inscriptions "Jahn 1813, Stein 1813, Arndt 1813, Görres 1821"—pointing to the death of these men for the German cause. Friedrich's picture *The Ice Sea (Das Eismeer)*, also called *Dashed Hope (Die gescheiterte Hoffnung)*, painted in the same year, is perhaps even more rousing. It portrays the wreck of a North Pole expedition, but on a symbolic level also implies the wreck of all the lofty national-religious ideas of the preceding years. It should be evident that such pictures would not win Friedrich favor with his superiors. When a professorship in landscape painting opened up at the Dresden Academy in 1824— a post Friedrich had long waited for—he was simply passed over by authorities because of his "unfavorable influence upon youth."[23] But even this did not bring Friedrich around. On the contrary, he became increasingly obstinate and would now wear only his Old German costume with an enormous blonde beard in order to appear as "Nordic-reserved" as possible. He had nothing but contempt for all those who conformed out of opportunism. From his standpoint, this included both courtly oriented classicists, who after a more ceremonial Empire phase in the course of the twenties turned to a Biedermeier trivialization, and spiritual reactionaries such as the Nazarenes, who largely placed themselves in the service of restorative-Catholicizing tendencies of the Metternichian system.

Friedrich experienced a real lift only one more time: in 1830, influenced by the July Revolution in Paris, rebellions broke out in Dresden in the course of which the folk began arming itself.[24] But when even this rebellion failed, the pictures of Friedrich became gloomier again and were given to the depiction of graves, coffins, owls, and other memorials of transitoriness. The last painting which stands out among these products of old age is the picture *Life Stages (Lebensstufen*—1835). Here on the Baltic coast, in the vicinity of Greifswald, an aged man stands with staff, fraternity cap, an ice-gray fur, and an Old German coat, staring steadfastly north. One also sees in fashionable Biedermeier attire a man and a woman, who make a fundamentally "less dignified" impression and create the same effect as the opportunists so hated by Friedrich. At their feet lay two small children, of whom the boy stretches a small Swedish flag toward the north, as if pointing symbolically to a better future. Since the children have failed, Friedrich now pins his never entirely faltering hope on the grandchildren.

But by 1835, who could even understand such a picture anymore? When Friedrich died in Dresden on May 7, 1840, he belonged not just to the poor, but also to the forgotten. While other old freedom fighters such as Arndt and Jahn were publicly rehabilitated during this period, the wheel of history had rolled right past him.

Even sadder, when he was rediscovered around 1900, it happened incorrectly. In the course of Wilhelminism and later of fascism, attempts were made either to assign him to the Romantics with their longing for distance, to make a precursor of Impressionism out of him, or to try to restrict him to his purely national components. A more objective study of Friedrich got underway only with great difficulty in the succeeding decades. But only if this perspective is given a real chance will the "national democrat" Friedrich finally be seen in the right light. And only then will we gain an important new insight into the spirit of those Wars of Liberation, which played a significant role in the political and ideological development of Germany.

NOTES

1. MEW 14, p. 31.
2. Cf. Hasko Zimmer, *Auf dem Altar des Vaterlandes: Religion und Patriotismus in der deutschen Kriegslyrik des 19. Jahrhunderts* (Frankfurt, 1971).
3. Cf. Friedrich Sengle, *Das deutsche Geschichtsdrama* (Stuttgart, 1952), p. 102.
4. A first attempt at a comprehensive presentation is undertaken by Konrad Kaiser, "Patriotische Kunst." In *Patriotische Kunst aus der Zeit der Volkserhebung 1813* (Berlin/GDR, 1953) pp. 8–47.
5. Cf. the list of 488 works by Friedrich presumed lost or not identifiable given by Werner Sumowski, *Caspar David Friedrich-Studien* (Wiesbaden, 1970), pp. 182–244.
6. Cf. Annedore Müller-Hofstede, *Der Landschaftsmaler Pascha Johann Friedrich Weitsch, 1773–1803* (Braunschweig, 1973), pp. 48 ff.
7. Cf. among the numerous works on this subject Andreas Aubert, *Caspar David Friedrich: Gott, Freiheit und Vaterland* (Berlin, 1915); Willi Geismeier, *Caspar David Friedrich* (Vienna, 1973); Gerhard Eimer, *Caspar David Friedrich* (Frankfurt, 1974); *Bürgerliche Revolution und Romantik: Natur und Gesellschaft bei Caspar David Friedrich,* ed. Berthold Hinz et al. (Giessen, 1976); Jost Hermand, "Das offene Geheimnis: Caspar David Friedrichs nationale Trauerarbeit." In Hermand, *Sieben Arten an Deutschland zu leiden* (Königstein, 1979), pp. 1–42.
8. Cf. Philipp Otto Runge, *Hinterlassene Schriften,* vol. 2 (Hamburg, 1840), p. 310.
9. *Kunst und Altertum,* 1817, Heft 2, pp. 5–62 and 133–62.
10. On a purely patriotic interpretation cf. Aubert; on a purely Christian interpretation, cf. Helmut Börsch-Supan and Karl Wilhelm Jähnig, *Caspar David Friedrich* (Munich, 1973).
11. Cf. Paul Wagler, *Die Eiche in alter und neuer Zeit* (Berlin, 1891), pp. 107–25.

12. Cf. Hans-Joachim Kunst, "Die politischen und gesellschaftlichen Bedingtheiten der Gotikrezeption bei Friedrich und Schinkel." In *Bürgerliche Revolution und Romantik,* ed. Hinz, pp. 17 ff.

13. Complete documentation on this controversy is to be found in *Caspar David Friedrich in Briefen und Bekenntnissen,* ed. Sigrid Hinz (Berlin/GDR, 1968), pp. 135–95.

14. Cf. on this point Friedrich Ludwig Jahn, *Deutsches Volkstum,* 2nd ed. (Leipzig, 1817), p. 350.

15. According to Kurt Karl Eberlein, "Kerstings patriotische Kunst," *Cicerone* 16 (1924), p. 849.

16. Hinz, pp. 79 ff.

17. Geismeier, p. 45.

18. Eberlein, *Caspar David Friedrich, der Landschaftsmaler* (Bielefeld, 1940), p. 26.

19. Cf. George L. Mosse, *The Nationalization of the Masses* (New York, 1975), pp. 76 ff.

20. Kunst, p. 28.

21. On the origins of the "Old German" costume, cf. Jahn, pp. 313 ff.; Ernst Moritz Arndt, *Über Sitte, Mode und Kleidertracht* (Frankfurt, 1814).

22. Hinz, p. 220.

23. Cf. Gerhard Eimer, *Caspar David Friedrich und die Gotik* (Hamburg, 1963), p. 20.

24. Cf. Hinz, pp. 58 ff.

Caspar David Friedrich: *Kreuz im Gebirge* (1808). Dresden, Gemäldegalerie. Marburg, Foto Marburg, Ernst von Hülsen Haus.

Caspar David Friedrich: *Hünengrab im Schnee* (1807). Dresden, Gemäldegalerie. Marburg, Foto Marburg, Ernst von Hülsen Haus.

Caspar David Friedrich: *Klosterfriedhof im Schnee* (1817–19). Lost. Marburg, Foto Marburg, Ernst von Hülsen Haus.

232

Georg Friedrich Kersting: *Die Kranzwinderin* (1815). Westberlin, Nationalgalerie.

Peter Krafft: *Erzherzog Carl in der Schlacht bei Aspern* (1815). Vienna, Heeresgeschichtliches Museum.

Heinrich Anton Dähling: *Abschied zweier freiwilliger Jäger von ihren Eltern* (1813). Schwerin, Staatliche Museen.

Josef Anton Koch: *Der Tiroler Landsturm* (1813). Schloss Cappenberg.

Ludwig Ferdinand Schnorr von Carolsfeld: *Cäcila Tschudi als Walküre* (1813). Madison, private collection.

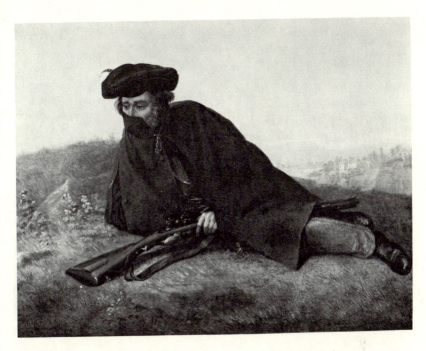

Georg Friedrich Kersting: *Auf Vorposten* (1815). Westberlin, Nationalgalerie.

Karl Friedrich Schinkel: *Dom über einer Stadt* (1814). Munich, Bayerische Staatsgemäldesammlungen.

Caspar David Friedrich: *Die gescheiterte Hoffnung* (1821). Hamburg, Kunsthalle.

Caspar David Friedrich: *Die Lebensstufen* (1835). Leipzig, Museum der Bildenden Künste. Marburg, Foto Marburg, Ernst von Hülsen Haus.

CHAPTER ELEVEN

The Nature and Function of Generational Discourse in France on the Eve of World War I

Paul F. Lachance

Intellectuals frequently express themselves in generational terms. Often they do so in passing as when in 1930 André Malraux lamented the bland formative years of his age group: "We grew up in a time of peace; we have not been tested by the shock of a war or revolution which would have been so useful to us."[1] Sometimes generations receive more extended treatment as in collective memoirs like Charles Péguy's *Notre jeunesse* (1910).[2] Now and then, a generational reading of the direction of history evokes a wider response. The "Consciousness III controversy" precipitated by Charles Reich's *The Greening of America* (1970) is an example from the recent past.[3] As an illustration of how intellectuals involved in the controversies of their time and addressing themselves to the public at large use the notion of generations, this essay examines a comparable debate in France immediately before World War I.

Beginning in 1912, the appearance of a new generation was widely remarked in the French press. It was pictured as radically different from the generation that had come of age in the fin de siècle. Journalists, novelists, and literary critics passionately discussed the significance of a shift in the sympathies of youth from Left to Right between 1890 and 1910. Some intellectuals reacted enthusiastically to this perceived shift, others negatively.[4] On the basis of their remarks, an anatomy of generational discourse can be worked out: its underlying structure, the permutations in interpretation it allows, and the functions it serves.[5] On a rudimentary level, the concept of generations implicit in the commentaries of prewar French intellectuals resembles that of social scientists. In both, age serves as the principle of social stratification. The basic units of society consist of individuals born in the same span of years and hence exposed to identical formative experiences during youth. The succession of age groups provides a scheme for charting the movement of history.[6] In a polemical context, generational discourse displays characteristics not suggested by theoretical models of generational consciousness. First of all, it is protean. Secondly, it is highly ideological.

Lewis Feuer is one theorist who insufficiently allows for the variety of interpretations possible using generational categories. Contrary to his assertion, "generational struggle, generational conflict, has been a universal theme of history,"[7] we shall see that not all statements about youth by older intellectuals reflect antagonism or resentment; some bespeak approval and even admiration. Generational consciousness is as variable as class consciousness. Just as Marxists insist on class struggle, corporatists dream of harmony, and liberals often deny the importance of class differences, so spokesmen for opposed ideological tendencies may be expected to picture the interaction of generations differently.

Since almost all commentators on generations between 1912 and 1914 had come of age in the fin de siècle, their remarks reveal the wide range of generational thinking within a single age group. Because their politics ranged from royalism to socialism, the effect of ideological preconceptions on generational discourse is also evident. The symbols these intellectuals used to describe youth of two different epochs were ideologically charged. How they manipulated generational symbols depended on their respective sociopolitical affinities.

Two ideologists of the nationalist Right, Henri Massis and Alfred de Tarde, set early in 1912 the frame of reference for much subsequent discussion of generations in French public opinion. Writing under the pseudonym of "Agathon," they began their series of articles in *l'Opinion* on "Les jeunes gens d'aujourd'hui" with the declaration: "There is something new about youth."[8] They meant that the young generation was "new" in comparison to the preceding generation. The first point to note about the structure of generational discourse is that it is necessarily comparative. Theoretically, there is no limit to the number of generations in a generational outlook. It depends on how far back in time one goes and the interval one posits between generations. Practically, between 1912 and 1914, only two active generations were objects of attention, an older generation that came of age in the 1890s and a new generation of 1910. The younger generation included anyone twenty years old or younger in 1905, the year of the Tangiers crisis; the older generation everyone else. Borderline cases were subsumed into one or the other of the two generations. Occasionally, to set off the qualities attributed to the generation of 1890, a third generation which had reached maturity during the Second Empire was cited; but it was no longer considered active on the eve of the war.[9]

By age the majority of commentators belonged to the generation of 1890.[10] However, they juxtaposed to youth of 1910 their own generation not as it was in 1912 but as it had been in its youth. Within their age group, the iconoclastic playwright Alfred Jarry rubbed shoulders with the Barrèsian Paul Acker, the socialist Hubert Lagardelle, and the unclassifiable Péguy.[11] The diversity of the generation of 1890 at maturity was too glaring to speak of a shared outlook. Members of the generation affirmed a more uniform mentality only as they looked backward to their youth. Equally noteworthy is that the other generation under comparison was just reaching maturity. Because very few youth in 1910 had begun to write or assume a role in society, older intellectuals felt free to speculate about their thoughts and future actions.

Of all types of consciousness, generational consciousness is the most indeterminate. Nationalism somehow makes the nation its central premise. Class refers to the division of wealth, status, and power in society. But there is no such specific focus in a generation. Its only determinant is time. Growing up in a particular historical context supposedly produces a common consciousness, a shared set of attitudes and beliefs. On the eve of World War I, generational outlooks were defined by symbols derived from the very different intellectual climates in which youth of 1890 and 1910 came of age.

The fin de siècle and the Dreyfus affair, superimposed and recalled fifteen to twenty years later, underlay depictions of young Frenchmen of that epoch as cosmopolitan at the expense of patriotism, anticlerical, avantgarde in their literary preferences, and Bohemian in lifestyle. Since 1905, the nationalist revival, feeding and fed by a premonition of war, the vogue of Bergson, critiques of the scientific ideal, defenses of classicism in art and education, and several notable conversions to Catholicism were perceived as new directions in French intellectual life. Contemporaries projected these developments onto the new generation, picturing it as fiercely patriotic, orthodox in its Catholicism, classical in its literary taste, and precociously mature. They used generational symbols to objectify their sense of a shift in the mood of the times.[12]

By the criteria of the day, the generation of 1890 was to the Left, that of 1910 to the Right. Rarely did propagandists of the Right, who most often approved the character of the new generation, call attention to the ideological connotations of the symbols used to describe it. On the other hand, the connotations were explicitly remarked by those to whom the new generation represented a threat. For Roger Dévigne, writing in a newspaper attentive to innovative tendencies in art and literature, youth were "Catholic and reactionary."[13] To radicals, their outlook amounted to "new words dissembling old ideas"; it was "very simply, under other names and with rejuvenated formulas, the politics of conservative traditionalism and monarchic nationalism."[14]

In using the terms *youth* and *generations* French intellectuals did not mean all the young but only a relatively narrow segment of the age group — young bourgeois males of Paris, for the most part in the universities or the upper classes of *lycées* and *collèges*. In 1912 there were 17,512 students at the University of Paris, compared to roughly 3,105,000 individuals between the ages of twenty and twenty-four in all of France.[15] Intellectuals were rarely troubled by the demographic insignificance of "educated" or "cultivated" youth. To admirers of the generation of 1910, what mattered was that it included those "who counted": the future elite of France.[16] Maurice Allard pointed out in *l'Humanité* the corollary to this proposition: "The other youth — working-class youth — does not count; its role is all marked out: to become in the barracks, the factory, and the workshop the slave of the former." But it served even this socialist's purposes to stereotype the sons of the bourgeoisie in the prevailing fashion. Under their dominion, he added, "the capitalist regime will soon reach its culmination. Don't complain. After culmination, the fall."[17]

The structure of generational discourse lent itself to use by intellectuals of widely varying ideological persuasions. All that was required was that the commentator take the step of projecting into two generations the intellectual moods of 1890 and 1910. That step taken, he could coo glowingly over the traits of the new generation, lament the change it represented, or take a more nuanced stance somewhere in between. Differing reactions led to different modes of explaining the two generations, depicting their relationship to each other, and judging the implications of youth for the future.

Most contemporaries accounted for the respective outlooks of the generations of 1890 and 1910 in one of four ways: (1) by the different intellectual climates in which each generation came of age; (2) by the long-term effects of the defeat of 1870; (3) by the influence of *maîtres* from a preceding generation; or (4) by the tendency of sons to revolt against their fathers. Rightists preferred the second and third types of explanation, Leftists the fourth, but as a rule an intellectual's ideological perspective determined less the type of explanation to which he had recourse than his manner of using it.

According to theorists of generational analysis, the young differ from adults in having no preconceived patterns of reaction based on past experience to determine how they relate to contemporary events. They are for that reason more impressionable, more susceptible to the influence of the prevailing intellectual atmosphere.[18] A similar logic was implicit in portrayals of the generations of prewar France in terms of intellectual moods. The Dreyfus affair and, in the cultural sphere, the cosmpolitan and libertarian atmosphere of Roger Shattuck's aptly labeled "banquet years," were commonly cited as formative experiences of the generation of 1890. The experiences seen as important for those coming of age after 1905 were fundamentally different. Their cult of physical strength and moral discipline was ascribed to the introduction of organized sports into France; their optimism, to the invention of the automobile and the airplane; and their nationalism, to the international tension following Tangiers.[19]

Use of the prevailing intellectual climate to account for the sentiments of youth lent itself equally readily to approving and disparaging views. Urbain Gohier did not regret the passing of the libertarian atmosphere which had given rise to the "fantasies and excesses" of intellectual youth at the end of the nineteenth century; nor did he hide his approval of the far different circumstances of 1912 in which the new generation was coming of age. He wrote that youth, foreseeing the outbreak of war, were acquiring through sports the qualities appropriate to waging it successfully: "The rigorous discpline of football, the hard fists of the boxer, steadfast wills."[20] An episode of "The New Dawn," the last book of Romain Rolland's *Jean-Christophe*, pictured the exacerbation of international tensions as having essentially the same effect on youth; but this time, reflecting the novelist's cosmpolitan ideals, the description was sarcastic: "The children of the nation who had never seen war except in books had no difficulty in endowing it with beauty. They became aggressive. Weary of peace and ideas, they hymned the anvil of battle, on which, with bloody fists, action would one day new forge the power of France."[21]

A second type of explanation, tracing the postures of the generation of 1890 back to the events of 1870–71, was inherently critical of that generation and hence preferred by commentators of the Right. Forty years afterward, one can still find French intellectuals who pretended to vividly recall childhood images of Paris "mutilated by the Prussian bombardment and the fires of the Commune."[22] The impact of the *année terrible* on members of the generation of 1890 not yet born in 1870 was explained by the argument that, passing their childhood, in its immediate aftermath they lacked the prior experience of an undefeated France. It is here that a third pre-1870 generation enters the interpretation. Until 1870, according to a moderate republican commentator, the wars of the Second Empire — in Italy, Crimea, Mexico — had been gratuitous from the point of view of national safety. The success of the Universal Exposition of 1867 had promoted the feeling that peace was triumphing through the marvels of industry. The fathers of the generation of 1890 had known for at least part of their lives an optimism, a calm, a security which their sons who grew up in a conquered France never knew.[23]

The Right ingeniously linked the outlook of the generation of 1890 to the childhood trauma of defeat. Just as Alfred de Musset had accounted for the pale and nervous character of the romantic generation of 1815 by the anxiety of mothers whose husbands and brothers were fighting in Napoleon's army, so many rightist intellectuals in the Third Republic argued that the distress and hardships of the Franco-Prussian war made the children of that era "neurasthenic" and "anemic."[24] On reaching adolescense, they affected the behavior of the *petit crevé* and read the *Journal des Abrutis.*[25] To compensate for lack of confidence in France as the military equal of Germany, they exaggerated the primacy of intellect over brute force and "took refuge in a pose of superior indifference."[26] These characterizations accorded neatly with popular notions of decadence whereby France, having passed its peak of strength and no longer capable of confronting a "young" nation like Germany, should console itself with the flowering of culture that is the last privilege of a moribund nation. The political postures of the generation of 1890, its attraction to humanitarian and internationalist doctrines, to pacifism and socialism, were judged as "masks for its pusillanimity."[27]

Besides accounting for the defects of the generation of 1890, the trauma of 1870 was used to explain a healthier psychology and more positive attitudes in the generation of 1910. Youth were said to have benefited from the concentration of all the negative consequences of the Franco-Prussian war in the generation of 1890. Agathon remarked that its effacement "prepared and made possible the present generation which, to quickly reconstruct life on new certitudes, has not had to overcome so many obstacles." It was as if the generation of 1890 were fated to contract the disease of defeatism in order to immunize future generations against it.[28]

Equally psychohistorical and especially favored by detractors of the older generation was the third type of explanation: the influence of *maîtres*. Paul Bourget established the terms in which the Right discussed the impact of positivist *maîtres* on the generation of 1890. First in his *Essais de psychologie contemporaine* (1883–85) and then in a novel *Le Disciple* (1889), he proposed and popularized the notion that the theories and dreams of one generation determine the temperament of the next.[29] They are communicated to young readers through the works of great authors, themselves unconscious of the psychological implications of their ideas. In Taine's determinism and Renan's relativism, in Stendhal's dispassionate dissection of character and in the perspectives of other *maîtres* from the positivist generation of 1850, he identified the source of the "maladies of soul" of educated youth of the 1880s: "It seems to me that all these works reveal a single influence — downhearted and, to say everything in a word, profoundly, unrelentingly pessimistic."[30]

Through Bourget, analysis of the deformed psychology of fin de siècle youth became from the 1880s onward a refrain in rightist critiques of French intellectual life. To this extent, the image of generations of 1912–14 built upon existing preconceptions.[31] By 1912 Bourget's thesis seemed to have received confirmation from the latest developments in French philosophy. Henri Bergson was in vogue because in the opinion of many of his contemporaries he had finally liberated them from the excesses of intellectualism, the "nightmare of pessismism" engendered by positivism. This made for a scheme of French intellectual history in which the sequel to the positivist certitude of the generation of 1850 was the relativism and scepticism of the generation of 1890, with its psychological dimension of pessimism and self-doubt, followed in turn by a new generation of 1910 which, with a little help from Bergson, found its way back to the certainties afforded by national and religious commitment.[32]

Many of the same intellectuals who explained the traits of the generation of 1890 by the influence of positivist *maîtres* were reluctant to adopt a similar type of explanation for the new generation of 1910. When the influence of *maîtres* on contemporary youth was acknowledged, it was practically always with qualifications, youth rejecting those aspects of their thought that still bore the marks of the debilitating climate of the 1890s.[33] To ascribe too much importance to *maîtres* was to diminish the new generation. One meaning of the "precocious maturity" said to characterize youth was that they spontaneously and instinctively arrived at the correct postures, which logically meant that their elders were superfluous.

Several commentators went so far as to deny to *maîtres*, particularly when the term meant academics, any role at all in forming the new generation. The nationalist polemicist Étienne Rey wrote that youth, "far from undergoing the influence of their educators, have either ignored or frankly opposed them, and have formed themselves from principles of action outside their education."[34] The direction of influence was sometimes said to run in the opposite direction. In a section of his study entitled "Conversion of the elders," Agathon contended that the daily encounters of Paul Desjardins with students at a Paris *lycée* caused him to cease advocating the ideas of Kant and Tolstoy and to become a patriot instead.[35]

Pushed further, denials that *maîtres* influenced the generation of 1910 passed over into a fourth type of explanation — the revolt of youth. For intellectuals of the Right who had recourse to this argument, the cause of revolt lay in the fundamental faults of a society created and perpetuated by republican generations — in the crises and corruption of parliamentary government and the alien intellectualism of a German-inspired education. These factors had been blamed for falsifying the hearts of the generation of 1890; now they were said to provoke revolt in the next generation. Speaking of foreign domination of the French economy and of French intellectual life, Charles Maurras proclaimed in July, 1912: "Young France of today is in complete and profound reaction against this double evil."[36]

When intellectuals of the Left used the explanation of revolt, there was a shift of emphasis. The gravity of ills of French society had nothing to do with the revolt of youth. It was instead but another instance of a universal law of reaction whereby every new generation opposes itself to the establishment, whatever its political coloration. The Radical senator and journalist Henri Bérenger used the metaphor of a pendulum that swung to the left and to the right with successive generations: "If youth of 1900 were socialist and anticlerical, it was because at the beginning of the Dreyfus affair socialism and anticlericalism were outlawed by the official world. When they invaded that world, youth naturally became Catholic and traditionalist."[37]

Cyclical views of history are normally associated with the Right. Paradoxically, leftists adopted this perspective in their commentaries on youth of 1910. The pendulum argument served to deflate the importance of a new generation stereotyped as rightist. Its appearance was thereby disconnected from any fundamental change in French society. It was reduced to a passing phenomenon. Depending on the sense in which it was used, a law of reaction implied either that the rebellion of youth would give way to different attitudes in adult age, or that the cycle of generations would bring about in the next generation a return to the ideas and principles of the generation of 1890. Bérenger was not unduly alarmed by the preferences of youth of 1910: "Let the Clergy and the Reaction retake power tomorrow. So soon shall we see students become again freethinkers and revolutionaries."[38]

Ideology also determined how intellectuals depicted the relationship between generations in the present. Rightists tended to approve and leftists to disapprove the rightist orientation of youth of 1910. Since the commentators belonged to the generation of 1890, attitudes of approval were equivalent to proclaiming the contemporary rapport of the older generation with youth; conversely, attitudes of disapproval denoted generational conflict.

The symbol of nationalism gave rise to the clearest statments of generational rapport. Writing in *Le Matin* of the reawakening of French pride, Georges Lecomte maintained: "Whether they belong to the up-and-coming generation or to that whose hairs are graying — and whose merit was at least to maintain intact the hopes born the day after the defeat — Frenchmen today are tired of self-distrust."[39] Similarly, Barrès spoke of how with time his generation had come to a realization of the majesty of "order," making possible an identity of outlook with youths of 1910 who, unlike his own generation, spontaneously recognized the virtues of order and discipline.[40] Other intellectuals felt that youths' return to Catholicism was duplicated, over a longer time span, by the preceding generation, and in part due to the same influences, especially that of Bergson.[41]

Harmony between generations in the present implied that the generation of 1890 was very different at maturity than during its youth. Indeed, it demanded confession by its members that they had been in error. They, not the young, were expected to acknowledge their folly. In some cases, disparagement was pushed to the point where good relations with youths of 1910 depended on the older generation's recognition that it could never hope to be their equal. "One must not fear to proclaim it," wrote Henri Lavedan in *l'Illustration,* "[the young man] is superior to his senior; he is worth more than him, he will go further, and will do more."[42] The implication of such an argument was that the generation of 1890 should make way for youth. Generational rapport depended entirely on the self-effacement of the older generation.

Rightist intellectuals did not represent youth as resentful toward their elders, at least on a personal level. Indeed, if the generation of 1890 had evolved to less reprehensible postures by 1912, there was no basis for the young generation to be in conflict with it.[43] In sharp contrast, leftist critics pictured the new generation as wilfully in revolt. The burden for lack of generational rapport fell on youth as the optic from which they were viewed changed. Beneath the reflections of Joseph Paul-Boncour that "in the space of ten years a movement of disaffection for many of the things we loved and wished to defend has gained a part of youth," one can detect a sentiment of arbitrary rejection.[44] Justin Godard, a Radical-socialist, spoke of the "spitefulness of unreasonable boys."[45]

Disapproving intellectuals projected whatever hostility they felt onto youth of 1910, posing themselves as objective observers of an unpleasant phenomenon. However, if Roger Martin du Gard's *Jean Barois* is indicative, freethinkers of the Dreyfus generation could lose their equanimity in the face of provocations from youth. Toward the end of the novel, the hero interviews Tillet and Grenneville, two characters who represent the opinions of Agathon. Barois is at first an amused and sarcastic host, but he becomes progressively more irritated: "The young men stood up; their attitude at once deferential and hostile exasperates Barois. His composure breaks against the impertinent grin of the two boys."[46] The relationship between generations was pictured as one of rapport by rightist admirers of youth, as one of conflict by their leftist critics. This reqired that the former stress the transformation of their generation from what it had been in its youth, at least to the point of acknowledging its errors, and that the latter posit the continuity of their youthful ideals.

When it came to envisaging the future through youth of 1910, many of the same intellectuals of the Right who proclaimed a change of heart within their own generation were less ready to face the possibility that the new generation, whose postures they so completely approved, might also reverse itself as it grew older. As for intellectuals unsympathetic to youth, the normal response was to admit that youth represented the future in the short run, but to deny that they announced a permanent redirection of the course of French history.

Parliamentary politics since the Dreyfus affair had offered little comfort to intellectuals of the Right. Laws passed in 1901 and 1904 to close down schools run by religious orders extended government support of the *école laïque*. Separation of church and state came in 1905. More effective controls were established over the army, and efforts were made to republicanize it. Each election in the prewar decade brought a larger majority for the Left, and there the SFIO made the most spectacular gains. Against these trends and developments, youth held out to the Right the promise of an about-face of destiny. One can sense the reinflation of hopes in Paul de Cassagnac's editorial in *l'Authorité:* "Oh! that these young men promptly became men. With them, by them, armed with this force curbing the 600 tyrants of Parliament, we can hope to remake France."[47] One can perceive a certain satisfaction in the editorial of *La Croix,* June 2, 1912, citing the Catholic renaissance among "educated youth" as proof that Inspector Payot had been rash in his prediction that the map of Catholic France would soon coincide with pockets of illiteracy.[48]

Most rightists were optimistic about what youth portended. To those who blamed France's slide into decadence on the cowardice and lack of energy of the bourgeoisie, youth promised a recovery of self-confidence in the elite. To intellectuals worried about the demographic disparity of France and Germany, the image of youth performed the same compensatory function as the notion of élan vital.[49] They saw in the nationalist and bellicose generation of 1910 future soldiers to fight the war felt to be on the horizon. The young generation signified that France had fully recovered from the defeat of 1870 and could reassert itself as a power of the first rank.[50]

A few intellectuals of the Right hesitated to foresee the future in the crystal ball of youth, either from a desire to be logically consistent with the transformation posited in the case of their own generation, a visceral antipathy to conjectures about the future, or a conception of the psychology of youth difficult to square with the adoption of enduring world views.[51] Several critics of the new generation also went against their preferences on the subject of youth and the future; but for them, the problem arose because youth could not be expected to change as they grew older. In answer to the question, "What does this 'avid, brutal, and well-trained' youth augur for the future?" the Sillionist Henri du Roure predicted a relapse into "the Bonapartist rut."[52] For Georges Normandy, who remained faithful to the pacifist convictions of his youth, "young Europe shows us that our dreams are still dreams and that to replace war by conferences is to replace a frightful thing by something they render ridiculous."[53]

Most intellectuals of the Left and Right found ways to remain optimistic about the future. Socialists could accept without alarm a reactionary youth elite. A hardened bourgeoisie was part of the scenario of the advent of socialism. Moreover, they insisted that the mentality of young workers was quite different from that of bourgeois youths.[54] Radicals made use of a similar argument in envisaging the near future. Maurice Faure placed his hopes in youth from the popular classes won over to the republic by the *école laïque*: "Outside the university, by thousands and hundreds of thousands, young Frenchmen, who have almost all been taught in our schools, know too well the advantages of the republic to show themselves, as citizens, ungrateful and unfaithful sons."[55]

A final type of argument employed by the Left to counter the Right's association of youth with the future was a corollary to the notion of a rhythm of generations. Henri Bérenger invoked a law of reaction whereby the following generation would cancel out whatever effect youth of 1910 might have in the immediate future. This was also the reply of Martin du Gard's Jean Barois to Agathonian youth. In his eyes, they represented an inevitable recoil from the advances of free thought. Their bourgeois status was endangered by the accelerated rate of progress. To their accusation that his so-called liberating truths had failed to free the majority of his generation, Barois retorted: "Perhaps, but they will liberate our descendants completely — and yours, gentlemen."[56]

In the reactions of commentators to youth of 1910, one can perceive the full gamut of possible generational attitudes. Intellectuals at odds with their own group at last felt justified by the appearance of a new generation in accord with their ideas. Others humbly confessed the folly of their youth and saluted a young generation wiser than their own. Among those who showed disapparoval, some posed as dispassionate observers of the unpleasant but transitory phenomenon of youthful rebellion; others did not conceal their bitter resentment that their values and accomplishments were arrogantly and presumptuously spurned by the new generation. In most cases, these diverse reactions followed the lines of ideological cleavage in the intellectual world of pre-1914 France.

It is not difficult to explain the recourse by intellectuals of the Right to generational symbols. Generations afforded them an alternative vision of society to that based on social class, a psychohistorical vision in which the ferment of change lay with an elite. Agathon justified restricting his survey to "cultivated youth" by the argument that, in the matter of generations, a numerical majority had only limited significance: "The secret to the future lies not in the multitude but in an innovating elite."[57] For the Right, suffering from a decade of electoral defeats, the new generation very conveniently represented a possibility of change deriving from the bourgeoisie itself and not measurable by elections.[58]

Associating reactionary ideas with the vigor of youth was a way of lending dynamism to the program of the Right. Two types of symbols were associated in the rightist image of French youth of 1910. On the one hand, its outlook was depicted as bourgeois and conservative: lack of interest in the social question or abstractions like "justice," hostility to the scientific ideal of reformers in the university, preference of traditional forms of Catholicism to Modernism and the *Sillon,* attraction to varieties of nationalism stressing the importance of order and authority. On the other hand, the terms used in describing the psychology of youth — energy, will, the taste for action — suggested the romantic and antipositivist nationalism of the young Barrès.[59] Use of metaphors drawn from aviation evoked the cult of dynamism and speed and unrestricted activism of avant-garde movements like Futurism.[60]

Then as always, youth was synonymous with modernity. Modernity however, can be adapted to the purposes of opposite ideological perspectives. Although the Right is usually identified with the principle of conservation as opposed to change, at certain moments in history its spokesmen define traditional postures as most in step with modern times — just as the Left has claimed legitimacy for its ideals by an appeal to a revolutionary tradition of the past. The image of youth reflected a recasting of the ideology of the French Right in terms of elements of the early twentieth century which could lend it renewed relevance: Barrèsian psychology, Bergsonian philosophy, the imminence of war, even popular sentiment toward sports and aviation.

To the extent that elements of French youth could be convinced to see themselves in terms of prevalent symbols, prewar generational discourse served for rightists the very pragmatic function of adding recruits to their movements. Almost from the outset, *Action Française* had recognized youth as a natural clientele for a mass movement of the Right. Henri Vaugeois wrote in 1903 of students whom he acknowledged as still drawn to either anarchism or socialism: "It will be the easiest thing in the world to lead *the 20,000 young men* to be found in the upper classes of the *lycées* and *collèges,* in the universities and the *grandes écoles,* back to the generative principles of French Order."[61] The extreme Right found that generational rhetoric fit well into a cross-class appeal. More conservative elements were content to appeal to bourgeois youth. As one of the coauthors of *Les jeunes gens d'aujourd'hui* later acknowledged, the Agathonian world-view was a myth intended for young Frenchmen: "An effective myth capable of exerting an influence, of orienting minds, of revealing youths to themselves."[62]

Although the generational symbols of prewar France accorded less naturally with views of society and history characteristic of the Left, many intellectuals at that end of the political spectrum also commented on the emergence of a new generation. The objectification in youth of 1890 and 1910 of the very different intellectual moods at the fin de siècle and on the eve of the Great War enabled the Left, which sensed the shift in mood as acutely as the Right, to articulate and react to it. Criticism and efforts to minimize the significance of a reactionary generation of 1910 reveal their state of mind in an intellectual climate antithetical to their preferences.

If intellectuals of both the Right and Left had recourse to a common store of generational symbols, it was also because those symbols could as easily be given positive as negative connotations. What one intellectual called a "renaissance of French pride," another could label a "renaissance of French chauvinism."[63] Generational discourse was not exclusive of other ways of describing society. For the Right, the young generation was most often a carrier for nationalist doctrines. For the Left, restriction of the term *generation* to *educated* youth meant that generational categories could be squared with class divisions.

In France just before World War I, interpretations of the Left were clearly defensive; this may have been due to a young generation considered more conservative than its predecessor. Where the outlooks attributed to generations are reversed — when youth is characterized to the Left and their elders to the Right — one may imagine inverse ideological patterns of interpretation. It will be the Right that insists on generational conflict and on youth changing as they grow older; the Left will put more stock in the content of the social critique attributed to youth and foresee the future through the new generation. The categories of generational thinking are most probably constant. Its specific form will vary with the response of intellectuals of divergent ideological viewpoints to shifts in intellectual mood over time.

NOTES

1. André Malraux, cited in Georges Liebert, "Répétitions et différences," *Contrepoint* (no. 1, May 1970), p. 12. Despite a number of empirical studies of literary, political, and social generations in French history, perception of generations at past moments in time and changes in peception over time have not been systematically examined. Nevertheless, examples of generational discourse between the French Revolution and World War I are interspersed throughout Albert Thibaudet, *Histoire de la littérature française de 1789 à nos jours* (Paris, 1936); François Mentré, *Les générations sociales* (Paris, 1920), esp. pp. 417–46; Claude Digeon, *La crise allemande de la pensée française, 1870–1914* (Paris, 1959). For the interwar period, see Micheline Tison-Braun, *La crise de l'humanisme*, 2 vols. (Paris, 1958–67), vol. 2, pp. 91–97; Jean-Louis Loubet del Bayle, *Les non-conformistes des années 30* (Paris, 1969), pp. 27–31. The special issue on "Jeunesse: histoire et mythologie" of *Contrepoint* (no. 1, May 1970), reveals how some contemporary French intellectuals use the concepts of "youth" and "generations."
2. Charles Péguy, *Notre jeunesse* (Paris, 1910).
3. Charles Reich, *The Greening of America: How the Youth Revolution Is Trying to Make America Liveable* (New York, 1970). For a sample of the debate over Reich's book, see Philip Nobile (comp.), *The Con III Controversy: The Critics Look at the Greening of America* (New York, 1971).
4. The commentaries of 1912–14 on the outlook of the new generation are frequently cited in histories of the Third Republic. Philippe Bénéton, "La généra-

tion de 1912-1914: image, mythe et réalité?" *Revue française de science politique* 21 (October 1971), pp. 981–1009, demonstrates the extent of the controversy over youth in public opinion. Every major newspaper from *l'Action Française* to *l'Humanité* devoted at least one editorial to the subject of youth. My own research is based on over 150 commentaries varying from paragraph-length responses to one of ten special surveys to novels and books on the theme.

5. The generational imagery is examined for what it reveals about the use by intellectuals of generational symbols, not as evidence of the actual thinking of youth. For a critique of the latter approach, undertaken by historians like H. Stuart Hughes, *Consciousness and Society* (New York, 1958), pp. 340–44, see Paul Lachance, "The Consciousness of the Generation of 1890 at Maturity: An Alternative Reading of the Image of French Youth in 1912–1914," *Europa* 2 (no. 1, Fall, 1978).

6. The classic formulation of generational theory is Karl Mannheim, "The Problem of Generations" (1923). In *Essays on the Sociology of Knowledge* (London, 1952)), pp. 286–319. The present state of generational theory is surveyed in Vera L. Bengston, Robert S. Laufer, and Michael Ferberg, "Time, Aging, and the Continuity of Social Structure: Themes and Issues in Generational Analysis," *Journal of Social Issues* 30 (no. 2, 1974), pp. 1–30.

7. Lewis S. Feuer, *The Conflict of Generations: The Character and Significance of Student Movements* (New York, 1969), p. 10.

8. Agathon (Henri Massis and Alfred de Tarde), "Les jeunes gens d'aujourd'hui," *l'Opinion* 5 (13 April 1912), p. 449. The survey was subsequently published as a book in January 1913. Subsequent references are to the eleventh edition of *Les jeunes gens d'aujourd'hui* (Paris, 1919).

9. Ibid., pp. ii, 2, 5. Agathon specified the age range of youth in 1912 as between 18 and 25, compared them to the "generation which arrived at the age of man towards 1885," and contrasted this generation — which had nothing to temper the impact of the defeat of 1870 — to the generation of the Second Empire, "strong in its materialist pride and scientific *credo*." There were variations, but Agathon's demarcation of the boundaries of the two generations of 1890 and 1910 is typical.

10. In a review of the major surveys on youth appearing in 1912, Georges le Cardonnel remarked that the age of respondents was between 30 and 50 and usually closer to 50. Georges le Cardonnel, "Une renaissance française," *Mercure de France* (no. 386, 16 July 1913), pp. 225–26. Of 110 intellectuals commenting on youth whose age in 1913 I have been able to determine, 62 (56 percent) fall in the age range of 30 to 50. The average age is 43.

11. Jarry and Péguy were born in 1873, Acker and Lagardelle in 1874. If the generation of 1890 is made to include all those born between 1855 and 1875, it includes Jaurès, Bergson, Barrès, Proust, and Maurras.

12. The symbols were sometimes developed at book length, as in Agathon, *Les jeunes gens* (the chapter headings were: "The Taste for Action," "The Patriotic Faith," "The Moral Life," "A Catholic Renaissance," and "Political Realism"), or Etienne Rey, *La Renaissance de l'orgueil français* (Paris, 1912). Other writers simply strung the symbols together without further elaboration. Consider the following commentary: "The skeptical and pessimistic generation of yesterday has been succeeded by a confident and gay generation, characterized by noble dignity and ardent patriotism. An unbelieving generation has been replaced by a generation that displays clearly idealistic, and often purely religious, tendencies." Jules Bertaut, (ed.), "La jeunesse d' aujourd'hui," *Le Gaulois* (1 June 1912).

13. Roger Dévigne, "Le malentendu à la mode," *Paris-Journal* (18 February 1913).
14. Maurice Faure, "Mots nouveaux et vieilles idées," *La Lanterne* (17 February 1913). If most writers of the Right did not call attention to youth as a generation of the Right, a few did. Pierre Hepp, in reply to Agathon, *Les jeunes gens,* pp. 231–32, remarked that the patriotism of youth seemed "to favor rather than contradict reactionary efforts." Agathon printed Hepp's remarks under the heading "l'Action française."
15. Emile Durkheim, "Organisation générale de l'Université de Paris," *La Vie universitaire à Paris* (Paris, 1918), p. 281. Parisian students represented slightly less than half of the total number of university students in France, 41,832 for 1911–13 according to "Partie retrospective," *Annuaire Statistique* 55 (Paris, 1939), cited by Antoine Prost, *L'enseignement en France, 1800–1967* (Paris, 1968) p. 243. The figure for the 20-24 age group is taken from D.R. Mitchell, *European Historical Statistics, 1750–1970* (New York, 1975), p. 37. The term *youth* was further restricted to *males.* Special public opinion surveys presented young women of 1910 as less militantly feminist than their counterparts at the turn of the century, but also as less Catholic and less authoritarian than young men of their age group. See Amélie Gayraud, *Les jeunes filles d'aujourd'hui* (Paris, 1914), pp. 6, 141–42; Fernand Laudet, "Enquête sur les jeunes filles," *La Revue Hebdomadaire* (12 April-14 June 1913).
16. Agathon, *Les jeunes gens,* p. iii; Rey, *Renaissance de l'orgueil français,* p. 153.
17. Maurice Allard, "La Cause," *l'Humanité* (2 May 1913).
18. Mannheim, "The Problem of Generations," pp. 293–94.
19. Examples of explanation by the atmosphere of French society in which the generations came of age are: Alphonse Séché, *l'Oreille sur le coeur* (Paris, 1916), p. 17 (on the Dreyfus affair); Henri Mazel, introduction to "Nos enfants: à quoi rêvent-ils? Que rêvons-nous pour eux?" *Revue des Français* 12 (January 1912), pp. 22–24 (on the libertarian and anarchist climate); Pierre de Coubertin, reply, ibid., pp. 227–28 (he saw in the young generation proof of the "perfect success" of his life-long dedication to the work of "rebronzing France" by means of sports); J. Bourdeau, "Le déclin de l'idéalisme en France," *Journal des Débats* 20 (9 May 1913), p. 878 (on the effect of sports and aviation); Pierre Baudin, "L'évolution de l'esprit français," conclusion to Mazel, "Nos enfants," *Revue des Français* 13 (July 1912), pp. 209–10 (on the changed international climate).
20. Urbain Gohier, "De la discipline," *Le Journal* (8 January 1912). In his comment that "the generation which will replace us differs from us as much as we differ from Frenchmen of the Second Empire," Gohier may reflect his own past as an antimilitarist. By 1912 he was writing for *La Libre Parole.*
21. Romain Rolland, "The New Dawn." In *Jean-Christophe,* trans. Gilbert Cannan (New York, 1938), p. 458. This part of the novel was written in 1912.
22. Hugues le Roux, "La culture de la force et la jeunesse d'aujourd'hui," *La Revue Hebdomadaire* (no. 26, 29 June 1912), p. 597. Paul Flat, "La jeune generation," *Figures et questions de ce temps* (Paris, n.d.), p. 348.
23. Le Roux, "Culture de la force," pp. 596–97.
24. Mazel, "Nos enfants," p. 21; Marcel Drouin, reply to Agathon, *Les jeunes gens,* p. 279.
25. Le Roux, "Culture de la force," p. 599.

26. Agathon, *Les jeunes gens,* p. 6.
27. Rey, *Renaissance de l'orgueil français,* pp. 17-18.
28. Agathon, *Les jeunes gens,* p. 5. Another variant of the argument was that with the passing of the momentary depression of French energies due to the defeat of 1870, the new generation represented the rebound of the French race to its normal state. The vocabulary used in speaking of the new generation — "reawakening" of patriotic instinct, being "led back" to Catholicism, "renaissance" of French pride, *revivescence* of the classical French type — suggests this line of reasoning.
29. Paul Bourget, *Essais de psychologie contemporaine* (Paris, 1883-85) and *Le Disciple* (1889). For a synopsis of Bourget's argument, see René Doumic, "Le bilan d'une génération," *Revue des Deux Mondes* 158 (15 January 1900), pp. 434 ff. The definitive work on the early Bourget is Michel Mansuy, *Un moderne: Paul Bourget, de l'enfance au disciple* (Paris, 1960).
30. Bourget, quoted in Agathon, *Les jeunes gens,* p. 2.
31. Paul Flat, "La jeune génération," pp. 349–50, is another example besides Agathon of citation of Bourget as the authority on the mentality of the generation of 1890. His terms of reference are to be found in many other authors. The archives of Librairie Plon reveal that after 1902 a new edition of *Essais de psychologie contemporaine* went through over 15,000 copies and a paperback edition of *Le Disciple* eventually totaled 496,000 copies.
32. Gaston Picard and Gustave-Louis Tautain, "Enquête sur M. Bergson et l'influence de la pensée sur la sensibilité contemporaine," *La Grande Revue* 83–84 (10 February-10 April 1914). See especially the replies of Raphael Cor, vol. 83, pp. 745–46, and Georges Matisse, vol. 83, p. 750. The phrase "nightmare of pessimism" is from the reply of Paul Naudet, vol. 84, p. 116. The dialectic of French history in which a Bergsonian pragmatism was the answer to the skepticism engendered by positivism is well summarized by Eugen Weber. "The Secret World of Jean Barois: Notes on the Portrait of an Age." In John Weiss (ed.), *The Origins of Modern Consciousness* (Detroit, 1965), esp. p. 100.
33. Agathon, *Les jeunes gens,* pp. 83–84. See also Henri Massis, *Évocations: souvenirs, 1905–1911* (Paris, 1931), pp. 87–96. Bourget made a similar point when speaking in 1914 of the influence of Emile Boutroux on youth: "They have overtaken even you, sir, in several respects. Many . . . are not satisfied to have laid bare the prejudice of scientism. They go where Pascal went." Paul Bourget, address to L'Académie Française for the reception of Emile Boutroux, 22 January 1914 (Paris, 1914).
34. Rey, *Renaissance de l'orgueil français,* pp. 160–61.
35. Agathon, *Les jeunes gens,* pp. 40–42.
36. Charles Maurras, cited by Raoul Girardet, *Le nationalisme français, 1871–1914* (Paris, 1966), p. 211.
37. Henri Bérenger, "La Jeunesse," *l'Action* (12 February 1913).
38. Ibid.
39. Geroges Lecomte, "La réveil de la fierté française," *Le Matin* (14 February 1913).
40. Barrès, cited in Agathon, *Les jeunes gens,* p. 283.
41. Albert Jounet, in Picard and Tautain, "Enquête sur Bergson," vol. 84, p. 115; Joseph Lotte, reply to Paul Barge, "Les signes d'une renaissance catholique dans la jeunesse contemporaine," *La Revue de la Jeunesse* 7 (1913), p. 278.

42. Henri Lavedan, "Celui d'aujourd'hui," *l'Illustration* (no. 3650, 8 February 1913), p. 103. Similarly, a reviewer of Ernest Psichari, *L'Appel aux armes* (1913), compared the novelist rather bluntly to his grandfather Renan: "The sons are made of better stuff than their fathers." The review appeared in *La Revue Française Politique et Littéraire* 2 (1913), p. 425.

43. Agathon, *Les jeunes gens,* p. 114.

44. Joseph Paul-Boncour, "Réponse à MM. Agathon," *Le Radical* (11 February 1913).

45. Justin Godart, "Les Jeunes," *La Lanterne* (15 February 1913).

46. Roger Martin du Gard, *Jean Barois* (Paris, 1913), p. 443.

47. Paul de Cassagnac, "Renaissance," *l'Autorité* (23 March 1913).

48. *La Croix,* (2 June 1912).

49. A.O., reply to Yvonne Sarcey, "Notre enquête sur la jeune génération," *Les Annales Politiques et Littéraires* (22 December 1912), p. 549. The compensatory function of the notion of *élan vital* was first described by John Bowditch, "The concept of *Élan Vital:* A Rationalization of Weakness ." In Edward Earle (ed.), *Modern France* (Princeton, 1951), p. 33.

50. Baudin, "L'évolution de l'esprit français," p. 210.

51. Paul Bourget, reply to Bertaut, "La jeunesse d'aujourd'hui" (1 June 1912); Abel Bonnard, "Père et fils," *Le Figaro* (12 March 1913).

52. Henri du Roure, reply to Agathon, *Les jeunes gens,* pp. 242–43.

53. Georges Normandy, "Les Jeunes," *Paris-Journal* (27 May 1913).

54. Allard, "La cause."

55. Faure, "Mots nouveaux."

56. Martin du Gard, *Jean Barois,* pp. 441–43.

57. Agathon, *Les jeunes gens,* pp. ii–iii.

58. Ibid., 95–96.

59. Zeev Sternhell, *Maurice Barrès et le nationalisme français* (Paris, 1972), esp. pp. 274 ff. In the imagery there was hardly any hint of the antibourgeois revolt of the young Barrès nor of the anti-Semitic and antiplutocratic rhetoric of his effort to appeal to the masses as a Boulangist and anti-Dreyfusard. The image of youth combined conservative postures with the psychology of the new nationalism minus whatever radicalism it had when originally developed by Barrès (who had himself grown more conservative).

60. The imagery of youth stops short of the radical rejection by futurists of everything dating from the past, the movement's disdain for the great masters, combative antitraditionalism, anticlassicism, and anticlericalism.

61. Henri Vaugeois, "A Nos Amis," *L'Action Française* 8 (1 January 1903), p. 5. "20,000 young men" is italicized in the article.

62. Henri Massis, *l'Honneur de servir: textes réunis pour contribuer à l'historie d'une génération, 1912–1937* (Paris, 1937), p. 11.

63. François Ponçet, reply to Agathon, *Les jeunes gens,* p. 171; Marcel Prévost, *Lettres à Françoise Maman* (Paris, 1912), p. 344.

CHAPTER TWELVE

Man in the Natural World: Some Implications of the National-Socialist Religion

Robert A. Pois

How can you find pleasure, Herr Kersten, in shooting from behind cover at poor creatures browsing on the edge of a wood, innocent, defenseless, and unsuspecting? It's really pure murder. Nature is so marvelously beautiful and every animal has a right to live .... You will find this respect for animals in all Indo-Germanic peoples. It was of extraordinary interest to me to hear recently that even today Buddhist monks, when they pass through a wood in the evening, carry a bell with them, to make any woodland animals they might meet keep away, so that no harm will come to them. But with us every slug is trampled on, every worm destroyed.[1]

Heinrich Himmler

The romantic origins of national-socialist ideology have been obvious to historians and political analysts for quite some time. American observers have tended to emphasize the politicalization of romanticism as that singularly German phenomenon which constituted an important step in the direction of Hitler's coming to power in 1933.[2] There is little reason to dispute these findings as important contributions to our understanding of how an apparently ingenuous permutation of mysticism could be developed into justification for racism and mass murder. It is also beyond dispute that in its ideational contents nazism was uniquely German — a product of German historical and psychogenetic circumstances.

It has not been unusual for historians to comment upon certain religious characteristics of the national-socialist movement. Such things as Hitler's extraordinary charismatic appeal to the mob, the nature of the Nuremberg party rallies, and the neopaganism of Himmler and his SS have been emphasized.[3] Authors have also pointed to an aspect of national-socialist religious thought which existed as a legacy of nazism's romantic heritage — a pronounced interest in nature.[4] This topic has usually been touched upon lightly. It is worth asking why so little attention has been paid to the most interesting view which the leading ideologues of nazi Germany had with regard to man's place in the natural world. Outside of the fact that some historians probably do not take this (or in some cases *any*) aspect of nazi ideology very seriously, there is another reason: in the character and tone of the nazi approach one can readily apprehend elements which demonstrate that national socialism was very much in the mainstream not only of German but of Western philosophical and religious developments.

That man needs religion for one reason or another, even as an extremely loosely organized symbolic or ritualistic system, is something so widely accepted as to be almost bromidic. Most bromides, of course, are open to attack, and generations of Marxists and Freudians have done their best. However, Marx's drawing of a well-nigh ontological line between *Entstehungsgeschichte* and true "human" history and Freud's occasional excursions into Comtean-like metahistorical speculations indicate the problems that confronted even these two seminal minds in attempting to adhere to their respective injunctions to dispense with the insidious "opiate" or archaic "illusion." It would appear that up until now and for the foreseeable future, men have needed and will continue to need some sort of recourse to a posited supermundane being or realm, however ill-defined, in order to provide existential and/or axiological content to existence. Yet it would be grossly erroneous to assume that Western man's need for such a recourse has been or will be met in the future by adherence to that supposed foundation of Western civilization, the Judeo-Christian tradition. While this tradition has been at least nominally *the* tradition of the West, it has within it certain fundamental characteristics with which human beings cannot be entirely comfortable. Of crucial importance for this essay are the following two: (1) the line between life and death (or earth and "heaven"); and (2) the line between man and nature.

As Ernst Cassirer has pointed out, primitive man, in the face of numberless challenges from an often hostile world, could not accept the reality of death. Primitive religion's belief in the continuity of life is "the strongest and most energetic affirmation of life that we find in human culture."[5] Mary Douglas, in her thought-provoking work *Natural Symbols,* argues that the notion that "primitive peoples" are inherently deeply religious is false.[6] Douglas does state that "there is no person whose life does not need to unfold in a coherent symbolic system."[7] In various circumstances, "coherent symbolic system[s]" assume the forms of well-articulated religions. In describing the religion of a New Guinea tribe, the Garia, a people who had a very loose, pragmatic view of the universe and of religion, which pretty much precluded the use of those moral restraints usually associated with religious beliefs, Douglas asserts that "religion was a technology for overcoming risk."[8] In a world in which, according to Cassirer, man strives to overcome death, or at the very least deal with it in a manner which diminishes its impact, any pattern of religious beliefs, no matter how sketchy or ill-defined its symbolic content, must be a partial articulation of a primal urge to "overcome risk." The gap posed by death, that cold, ultimately disquieting frontier between finite and infinite, was the primary challenge to which even the most pragmatic and nonnormative religions had to respond.

While often more emphasis is placed on the hyphen than on either Judeo or Christian, one cannot deny that for both Jews and Christians a hiatus between finite man and an infinite God does exist and that this hiatus must necessarily be described by the term *death*.[9] The Judeo-Christian tradition, like many others, accepts the immortality of the soul. Life is largely rationalized through an assumed justification or condemnation of one's particular life to take place in some period or level of existence to come. However, there appears to be some psychic mechanism that refuses to be comforted by such assumptions. Mankind seems unable to accept its finitude, the ontological border of which is death.[10] If we accept Cassirer's contention that man originally "became religious" to avoid having to confront death (through denying its reality), we must see that the Judeo-Christian tradition flies in the face of certain, at times impalpable but nonetheless real, psychic needs.

The line drawn between man and nature by the Judeo-Christian tradition is due primarily to the influence of the Mosaic Code, which caused Hegel (and quite a few others less kindly disposed toward Judaism) to condemn the Jewish faith as too abstract and unnatural. Orthodox Christianity has not—nor could it have—dispensed with this code, by virtue of which man is elevated to the position of being, as the psalmist put it, "little lower than the angels." Man has awesome responsibilities to nature. None of God's creatures can be taken for granted, and a substantial portion of Orthodox Jewish family life revolves around the stringent injunction that one must not eat a calf in its mother's milk. Yet the general attitude toward nature central to Judaism—and through it to Christianity also, albeit to a lesser degree—sees it as apart from God. Man, of course, is as well. But by being made in the image of the divine, man must be seen as ontologically superior to nature.[11] The responsibilities inherent in so elevated but uncomfortable a position—ensconced somewhere between the natural world and the Kingdom of God—must be great indeed, and men have rebelled against this demanding role. According to some observers, such neopagan revivals as the search for Aryan roots and national socialism can be viewed as rebellions of this nature.[12] In most Western countries today, many appear to be in full flight from the two stringent principles described above—the acceptance of a qualitative distinction between an infinite God and finite men (acceptance of the reality of death) and avowal of man's divinely determined separation from nature. This will be considered again later. Now we will turn to those aspects of national-socialist religion germane to this discussion.

While national socialism did not survive long enough to implement some of the more thoroughgoing anti-Christian aspects of its ideology (or *Weltanschauung* [worldview], since most of the writings and comments we will be considering use this term), there can be no doubt that these views were taken seriously, at times painfully so, by those national socialists who either created policy or were in positions to affect it. Further, the national socialist approach to religion served to rationalize mass murder.

In *Mein Kampf,* Hitler was not particularly concerned with religion. Yet a foreshadowing of what would become the national-socialist "religion of nature" was present. Hitler deprecated the role of humanity in a universe run according to pitiless natural laws. In decrying pacifism as contrary to established natural laws of survival, he stated: "At this point, someone or other may laugh, but this planet once moved through the ether for millions of years without human beings, and it can do so again some day if men forget that they owe their higher existence, not to the ideas of a few crazy ideologists, but to the knowledge and ruthless application of Nature's stern and rigid laws."[13] It was Hitler's belief in (1) the existence of these "stern and rigid" natural laws and (2) the necessity for men to apply them to areas of human existence which allowed him to declare that the preservation of inferior human races was against nature. "Nature," he said, "usually makes certain corrective decisions with regard to the racial purity of earthly creatures. She has little love for bastards."[14] Nature also served another purpose for Hitler. It enabled him to rationalize the emergence of the true political leader on the basis of a crudely apprehended "natural selection." As he put it: "Natural development finally brought the best man to *the* place where he belonged. This will always be so and will eternally remain so, as it always has been so . . . the most powerful and swiftest will . . . be recognized, and will be the victor."[15]

Here Hitler did not refer to religion per se. However, he had deified nature, and identified God (or Providence) with it. In this he agreed with Alfred Rosenberg, whose 1930 work *Der Mythus des 20. Jahrhunderts,* contained detailed descriptions of the "Nordic" religion and how it differed from the Judeo-Christian religious conception. Before considering Rosenberg's views, we might add a disclaimer. As Joachim Fest has pointed out, few people seemed to take Rosenberg's ponderous musings very seriously, particularly after the nazis came to power.[16] Hitler himself, who usually enjoyed posing as a sort of latter-day Renaissance man, admitted that he could read very little of the *Mythus.* Nevertheless, Rosenberg's view of religion, either because or in spite of him, was widely held by most committed national socialists.[17] In the *Mythus* of 1930, Rosenberg sharply distinguished between the religion of the Jews (and insofar as much was carried over into the New Testament, orthodox Christianity as well) and what he liked to refer to as "Nordic religion." He criticized belief in "a remote and fearful God, enthroned over all, the Jahweh of the so-called Old Testament . . . to whom one prays in fear and praises in trembling."[18]

The rejection of what Rosenberg called the "monstrous principle" which declared that God created the world from nothing was particularly important. For Rosenberg, this Jewish idea, which also constituted the foundation of Catholic beliefs, was rooted in a pernicious dualism. God created a world that was separate from him. Such a world was unnatural, since nature and its rules were relegated to a secondary position. Belief in Judeo-Christian dualism could only lead to a situation in which the "natural-grown Being of nature" would be crippled. "These spiritual and racial cripples will then be collected under the Catholic roof."[19] Rosenberg opposed to this an Aryan-Nordic race soul whose monistic religious tenets, which posited an eternal "order principle" struggling against chaos, were rooted in India. The ordering principle was nature itself, the form in which Providence found its only expression. In his view, man did not relate to any extrinsic or transcendental deity. As a creature of nature, the ordering principle of life lived within him. "Odin was and is dead," according to Rosenberg, but "the German mystic discovered this 'strength from above' in his own soul. Divine Valhalla arose from the infinite, misty vastness buried in the human breast."[20]

Rosenberg differed from Hitler in that he was much more seriously concerned with creating (or perhaps in his eyes, rediscovering) a mythos which could serve those purposes normally assigned to orthodox religion. For Hitler, far more attuned to political realities than his more esoteric colleague, religious concerns were always tied to those of a practical nature. Rosenberg, in his sustained attacks on the Judeo-Christian tradition, went a bit further than Hitler with respect to theological issues. However, both Hitler and Rosenberg believed in the deification of nature and in certain natural qualities which elevated some men above all others.

The national-socialist ideologues sought to bring together "religious" and "scientific" concerns. The national-socialist Weltanschauung seemed to allow for a bridging of the gap between spirit and matter through deification of nature. For example, a biology pedagogy book suggested that the teaching of biology should emphasize the total view of things. "The metabolic changes in a closed biotic community reveal a meaningful plan in the greater occurrences of nature." Thus it was possible to arrive "at a concept of nature that does not conflict with religious experience, whereas this was necessarily the case with the former purely mechanistic attitude."[21] The same text argued that the study of man, anthropology, had to take place within a biological context. Anthropocentric views in general had to be rejected. They would be valid only "if it is assumed that nature has been created only for man. We decisively reject this attitude. According to our conception of nature, man is a link in the chain of living nature just as any other organism."[22]

This "chain of living nature" was central to the national-socialist Weltanschauung. The place of humanity in the chain received clear definition in the term handbook used in the SS Junkerschule at Bad Tölz:[23] "The concept of humanity [Menschheit] is biological nonsense."[24] After all, in the natural world there was no *Tierheit*.[25] Man the species and *not* humanity was part of nature, a fact recognized by the national-socialist Weltanschauung. This Weltanschauung was a dynamic that did not recognize rest. "In this regard," the pamphlet continued, "nature gives us the best examples." The handbook further declared that "the body must assimilate to the environment; certainly in wearing apparel, dress, and temperature."[26] All life was struggle, and hence the national-socialist Weltanschauung was simply a recognition of natural laws.[27]

The emphasis was on the cruel struggle for existence, one in which the most "natural" of peoples would survive. Nature was merciless and showed no pity to those who could not respond to its at times seemingly overwhelming challenges. In such a struggle, there was no room for pity because "pity obscures the principle of selection."[28] The principle of selection suggested the Darwinian belief in descent from a common ancestor, but the handbook concluded that "it is a completely false conception that man has descended from apes," or "that man and apeman stem from a [common] source."[29] As the Bad Tölz handbook envisioned it, life was a struggle between the several major races, the most "natural" of which would win. In this context, the Christian Weltanschauung was singularly inappropriate, since it was based on a "false division" between body and soul and on the assumption that all bodies and all souls were equal before God.[30]

As this national-socialist ideologue saw it, religion and science had been bound together in a Weltanschauung congruent with a nature of which it was the highest possible expression. This Weltanschauung was neither overly spiritual nor overly materialistic, but rather could be summed up in the engaging phrase "everything is life" or, as was often more simply written, "nature." Spiritual, i.e., *overly* spiritual people captured by traditional religious notions, believed in the one God who created a world which he now ruled with caprice and harshness. Materialists were either coldly deistic or out-and-out atheists. The "life-affirming" (to use a favorite pharse) national-socialist Weltanschauung saw God's and Nature's power as one and the same. To ask for the source of life was absurd. Its beginnings were unclear. But we do know, as the Bad Tölz document put it, that "we are the bearers and shapers of eternal life."[31] Since the gap between spiritual and mundane worlds had been bridged by the national-socialist Weltanschauung and since a nature-bound people was, by definition, bound to the highest of spiritual principles, it followed that the "*Volk* is the religion of our time."[32]

Amidst the crudely pantheistic and badly protoexistentialist verbiage, one idea emerged with some clarity—that national socialism was based upon a "life-affirming" principle which was the principle of nature itself. The writings of Hitler and Rosenberg and the Bad Tölz document all point to this. This can also be seen in Brachmann's address to the Religionswissenschaftliche Institut at Halle. The topic of the lecture was the conflicting ideologies of East and West. Throughout the address, Brachmann attacked the "otherworldliness" and legalisms he saw as inherent in the Eastern, Judeo-Christian tradition. Eastern religion was based on restrictions and fear; it was based on a spiritual condition which had lost the instinct for life (or perhaps never had it in the first place).[33] Oriental religiosity, according to Brachmann, was based in all of its forms (but most particularly in Judaism and Pauline Christianity) upon a "denial of everything living."[34] There was a fear of life itself. Such a conception of life, which emphasized its emptiness next to the opulent grandeur of God, was suitable for a nomadic people, unhappily rootless in the wastes of Asia. Brachmann opposed to this the rooted, farming life, responsible for a view of the world in which all material elements—the soil, cattle, etc.—were holy. According to Brachmann, what was holy for the rooted—presumably Nordic-European farmer—did not serve to separate men from nature.[35]

Through the capricious triumph of the Judeo-Christian tradition and thus of the Jewish God the European spirit had been enslaved by religious principles inherently foreign to it. The healthy "peasant religion" was just now beginning to emerge. As an example of the sort of spirit that it would have to combat, Brachmann cited Moses, who before he could marry the daughter of Jethro had to circumcise himself—sacrifice his manhood to a "god of the wastes."[36] It was this type of God whom John the Baptist brought into the New Testament. A religious Weltanschauung of this nature, based on fear of a God of caprice, was necessarily dependent on revelation. The Indo-Germanic religious Weltanschauung took its point of departure from men and was apotheosized in that German sense of "inwardness" responsible for attempting to bring certain aspects of the Judeo-Christian tradition back into harmony with nature through the cult of the Virgin Mary. The robust glorification of mother and child, Brachmann stated, was hardly characteristic of the Oriental world.[37] When we "give thanks," it must be not to some capriciously tyrannical God of the wastes but rather to that which demonstrates to us the congruity of "man and life."[38]

The national-socialist Weltanschauung was celebrated as providing for a true "religion of life." The old dualism could now be overthrown, and in its place one could posit something for which such hoary precursors of national socialism as Wilhelm Marr, Eugen Dühring, and Houston Stewart Chamberlain had argued— a religious belief congruent with those laws of nature in which a true *Volksgemeinschaft* (folk community) would develop to fruition. The liberation from Judeo-Christian dogma would be apotheosized in the transcendence of—to use a common phrase at the time —"life-alien" (*Weltfremden*) usages. In an SS document of 1936, *Die geschichtliche Entwicklung der deutschen Reichseinheit* (the historical development of German imperial unity), several songs for SS festivals were suggested. One of them captured the sense of liberation from the Judeo-Christian tradition. In Asian "wastes," (i.e. the Holy Land)

> Verblutete deutsche Wehr
> Die Zeit verging, doch der Pfaffe blieb,
> Den Volk die Seele zu rauben,
> Und ob er es römisch, Lutherisch trieb,
> Er Lehrte den jüdischen Glauben.[39]

A second song, entitled "Juden raus, Papst hinaus" ("Jews out, Pope away"), developed this theme further:

> Nein, wir haben nicht geblutet namenlos und ohne Ruhm,
> Das der deutschen Art verjudet weiter durch der Christentum.

Now the German Volk had been liberated from Judeo-Christian enslavement ("Wir sind frei von Berge Sinai" ["We are free from Mount Sinai"]), and there was no further need for a church, since German men and women would be living in accord with the laws of nature ("Sonnenrad führt uns allein").[40]

The significance of the national-socialist theological revolution can perhaps be disputed. After all, despite the Bad Tölz documents, the rather childlike attacks on the Judeo-Christian tradition, and the various Hitler youth sun and fire festivals, Germany remained nominally Christian, and the desires of some, such as Martin Bormann, that war be declared on Christianity were never implemented, if only because there was not ample opportunity to do so. However, leading national socialists accepted the anti-Christian (to say nothing of anti–*Judeo*-Christian) Weltanschauung of the movement and were able to rationalize many of their actions in terms of it. Hitler may have mocked Rosenberg for his garbled neologisms, and Bormann may well have despised minor party philosophers such as Brachmann, Krieck, and Wagner (to say nothing of the "major" one, Rosenberg); but all were united in the belief that national socialism represented a new philosophy of life in which a fundamental understanding of the laws of life made it possible for science and religion to be brought together and the cleft between heaven and earth bridged.

We can get a good idea of this by considering some comments of Martin Bormann. In a 1942 piece on national socialism and Christianity, he emphasized the incompatibility of "national socialist and Christian concepts." National socialism, Bormann declared, was based on "scientific foundations," while Christianity's principles laid down almost two thousand years ago "have increasingly stiffened into life-alien dogmas."[41] National socialism must always be guided by science, and instead of conceiving of God as being some sort of "manlike being" sitting up somewhere in the heavens, the new Weltanschauung viewed it as some sort of force which governed heavenly spheres other than our "unimportant earth":[42] "The assertion that this world-force can worry about the fate of every individual, every bacillus on earth, and that it can be influenced by so-called prayer or other astonishing things is based either on a suitable dose of naiveté or on outright commercial effrontery."[43] The "God" of which Bormann was speaking was the God of a fairly substantial number of people. Bormann deprecated the notion of the divinity of man, there being no "manlike being" in whose image he had been created. In place of divine humanity and a presumably superannuated God, there was life itself, whose fundamental scientific truths had been grasped in national socialism. The more "mystically inclined" Heinrich Himmler persistently attacked Christianity for its notion that men should dominate the world. In place of this, he offered a presumably Old German belief in the interrelationship between macro- and microcosms. "Man," Himmler maintained in a June 9, 1942 speech to SS chiefs in Berlin, "is nothing special," only a piece of Earth.[44]

In all this, there was the implicit or explicit notion that while "man" was nothing, some *men* were unto gods. These were those humans fortunate enough to be endowed with a Weltanschauung rooted in the laws of nature. Such people had a life-bound idealism. This notion came out strongly in a February 17, 1944 speech by Robert Wagner at the Unviersity of Strassburg. During the course of his address, Wagner posed "the ideas and idealism of the national-socialist Weltanschauung against the suicidal struggle of the democratic historical era" charactized by materialistic self-seeking.[45] Men, Wagner maintained, "cannot build their concepts of life upon foundations of egotistical wishes or abstract theories alien to life, but only upon recognizable laws of nature."[46] There had been the call "back to nature," and now this process had been completed by national socialism and Adolf Hitler. National socialism was nothing else than the grasping of natural laws through "a spirit of genius" (presumably Hitler).[47] Time and again Wagner returned to the theme that the national-socialist Weltanschauung was nothing other than "authentic, true knowledge, or better said, knowledge of nature." So closely did the Weltanschauung of Hitler adhere to the laws of life, that it was itself in a state of perpetual development: "The Führer has consciously avoided allowing his national socialism to develop into a stationary doctrine. It should and must remain a revolutionary idea. Each doctrine leads all too easily to dogmatism and through that to alienation from the world."[48] In these lines, Wagner captured something that helps explain the extraordinary success of national-socialist ideology—an impressive balance between belief in posited eternal natural truths and a pragmatism which allowed for a great deal of flexibility in determining how such truths should be applied to the world of men.

As we have thus far considered it, the national-socialist "religion" emphasized two fundamental points: (1) the necessity of overcoming the gap between the worldly and otherworldly (hence between the traditional realms of science and religion); and (2) the necessity of seeing man as part of nature and subject to the pitiless judgment of natural law. In the first instance, the national-socialist Weltanschauung emphasized a crude Hegelianism—man's search for infinitude within his own breast. The national socialists differed from Hegel in their insistence that not all men could do this, since most adhered to "life-alien" doctrines such as the Judeo-Christian tradition, which in turn pointed to a lack of "soulish," natural qualities. The second point, the emphasis upon man's role in and *of* nature was, at least in the eyes of national socialists, inextricably intertwined with the first. Having produced, as they saw it, a Weltanschauung that allowed two of the most disturbing dualisms in human existence to be overcome—the gaps between body and spirit and man and nature—it is not surprising that nazi ideologists took their beliefs extremely seriously. Under these circumstances, it can be easily understood why a September 1940 quarrel in the Gräberfürsorge (grave caretaker) office of the SS over whether the graves of fallen SS men should be marked with a so-called *Tyr-rune* or a *Man-rune* ended up involving the attention of Himmler himself.[49] One can also appreciate why, at a time when the war was all but lost—December 15, 1944—Rosenberg could still be so deeply concerned over the correct appreciation of the significance of the national-socialist Weltanschauung that he would send a twelve-page letter of instruction on the subject to the SD office.[50] Perhaps for the individual German soldier in 1944, fighting desperately against impossible odds, the Weltanschauung issue may well have seemed irrelevant. But from the point of view of the national-socialist leadership it was not, for the war they had chosen to bring upon Europe was largely concerned with the triumph of a Weltanschauung which embodied the hopes and ambitions of *some* of those estranged from Judeo-Christian tenets.

Yet the national-socialist Weltanschauung embodied elements that have existed as Western civilization's alter ego for some time. Joachim of Fiore was only one representative, albeit perhaps the most intellectually respectable, of a chiliastic tradition which, while not consciously anti-Christian (those prominent in it often claimed to be the true Christians), nevertheless was most uncomfortable with the orthodox Christian view of eschatology and eternal life. A succession of false messiahs and embodiments of the Holy Ghost from Montanus of Phrygia to the pseudo Baldwin of Flanders sought to demonstrate that the Kingdom of Death could be transcended in the here-and-now and spiritual truth realized through violent social action. The Manichean tradition, never completely reconciled to the delicate and at times seemingly artificial balance between body and spirit proffered by the Judeo-Christian tradition denounced it in favor of a radical permutation of Gnosticism, something that had to occasion the Albigensian Crusade of the thirteenth century.[51] Theosophical societies, spiritualists, and purveyors of various forms of Eastern mysticism are as prominent as ever before throughout the West and in some places, e.g. the United States, probably more so than previously. The Judeo-Christian tradition remains the "official" tradition of Western civilization, but its hold is as tenuous as it has always been. While German historical circumstances and conditions were responsible for bringing the National Socialists to power, that element of the national-socialist Weltanschauung which rejected the Judeo-Christian separation between finite and infinite—and hence implicitly rejected the reality of death—had a long pedigree in the history of Western civilization. That there could be such a tradition should not be particularly startling if one accepts Cassirer's contention that the rejection of death constituted the primary motive for primitive man's turning to religion in the first place.

From the point of view of those living in the last quarter of the twentieth century, the second element of the national-socialist Weltanschauung which we have considered—emphasis on man's role in and *of* nature—is perhaps of greater importance. Here too, the nazi ideologists were drawing upon a long and well-established tradition. The dichotomy between a human world—inherently divine due to man's being made in God's image—and a natural world—over which man presumably has some degree of control—has never been particularly comfortable. First, the axiological charge to man as a singularly divine creature, situated somewhere between heaven and earth, is immense. Second, the notion that man having certain powers over nature is responsible for it in some way (rather than simply adjusting to certain "natural laws" beyond his control) places a great burden upon him. It is a far easier choice to see man as not being apart from nature, much less above it, but *of* nature. This approach has not been confined to romantics in full flight from modernity. As Leon Poliakov has pointed out, the stripping of man of his divinity began with the crude scientism of the Enlightenment.[52]

For such thinkers as Linnaeus, Buffon, Voltaire, Meiners, and Kant, there was a natural order of men just as there was of animals and things. While all men were part of nature, some were higher up on the developmental ladder. With the rise of modern nationalism and its partial reinforcement through the development of the Aryan myth, something for which the Frenchman Gobineau was to some extent responsible, the crude scientism of eighteenth-century phylogenetic speculation was partly replaced by more baldly ethnocentric concerns. In all this, the New World made no mean contributions. Gobineau's writings, at first not taken seriously in France, were translated into English to justify slavery, while the American war against Mexico (1846–48) was rationalized in racial terms.[53] By the end of the nineteenth century the "scientific" explanations of Enlightenment thinkers were supplanted by those provided by protoanthropologists, geographic determinists, theosophists, and phrenologists. While the West remained officially committed to the Judeo-Christian tradition and often rationalized imperialism in its name, the Mosaic Code central to this tradition was being strenuously attacked from all sides. Vulgar interpretations of the Darwinian tradition were useful in these efforts, though the submergence of man in the world of nature antedated these to a great extent.

Though eschewing notions of race and racial supremacy, modern environmental concerns are partly rooted in this tradition. National-socialist ideologues were concerned that man, or at least some men, live in harmony with the environment. Just because something happens to have been emphasized by people as uncongenial as the nazis does not make it wrong. Man is rooted in the natural world, a world too often viewed as an object for exploitation. In their own version of the "natural religion," the national socialists exemplified a pernicious tendency that must be of special concern for anyone who chooses to see man exclusively as a product of some deified nature.

The tendency is the following: to see some men as less "natural" than others or as being in a border area between animate and inanimate forms. Of course, it is not necessary that this happen. However, should the conception of man as being merely a slightly more intelligent—and hence less likable—animal be applied within social and political contexts, then in a world replete with tensions and hatreds, avoidance of drawing certain crudely affirmed conclusions could become difficult or impossible. Pitiless massacre and rapine has occasioned the spread of religious movements which, hypothetically at least, accepted mankind's divinity. However, there was at least an ethical or axiological counterbalance in the conception that human life was to be valued as such. Nevertheless, murder as a part of public policy was not part of the Medieval vision, and the process of conversion precluded the racist concept of the permanently tainted soul.[54]

It is only with the reduction of men to being simple products of nature, or pieces of earth, in Himmler's eyes, that the following description of a people could have been offered: "From all this it follows that Judaism is part of the organism of mankind just as, let us say, certain bacteria are part of man's body, and indeed the Jews are as necessary as bacteria . . . mankind needs the Jewish strain in order to preserve its vitality until its early mission is fulfilled. . . . . It will collapse only when all mankind is redeemed."[55] Only with the overthrow of the Mosaic Code could Goebbels have described a people in the following manner: "*Judentum*," he said, was not just a nation, "it is a singular, social-parasitic phenomenon," a poisoner of other cultures.[56]

At a time in which a well-justified religious scepticism has not eliminated man's need for supermundane assurances—How can one prevent such events from taking place? There probably is no single answer to this dilemma, but perhaps one can bear in mind that, even stripped of its ceremonial garments, the Judeo-Christian tradition has served to impress upon us a realistic appreciation of man's peculiar position of being a "thinking animal" (and unlike that posited by classical speculators, blessed in its finitude) suspended between a natural world toward which he must show responsibility and a spiritual world in terms of which all responsibility must be rationalized.

NOTES

1. From Felix Kersten, *The Kersten Memoirs, 1940–1945* (London, 1956/New York, 1957), as quoted in Joachim C. Fest, *The Face of the Third Reich: Portraits of the Nazi Leadership,* trans. from the German by Michael Bullock (New York, 1970), p. 121.
2. See Peter Viereck, *Metapolitics: The Roots of the Nazi Mind* (New York, 1961); Hans Kohn, *The Mind of Germany* (New York, 1960); Fritz Stern, *The Politics of Cultural Despair* (New York, 1961); George L. Mosse, *The Crisis of the German Ideology* (New York, 1964). In his excellent psychohistorical study *The Psychopathic God: Adolf Hitler,* Robert G.L. Waite has recently (1977) reemphasized romanticism as constituting a major portion of the intellectual background both for national socialism in general and for Hitler's very personal sublimations.
3. An excellent description of Hitler's impact on the mob is to be found in William L. Shirer's *Berlin Diary: The Journal of a Foreign Correspondent, 1934–1941* (New York, 1941), pp. 14–16. An important discussion of Hitler's mass appeal can be found in Walter C. Langer, *The Mind of Adolf Hitler* (New York, 1973), esp. pp. 206–10. Albert Speer's memoirs, *Inside the Third Reich* , trans. from the German by Richard Winston and Clara Winston (New York, 1970), are still the best source for investigating the planning and staging of the Nüremberg rallies. See esp. pp. 27–28, 58–59. On Himmler's religious concerns see Josef Ackermann, *Himmler als Ideologe* (Göttingen, 1970); Willi Frischauer, *Himmler: The Evil Genius of the Third Reich* (Boston,

1953), esp. pp. 40–42; Roger Manvell and Heinrich Fraenkel, *Heinrich Himmler* (London, 1965), esp. pp. 46–49, 177–78; Heinz Höhne, *The Order of the Death's Head: The Story of Hitler's SS,* trans. from the German by Richard Barry (New York, 1970), esp. pp. 144–45, 153–55; *Reichsführer! Briefe an und von Himmler* (Stuttgart, 1968), esp. pp. 11–12 of Helmut Heiber's excellent introduction. Joachim Fest's previously cited work contains material of interest. George L. Mosse, *The Nationalization of the Masses* (New York 1975), is a most interesting study of the background for national-socialist symbolism; J.P. Stern, *Hitler: The Führer and the People* (Berkeley, 1974), has much to say about the religious appeal of Hitler.

4. As an example of this see Frischauer, p. 26.
5. Ernst Cassirer, *An Essay On Man: An Introduction to a Philosophy of Human Culture* (New York, 1953), p. 112.
6. Mary Douglas, *Natural Symbols: Explorations in Cosmology* (New York, 1970), p. x.
7. Ibid., p. 50.
8. Ibid., p. 126.
9. In the Christian tradition, Christ is God-as-Man—the infinite becoming finite to suffer for the accumulated sins of humanity. Orthodox Christianity does not see this as pointing to a substantial identification of man and God. Both Joachim of Fiore (1145–1202) and G.W.F. Hegel are often pointed out as having done this. But Hegel was talking about man's discovering infinitude in the species while Joachim, through his "Age of the Spirit," which presumably would usher in the millenium, found it relatively easy to dispense with Christ and the orthodox Christian tradition altogether. For a brief but pithy consideration of some of the problems raised by Joachim of Fiore's flirtations with chiliastic thinking, see Norman Cohn, *The Pursuit of the Millenium* (New York, 1961), pp. 98–101.
10. The classic modern study of this problem is Sigmund Freud's, "Thoughts for the Times on War and Death." In *Standard Edition of the Complete Psychological Works,* vol. 14, ed. James Strachey (London, 1957). Freud's contention that man cannot envision his own death except by observing it as a spectator (hence not really dead) has been modified to some extent by Robert Jay Lifton in his *History of Human Survival* (New York, 1971). See esp. pp. 172–73.
11. The Old Testament distinction between men and animals is very well demonstrated in the Book of Judges 7, where Gideon has been enjoined by God to employ a most interesting test in determining who was to be selected to fight the Midianites. Ten thousand men were taken to the banks of a river and told to drink from it. The three hundred who used their hands to bring water to their mouths were chosen. The nine thousand seven hundred others, who bent down and with their tongues lapped up the water "as a dog," were not selected. To drink "as a dog" suggested that one did not view himself as a man and hence was a likely candidate for slavery.
12. As an example of this see Leon Poliakov, *The Aryan Myth,* trans. from the French by Edmond Howard (New York, 1974), pp. 329–30. On the problems created by the Jewish "god of conscience," who demanded control over "natural" instincts and was opposed to somewhat more pliable gods of nature, see Bernhard Berliner's essay "On Some Religious Motives of Anti-Semitism." In Ernst Simmel (ed.), *Anti-Semitism: A Social Disease* (New York, 1946), pp. 79–84.

13. Adolf Hitler, *Mein Kampf,* trans. from the German by Ralph Mannheim (Boston, 1943), p. 288. Hitler's apparent belief in the ether theory is most interesting. One can assume that he was ignorant of the Michelson-Morley experiment of 1887 in which the Earth's movement through an assumed ether medium could not be detected. Even if he had known about this, he might well have discounted the validity of the experiment, since one of those involved in it, Albert Abraham Michelson, was a German-born Jew.

14. Ibid., p. 400.

15. Ibid., p. 512. Hitler's emphasis.

16. Fest, pp. 165–70, 174.

17. By "committed national socialists" one means those who accepted the nazi ideology or Weltanschauung to the point of utilizing it at the very least to rationalize the activities undertaken by the National-Socialist party and the state which served as its vehicle. A recent quantitative study which has called into question some of the basic assumptions regarding national socialism has confirmed that the most fundamental aspect of the nazi Weltanschauung, political anti-Semitism, was the most important conscious motivating factor for those prominent in the movement. See Peter H. Merkl, *Political Violence under the Swastika: 581 Early Nazis* (Princeton, 1975), pp. 503–4, 628.

18. Alfred Rosenberg, *Selected Writings* (London, 1970), p. 114.

19. Ibid., p. 117.

20. Ibid., p. 119.

21. Paul Brohmer, *Biologieunterricht und völkische Erziehung* (Frankfurt, 1933), as quoted in George L. Mosse (ed.), *Nazi Culture* (New York, 1965), pp. 83–84.

22. Ibid., p. 87. For another example of the national-socialist effort to root man firmly within the natural world, see Alfred Baeumler's 1939 lecture in which the nineteenth-century "racial scientist" Ludwig Woltmann was extolled for recognizing that man "must be understood *as a part of nature.*" Institut für Zeitgeschichte, reel no. MA 608, frame 55871. Baeumler's emphasis.

23. The school was established in 1932. From 1935 on, units that would become part of the Waffen SS were trained there. The date of this handbook is not known, but internal evidence would suggest 1936.

24. Untitled material concerning Weltanschauliche Erziehung, Institut für Zeitgeschichte, reel no. MA 332, frame 2656648.

25. Ibid.

26. Ibid., 2656651

27. Ibid., 2656652

28. Ibid., 2656653

29. Ibid., 2656652. If one believed in the superiority of a given race, the common ancestor theory had to be combatted. It is a weakness of Daniel Gasman's *The Scientific Origins of National Socialism* (New York/London, 1971), concerned with establishing links between Ernst Haeckel's Monist League and national socialism, that, outside of briefly alluding to it on page 173, the author never considers this problem in depth. For a fine treatment of this problem see Gunter Altner, *Weltanschauliche Hintergrunde der Rassenlehre des dritten Reiches* (Zürich 1968), pp. 23–25.

30. Ibid.

31. Ibid., 2656673

32. Ibid.

33. Institut für Zeitgeschichte, reel no. MA 45 1172, 250-c-10/5, pp. 3–4. The date of this lecture is not given, but was probably between 1934 and 1935.

34. Ibid., p. 6.

35. Ibid., p. 8.

36. Ibid., p. 9.

37. Ibid., p. 13.

38. Ibid., p. 16.

39. Bundesarchiv, Sammlung-Schumacher, group 14, no. 447. Composer's emphasis.

40. Ibid. Various forms of sun and fire worship had been of some significance in earlier youth and folkish movements. See George L. Mosse, *The Crisis of German Ideology* (New York, 1964); Walter Laqueur, *Young Germany* (London, 1962).

41. Martin Bormann, from *Kirchliches Jahrbuch für die evangelische Kirche im Deutschland, 1933–1944* (Gutersloh, 1948), as quoted in Mosse, *Nazi Culture*, p. 244.

42. Ibid., pp. 244–45.

43. Ibid., p. 245.

44. Heinrich Himmler, *Geheimreden: 1933 bis 1945* (Frankfurt/Berlin, 1974), p. 160.

45. Institut für Zeitgeschichte, reel no. MA 138/1, frame no. 301767.

46. Ibid.

47. Ibid., 301768.

48. Ibid., 301789.

49. After an exchange of communications between an apparent expert in this area, a man named Willigut, and R. Brandt of Himmler's office, Himmler decided that SS graves should be marked either with a traditional cross or with a *Man-rune*. The reason for choosing the latter was that it was a Lebens-rune, suggestive of immortal life for those fallen for the Fatherland. The *Tyre-rune,* while suggestive of an eternal *Kreislauf,* did not convey so optimistic a prospect for the individual soldier. See Bundesarchiv, Sammlung-Schumacher, group 14, no. 447.

50. Institut für Zeitgeschichte, reel no. MA 558, frames 9380476-9380488. To put this in some perspective, we can recall that this letter was dispatched just one day before the ill-fated Ardennes offensive was launched.

51. Large numbers of occultists who seek to explain nazism in terms of various uncouth, supernatural forces believe that there is a connection between Hitler and the Albigensians. As an example of this, see Angebert's *The Occult and the Third Reich* (New York, 1975).

52. Poliakov, *The Aryan Myth*, ch. 8.

53. Gobineau had been pessimistic about the survival of the Aryan race. Defenders of American slavery, as one might imagine, preferred happy endings. Hence Gobineau's writings were edited by Holz, his translator, in such a fashion as to create one. Slavery's defenders often utilized biblical arguments to support their case. The Bible also served the Abolitionist cause. Arguments rooted in "scientific racism" could be countered only by formal scientific analyses, the sorts of things with which the average lay person would not be concerned.

54. One could offer the notion of original sin, something that is part of the Christian but not the Jewish tradition. But this applied to all peoples, Christians included. While murder and annihilation as part of a conscientiously carried out policy were absent in the West, such was not the case with regard to the Mon-

gols, a people singularly removed from the Judeo-Christian tradition. Estimates as to the lives taken in the Mongol massacres range up to ten million, which demonstrates that what these people lacked in technology, they more than compensated for in enthusiasm.

55. *Dietrich Eckart: Ein Vermächtnis* (Munich, 1928), in George L. Mosse, *Nazi Culture*, p. 77.

56. Taken from a letter sent to all *Gauleiters*— for purposes of propaganda— dated September 30, 1941, Bundesarchiv, Sammlung-Schumacher, group 13, no. 382. The view of Jews as representing some sort of disease was amply precedented, particularly in the writings of Paul de Largarde.

PART IV

Teaching and Politics: George Mosse in the Pulpit

CHAPTER THIRTEEN

GLM: An Appreciation

Sterling Fishman

It is a Sunday afternoon. George Mosse sits at his large, cluttered desk pecking vigorously at his typewriter. His concentration is intense. The telephone rings. He pecks on determined to complete his sentence, if not his thought. The telephone rings more urgently. By the time George turns to it, the telephone has missed a beat. "Hello . . . I have it, David," he says. George switches from English to German. His sister, Hilde, is calling from New York to find out when to expect him.

A few snowflakes detach themselves from the lead-gray December sky and descend through the tall oak trees in the garden. Despite the entire wall of glass beside George's desk, the fluorescent lights of the study burn brightly through most of the brief, daylight hours. Three walls of this library-sized room are a bibliophile's dream. Ceiling-high shelves are packed with a lifetime of learning. One of the country's leading Reformation scholars bought this house more than two decades ago and later built this room. In this room he transformed himself into a student of what he had experienced, the catastrophe of Europe in this century. The book titles bear witness to this change. Hundreds of works documenting the religious strife of an earlier European era suddenly give way to a wall of modern titles bearing evidence of recent European racial and national conflicts. Jewish intellectuals, their creativity and their diaspora fill another tier of shelves with books. In this section, an entire shelf of titles, more than twenty including translations, bears the name of George L. Mosse as author. To the left of this shelf is another which holds equal pride of place in this library. These are the works of George's students.

"Yes," George is saying in German on the phone, "I shall be arriving on Christmas day. . . . Yes, I know that taxis are impossible to find in New York on Christmas day, but there is no need to send a limousine to get me.

. . . Oh, all right. Then I'll go to the hotel first before meeting you for dinner."

Hanging in one of those few clearings in this forest of shelves and books is a portrait of a different George from the one who now returns to his typewriter. A ten year old "Gerhard" faces a sixty-year-old George. The boy is unmistakably the father of the man; the eyes are the same. In many respects, George's face retains a certain childlike quality — especially its rounded shape. Of course, the thick glasses George now wears tell the tale of advancing years as do the patches of gray hair on either side of a bald pate.

Half a century earlier, one can only imagine the mischievous boy who was told he must sit for a portrait. Gerhard was one of three siblings who would one day inherit the Mosse publishing house enterprises and fortune. His maternal grandfather had built a publishing empire with the *Berliner Tageblatt,* one of Germany's leading newspapers, as its centerpiece. George grew up in a world of wealthy, assimilated Berlin Jewry. He had a nanny and was destined to attend the fashionable but somewhat outré Salem boarding school on the Bodensee in the far south of Germany, almost on the Swiss border. He recalls that he was never permitted the childhood delight of traveling on a tram until he was thirteen; otherwise always in a chauffeured car.

In retrospect, we know that the days of the Weimar world were numbered, that the secure, middle-class world of assimilated Berlin Jews would soon become an anxious world of swastikas and brown shirts. The mature George bearly recalls the slippage. In discussing those prenazi days with him, I have never detected a moment of serene nostalgia. Unlike so many political émigrés, George does not surround himself with mementos of bygone summer days. Several Medici tapestries which once hung in the Mosse house in Berlin now hang in George's Madison living room, and an oil portrait of Rudolf Mosse hangs over his bed, but these have intrinsic historic or artistic value for him. George does not burden himself with memories.

George's own recollections about leaving Germany sound more adventurous than furtive. Given the antinazi stance which the Mosse newspapers had taken, the family was forced to flee to Switzerland in the first days after Hitler became chancellor in January 1933. The fourteen-year-old George was in boarding school at the time; Switzerland was only a ferryboat ride away. The family sent the chauffeur for him. George does not recall the exact date, but does remember that he crossed the German border only fifteen minutes before midnight, when a new law requiring an exit visa was to go into effect. "Well, I managed to get out only because of the German penchant for order," he says casually. "That is really what I owe my life to, because I remember them [the border guards] looking at each other and raising their eyebrows when I went to give my passport."

Thus the teenage George became a refugee. Paris, which became his new home, was exhilarating and exciting for him. Given the family connections and George's knowledge of French, he never suffered the immediate pangs of being a "displaced person." Whereas he previously spent the school year enduring the Spartan life of boarding school in Salem, he was now enrolled in the Bootham School in York, England, there also to suffer the cold water rigors which were meant to "harden" the pampered children of the well-to-do. Summers he spent in Paris or traveling with his family to such places as Corsica and Italy. The Italian Fascists, he remembers, were quite hospitable to Jews. And the family waited, hoping that the nazi madness would pass and permit its return to Berlin. On one occasion his father returned to Berlin where he was offered Aryanization by propaganda minister Goebbels. He wisely refused.

Meanwhile, the young Gerhard became George and learned the ways of English life. He tramped through the countryside of York and collected pence and shillings for refugees of the Spanish Civil War. As European life unraveled, George found a secure haven in England. His Bootham School report cards indicate only that a refugee German boy was doing well in English, but not so well in music and math (George does not even recall having studied the latter). George credits his history master, Leslie Gilbert, with sparking his interest in the past. According to George, Gilbert was a superb teacher who launched the careers of many future historians.

Up to this point, the making of George Mosse the historian appears deceptively easy. Perhaps it was. However, we should not minimize the ill winds and rocky shoals which attended his setting forth. Destined at birth for a secure place in the family lineage and firm, raised amid the stout walls and bric-a-brac of a well-to-do German family, George was barely aware of himself as a Jew. Suddenly his destiny and fortune disappeared and he was cast into exile because he was Jewish. Becoming a refugee was undoubtedly a wrenching experience for the wealthy as well as the poor. No one who has crossed a border with George, even to Mexico, can say otherwise.

In recent years George has begun to reminisce more frequently about these early years. Those who feel they know him well still know relatively little about his childhood and youth. We know that his father divorced George's mother and married his governess once the strictures of Berlin life were broken. At this writing, the latter still lives in Berkely, although ailing, while the former died just a few years ago. George's father died in 1946. In the fall of 1937, George left Bootham and went to Cambridge to read history in Downing College. He had just turned nineteen.

GEORGE THE SCHOLAR

Given the years in which the young George reached maturity, one might expect to find the stamp of either rancour or ideological rigidity in his personality and early writings; rancour born of exile and rigidity born of ideological commitment. Those were the years when Marxism strongly attracted many of George's contemporaries who opposed fascism. One finds not a trace of anger or ideology in reading George's books and articles.

Not that any of George's early mentors were ideologues, at least not in the contemporary sense. They often dealt with eternal verities of a different sort — God, man, kinship, human nature, and the relationships between these eternal abstractions. This group of historians included George Macauley Trevelyan, Helen Maude Cam, and Bernard Manning in England, and William Lunt, and especially Charles Howard McIlwain in America. Through them George became interested in the tension that exists between the world of ideas and the world of political and social realities. His first ventures in historical scholarship include a book, originally his Harvard dissertation, describing the development of constitutional theories in Elizabethan England and a fascinating work on Puritan casuistry. In the latter he shows how even the adherents to that most sober and somber theology made theological accomodations in the name of survival — a "Holy Pretence" as George entitled it.

For those who know only the contemporary George, it may be difficult to imagine him as a Reformation scholar. It might also appear that George suddenly interrupted a successful career researching and writing about gentle lawyers and divines of a more distant past to tackle the roots of modern barbarism; as if George in mid-life began to probe his own refugee predicament. Such a view would ignore the continuities in George's development.

From the outset of his career George evinced a keen interest in the cultural symbols which mediate between abstract beliefs and popular piety. This has proved to be his most enduring historical concern. As a Reformation scholar, he became quickly fascinated with the baroque period because of its dramatic symbolic elements — the canonization and cult of St. Theresa, the sculpture of Bernini, and especially the highly theatrical baroque church.

I recall a trip to Mexico with George and Dick Soloway in 1956, when George was in search of expressions of the baroque. Struck by the inevitable intestinal plight of North American travelers, we took refuge in the small town of Zamora. Undaunted, George attended mass twice each day in the local baroque church. Our unscheduled stop permitted him to study religious rituals which several centuries had not altered. The local Indians must have marveled at the piety of this round-faced, bespectacled "gringo."

A few years later, when George turned his full attention to the study of modern mass movements, his work was informed by his study of baroque religious rites. However broad the chronological spectrum of his interests, strong threads of continuity run through his works. He has demonstrated that, although the prevailing ideological systems may change, popular piety with all its rites and rituals persists. George has shown how the cultural symbols of popular belief blur the distinction between religious and secular beliefs. For example, bawdy drinking songs were transformed by Reformation religious reformers into religious hymns; later, in a different age, they became modern military anthems. George's most recent work on the religious symbolism of World War I provides an excellent example of this. One can easily picture the baroque George prowling among the monuments and the gravestones of the Great War. His books on the rise of national socialism are proof of the point.

George does not really subscribe to any particular historiographical school. When cross-examined as in the Mike Ledeen interview of several years ago, he may label himself a Hegelian, but then quickly qualifies this term beyond recognition. George's historical genius does not rest on his commitment to theoretical models. He is an artist with a vision rather than an architect with a carefully drawn plan. He combines the intuitive leap with careful research. More than most of us, Goerge trusts his historical intuition. Cold stones and archives do not speak to George the historian; they provide the material to prove or disprove an idea. He leans further in this direction than any professional historian I know, and with remarkable results. Occasionally, especially when he is testing a new idea, he makes apparently outrageous assertions and thereby invites the criticism of colleagues and students. In modified form and beautifully documented, these ideas frequently become the convincing thesis of a future major work. No one who knows George will ever dismiss these highly imaginative ideas.

Thus George the historian is the marvel of his colleagues and friends. Defying categorization, he selects important and highly original themes on which to write. In so doing he almost recklessly trusts his intuition, but then carefully unearths a startling variety of sources to support his ideas. He has the instincts of a great composer and seems to sense the form the completed work will take. With remarkable efficiency, born of devotion to his vision, he assembles a variety of fragments into a well orchestrated opus. We are spoiled by the apparent ease with which he does this.

GEORGE THE PERSONALITY

George Mosse the historian is a playful man. His imagination can be pressed into scholarly service, but also provides him with a lively sense of humor. Whether on the podium or at the dinner table, he loves to play. His

eyes sparkle as he tells a tale in which he is the butt of the humor —
George seems to delight in laughing at himself — or as he gently teases
students or friends. Never mind that his stories grow more elaborate and
improbable with every telling — George delights his listeners. As he describes his flight to Guatemala with a cow and chickens on board the
plane, we are hearing the stories of the still mischievous boy named Gerhard.

George's tales and deeds often make him seem eccentric. In the best
sense of the term, perhaps he is. He has a sense of the dramatic and the absurd which has made him the subject of countless anecdotes. Each generation of his students shares a common store of these, as do his colleagues
and friends. The tales usually portray George as the German intellectual
confronting life in a middle-sized, Midwestern academic community. In
these anecdotes the great scholar does not quite comprehend the local folk-
ways and mores.

We all have our favorite "George stories"; I will indulge in recounting
just one. The setting is a Saturday evening long ago. The time was dusk
and I was preparing to go out when the telephone rang. It was an excited
George who told me that the lights had just gone out in his house. I reas-
sured him as best I could that all would be well and headed quickly for 36
Glenway Strasse, purchasing a couple of fuses en route. When I arrived, I
asked George what he was doing when the lights went out and he told me
that he had just settled down to watch "December Bride" on television. I
unplugged the TV which smelled faintly of smoke and asked George where
I could find the fuse box. He replied with a look that said, "How should I
know that, I'm not a mechanic or an electrician."

I led the way into the basement lighting matches as I went. George followed expressing great curiosity at my search. No fuse box in the basement. We went into the garage which by now was totally dark. Out of
matches, I reached into George's Ford and turned on the car headlights. At
last the fuse box. As I replaced the burned-out fuse, George mumbled
something about "pragmatic American genius." Before leaving the
brightly relit house, I firmly admonished George against playing the television set until he had it repaired; otherwise, the house might burn down. He
thanked me graciously and I left. By Monday George was telling people
that I had saved his life by preventing a terrible conflagration.

GEORGE THE TEACHER

I first encountered George Mosse the teacher on the bulletin board outside the old history office in Bascom Hall. By means of great exertions un-
beknownst to a new student, the Wisconsin historians had lured George to
leave Iowa City for Madison. His arrival was heralded by a clipping posted

in Bascom Hall. As it happened, George was departing from Iowa at the height of its football fame. The football coach had just completed an especially successful season and had been rewarded with a new car by his grateful fans. According to the Associated Press report, the equally grateful students of a young history professor, while unable to raise enough to buy a car, had presented their hero with a gold-plated key to his Ford; not out of disdain for football, but out of admiration for their teacher. In the fall, that car filled with books and baggage, the gold-plated key in the ignition and George Mosse at the wheel, crossed the Mississippi and headed for Madison.

George began at Madison by offering a two-year sequence in European cultural history. Although I had read the clipping on the bulletin board that summer, apparently not too many others had. One's fame as a teacher seldom transfers from one university to another. Only thirty of us heard those first lectures given by George on the Reformation. Although most of us did not know that Geroge was accustomed to lecturing to many hundreds at Iowa, we could tell that his voice could fill larger lecture halls than ours. By the end of the second year of the cultural history sequence, our numbers had risen to nearly two hundred. George Mosse, the Madison legend, had been launched.

At Iowa George had perfected his style. He brought with him a booming voice with dramatic modulation, clear, slightly accented diction, memorable descriptions, powerful phrasing, and the ability to make transcendent ideas comprehensible and personal. If George had chosen to be an evangelist and used his oratorical gifts for converting the faithless, he could have conducted a successful cross-country crusade — although it is hard to picture him in that role. George did not practice demagoguery with his students, but he has always been able to reach his most passive hearers. Without employing oversimplifications he has been able to make the ideas of even Calvin or Hegel exciting and personally meaningful.

Who can forget George, standing as erect as a Prussian next to the podium, pausing in his lecture, and turning in a personal manner to address a particular constituency: "For those of you who are Marxists"; or "for those of you from Scarsdale" (or Dubuque, or Wausau). Inevitably, an important idea would be made pertinent and become indelibly etched in one's *tabula rasa*. Sometimes he would even use a sense of the outrageous to make his point — perhaps deliberately to provoke some of his listeners. And usually with a touch of good natured humor. I doubt if any of George's thousands of students have ever forgotten their course with him, and more important, I suspect that most of them still remember some of what he had to say. How many mothers and fathers in Iowa, Wisconsin, and elsewhere in recalling their college days must describe a course with George Mosse.

Great virtuoso lecturers with a dramatic flair, often highly praised by students, are frequently criticized by colleagues for valuing style and technique over content, or for catering to the whims of the crowd. Similarly, such lecturers are often seen as mediocre in small classes or seminars, able only to declaim and not to teach, unable to translate public charisma into personal warmth. None of these criticisms apply to George.

In twenty-five years at Wisconsin, I know of no teacher who was more universally praised by students and faculty for his outstanding teaching than George Mosse. This praise applies on every level and in every situation. Nor do I know of any teacher more willing to teach than George Mosse; he is a professor eager to profess. Wherever there is a lecture hall or seminar room, a throng or select band, George will sally forth. In this, a typical semester, George has been lecturing thrice weekly on European cultural history since 1870, holding an undergraduate seminar on sexuality, and has traveled to New York, Norman, Oklahoma, Boston, and Milwaukee for guest lectures. In Oklahoma, besides visiting every local cowboy landmark and some that only exist in the vivid imagination of a Gerhard weaned on Karl May Western novels, George delivered six lectures in half as many days. In addition he delivered a paper to the German Workshop in Madison and spoke to half a dozen student and faculty groups.

This is not due entirely to a selfless commitment. His ego requires a forum. He clearly derives enormous personal satisfaction from public speaking. He knows that he is gifted, informative, and entertaining. As with any good virtuoso, George enjoys testing and confirming his talent. While at Iowa he frequently traveled to small towns to help commemorate important local events — high school commencement, Reformation Day, etc. One can only imagine the effect he might have had on such communities. I daresay no one slumbered in his seat when George spoke. Despite his secularity, I can imagine that church attendance rose markedly for several weeks following George's appearance. George can make even a secular message seem prophetic.

As a graduate teacher, George's aim was to eliminate banal pleasantries from his seminar. In its place he insisted on constructuve criticism. How well I remember George's first seminars in Madison. We were a mixed group of graduate students working on a variety of themes in a wide range of languages and sources. John Thayer was uncovering the roots of Italian fascism; Margaret Donovan read Russian existentialists; Dick Soloway, French fascists; Norman Coombs was writing on Anglican socialist clerics; and Sy Drescher was already involved with de Tocqueville. Somehow George Mosse managed to harness these diverse interests and create a valuable seminar. He urged us not to be too kind or gentle to one another in our criticism — and we weren't. But he never allowed us to be unduly and unfairly harsh either. We all remember the shock of confronting our critical colleagues in those early sessions. Sy Drescher recalls that he was ready to leave Madison and return to New York following the seminar discussion of his first paper. My reactions to a first effort on my part, a paper on Oswald Spengler, were similar. George's own comments were critical and constructive. The aim was excellence and he inspired us to achieve it.

GEORGE THE JEW

One of the most enigmatic questions concerning George Mosse involves his Judaism: What role does being a Jew play in his life? Although he might even scoff at the question, it is clearly an important one. He was raised in an assimilated German-Jewish family where mixed marriages and religious converts were not unknown. It was the Nazis who made George actuely aware of his Jewish origins. At fourteen he became a reluctant Jewish refugee. Although a nonobservant Jew today, George offers a course in Jewish history, actively identifies with Jewish cultural and social life, and holds a professorial chair at The Hebrew University in Jerusalem. However minimally aware he was of being a Jew as a boy, he identifies today with the Jewish community. Being Jewish has had a profound effect on his personal life as well as on his scholarly career.

I vividly recall an evening in George's living room in 1956, when the evening news was filled with reports of how the United States was pressing Israel to pull back from the Suez Canal. Never having discussed Israel with George previously, I was surpised to hear him describe how important it was, even for American Jews, to have a land of refuge. One never knew, he said, when you might have to flee from anti-Semitism. Israel deserved our support. Of course, he was being critical of the "moral politics" of John Foster Dulles, but he was also saying that a Jew should keep his suitcase available and partially packed. Several of us accused George of being a Zionist, which to some in those days was a rather serious accusation. George never rejected our label.

George's own views on Israel are far from clear-cut. He has often been critical of Israeli foreign policy and once returned from Israel following the 1967 Israeli victories and referred to the Jewish state as the "Prussia of the Middle East." Clearly George's identification with Judaism has directed his research interests as well. He has written extensively on such topics as the relationship of Germans and Jews, the role of the Jewish intellectual in modern Western cultures, and Jewish refugee historians. Asked to make sense of this, I believe that George would respond by saying that the course of history, in some dialectical fashion, has determined that he will be Jewish. And so he is that.

GEORGE THE FRIEND

On bright winter days George goes past my door with his latest dog Chelsea tugging at his leash. The erect manner in which George walks and holds himself — a reminder of his Prussian origins — causes him to appear larger than he is. On such days he wears a dark wool overcoat and a hat with earflaps. The flaps are often awry, one hanging loose and the other thrust high. He is the alert master of a skittish dog stopping at trees along the way.

Frequently master and beast explore the nearby cemetery on their rounds. Last summer's harvest of leaves lies thick on the ground between the tombstones. While the dog thrusts his nose in crackling piles of leaves George Mosse the cultural historian reads the epitaphs of departed Madisonians. Later, homeward bound, George stops to chat with me and shares the results of his cemetery research. Usually, he has composed an epitaph for himself. "I think it should just read, 'George Mosse — historian,'" he says. Following a cup of tea, I accompany George to the end of the driveway. He and Chelsea go down the road through the long shadows. George the émigré, George the scholar, George the professor, is also George the dear friend. "George," I said to him before he left, "when Goethe said that we are entering an age which would be devoid of great individual personalities, he didn't know that you would be coming along."

CHAPTER FOURTEEN
With George Mosse in the 1960s

Paul Breines

Around 1966 or 1967 in the history department at the University of Wisconsin in Madison there circulated a little story that is symptomatic of both a part of George Mosse's career and the experience of those who studied with him during the 1960s. It was said that in an application for graduate study, a candidate had included among his reasons for wanting to study European cultural history the desire to live among Professor Mosse's students. Fact or fiction, the tale is surely plausible. By the mid-1960s it was well known along the academic grapevine that the University of Wisconsin's history department was the site of some substantial scholarly and political developments, and that George Mosse, along with his colleagues William Appleman Williams and Harvey Goldberg, was close to their center. And if Mosse's students did not constitute a real circle or — since we were virtually without exception males — a young *Männerbund* of the type on which he often lectured, there nevertheless was a certain coherence and élan among us. This excited self-consciousness stemmed from the mixture of Mosse's impact as teacher and historian, the special features of the 1960s, and our own needs and fantasies as a young generation of aspirant intellectuals. How far, and for that matter, *how* the little glow of this experience spread may be hard to determine, but here and there spread it did, and one is not surprised that the young man in the story wanted to get inside.

In the personal recollections that follow, I focus on two related dimensions of the experience of being a student of George Mosse during the early and mid-1960s, dimensions which do not enable me to tell the whole story, but which are at least of more than merely personal significance. They are Jewishness and leftism, which is initially somewhat odd since George Mosse was neither a leftist nor, through most of the 1960s in Madison, an active Jew. Nevertheless, his relation to leftist students and his specific mode of Jewishness were at the heart of what transpired around him, even for many of his students who were neither leftists nor Jews. There were of course other factors at the University of Wisconsin and in the decade as a whole, some of which will be noted below; needless to say, Mosse did not influence his students in a vacuum. Yet for many of us, even when we disagreed with him most vehemently, he was the one who transmitted the key values, images, and secrets with which we tried to form ourselves as (Jewish or Judeophile) leftist intellectuals.

Was this George Mosse's intention? In one sense, emphatically not. Active in the reform wing of the Wisconsin State Democratic party, Mosse seemed a political liberal, and like many such academics at the time, he possessed the prerequisites for standing fast against radicalism. He could hardly have been its guide or guru, and he never was. But as these pages will depict, it belongs to the specificity of George Mosse's person and career that he responded with critical sympathy and real engagement to the emergent student leftism of the 1960s. Similarly, while until late in the decade he did not actively promote Jewish themes, certainly never religious ones, there was nonetheless something very Jewish about him — his intellect, his pedagogy, and Jews were preponderant among his students, as we were among the Left in the early and middle years of the decade.

These facts, yet to be explained, yield another preliminary question. George Mosse is primarily and rightly known as a scholar, an historian of ideologies, not as an ideologue or even a public figure, yet it is in these latter terms that I have begun to discuss him. The plain fact, to which anyone who has spent time at the University of Wisconsin could attest, is that he has amply filled these roles as well, if in a special manner. This is not only because his lectures became, as the 1960s progressed, events on the campus, part of the dramaturgy of the student movement. For one thing, and this is a measure of the richness of the story, George Mosse's lectures were more often than not directed *against* the Left — which meant that he took us seriously and that he had little patience with the claim that teaching must be neutral, devoid of values. As a public figure, then, it could be said for introductory purposes that George Mosse, though never *on* the Left, as were his colleagues Goldberg and Williams, was nevertheless linked to us because he was consistently if polemically *present for* the Left; *there* not only to debate and challenge, which he did with gusto, but to share. To share in what? In camaraderie. George Mosse's deeper if more narrow links to the Left developed through his private rather than his public figure; through friendships with leftist colleagues and students. This historian of ideologies, who has unrelentingly stressed their primacy in history, has lived according to the assumption of their weakness in personal life.

To try to look more closely at these matters, two shifts in gear are in order: one toward a sketch of the historical context, specifically, the unique situation of the history department at the University of Wisconsin; the other toward the more personal context, some words on what it has meant to me to have been a student of George Mosse. For some, the state of Wisconsin is politically notable as the home turf of Senator Joseph McCarthy, infamous hunter of communists in the early cold-war years. But it has its other credentials, including such progressives as Senator Robert La-Follette and William T. Evjue, founding editor of the once muckraking *Capital Times;* a strong socialist movement in the early decades of this century, especially around Victor Berger in Milwaukee; later an active state branch of the Communist party, U.S.A., and so forth.

That the University of Wisconsin, too, should have a certain heritage of academic radicalism is thus not surprising. This reaches back at least to the turn of the century when John R. Commons founded the country's first school of labor history; to Alexander Mickeljohn, iconoclastic and experimental university president in the 1930s; and to such beleaguered leftist faculty in the 1940s as the Marxist Alban Winspear, author of *The Genesis of Plato's Thought.* In the post–World War II years the history department in particular gathered a handful of independent-minded and sometimes leftist scholars, among them the Americanists Merrill Jensen, Howard Beale, Fred Harvey Harrington, and William Best Hesseltine, who created a certain space for critical reappraisals of the national past. New blood was infused by two graduate students who in the 1950s and early 1960s returned to the university to teach history — the socialists William Appleman Williams and Harvey Goldberg, with Mosse arriving in 1955. While the history department was emerging as the main vessel bearing and altering older radical traditions, the sociology department counted among its faculty the German émigré and idiosyncratic thinker Hans Gerth, with whom C. Wright Mills had studied in the early 1940s.

These are but some highlight personalities of a story that awaits its interpreter, although much of the story *is* one of the coming together of teachers and students, the ties and tensions among them being central to the transmission of ideas. In the absence of that larger picture, three summary notes may do. The first is that the University of Wisconsin crystallized some of the state's rich political dynamics and in so doing provided the historical terrain for the fusion of oppositional activism and thought which was to flourish in the 1960s. The second point concerns the vital place in this context of the history department, a politically and morally charged milieu which, in the rapidly shifting climate of the late 1950s and early 1960s, helped give birth to the New Left in Madison. The last point is that the state's and the university's radical tradition, while hardly dominant, nevertheless served as a magnet that attracted students from among the children of leftist Jews from New York.

The precise bearer of the transition from these earlier developments to those of the 1960s was the group of graduate students around William ApplemanWilliams who in 1959 constituted the journal *Studies on the Left*. Its history ought soon to be written. Drawing on Williams's revisionist interpretations of American foreign policy, encouraged by Hans Gerth, and inspired by awareness that their efforts were part of a broader if embryonic national and international New Left, the *Studies* group accomplished several important things. It advanced the idea of a post-Stalinist and postliberal humanistic Marxism (many of the editors were former members of the Communist party), stressing its pertinence to American life. It highlighted the importance of historical thought and criticism, presenting, against the backdrop of the impacted academic conformity of the postwar years, models of critical intellectual activity. And of special importance to the handful of younger students who came to circulate around *Studies on the Left,* is that the journal's associates were among our teachers, not in classrooms but amidst a dynamic little marginal and oppositional community, with the Socialist Club (membership: approximately two dozen) being its focal point.

When I came to the University of Wisconsin as a freshman in 1959, neither *Studies,* the Socialist Club, the history department, nor Mosse were concepts to me. Before too long they would be, and would constitute a milieu that changed my life and those of others in my generation. Some brief background may clarify aspects of the change. My parents are second generation Americans from East European artisan Jewish families. Born and raised in New York City, they became thoroughly modern in relation to their past — our home was irreligious; its ties to Jewish custom and tradition almost nonexistent. In the early 1950s we were part of the exodus to the suburbs, and my parents imposed no restraints on my complete and happy integration into the upper–middle-class life of Scarsdale. If my conscious links to things Jewish had been loosened from the start, I was likewise only dimly aware that I was a kind of closet leftist. Unlike other New York-born "red diaper babies" (children of leftists) I would later meet in Madison, I was largely oblivious to politics, and never felt myself politically at odds with neighbors or friends. On the other hand, I knew my parents were different and I admired the fact that they lived, even in Scarsdale, by more bohemian and less commercial values than did the parents of my friends. I also read and loved the novels of Howard Fast, then a communist, and noticed *I.F. Stone's Weekly, Monthly Review,* and *The Nation* on my parents' reading table, though I do not recall reading them. Had anyone scratched my surface, they would have found a young socialist, but no one did, least of all me.

While I was devoted to numerous of my high-school teachers, I never thought of myself as an intellectual, but instead pursued both sports, where

I found my role models, and a social life among the popular crowd in my class, which graduated in 1959. Scarsdale, whose Jewish population was growing at the time, offered among its many amenities a civil and classy brand of anti-Semitism, which now and then erupted into a minor incident —a Jew having difficulty purchasing a home or being excluded from a country club. To this my response was a mixture of concern and evasion through the time-honored strategy of (Jewish) self-denial. Toward my older, more visibly Jewish relatives, I reacted similarly with a combination of affection and fascination, whose sources eluded me, and repulsion, whose source was clear: ties to them in the Scarsdale context would have made me an outsider, an "other," a Jew. Yet while my closest friends were not all Jews, most of them were. In a sense, I was an all around latent person: latent leftist, latent intellectual, latent Jew. The one mode of "otherness" I did choose was both impossible and rather tame. Norman Mailer termed the more volatile version of this choice the "White Negro," which for me consisted of a passion for Black basketball, rock and roll and gospel music, and a general feeling of admiration and empathy for Black people, very few of whom I actually knew. In any case, at age eighteen I recognized I would probably not go on to become a Black person, but was sure of little else. Originally planning to attend a small New England liberal arts college, I switched at the last moment to the University of Wisconsin when a Scarsdale teacher I liked spoke highly of his summer school experience there and, when my parents, familiar with the outlines of the university's traditions, endorsed the idea.

My discovery of George Mosse, the history department, and the group of mostly Jewish intellectuals from New York around *Studies on the Left* and the Socialist Club would amount to something like a return to the home I never realized I had been looking for. It was not an immediate discovery. My initial choice, more closely tied to Scardsale experiences, was to join a fraternity, Pi Lambda Phi. It was a Jewish fraternity many of whose members tended not to look especially Jewish and generally paid special attention to parties with non-Jewish sororities. Without grasping it all at the time, my own impulses to deny my Jewishness—to be a Gentile— fit in well. The experience was sufficiently common to have found its way into a little song, a Jewish mama's lament over her son's fate in Zeta Beta Tau, a fraternity roughly similar to Pi Lambda Phi in this context: "Oi, oi, oi, for Zeta Beta Toi/ Vot have you done to my little Jewish boy?/ I send him off to college to learn to read and write/ And now he's dating Schikses every Friday night."

Not long after I became a fraternity "pledge," I began to grow impatient with Pi Lambda Phi's rituals, pressures, and social conformism. In large part, this was the work of a girl friend, who I would later marry and who influenced me greatly in new directions. It was also a sign of the times, since of the twenty-five-odd boys who pledged Pi Lambda Phi in 1959, only three or four were fraternity members when our class graduated in 1963, by which time the whole fraternity system had all but dissolved at the University of Wisconsin.

I mention Pi Lambda Phi because it was through it that I first learned of George Mosse; and it was through Pi Lambda Phi that Mosse had among his first, if now amusing, ties to incipient student radicalism. While still a pledge I learned that in the previous year the fraternity had passed through a crisis culminating in the expulsion of a group of dissidents along with Pi Lambda Phi's faculty advisor, Professor George L. Mosse. The group, with Mosse's backing, had tried to institute reforms in the inane and sometimes lethal initiation rites inducting pledges into full membership. When the normal channels failed to work, so the story has it, the dissidents attempted a little coup d'état by sneaking a university administrator into one of the "Hell Week" events to observe and report. The plot was discovered; the culprits, having failed to build a sufficient base, were duly expelled. Some members of the defeated opposition, most of whom happened to be history students, moved to an apartment where, on leaving Pi Lambda Phi myself, I would spend some time and get reminders to take one of Professor Mosse's history courses.

I soon did and the experience became part of the little whirl of conflicting ideas, values, and styles in which I found myself, having suddenly bounced out of my several high-school closets. Somewhere among the microfiche storage at the University of Wisconsin is documentary evidence that I did not pay an inordinate amount of attention to many of my courses. Most of my initial college education came from the little leftist student ghetto whose life I fervently embraced: its bohemianism, the books and pamphlets— I became a bibliomaniac with little time to read—the folk music, the attempt to live by humane ethics, the will to end class society, the newly felt guilt at having come from Scarsdale. What was then known as "History 3," Mosse's popular introductory course on nineteenth- and twentieth-century Europe, was the one course with real attraction for me. I entered it armed with a newly found militant Marxism.

At the time (1959–60), George Mosse was at work on his textbook *The Culture of Modern Europe*. Its focus on the importance of myth and symbol, popular culture, and the rise of mass politics was reflected in his lectures, as was his hostility to Marxism as a method, although he presented Marxism with real force as part of the search for wholeness in modern life —one of many of his ideas which I internalized without at first realizing it. With tales of his Pi Lambda Phi adventures and accounts of his lecturing prowess in mind, he loomed as a mythical figure in my eyes. On actually meeting him, I felt in the presence of someone very important and powerful; sitting in his lectures amplified the feeling. Stocky and robust, bedecked in tweeds, the big, curved pipe hanging from his mouth, the erect posture, the resonant voice with its mix of German and British accents, the twinkly eyes, and the slightly dishevelled aspect—so learned a man, I believed, could hardly be attentive to appearances—these were among the accoutrements of a charismatic figure. From the moment he gripped the lectern with two firmly straightened arms until he completed his slow pacing to and fro on the lecture platform, one felt, and I was hardly alone in feeling it, that one had not merely heard something important about history, but had actually been in contact with it.

As these notes indicate, I am an impressionable person, and was especially so at age nineteen. Again without recognizing the fact at first, I had decided not merely that I was going to take more courses with George Mosse, but that I wanted to *be* what he was. Yet I also wanted to be, or be like, Martin Sklar, the brilliant Williams student, editor of *Studies on the Left,* occasional manual laborer, and generally the grey eminence of the student Left in Madison. With some embarrassment I will report that I bought a pipe like Mosse's, and his tobacco as well; and a hat like Sklar's, along with replicas of his specific fountain pen and yellow writing paper, as if this would enable me to produce comparable reams of vital, unpublished contributions to Marxist theory. Though embarrassing to recount, I have wondered often both about how prevalent in the dissemination of ideas are such mimetic impulses, and about their real sources.

At least one story involving Martin Sklar seems worth telling here since, although quite obscure, it seems representative of an important dimension of the student Left experience in Madison in the early 1960s. In the summer of 1961 I had decided to go to Mississippi to participate in the Freedom Rides, then the main focus of the Civil Rights movement. A small send-off party was arranged for the occasion, and to my great honor, Sklar graced it with his presence. Amidst the little fanfare, he took me aside to convey the message that, while he fully respected my decision, he thought it worth my considering the idea of remaining in Madison in order to carry on theoretical work. There is no shortage of activists, he advised, but of theoreticians. I held my ground and went South, unable to communicate at the time my utter delight at being considered capable of something as magisterial as theoretical work. It is probably true that only Martin Sklar could have said what he said, yet the episode seems to capture certain essentials of a larger story. It captures, for example, the extent to which the connections between the history department and the Left milieu generated a (relatively) unique respect for intellectual activity, for books, for thought.

George Mosse himself was in the early 1960s generally remote from the activities of the campus Left. If sympathetic to the Civil Rights and peace efforts of the time, he did not share in our enthusiasm for the Cuban Revolution or for C. Wright Mills and Jean-Paul Sartre. Yet I saw no particular contradictions between my complete involvement in the efforts of the Left and the increasing attention I was paying to Mosse's courses, which may be more a commentary on my own case than on the circumstances. For example, what in retrospect was probably my most formative intellectual experience—attendance in 1961 in the twentieth-century semester of Mosse's renowned four-semester course on European cultural history— came simultaneously with my reading Maurice Cornforth's *Historical Materialism* and Emile Burns's *Handbook of Marxism*, two manuals by British Communist party theorists of the 1930s and 1940s. There I was, trying to master the fundamentals of orthodox Marxism while emoting over Nietzsche, too enthusiastic to bother with the gaps between them.

Yet it was in Mosse's cultural history course that I and a handful of friends first learned of Burns, Cornforth, Christopher Caudwell, Arthur Koestler, André Malraux, Georg Lukács, German Expressionism, Antonio Gramsci, the debates between Sartre and Camus, Martin Buber, Wilhelm Reich, and others. Two recently published books assigned in the course were of special importance to us. Along with Mosse's own commentary, H. Stuart Hughes's *Consciousness and Society* introduced the neoidealist and neoromantic critiques of positivism and materialism, while George Lichtheim's *Marxism* opened my eyes to some major dilemmas in the ideas I had until then embraced. The course itself attracted some three hundred students who packed into what was then one of the largest lecture halls on the campus. We leftists amounted to perhaps a dozen. Nevertheless, it was more often than not to one of us or to us as a group that Mosse addressed himself, now and then speaking as if the room were filled with leftist students for whom the problems of, say, Sartre's ties to French communism were a vital matter.

On a number of occasions, a lecture would be followed by a trek to the student union cafeteria or terrace, with Mosse in heated debate with several of the leftist graduate students in the course, surrounded by a handful of us undergraduates. The subsequent lecture often turned out to be a continuation of one of these colloquies. What all of this was like to the majority of students attending I cannot say, except to note that the course was immensely successful and its enrollment grew in the next years. For the few of us on the Left, the experience was unique, though at the time we had no way of knowing how unique. On the one side, we were in combat with Mosse and his constant debunking of the shibboleths of leftist intellectuals in Europe—his criticism of the antileftist assumptions of the bulk of the class were few and far between; on the other side, the course as a whole was in many respects a kind of internal leftist discussion, and as such of great meaning to us.

Recalling this experience and Mosse's role in it makes me realize that his own political standpoint was or perhaps has along the way developed into something more complex than that of a liberal Democrat who, for reasons of personal friendships and attractions, undertook lively exchanges with leftist students. Already in the cultural history course (1961), for example, George Mosse showed a certain weakness for those figures he termed "Marxists of the heart," a phrase adopted by C. Wright Mills in his book *The Marxists*. For Mosse, these included Jean Jaurès, the German neo-Kantian socialists, Ernst Toller, Gustav Landauer, and others. I say he showed a weakness for them because the affinities I believe were there were well hidden beneath criticism of the political ineffectiveness of the individuals and groups involved, above all in the age of mass movements and manipulation. That he nonetheless saw in the Marxists of the heart spirits kindred to his own is not something I can prove. Yet, for example, one need not read very far between the lines of his essay from later in the decade, "Left-wing Intellectuals in the Weimar Republic," the final chapter of *Germans and Jews,* to notice more than a little sympathy for the generally pacifist, ethically idealist socialism of such figures as Carl von Ossietzsky and Carlo Roselli. The essay resurrects them as forerunners of the New Left, and to a degree at least suggests one of the ways the student movement of the 1960s influenced George Mosse's scholarship and view of the world.

It could even be said without stretching the matter too far that, while he has neither broadcast the fact nor even made it explicit, George Mosse has in his own way sought to contribute to the tradition of Marxism of the heart. That he has done so as a teacher through his vigorously critical engagement with the student Left is, I hope, reasonably clear. But beyond this, he has offered something specific and dense through his scholarship. With real if implicit concern, his studies of nazism, racialism, the politics of mass dramaturgy *(Nationalization of the Masses),* and his forthcoming works pose a sharp and perhaps unmeetable challenge to humanistic socialism. For the latter has not only been inept at generating the symbolic and manipulative techniques of mass politics; it has rejected them from the outset. Yet in the present age, those are the triumphant techniques. While Mosse is no advocate of such techniques, his historical studies point to two vital tasks facing the humanistic socialism to which he has been closer than he reveals: intensive study of the history of popular culture as the soil from which modern mass movements have sprung; and investigation of the symbols, images, and fantasies adequate to a movement for change that is at once massive and humane. As remote and even as ludicrous as such a quest might appear to be, I believe it stems directly from George Mosse's historical work, and that if you were to press the point, he would finally admit it.

It is now time to take up the Jewish question. The student Left at the University of Wisconsin in the early 1960s was predominantly Jewish. Yet there was little if anything in the way of systematic discussion of this theme in the Socialist Club or around *Studies on the Left*. Later, after its relocation in New York City, the journal did carry Norman Fruchter's fine and controversial commentary on "Arendt's Eichmann and Jewish Identity." The public silence was largely due to a reluctance to amplify the obvious fact of the Left's mostly Jewish membership, but also because none of the Jews was actively Jewish. We considered ourselves first of all leftists. I recall no one who was religious, no "radical Seders," and no Zionists. Typical of the situation and sensibility involved was the appearance in our milieu in 1962 of one Doug Korty, a freshman from Ohio, ruggedly handsome, blond, blue-eyed and — we thanked our stars — socialist, whom we (and he) happily dubbed our token Goy, although he was only the most Aryan specimen among the non-Jews in our circle.

The question of Jews on the Left, in other words, was relegated to jokes and passing remarks. So, for example, what the non-Jews thought about being among the Jews, a reversal of the usual picture, I do not precisely know. Perhaps none of us relished the prospect of admitting that racial-historical fantasy played a role in our lives, especially since we were all antiracists, active in civil rights, mostly rationalists with little conscious sympathy for myth and stereotype. But there were signs, briefly touched on in private conversation, marking the regions we by-passed. Among these was the fact that some White Gentiles who gravitated toward the Left in the early 1960s (and at other times and places), did so in part out of a kind of Judeophilism, an effort to find a new vitalism and identity through contact with Jews and Jewishness, specifically with the stereotypes of Jewish leftism, intellectualism, and history as an oppressed people, with the attraction of an alleged Jewish sexuality playing some sort of role in the story. As an assimilated, secular, middle-class Jew, I was drawn to the leftist milieu in Madison for these same reasons. Becoming a leftist there meant also becoming a Jew, though once again, with only dim self-consciousness.

There was one significant form in which the issue of Jew and non-Jew on the Left was addressed in Madison, and in this connection George Mosse occupied a prominent place. The issue unfolded as a counterpoint between several key faculty personalities, with William Appleman Williams on one side and George Mosse and Harvey Goldberg on the other. The three were good friends and far from intending to represent polar currents. In any case, among their students there was a certain awareness of cultural differences, which in turn had substantial bearing on the ways in which we tried to define our heritage or mythology as leftists.

In appearance and style, quirks and background (born in Iowa, athlete, decorated naval captain, and so on), for example, William Appleman Williams was robustly American. Although he always noted his intellectual debts to European social theory, it was hard to miss the homespun character of his radicalism and his consistent efforts to discover forerunners, including those he deemed thoughtful, independent-minded conservatives, in the American past. In the early 1960s, many, though by no means all his students (a few of whom were not on the Left) were Jews from New York. His most dedicated and able publicist among undergraduates in the early 1960s, Fred Ciporen, was a veritable archtype of *Yiddishkeit,* and indeed spoke Yiddish as his first language. There was some, if never extensive, discussion of the matter. I myself, something of an expert in escapist strategies in this context, was one of those who contended, in small private discussions, that leftist Jews who identified with Williams were trying to submerge their Jewishness in his very American socialism or even his socialist Americanism. Others deemed the whole question an idiotic subterfuge, insisting that what mattered was the critical content of Williams's thought, its applicability to our political present. While a few others contended that historiography and deeply ethical socialism amounted to a kind of realization of historical Jewish socialism in the American context.

For what it may be worth, my own position here reflected not so much a heightened Jewish consciousness, though partly that, as it did an increasingly hostile attitude toward things American. This attitude in turn was only partly based on outrage at what I was learning about America's role in world affairs. It stemmed equally if not more so from a growing Europophilism, specifically, a belief in the superiority of German idealist culture, which it was not George Mosse's aim to promote, although he was clearly the source. For a number of my friends, the key role was played by Harvey Goldberg, who with extraordinary intensity introduced the Madison Left to European and world socialist history. The fact that the two Europeanists were Jews is accidental, but the same cannot be said of its implications. Interest in Mosse and Goldberg, while in my own and other cases never excluded real enthusiasm for Williams's work, entailed a rejection of America, a spiritual flight to a historical fantasy world of European, partly Jewish leftist politics and culture.

Two points bear repeating: there were Jews among us who sought an American leftist heritage, and non-Jews who looked to European and Jewish currents for inspiration. Second, none of this was the aim of the teachers—Williams, Goldberg, and Mosse. For example Harvey Goldberg, whose lectures on the sansculottes, comparative revolutions, and French social history often flowed into chanted messages of redemption reminding me of cantors and rabbis I had never known or seen, was the representative of socialist internationalism in our midst. He was preoccupied with Jean

Jaurès, whose biography he was completing, rather than with Jewish matters. Similarly Mosse, who in the 1970s would become active in Jewish studies in connection with his half-time teaching in Jerusalem, was in the early and mid-1960s not doing anything explicitly Jewish. Nevertheless, as I would realize only later, Mosse in particular was involved in contributing to the formation of a leftist-Jewish identity in Madison.

On graduating in 1963, I left Madison for Cornell, following my wife-to-be who had received a grant to study city planning there. Wini Breines, whose background was roughly similar to my own and who shared the experiences recounted here, was never seduced by the Jewish-leftist mystique. In Madison, for example, Williams and the American cultural historian William Taylor exerted a sharper influence on her thinking. For the moment, there is but one aspect of the move to Cornell that needs mention since it bears on my previous and future relation to George Mosse. There Sam Weber and Shierry Weber, who had begun their translation into English of T.W. Adorno's *Prismen,* would introduce us to the Frankfurt School. This coincided with publication of Marcuse's *One Dimensional Man,* which we read with the fervor of a kind of great awakening. I could not yet even read German, yet the "critical theory of society" made sense of everything: my Madison past, the present realities of America and the world, and my future tasks. It seemed the body of ideas I had been fated to find. I became a disciple.

In the summer of 1965, we left Ithaca for Europe, as dropouts of sorts, although Wini had completed her planning degree. Part of our aim was to go to Frankfurt to learn from Adorno, Horkheimer, and the emergent German New Left. We met and stayed briefly with the little group of American students, including Jeremy Shapiro, who were studying at the Institute for Social Research. I went to one Adorno lecture, and hung on every word with no idea of what any one of them meant. Wondering whether the *Polizei* would see I was a Jew and take me away; actually stopped and reprimanded by a pedestrian for starting to cross a street against a red light; I nevertheless believed I had arrived in my cultural-political home. As things turned out, we did not remain in Frankfurt, but traveled and finally settled in Vienna, among other things to learn German at last. Within six months, the problem arose that the American Selective Service had, in connection with stepping up the war against Vietnam, dropped the marital deferment, leaving the student deferment as my one bet to stay out of the draft.

In the early winter of 1965, aid arrived in the person of George Mosse, who had come to Vienna to attend the International Conference of the Historical Sciences. He encouraged me to return to Madison for graduate work with him and, more than that, proposed a project: a study of Gustav Landauer. We made plans to return to that other homeland, while I started gathering Landauer material from the library. Then, during a brief visit to

Prague, Wini found an original Landauer book in an *Antiquariat* in the Jewish quarter. Evidently a plan in the hands of higher forces was being played out. It helped that this was still a time when strong-minded women could accept following their men.

By 1966 Madison had both changed and remained the same. The outlines of the political changes can be assumed: the flowering of the student revolt and counterculture, the antiwar movement, and Black nationalism. Mosse, Goldberg, and Williams were still there, and while we were gone Mosse and Williams had presented their joint seminar on Marxism, one product of which was Williams's fine and neglected book *The Great Evasion.* Though I can say nothing about the seminar specifically, it was nevertheless symptomatic of the unity among some differences in the leftist milieu in the history department. In addition, the late George Haupt had arrived as a guest lecturer. A Rumanian Jew, survivor of Auschwitz, ex-communist, Haupt was a déraciné intellectual par excellence. Another new addition was Paul Buhle, a history graduate student and editor of the journal *Radical America,* which became a focal point for numerous discussions and debates among those of us on the Left who were looking for indigenous working-class traditions, and those of us who had adopted European intellectual progenitors.

The whole atmosphere was highly charged, not just with the energy of historical and cultural debate, whose participants were rather few, but by a rapidly growing political movement. This is not the place to recount the latter, with the exception of one note. George Mosse's relation to the burgeoning student activism in 1966–67 was complex, yet ultimately defined by his solidarity. Opposed to the Vietnam war and sympathetic to many of our impulses, Mosse was openly critical of the increasing use of confrontation strategies. The John Bascom Professor of History was not known on campus or in the city of Madison as a sponsor of the student Left. Yet in the emergency faculty meetings held in response to the student takeover of the administration building over the issue of university involvement in the draft, and then after the massive police assault against the sit-in blocking Dow Chemical Corporation recruitment in university buildings, it was George Mosse who presented the major speeches on our behalf. Distancing himself from our tactics, he proclaimed his solidarity with our goals and impulses, while chastising his colleagues for their preoccupation with business as usual. They were not leftist speeches, but Mosse speeches.

In the meantime, I was taking some steps toward putting George Mosse and his role in my life and in those of some of my friends into somewhat clearer perspective. In the heady 1966–67 period, while at work on the Master's thesis on Gustav Landauer, I read Isaac Deutscher's essay "The Non-Jewish Jew," which enabled me to place myself, Landauer, the Frankfurt School, and Mosse as well into a meaningful historical frame.

At the time, my emotions were spilling out of the frame. Research into Landauer sent me into raptures of identification and historical fantasy, partly because Landauer's own case as a Jew was complex, hesitant, and critical. For a brief while I was convinced by the claim of one Fritz Kahn, a leftist Jew, whose *Die Juden als Rasse und Kulturvolk* (1921), a book later cited often by nazis, argued that from Christ through Spinoza, Marx, and Landauer, radicalism flowed in Jewish blood. Also thanks to George Mosse, I was able to interview Gershom Scholem, who as a young man had met Landauer shortly before World War I. Several hours in Scholem's presence sent my brain into an orbit of Jewish mysticism, anarcho-leftism, and related forms of esoteric belief. When in 1967 our daughter was born within hours of Gustav Landauer's birthday, I was certain that numerological messages were being sent by my racial-political ancestors.

It is characteristic that, although George Mosse had by then become a Zionist of sorts, he never exerted any pressure on me in that direction. Clearly, Mosse could have been a *Grossmeister,* a domineering intellect and persona surrounded by adoring disciples. By choice he never was. In his graduate seminars, for example, he nurtured debate rather than consensus, and showed little patience with intellectual mimicry. In personal-intellectual relations as well, he was supportive rather than overbearing. For what my own case is worth in this context, he had definite reservations regarding my choice of a dissertation study of the Marxian theory developed in the early 1920s by Georg Lukács and Karl Korsch. He made those reservations clear and then did what he could to help get me launched with the work. Although I did not think of it in these terms at the time, that work entailed opting for leftism rather than Jewishness, although Lukács, in whom I was primarily interested, exemplified the type of the non-Jewish Jew. On returning to Madison in 1972 to defend the finished dissertation, one of the examiners was quick to comment: "This is not a Marxist work; it is a Mosse work."

Whatever that says about me is not as interesting as what it says about Mosse, what he embodied for me and my generation of his students, especially those of us who were both leftists and Jews. The simple part is that he was the living agent of a German-Jewish intellectual culture which, against the backdrop of what we perceived as an American desert, was immensely seductive. But his Jewishness was not very Jewish, that is, it was German rather than Yiddish. This appealed to assimilated American Jews like myself, as well as to non-Jewish Judeophile students. The experience of those of Mosse's students who came from lower-class Yiddish backgrounds was quite different in this regard. Of special importance to all of us, I believe, was Mosse's sense of detachment from himself; his capacity to look at himself as well as at us, his students, with a historical-critical eye, locating our efforts in the contours of the situations and quests of

Western intellectuals in the modern era. This enabled us to impart a certain histrionic aura and sense of importance to what we were doing. It also encouraged us in the opposite direction, toward a somewhat better sense of self-irony and tolerance.

In December 1979, some twenty years after first meeting George Mosse, I was able to hear him present the keynote address to the Annual Conference of the American Association of Jewish Studies held in Boston. His topic was "The German-Jewish Dialogue"; his audience was composed mostly of Zionist and religious Jewish scholars. His argument, leaving aside its complexity and scope, was that, alongside Zionism and religious Judaism there exists a Jewish intellectual heritage which the more Jewish Jews would do well to recognize. It is a heritage, he argued, of critical, cosmopolitan, humanistic intellect grounded in the classical German idealist concept of *Bildung,* humane cultivation of one's self and world. In its fold, Mosse placed selected liberal and leftist intellectuals from the nineteenth and twentieth centuries, suggesting further that this tradition inspired certain currents among the New Left in the 1960s. Two thoughts passed through my mind as I listened, noting the signs of dissent that would erupt in the discussion period— a typical Mosse lecture. First, I was touched to realize that he was in part talking about his students and I wished more of us had been present. Then occurred the thought that put much of my twenty years' association with George Mosse into context: he is talking about himself, about *his* heritage, the one he has given us.

About the Contributors

STEVEN E. ASCHHEIM is Florence T. May Visiting Professor of Judaic Studies at Reed College. He has taught variously in Jerusalem, the University of Maryland, and the University of Wisconsin. He has published for the Jewish Agency, the *Jewish Journal of Sociology*, and his work *Strange Encounter: The East European Jew in German and German Jewish Consciousness, 1800–1923*, from which the present contribution derives, is being prepared for publication.

PAUL BREINES teaches modern European intellectual history at Boston College, where he is also director of Graduate Studies. He is a member of the editorial group of *Telos* and a corresponding editor of *Theory & Society*. He is coauthor (with Andrew Arato) of *The Young Lukács and the Origins of Western Marxism*.

SEYMOUR DRESCHER is professor and chairman of the History Department as well as professor of sociology at the University of Pittsburgh. He has also taught at Harvard University. He has been a Fulbright scholar, a senior fellow of the National Endowment for the Humanities, a Guggenheim fellow, and a resident scholar at the Rockefeller Foundation's Bellagio Study Center. He is the editor of *Tocqueville and England*, and author of *Tocqueville and Beaumont on Social Reform* and *Dilemmas of Democracy: Tocqueville and Modernization* (the latter dedicated to George L. Mosse). He is also the author and editor of a number of studies on slavery and abolition, most notably *Econocide: British Slavery in the Era of Abolition* and (coeditor) *Anti-Slavery, Religion, and Reform*.

STERLING FISHMAN has studied under George Mosse and is presently his colleague as a professor of history and educational policy studies at the University of Wisconsin, Madison. He has taught at the State University of New York, Binghamton, and at Douglass College (Rutgers University). He is the editor of *Teacher, Student, and Society*, and the author of *The Struggle for German Youth, 1890–1914*, as well as of numerous articles.

DAVID GROSS is associate professor of history at the University of Colorado, Boulder. His work includes *The Writer and Society: Heinrich Mann and Literary Politics in Germany, 1890–1940*, and several articles on the nature of mass culture and the theory of cultural criticism in the twentieth century. He is currently working on a book on the concept of memory in modern European thought. He is an associate editor of *Telos*.

JOST HERMAND is professor of German and Vilas Research Professor of German at the University of Wisconsin. He has been visiting professor at Harvard University, the University of Texas at Austin, the University of Bremen, the University of Giessen, and the Free University of West Berlin. His major publications include *Epochen deutscher Kultur von der Gründerzeit bis zum Expressionismus*, 5 volumes (with Richard Hamann); *Kunstwissenschaft und Literaturwissenschaft*; *Interpretative Synthesis: The Task of Literary Scholarship*; *Von Mainz nach Weimar*; *Pop International*; *Der Schein des schönen Lebens*; *Der frühe Heine*; *Die Kultur der Weimarer Republik* (with Frank Trommler); *Sieben Arten an Deutschland zu leiden*; *Orte. Irgendwo. Formen utopischen Denkens*; *Konkretes Hören: Zum Inhalt der Instrumentalmusik*.

TIM KECK is chief of Equal Employment Opportunity at Ramstein Air Base, Germany. He also teaches history, philosophy, and women's studies at the University of Maryland, European Division. He has been a Ford fellow and a Fulbright fellow, and has published articles in *Archiv für Sozialgeschichte* and the *Social Science Journal*. He is currently working on a study of neo-Kantians in Wilhelmian Germany.

ALFRED H. KELLY has studied under George Mosse and has taught at Virginia Commonwealth University and the University of Richmond. He is currently assistant professor of history at Hamilton College in Clinton, New York. His fields of interest are modern European intellectual history and modern Germany. He is the author of *The Descent of Darwin: The Popularization of Darwinism in Germany, 1860–1914*.

H.G. KOENIGSBERGER is professor of history at the University of London King's College and president of the International Commission for the History of Representative and Parliamentary Institutions. He has taught at various universities in Northern Ireland, England, and the United States. His principal publications include *The Practice of Empire*; *Europe in the Sixteenth Century* (with George L. Mosse); *Estates and Revolutions*; *The Habsburgs and Europe*; and *Politics and Civilization in Early Modern Europe*.

PAUL F. LACHANCE is assistant professor at the University of Ottawa, where he teaches European and American history. He has contributed articles to *Europa: A Journal of Interdisciplinary Studies*; *Plantation Soci-*

ety in the Americas; and to the review of the Société Haïtienne d'Histoire, de Géographie et de Géologie. His current interest is in French cultural persistence in late Spanish and early American Louisiana.

ROBERT A. NYE is professor of history at the University of Oklahoma, Norman. Among his works are *The Origins of Crowd Psychology: Gustave LeBon and Mass Democracy in the Third Republic; The Anti-Democratic Sources of Elite Theory: Pareto, Mosca, Michels*; and the introduction to the Transaction edition of Gustave LeBon's *The French Revolution and the Psychology of Revolution*. He is currently working on a book on crime and social pathology in France in 1850–1920.

ROBERT A. POIS is professor of history at the University of Colorado, Boulder. His main areas of interest are historiography, Weimar Germany, German Expressionism in the plastic arts, and the nature and roots of national-socialist ideology. He is the editor of *Alfred Rosenberg: Selected Writings*, and the author of *Friedrich Meinecke and German Politics in the Twentieth Century* and *The Bourgeois Democrats of Weimar Germany*, as well as of articles and reviews in various professional journals.

ANSON RABINBACH has studied under George Mosse and is currently teaching history at Princeton University. His publications include a study of the national socialist bureau of "beauty of labor," articles on the theory of fascism, and essays on German culture between the wars. A recently completed book entitled *The Crisis of Austrian Socialism: Otto Bauer and the Left Opposition, 1927–1934* will appear shortly. His current research is on the social and cultural perception of fatigue and the working body at the end of the nineteenth century. He is an editor of *New German Critique: An Interdisciplinary Journal of German Studies.*

DAVID SABEAN is a research associate at the Max-Planck-Institute for History in Göttingen, West Germany. He has taught at the University of East Anglia and the University of Pittsburgh, where he is an adjunct associate professor. He has published a book and several articles on the German Peasant War of 1525. He is coediting two volumes on anthropology and history. His present research centers on the study of a South German village in 1500–1870, and he is writing a book on family and kinship.

JOAN WALLACH SCOTT is Nancy Duke Lewis University Professor and professor of history at Brown University. She has taught at the University of Illinois at Chicago Circle, Northwestern University, and the University of North Carolina, Chapel Hill. She is the author of *The Glassworkers of Carmaux: French Craftsmen and Political Action in a*

Nineteenth Century City and coauthor (with Louise A. Tilley) of *Women, Work, and Family*. She is currently working on a study of working-class family, politics, and culture in nineteenth-century France.

ALLAN SHARLIN is assistant professor of sociology at the University of California, Berkeley. He works in the areas of historical sociology, demography, and social theory, and has published articles in *Past and Present*, *Population Studies*, and the *American Journal of Sociology*, among others. He is currently working on a book entitled "From Estates to Bourgeois Society: The Transformation of Social Structure in Frankfurt, 1815–1864," and on a project on the demography of early modern European cities.

RICHARD ALLEN SOLOWAY is professor of history at the University of North Carolina, Chapel Hill. He has also taught at the University of Michigan. He is the author of *Prelates and People: Ecclesiastical Social Thought in England, 1783–1852* and *Birth Control and the Population Question in England, 1877–1930* (forthcoming).

Index